Ford Ka
Owners Workshop Manual

M R Storey

Models covered

(5637 - 208)

Hatchback with 1.2 litre (1242cc) petrol engine

Does NOT cover diesel engine models

© Haynes Publishing 2014

A book in the **Haynes Owners Workshop Manual Series**

ABCDE
FGHIJ
KLMNO
PQRST

Printed in the USA

Haynes Publishing
Sparkford, Yeovil, Somerset BA22 7JJ, England

Haynes North America, Inc
861 Lawrence Drive, Newbury Park, California 91320, USA

Haynes Publishing Nordiska AB
Box 1504, 751 45 UPPSALA, Sverige

ISBN **978 0 85733 637 8**

British Library Cataloguing in Publication Data
A catalogue record for this book is available from the British Library.

Printed using 33-lb Resolute Book 65 4.0 from Resolute Forest Products Calhoun, TN mill. Resolute is a member of World Wildlife Fund's Climate Savers programme committed to significantly reducing GHG emissions. This paper uses 50% less wood fibre than traditional offset. The Calhoun Mill is certified to the following sustainable forest management and chain of custody standards: SFI, PEFC and FSC Controlled Wood.

Contents

Contents

REPAIRS AND OVERHAUL

Engine and associated systems

Transmission

Brakes and suspension

Body equipment

Wiring diagrams

REFERENCE

Index

The new Ford Ka was introduced in the UK in October 2008 and is based on the Fiat 500/Panda model. All the running gear is Fiat based, as are the engine and transmission. Ford have acknowledged that the car is 80% Fiat. The Ka is produced alongside the Fiat models in Poland.

The major changes from the Fiat versions are to the body style and the interior. Ford also made some minor changes to the rear suspension and adjusted the engine tune (by amending the engine management software) to give the drive more of a Ford 'feel'.

The Ka is only available as a three door hatchback and with a choice of petrol or diesel engines. Note that the diesel engines are not covered by this manual.

The petrol engine is a four-cylinder single overhead camshaft (SOHC) 8-valve configuration, in-line type. The Ka is only available with a 5-speed manual gearbox.

All models have front-wheel-drive with fully-independent front suspension, and semi-independent rear suspension with a torsion beam and trailing arms.

A wide range of standard and optional equipment is available within the range to suit most tastes including air conditioning, remote central locking, electric windows, electric sunroof, anti-lock braking system, electronic alarm system and supplemental restraint systems.

For the home mechanic, the Ka is a relatively straightforward vehicle to maintain, and most of the items requiring frequent attention are easily accessible.

Your Ford Ka manual

The aim of this manual is to help you get the best value from your vehicle. It can do so in several ways. It can help you decide what work must be done (even should you choose to get it done by a garage), provide information on routine maintenance and servicing, and give a logical course of action and diagnosis when random faults occur. However, it is hoped that you will use the manual by tackling the work yourself. On simpler jobs, it may even be quicker than booking the car into a garage and going there twice, to leave and collect it. Perhaps most important, a lot of money can be saved by avoiding the costs a garage must charge to cover its labour and overheads.

The manual has drawings and descriptions to show the function of the various components, so that their layout can be understood. Then the tasks are described and photographed in a clear step-by-step sequence.

References to the 'left' or 'right' are in the sense of a person in the driver's seat, facing forward.

Acknowledgements

Thanks are due to Draper Tools Limited and Auto Service Tools Limited (asttools.co.uk), who provided some of the workshop tools, and to all those people at Sparkford who helped in the production of this manual.

We take great pride in the accuracy of information given in this manual, but vehicle manufacturers make alterations and design changes during the production run of a particular vehicle of which they do not inform us. No liability can be accepted by the authors or publishers for loss, damage or injury caused by any errors in, or omissions from, the information given.

Working on your car can be dangerous. This page shows just some of the potential risks and hazards, with the aim of creating a safety-conscious attitude.

General hazards

Scalding

• Don't remove the radiator or expansion tank cap while the engine is hot.
• Engine oil, transmission fluid or power steering fluid may also be dangerously hot if the engine has recently been running.

Burning

• Beware of burns from the exhaust system and from any part of the engine. Brake discs and drums can also be extremely hot immediately after use.

Crushing

• When working under or near a raised vehicle, always supplement the jack with axle stands, or use drive-on ramps.
Never venture under a car which is only supported by a jack.
• Take care if loosening or tightening high-torque nuts when the vehicle is on stands. Initial loosening and final tightening should be done with the wheels on the ground.

Fire

• Fuel is highly flammable; fuel vapour is explosive.
• Don't let fuel spill onto a hot engine.
• Do not smoke or allow naked lights (including pilot lights) anywhere near a vehicle being worked on. Also beware of creating sparks (electrically or by use of tools).
• Fuel vapour is heavier than air, so don't work on the fuel system with the vehicle over an inspection pit.
• Another cause of fire is an electrical overload or short-circuit. Take care when repairing or modifying the vehicle wiring.
• Keep a fire extinguisher handy, of a type suitable for use on fuel and electrical fires.

Electric shock

• Ignition HT and Xenon headlight voltages can be dangerous, especially to people with heart problems or a pacemaker. Don't work on or near these systems with the engine running or the ignition switched on.

• Mains voltage is also dangerous. Make sure that any mains-operated equipment is correctly earthed. Mains power points should be protected by a residual current device (RCD) circuit breaker.

Fume or gas intoxication

• Exhaust fumes are poisonous; they can contain carbon monoxide, which is rapidly fatal if inhaled. Never run the engine in a confined space such as a garage with the doors shut.
• Fuel vapour is also poisonous, as are the vapours from some cleaning solvents and paint thinners.

Poisonous or irritant substances

• Avoid skin contact with battery acid and with any fuel, fluid or lubricant, especially antifreeze, brake hydraulic fluid and Diesel fuel. Don't syphon them by mouth. If such a substance is swallowed or gets into the eyes, seek medical advice.
• Prolonged contact with used engine oil can cause skin cancer. Wear gloves or use a barrier cream if necessary. Change out of oil-soaked clothes and do not keep oily rags in your pocket.
• Air conditioning refrigerant forms a poisonous gas if exposed to a naked flame (including a cigarette). It can also cause skin burns on contact.

Asbestos

• Asbestos dust can cause cancer if inhaled or swallowed. Asbestos may be found in gaskets and in brake and clutch linings. When dealing with such components it is safest to assume that they contain asbestos.

Special hazards

Hydrofluoric acid

• This extremely corrosive acid is formed when certain types of synthetic rubber, found in some O-rings, oil seals, fuel hoses etc, are exposed to temperatures above 4000C. The rubber changes into a charred or sticky substance containing the acid. *Once formed, the acid remains dangerous for years. If it gets onto the skin, it may be necessary to amputate the limb concerned.*
• When dealing with a vehicle which has suffered a fire, or with components salvaged from such a vehicle, wear protective gloves and discard them after use.

The battery

• Batteries contain sulphuric acid, which attacks clothing, eyes and skin. Take care when topping-up or carrying the battery.
• The hydrogen gas given off by the battery is highly explosive. Never cause a spark or allow a naked light nearby. Be careful when connecting and disconnecting battery chargers or jump leads.

Air bags

• Air bags can cause injury if they go off accidentally. Take care when removing the steering wheel and trim panels. Special storage instructions may apply.

Diesel injection equipment

• Diesel injection pumps supply fuel at very high pressure. Take care when working on the fuel injectors and fuel pipes.

⚠ *Warning: Never expose the hands, face or any other part of the body to injector spray; the fuel can penetrate the skin with potentially fatal results.*

Remember...

DO

• Do use eye protection when using power tools, and when working under the vehicle.

• Do wear gloves or use barrier cream to protect your hands when necessary.

• Do get someone to check periodically that all is well when working alone on the vehicle.

• Do keep loose clothing and long hair well out of the way of moving mechanical parts.

• Do remove rings, wristwatch etc, before working on the vehicle – especially the electrical system.

• Do ensure that any lifting or jacking equipment has a safe working load rating adequate for the job.

DON'T

• Don't attempt to lift a heavy component which may be beyond your capability – get assistance.

• Don't rush to finish a job, or take unverified short cuts.

• Don't use ill-fitting tools which may slip and cause injury.

• Don't leave tools or parts lying around where someone can trip over them. Mop up oil and fuel spills at once.

• Don't allow children or pets to play in or near a vehicle being worked on.

The following pages are intended to help in dealing with common roadside emergencies and breakdowns. You will find more detailed fault finding information at the back of the manual, and repair information in the main chapters.

If your car won't start and the starter motor doesn't turn

☐ Open the bonnet and make sure that the battery terminals are clean and tight (pull up the positive terminal cover for access).

☐ Switch on the headlights and try to start the engine. If the headlights go very dim when you're trying to start, the battery is probably flat. Get out of trouble by jump starting (see next page) using a friend's car.

If your car won't start even though the starter motor turns as normal

☐ Is there fuel in the tank?

☐ Has the engine immobiliser been deactivated? This should happen automatically, on inserting the ignition key. However, if a replacement key has been obtained (other than from a Ford dealer), it may not contain the transponder chip necessary to deactivate the system. Even 'proper' replacement keys have to be coded to work properly – a procedure for this is outlined in the vehicle handbook.

☐ Is there moisture on electrical components under the bonnet? Switch off the ignition, then wipe off any obvious dampness with a dry cloth. Spray a water-repellent aerosol product (WD-40 or equivalent) on ignition and fuel system electrical connectors like those shown in the photos. Pay special attention to the ignition coil wiring connector and HT leads (where applicable).

A Check the security and condition of the battery terminals – pull up the cover for access to the positive terminal.

B Remove the air filter housing and check the wiring plug and HT leads at the coil pack.

C Check the security of the ECU wiring plugs.

D Check that none of the engine compartment fuses have blown.

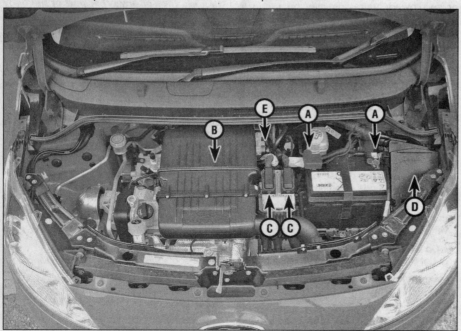

Check that electrical connections are secure (with the ignition switched off) and spray them with a water-dispersant spray like WD-40 if you suspect a problem due to damp.

E Check the throttle body connections.

Jump starting

Jump starting will get you out of trouble, but you must correct whatever made the battery go flat in the first place. There are three possibilities:

1 *The battery has been drained by repeated attempts to start, or by leaving the lights on.*

2 *The charging system is not working properly (alternator drivebelt slack or broken, alternator wiring fault or alternator itself faulty).*

3 *The battery itself is at fault (electrolyte low, or battery worn out).*

When jump-starting a car, observe the following precautions:

✓ Before connecting the booster battery, make sure that the ignition is switched off.

Caution: Remove the key in case the central locking engages when the jump leads are connected

✓ Ensure that all electrical equipment (lights, heater, wipers, etc) is switched off.

✓ Take note of any special precautions printed on the battery case.

✓ Make sure that the booster battery is the same voltage as the discharged one in the vehicle.

✓ If the battery is being jump-started from the battery in another vehicle, the two vehicles MUST NOT TOUCH each other.

✓ Make sure that the transmission is in neutral (or PARK, in the case of automatic transmission).

Budget jump leads can be a false economy, as they often do not pass enough current to start large capacity or diesel engines. They can also get hot.

1 Connect one end of the red jump lead to the positive (+) terminal of the flat battery

2 Connect the other end of the red lead to the positive (+) terminal of the booster battery.

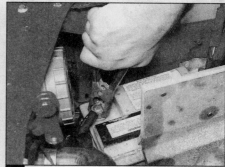

3 Connect one end of the black jump lead to the negative (-) terminal of the booster battery

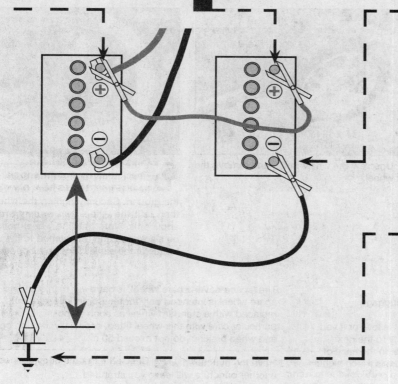

4 Connect the other end of the black jump lead to a bolt or bracket on the engine block, well away from the battery, on the vehicle to be started.

5 Make sure that the jump leads will not come into contact with the fan, drive-belts or other moving parts of the engine.

6 Start the engine using the booster battery and run it at idle speed. Switch on the lights, rear window demister and heater blower motor, then disconnect the jump leads in the reverse order of connection. Turn off the lights etc.

Wheel changing

Note: *The models covered by this manual are equipped with either a spare wheel or an 'Automatic Fix & Go' tyre repair kit. Follow the relevant procedure.*

 Warning: Do not change a wheel in a situation where you risk being hit by other traffic. On busy roads, try to stop in a lay-by or a gateway. Be wary of passing traffic while changing the wheel – it is easy to become distracted by the job in hand.

Preparation

- ☐ When a puncture occurs, stop as soon as it is safe to do so.
- ☐ Park on firm level ground, if possible, and well out of the way of other traffic.
- ☐ If you have one, use a warning triangle to alert other drivers of your presence.
- ☐ Use hazard warning lights if necessary.
- ☐ Apply the handbrake and engage first or reverse gear.
- ☐ Chock the wheel diagonally opposite the one being removed – a couple of large stones will do for this. Some models are supplied with a wheel chock in the car's tool kit – pull and twist the two halves of the chock to form the triangular shape.
- ☐ If the ground is soft, use a flat piece of wood to spread the load under the jack.

Changing the wheel

1 The spare wheel and tools are stored in the luggage compartment. Fold back the floor covering and lift up the cover panel. Unscrew the retaining bolt, and lift out the tool container, followed by the spare wheel.

2 Where applicable, using the screwdriver provided, prise off the wheel trim or centre cover for access to the wheel bolts. Models with alloy wheels may have special locking bolts – these are removed with a special tool, which should be provided with the wheel brace (or it may be in the glovebox).

3 Slacken each wheel bolt by a half turn, using the wheel brace. If the bolts are too tight, DON'T stand on the wheel brace to undo them – call for assistance from one of the motoring organisations.

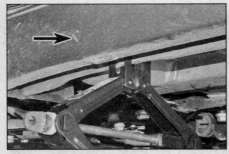

4 Two jacking points are provided on each side – use the one nearest the punctured wheel. Locate the jack head at the point in the lower sill flange indicated by the indentation in the metal sill (don't jack the vehicle at any other point of the sill, nor on a plastic panel). Turn the jack handle clockwise until the wheel is raised clear of the ground.

5 Unscrew the wheel bolts, and remove the wheel.

6 Fit the spare wheel, and screw in the bolts. Lightly tighten the bolts with the wheel brace, then lower the vehicle to the ground. Securely tighten the wheel bolts, then refit the wheel trim or centre cover, as applicable. Note that the wheel bolts should be slackened and retightened to the specified torque at the earliest possible opportunity.

Finally . . .

- ☐ Remove the wheel chocks.
- ☐ Stow the punctured wheel and tools back in the luggage compartment, and secure them in position.
- ☐ Check the tyre pressure on the tyre just fitted. If it is low, or if you don't have a pressure gauge with you, drive slowly to the next garage and inflate the tyre to the correct pressure. In the case of the narrow 'space-saver' spare wheel this pressure is much higher than for a normal tyre.

- ☐ The 'space-saver' spare wheel, is narrower than standard. This spare wheel is intended only for temporary use, and must be replaced with a standard wheel as soon as possible. Drive with particular care with this wheel fitted, especially through corners and when braking; do not exceed 50 mph.

- ☐ Have the punctured wheel repaired as soon as possible, or another puncture will leave you stranded.

Automatic Fix & Go tyre repair kit

Note: *The models covered by this manual are equipped with either a spare wheel or an 'Automatic Fix & Go' tyre repair kit. Follow the relevant procedure.*

 Warning: Do not change a wheel in a situation where you risk being hit by other traffic. On busy roads, try to stop in a lay-by or a gateway. Be wary of passing traffic while changing the wheel – it is easy to become distracted by the job in hand.

Preparation

☐ When a puncture occurs, stop as soon as it is safe to do so.

☐ Park on firm level ground, if possible, and well out of the way of other traffic.

☐ Use hazard warning lights if necessary.

☐ If you have one, use a warning triangle to alert other drivers of your presence.

☐ Before attempting to repair the puncture, note the following.
● *The kit can be used to repair tyres with damage to the tread or shoulder up to a maximum diameter of 4 mm. Damage to the tyre sidewall cannot be repaired.*
● *Do not operate the compressor for more than 20 minutes at a time or it may overheat.*

● *This repair is designed for temporary use only. Have the damaged tyre replaced at the earliest opportunity.*
● *Put on gloves (supplied in the kit) before commencing the repair. The sealant can be harmful if it comes into contact with skin, eyes, etc.*

Changing the wheel

1 The tyre repair kit and tool kit are stored in the luggage compartment. Fold back the floor covering and lift up the cover panel.

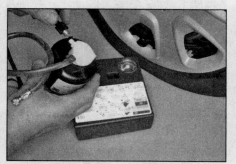

2 Attach the bottle of sealant to the compressor.

3 Fit the bottle of sealant to the housing in the compressor.

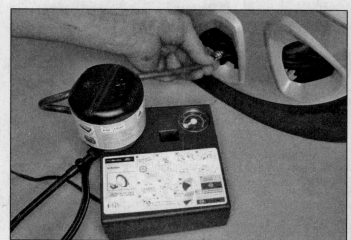

4 Remove the valve cap from the relevant tyre and then attach the flexible filler tube to the tyre valve. Tighten the retaining ring nut. Start the engine, then switch on the compressor and inflate the tyre to the pressure specified at the end of this Chapter. If after 5 minutes it's still impossible to achieve a pressure of at least 1.5 bar, disconnect the filler tube and roll the car forwards/backwards approximately 10 metres to redistribute the sealant within the tyre, then repeat the inflation procedure. If it's still not possible to achieve 1.5 bar, the tyre is too badly damaged, and having the vehicle recovered is the only option.

5 Apply the warning sticker to the steering wheel. With the tyre correctly inflated, disconnect the filler tube, and refit the valve cap. Check the pressure again after 10 minutes of driving.

Identifying leaks

Puddles on the garage floor or drive, or obvious wetness under the bonnet or underneath the car, suggest a leak that needs investigating. It can sometimes be difficult to decide where the leak is coming from, especially if an engine undershield is fitted. Leaking oil or fluid can also be blown rearwards by the passage of air under the car, giving a false impression of where the problem lies.

⚠ **Warning: Most automotive oils and fluids are poisonous. Wash them off skin, and change out of contaminated clothing, without delay.**

 HAYNES HiNT *The smell of a fluid leaking from the car may provide a clue to what's leaking. Some fluids are distinctively coloured. It may help to remove the engine undershield, clean the car carefully and to park it over some clean paper overnight as an aid to locating the source of the leak. Remember that some leaks may only occur while the engine is running.*

Sump oil

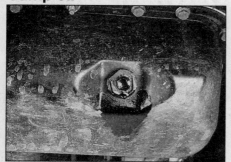

Engine oil may leak from the drain plug...

Oil from filter

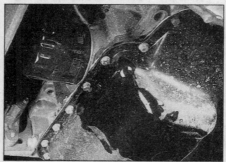

...or from the base of the oil filter.

Gearbox oil

Gearbox oil can leak from the seals at the inboard ends of the driveshafts.

Antifreeze

Leaking antifreeze often leaves a crystalline deposit like this.

Brake fluid

A leak occurring at a wheel is almost certainly brake fluid.

Power steering fluid

Power steering fluid may leak from the pipe connectors on the steering rack.

Towing

When all else fails, you may find yourself having to get a tow home – or of course you may be helping somebody else. Long-distance recovery should only be done by a garage or breakdown service. For shorter distances, DIY towing using another car is easy enough, but observe the following points:

☐ Use a proper tow-rope – they are not expensive. The vehicle being towed must display an ON TOW sign in its rear window.

☐ Always turn the ignition key to the 'on' position when the vehicle is being towed, so that the steering lock is released, and the direction indicator and brake lights work.

☐ The towing eye is of the screw-in type, and is found in the spare wheel well. The towing eye screws into a threaded hole, accessible after prising out a cover on the right-hand side of the bumpers (see illustration).

☐ Before being towed, release the handbrake and make sure the transmission is in neutral.

☐ Note that greater-than-usual pedal pressure will be required to operate the brakes, since the vacuum servo unit is only operational with the engine running.

☐ The driver of the car being towed must keep the tow-rope taut at all times to avoid snatching.

☐ Make sure that both drivers know the route before setting off.

☐ Only drive at moderate speeds and keep the distance towed to a minimum. Drive smoothly and allow plenty of time for slowing down at junctions.

Introduction

There are some very simple checks which need only take a few minutes to carry out, but which could save you a lot of inconvenience and expense.

These checks require no great skill or special tools, and the small amount of time they take to perform could prove to be very well spent, for example:

☐ Keeping an eye on tyre condition and pressures, will not only help to stop them wearing out prematurely, but could also save your life.

☐ Many breakdowns are caused by electrical problems. Battery-related faults are particularly common, and a quick check on a regular basis will often prevent the majority of these.

☐ If your car develops a brake fluid leak, the first time you might know about it is when your brakes don't work properly. Checking the level regularly will give advance warning of this kind of problem.

☐ If the oil or coolant levels run low, the cost of repairing any engine damage will be far greater than fixing the leak, for example.

Underbonnet check points

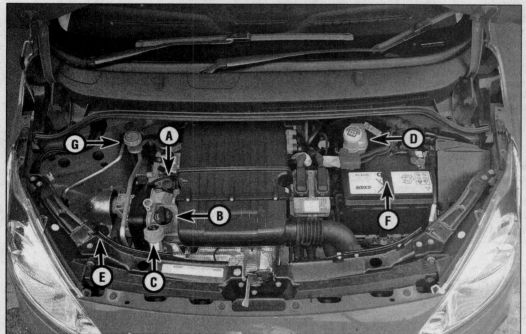

◀ **Ka engine**

A *Engine oil level dipstick*
B *Engine oil filler cap*
C *Coolant expansion tank*
D *Brake fluid reservoir*
E *Screen washer fluid reservoir*
F *Battery*
G *Clutch fluid reservoir*

Engine oil level

Before you start

✔ Make sure that the car is on level ground.
✔ Check the oil level before the car is driven, or at least 10 minutes after the engine has been switched off.

 If the oil is checked immediately after driving the vehicle, some of the oil will remain in the upper engine components, resulting in an inaccurate reading on the dipstick.

The correct oil

Modern engines place great demands on their oil. It is very important that the correct oil for your car is used (see *Lubricants and fluids*).

Car care

● If you have to add oil frequently, you should check whether you have any oil leaks. Place some clean paper under the car overnight, and check for stains in the morning. If there are no leaks, then the engine may be burning oil, or the oil may only be leaking when the engine is running.

● Always maintain the level between the upper and lower dipstick marks. If the level is too low, severe engine damage may occur. Oil seal failure may result if the engine is overfilled by adding too much oil.

1 The dipstick is located on the right-hand side of the engine (see *Underbonnet check points* for exact location). Withdraw the dipstick. Using a clean rag or paper towel, remove all oil from the dipstick.

3 Oil is added through the filler cap. Unscrew the cap . . .

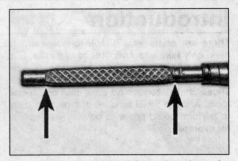

2 Insert the clean dipstick into the tube as far as it will go, then withdraw it again. Note the oil level on the end of the dipstick, which should be between the MAX and MIN marks. If the oil level is only just above, or below, the MIN mark, topping-up is required.

4 . . . and top-up the level; a funnel may be useful in reducing spillage. Add the oil slowly, checking the level on the dipstick often, and allowing time for the oil to fall to the sump. Add oil until the level is just up to the MAX mark on the dipstick – don't overfill (see *Car care*)

Coolant level

 Warning: Do not attempt to remove the expansion tank pressure cap when the engine is hot, as there is a very great risk of scalding. Do not leave open containers of coolant about, as it is poisonous.

Car care

● With a sealed-type cooling system, adding coolant should not be necessary on a regular basis. If frequent topping-up is required, it is likely there is a leak. Check the radiator, all hoses and joint faces for signs of staining or wetness, and rectify as necessary.

● It is important that antifreeze is used in the cooling system all year round, not just during the winter months. Don't top up with water alone, as the antifreeze will become diluted.

1 The coolant level varies with the temperature of the engine, and is visible through the expansion tank. When the engine is cold, the coolant level should be between the MAX and MIN marks on the side of the reservoir. When the engine is hot, the level may rise slightly above the MAX mark.

2 If topping-up is necessary, wait until the engine is cold. Slowly unscrew the expansion tank cap, to release any pressure present in the cooling system, and remove it.

3 Add a mixture of water and antifreeze to the expansion tank until the coolant level is halfway between the level marks. Use only the specified antifreeze – if using Ford antifreeze, make sure it is the same type and colour as that already in the system. Refit the cap and tighten it securely.

Brake and clutch fluid level

All models have a hydraulically-operated clutch which on some models uses the same fluid as the braking system, whereas on others the fluid is stored in a separate reservoir.

⚠️ **Warning:**
• **Brake fluid can harm your eyes and damage painted surfaces, so use extreme caution when handling and pouring it.**
• **Do not use fluid that has been standing** *open for some time, as it absorbs moisture from the air, which can cause a dangerous loss of braking effectiveness.*
• *The fluid level in the reservoir will drop slightly as the brake pads wear down, but the fluid level must never be allowed to drop below the MIN mark.*

Before you start

✔ Make sure that your car is on level ground.

Safety first!

● If the reservoir requires repeated topping-up this is an indication of a fluid leak somewhere in the system, which should be investigated immediately.

● If a leak is suspected, the car should not be driven until the braking system has been checked. Never take any risks where brakes are concerned.

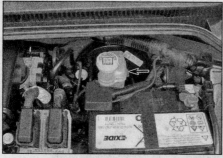

1 The brake fluid reservoir is located on the left-hand side of the engine compartment.

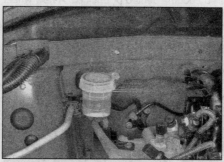

2 On models with a separate clutch fluid reservoir, it's located on the right of the engine compartment.

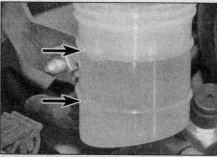

3 The MAX and MIN marks are indicated on the side of the reservoir. The fluid level must be kept between the marks at all times. Clutch fluid reservoir . . .

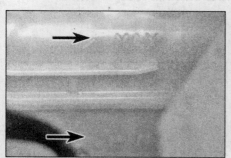

4 . . . and brake fluid reservoir.

5 If topping-up is necessary, first wipe clean the area around the filler cap to prevent dirt entering the hydraulic system. Unscrew the reservoir cap and carefully lift it out of position. Inspect the reservoir; if the fluid is dirty, the hydraulic system should be drained and refilled (see the relevant part of Chapter 1).

6 Carefully add fluid, taking care not to spill it onto the surrounding components. Use only the specified fluid; mixing different types can cause damage to the system. After topping-up to the correct level, securely refit the cap and wipe off any spilt fluid.

Tyre condition and pressure

It is very important that tyres are in good condition, and at the correct pressure - having a tyre failure at any speed is highly dangerous. Tyre wear is influenced by driving style - harsh braking and acceleration, or fast cornering, will all produce more rapid tyre wear. As a general rule, the front tyres wear out faster than the rears. Interchanging the tyres from front to rear ("rotating" the tyres) may result in more even wear. However, if this is completely effective, you may have the expense of replacing all four tyres at once!

Remove any nails or stones embedded in the tread before they penetrate the tyre to cause deflation. If removal of a nail does reveal that the tyre has been punctured, refit the nail so that its point of penetration is marked. Then immediately change the wheel, and have the tyre repaired by a tyre dealer.

Regularly check the tyres for damage in the form of cuts or bulges, especially in the sidewalls. Periodically remove the wheels, and clean any dirt or mud from the inside and outside surfaces. Examine the wheel rims for signs of rusting, corrosion or other damage. Light alloy wheels are easily damaged by "kerbing" whilst parking; steel wheels may also become dented or buckled. A new wheel is very often the only way to overcome severe damage.

New tyres should be balanced when they are fitted, but it may become necessary to re-balance them as they wear, or if the balance weights fitted to the wheel rim should fall off. Unbalanced tyres will wear more quickly, as will the steering and suspension components. Wheel imbalance is normally signified by vibration, particularly at a certain speed (typically around 50 mph). If this vibration is felt only through the steering, then it is likely that just the front wheels need balancing. If, however, the vibration is felt through the whole car, the rear wheels could be out of balance. Wheel balancing should be carried out by a tyre dealer or garage.

1 Tread Depth - visual check
The original tyres have tread wear safety bands (B), which will appear when the tread depth reaches approximately 1.6 mm. The band positions are indicated by a triangular mark on the tyre sidewall (A).

2 Tread Depth - manual check
Alternatively, tread wear can be monitored with a simple, inexpensive device known as a tread depth indicator gauge.

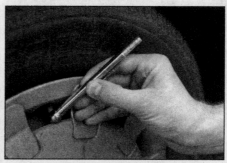

3 Tyre Pressure Check
Check the tyre pressures regularly with the tyres cold. Do not adjust the tyre pressures immediately after the vehicle has been used, or an inaccurate setting will result.

Tyre tread wear patterns

Shoulder Wear

Underinflation (wear on both sides)
Under-inflation will cause overheating of the tyre, because the tyre will flex too much, and the tread will not sit correctly on the road surface. This will cause a loss of grip and excessive wear, not to mention the danger of sudden tyre failure due to heat build-up.
Check and adjust pressures
Incorrect wheel camber (wear on one side)
Repair or renew suspension parts
Hard cornering
Reduce speed!

Centre Wear

Overinflation
Over-inflation will cause rapid wear of the centre part of the tyre tread, coupled with reduced grip, harsher ride, and the danger of shock damage occurring in the tyre casing.
Check and adjust pressures

If you sometimes have to inflate your car's tyres to the higher pressures specified for maximum load or sustained high speed, don't forget to reduce the pressures to normal afterwards.

Uneven Wear

Front tyres may wear unevenly as a result of wheel misalignment. Most tyre dealers and garages can check and adjust the wheel alignment (or "tracking") for a modest charge.
Incorrect camber or castor
Repair or renew suspension parts
Malfunctioning suspension
Repair or renew suspension parts
Unbalanced wheel
Balance tyres
Incorrect toe setting
Adjust front wheel alignment
Note: *The feathered edge of the tread which typifies toe wear is best checked by feel.*

Battery

Caution: Before carrying out any work on the vehicle battery, read the precautions given in 'Safety first!' at the start of this manual.

✔ Make sure that the battery tray is in good condition, and that the clamp is tight. Any 'white' corrosion on the terminals or surrounding area can be removed with a solution of water and baking soda; thoroughly rinse all cleaned areas with water. Any metal parts damaged by corrosion should be covered with a zinc-based primer, then painted.

✔ Periodically check the charge condition of the battery. On the original-equipment battery, the state of charge may be shown by an indicator 'eye' in the top of the battery, which should be green – if the indicator is clear, or red, the battery may need charging or even renewal (see Chapter 5A).

✔ If the battery is flat, and you need to jump start your vehicle, see *Roadside repairs*.

 HAYNES HiNT *Battery corrosion can be kept to a minimum by applying a layer of petroleum jelly to the clamps and terminals after they are reconnected.*

1 The battery is located in the left-hand front corner of the engine compartment – prise up the plastic cover over the positive terminal. The exterior of the battery should be inspected periodically for damage such as a cracked case or cover.

2 Check the tightness of battery clamps to ensure good electrical connections. You should not be able to move them. Also check each cable for cracks and frayed conductors.

3 If corrosion (white, fluffy deposits) is evident, remove the cables from the battery terminals, clean them with a small wire brush, then refit them. Automotive stores sell a tool for cleaning the battery post . . .

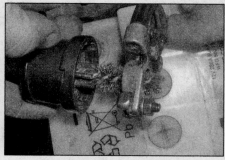

4 . . . as well as the battery cable clamps

Wiper blades

● Only fit good-quality blades.
● When removing an old wiper blade, note how it is fitted. Fitting new blades can be a tricky exercise, and noting how the old blade came off can save time.
● While the wiper blade is removed, take care

not to knock the wiper arm from its locked position, or it could strike the glass.
● Offer the new blade into position the same way round as the old one. Ensure that it clicks home securely, otherwise it may come off in use, damaging the glass.

Note: *Fitting details for wiper blades vary according to model, and according to whether genuine Ford wiper blades have been fitted. Use the procedures and illustrations shown as a guide for your car.*

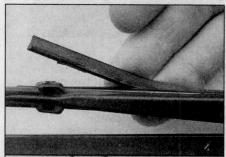

1 Check the condition of the wiper blades; if they are cracked or show any signs of deterioration, or if the glass swept area is smeared, renew them. Wiper blades should be renewed annually, regardless of their apparent condition.

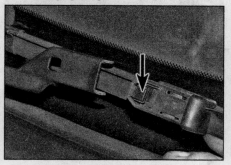

2 To remove a windscreen wiper blade, pull the arm fully away from the glass until it locks. Press the release button with your fingers and slide the blade out of the arm's hooked end.

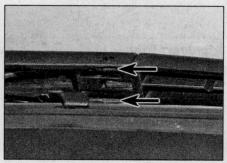

3 Don't forget to check the tailgate wiper blade as well. Remove the blade by prising apart the blade casing.

Washer fluid level

● The windscreen washer reservoir also supplies the tailgate washer jet, where applicable. On models so equipped, the same reservoir also serves the headlight washers.

● Screenwash additives not only keep the windscreen clean during foul weather, they also prevent the washer system freezing in cold weather – which is when you are likely to need it most. Don't top-up using plain water as the screenwash will become too diluted, and will freeze during cold weather.

Caution: On no account use engine coolant antifreeze in the screen washer system – this may damage the paintwork.

1 The washer fluid reservoir filler neck is located on the right-hand side of the engine compartment. The washer level cannot easily be seen. Remove the filler cap, and look down the filler neck – if fluid is not visible, topping-up may be required.

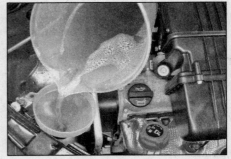

2 When topping-up the reservoir, add a screenwash additive in the quantities recommended on the additive bottle.

Electrical systems

✔ Check all external lights and the horn. Refer to the appropriate Sections of Chapter 12 for details if any of the circuits are found to be inoperative.

✔ Visually check all accessible wiring connectors, harnesses and retaining clips for security, and for signs of chafing or damage.

> **HAYNES HiNT**
> *If you need to check your brake lights and indicators unaided, back up to a wall or garage door and operate the lights. The reflected light should show if they are working properly.*

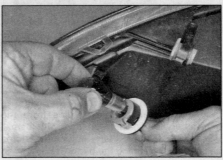

1 If a single indicator light, brake light or headlight has failed, it is likely that a bulb has blown and will need to be renewed. Refer to Chapter 12 for details. If both brake lights have failed, it is possible that the switch has failed (see Chapter 9).

2 If more than one indicator light or tail light has failed, it is likely that either a fuse has blown or that there is a fault in the circuit (see Chapter 12). The main fusebox is located in the glovebox and is accessed by opening the glovebox and removing the panel at the rear of the glovebox.

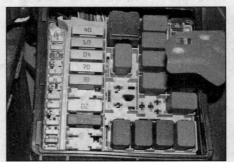

3 The auxiliary fusebox is located next to the battery – unclip and remove the cover for access.

4 To renew a blown fuse, simply pull it out and fit a new fuse of the correct rating (see Chapter 12). Spare fuses, and a fuse removal tool, are provided in the auxiliary fusebox. If the fuse blows again, it is important that you find out why – a complete checking procedure is given in Chapter 12

Lubricants and fluids

Engine . . . . Multigrade engine oil, fully-synthetic, viscosity
SAE 5W/40 to ACEA C3 or better

Manual transmission . . . . 75W-90 Gear oil (Ford Part 1565898)

Cooling system. . . . . Havoline XLC

Brake/clutch fluid reservoir. . . . . Hydraulic fluid to DOT 4

Tyre pressures (cold)

Note: *Pressures apply to original-equipment tyres, and may vary if any other make or type of tyre is fitted; check with the tyre manufacturer or supplier for correct pressures if necessary.*

	Front	Rear
Normal load (up to 3 passengers)		
165/65 R14, 175/65 R14 195/50 R15 and 195/45 R16 .	2.0 bar (29 psi)	2.0 bar (29 psi)
Fully laden		
165/65 R14, 175/65 R14 195/50 R15 and 195/45 R16 .	2.3 bar (33 psi)	2.5 bar (34 psi)
Space-saver temporary spare tyre		
All models.	2.8 bar (41 psi)	2.8 bar (41 psi)

Chapter 1
Routine maintenance and servicing

Contents

Degrees of difficulty

Easy, suitable for novice with little experience

Fairly easy, suitable for beginner with some experience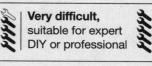

Fairly difficult, suitable for competent DIY mechanic

Difficult, suitable for experienced DIY mechanic

Very difficult, suitable for expert DIY or professional

Lubricants and fluids

Refer to end of *Weekly checks* on page 0•18

Capacities

Engine oil (including filter)	2.8 litres
Cooling system	4.85 litres
Manual transmission	1.65 litres
Fuel tank	35.0 litres

Engine

Auxiliary drivebelt tension:
  Models without air conditioning .... 5.0 mm deflection midway between pulleys
  Models with air conditioning .... Controlled by automatic tensioner
Valve clearances (cold):
  Intake .... 0.35 ± 0.05 mm
  Exhaust...................................... 0.45 ± 0.05 mm
  Cam follower (tappet) shim sizes .... 3.20 to 4.70 mm in increments of 0.05 mm

Cooling system

Antifreeze mixture (50% antifreeze) .... Protection down to −35°C
Note: *Refer to antifreeze manufacturer for latest recommendations.*

Ignition system

Ignition timing... Refer to Chapter 5B

Spark plugs:

	Type	Electrode gap
All engines	NGK ZKR7A-10	Pre-set

Remote control

Battery type CR2032

Brakes

Brake pad lining minimum thickness	1.5 mm
Brake shoe friction material minimum thickness	2.0 mm

Torque wrench settings

	Nm	lbf ft
Roadwheel bolts:		
Steel wheel	85	63
Aluminium wheel	110	81
Spark plugs	25	18
Sump drain plug	20	15
Transmission oil filler plug	20	15

The maintenance intervals in this manual are provided with the assumption that you, not the dealer, will be carrying out the work. These are the minimum maintenance intervals recommended by us for vehicles driven daily. If you wish to keep your vehicle in peak condition at all times, you may wish to perform some of these procedures more often. We encourage frequent maintenance, because it enhances the efficiency, performance and resale value of your vehicle.

When the vehicle is new, it should be serviced by a dealer service department (or other workshop recognised by the vehicle manufacturer as providing the same standard of service) in order to preserve the warranty. The vehicle manufacturer may reject warranty claims if you are unable to prove that servicing has been carried out as and when specified, using only original equipment parts or parts certified to be of equivalent quality.

Every 250 miles or weekly

☐ Refer to *Weekly checks*

Every 6000 miles or 6 months – whichever comes first

☑ Renew the engine oil and filter (Section 2)

Note: *Frequent oil and filter changes are good for the engine and we recommend that the oil and filter are renewed more frequently than Ford recommend, especially if the vehicle is used on a lot of short journeys.*

Every 12 000 miles or 12 months – whichever comes first

In addition to the items listed above, carry out the following:
☐ Check the condition and tension of the auxiliary drivebelt (Section 3)
☐ Hose and fluid leak check (Section 4)
☐ Check the front brake pads for wear (Section 5)
☐ Check the condition of the driveshaft gaiters (Section 6)
☐ Check the steering and suspension components for condition and security (Section 7)
☐ Check the underbody and sealant for damage (Section 8)
☐ Check the condition of the exhaust system and its mountings (Section 9)
☐ Check and if necessary adjust the handbrake (Section 10)
☐ Renew the pollen filter (Section 11)
☐ Lubricate all hinges and locks (Section 12)
☐ Carry out a road test (Section 13)

Every 24 000 miles or 2 years – whichever comes first

In addition to the items listed above, carry out the following:
☐ Check and if necessary adjust the valve clearances (Section 14)
☐ Renew the spark plugs (Section 15)
☐ Check the condition of the spark plug HT leads (Section 16)
☐ Check the engine management system (Section 17)
☐ Renew the brake fluid (Section 18)
☐ Renew the engine coolant (Section 19)

Every 36 000 miles or 3 years – whichever comes first

In addition to the items listed above, carry out the following:
☐ Renew the air filter element (Section 20)
☐ Check the condition of the timing belt (Section 21)
☐ Check and if necessary top-up the manual transmission oil level (Section 22)
☐ Check the rear brake shoes for wear (Section 23)

Every 48 000 miles or 4 years – whichever comes first

In addition to the items listed above, carry out the following:
☑ Renew the timing belt (Section 24)*
☐ Check the operation of the evaporative loss system (Section 25)
☐ Check the condition and operation of the crankcase emission control system (Section 26)
☐ Renew the remote control battery (Section 27)
☐ Renew the auxiliary drivebelt (Section 3)*

* Note: *Although the normal interval for timing belt and auxiliary drivebelt renewal is 62,500 miles (or 5 years), it is strongly recommended that the belts are renewed at 48 000 miles on vehicles which are subjected to intensive use, ie, mainly short journeys or a lot of stop-start driving. The actual belt renewal interval is therefore very much up to the individual owner, but bear in mind that severe engine damage will result if the timing belt breaks.*

Underbonnet view

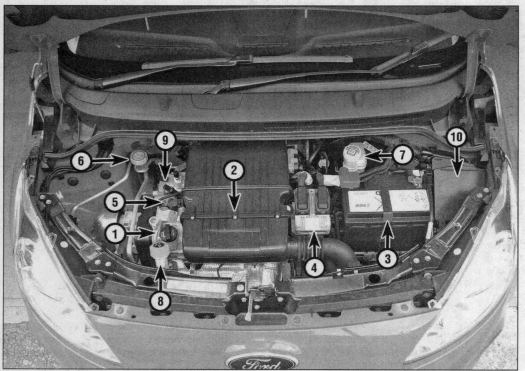

1 Oil filler cap
2 Air filter housing
3 Battery
4 Engine management ECU
5 Engine oil level dipstick
6 Clutch fluid reservoir
7 Brake fluid reservoir
8 Coolant expansion tank cap
9 Fuel pressure release valve
10 Engine compartment fuse/relay box

Front underbody view

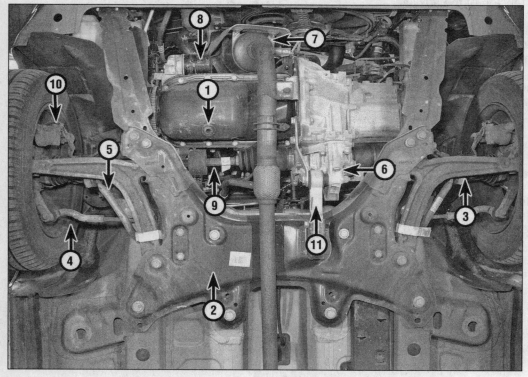

1 Engine oil drain plug
2 Front subframe
3 Lower arm
4 Steering track rod end
5 Anti-roll bar
6 Transmission drain plug
7 Catalytic converter
8 Engine oil filter
9 Driveshaft
10 Brake caliper
11 Rear engine mounting link

Rear underbody view

1 Fuel tank
2 Handbrake cable
3 Rear silencer
4 Coil spring
5 Rear axle
6 Fuel filler pipe
7 Shock absorber
8 Brake pipe

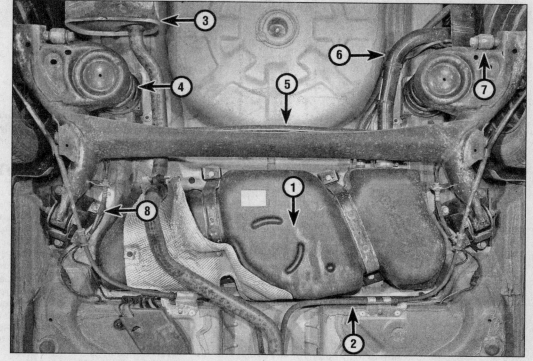

Maintenance procedures

1 Introduction

1 This Chapter is designed to help the home mechanic maintain his/her vehicle for safety, economy, long life and peak performance.

2 The Chapter contains a master maintenance schedule, and Sections dealing specifically with each task in the schedule. Visual checks, adjustments, component renewal and other helpful items are included. Refer to the accompanying illustrations of the engine compartment and the underside of the vehicle for the locations of the various components.

3 Servicing your vehicle in accordance with the mileage/time maintenance schedule and the following Sections will provide a planned maintenance programme, which should result in a long and reliable service life. This is a comprehensive plan, so maintaining some items but not others at the specified service intervals will not produce the same results.

4 As you service your vehicle, you will discover that many of the procedures can, and should, be grouped together, because of the particular procedure being performed, or because of the proximity of two otherwise unrelated components to one another. For example, if the vehicle is raised for any reason, the exhaust can be inspected at the same time as the suspension and steering components.

5 The first step in this maintenance programme is to prepare yourself before the actual work begins. Read through all the Sections relevant to the work to be carried out, then make a list and gather all the parts and tools required. If a problem is encountered, seek advice from a parts specialist, or a dealer service department.

Regular maintenance

6 If, from the time the vehicle is new, the routine maintenance schedule is followed closely, and frequent checks are made of fluid levels and high-wear items, as suggested throughout this manual, the engine will be kept in relatively good running condition, and the need for additional work will be minimised.

7 It is possible that there will be times when the engine is running poorly due to the lack of regular maintenance. This is even more likely if a used vehicle, which has not received regular and frequent maintenance checks, is purchased. In such cases, additional work may need to be carried out, outside of the regular maintenance intervals.

8 If engine wear is suspected, a compression test (refer to Chapter 2A) will provide valuable information regarding the overall performance of the main internal components. Such a test can be used as a basis to decide on the extent of the work to be carried out. If, for example, a compression test indicates serious internal engine wear, conventional

maintenance as described in this Chapter will not greatly improve the performance of the engine, and may prove a waste of time and money, unless extensive overhaul work is carried out first.

9 The following series of operations are those usually required to improve the performance of a generally poor-running engine:

Primary operations

a) Clean, inspect and test the battery (See 'Weekly checks').
b) Check all the engine-related fluids (See 'Weekly checks').
c) Check the condition and tension of the auxiliary drivebelt(s) (Section 3).
d) Check the condition of all hoses, and check for fluid leaks (Section 4).
e) Renew the spark plugs (Section 15).
f) Inspect the ignition HT leads (Section 16).
g) Check the condition of the air filter, and renew if necessary (Section 20).

10 If the above operations do not prove fully effective, carry out the following secondary operations:

Secondary operations

11 All items listed under Primary operations, plus the following:

a) Check the charging system (Chapter 5A).
b) Check the ignition system (Chapter 5B).
c) Check the fuel system (Chapter 4A).
d) Renew the ignition HT leads (Section 16).

2.3 Engine oil drain plug location (arrowed)

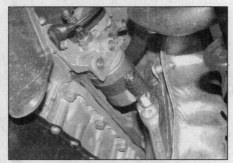

2.7 Using an oil filter removal tool to initially slacken the oil filter

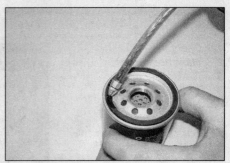

2.9 Apply a light coating of clean engine oil to the sealing ring on the new filter

Every 6000 miles or 6 months – whichever comes first

2 Engine oil and filter renewal

1 Frequent oil and filter changes are the most important preventative maintenance which can be undertaken by the DIY owner. As engine oil ages, it becomes diluted and contaminated, which leads to premature engine wear.

2 Before starting this procedure, gather all the necessary tools and materials. Also make sure that you have plenty of clean rags and newspapers handy to mop-up any spills. Ideally, the engine oil should be warm, as it will drain better, and any impurities suspended in the oil will be removed with it. Take care, however, not to touch the exhaust or any other hot parts of the engine when working under the vehicle. To avoid any possibility of scalding, and to protect yourself from possible skin irritants and other harmful contaminants in used engine oils, it is advisable to wear gloves when carrying out this work. Access to the underside of the vehicle will be greatly improved if it can be raised on a lift, driven onto ramps, or jacked up and supported on axle stands (see *Jacking and vehicle support*). Whichever method is chosen, make sure that the vehicle remains level, or if it is at an angle, that the drain plug is at the lowest point.

3 Slacken the drain plug about half a turn using a 12 mm Allen key/bit **(see illustration)**. Position the draining container under the drain plug, then remove the plug completely.

4 Allow some time for the old oil to drain, noting that it may be necessary to reposition the container as the oil flow slows to a trickle.

5 After all the oil has drained, wipe off the drain plug with a clean rag, then clean the area around the drain plug opening and refit the plug. Tighten the plug to the specified torque.

6 Move the container into position under the oil filter, which is located on the front right-hand side of the engine.

7 Using an oil filter removal tool if necessary, slacken the filter initially, then unscrew it by hand the rest of the way **(see illustration)**. Empty the oil in the old filter into the container.

8 Use a clean rag to remove all oil, dirt and sludge from the filter sealing area on the engine. Check the old filter to make sure that the rubber sealing ring has not stuck to the engine. If it has, carefully remove it.

9 Apply a light coating of clean engine oil to the sealing ring on the new filter, then screw it into position on the engine **(see illustration)**. Tighten the filter firmly by hand only – **do not** use any tools.

10 Remove the old oil and all tools from

under the car then lower it to the ground (if applicable).

11 Withdraw the dipstick, and remove the oil filler cap from the cylinder head cover. Fill the engine, using the correct grade and type of oil (see *Lubricants and fluids*). An oil can spout or funnel may help to reduce spillage. Pour in half the specified quantity of oil first, then wait a few minutes for the oil to run to the sump. Continue adding oil a small quantity at a time until the level is up to the MAX mark on the dipstick. Refit the filler cap.

12 Start the engine and run it for a few minutes; check for leaks around the oil filter seal and the sump drain plug. Note that there may be a delay of a few seconds before the oil pressure warning light goes out when the engine is first started, as the oil circulates through the engine oil galleries and the new oil filter before the pressure builds-up.

13 Switch off the engine, and wait a few minutes for the oil to settle in the sump once more. With the new oil circulated and the filter completely full, recheck the level on the dipstick, and add more oil as necessary.

14 Dispose of the used engine oil and filter safely, referring to *General repair procedures* in the Reference Chapter. Do not discard the old filter with domestic household waste. The facility for waste oil disposal provided by many local council refuse tips generally has a filter receptacle alongside.

Every 12 000 miles or 12 months – whichever comes first

3 Auxiliary drivebelt check and renewal

1 A single, multi-ribbed auxiliary drivebelt is used on all models. The belt drives the

alternator, or alternator and air conditioning compressor according to equipment fitted. On models without air conditioning, the belt is adjusted manually, whereas on models with air conditioning adjustment is by means of an automatic spring-loaded tensioning mechanism.

Checking

2 Firmly apply the handbrake, then jack up the front of the car and support it securely on axle stands (see *Jacking and vehicle support*). Remove the right-hand front wheel roadwheel.

3 Undo the retaining bolts and remove the

3.3 Undo the bolts (arrowed) and remove the bracket

3.7a Alternator lower pivot bolt (arrowed) . . .

3.7b . . . and upper adjustment bolts (arrowed)

3.13 Undo the bolts (arrowed) and remove the belt guard

3.14 Rotate the tensioner (arrowed) clockwise against the spring pressure

support bracket between the front subframe and vehicle body prior to removing the wheel arch liner panel **(see illustration)**.

4 Using a socket on the crankshaft pulley bolt, rotate the crankshaft so that the full length of the drivebelt can be examined. Look for cracks, splitting and fraying on the surface of the belt; check also for signs of glazing (shiny patches) and separation of the belt plies. If damage or wear is visible, the belt should be renewed. Note that Ford recommend changing the belt at 5 years regardless of condition.

5 If the condition of the belt is satisfactory, where applicable check the drivebelt tension as described below.

Renewal

Models without air conditioning

6 If not already done, proceed as described in paragraphs 2 and 3.

7 Slacken the alternator lower pivot bolt and the upper adjustment bolts **(see illustrations)**. Swivel the alternator towards the engine and slip the drivebelt off the alternator pulley.

8 Unbolt and remove the crankshaft TDC sensor from the front of the engine (refer to Chapter 4A, Section 9).

9 Remove the drivebelt from the crankshaft pulley.

10 When renewing a drivebelt, ensure that the correct type is used. Fit the belt around the two pulleys then swivel the alternator outwards to take up any slack in the belt.

11 Refit the crankshaft TDC sensor, then adjust the drivebelt tension correctly as described below.

Models with air conditioning

12 If not already done, proceed as described in paragraphs 2 and 3.

13 Undo the two bolts and remove the drivebelt guard **(see illustration)**.

14 Using a socket or spanner on the drivebelt tensioner pulley retaining bolt, rotate the tensioner clockwise against the spring pressure to release the tension from the belt **(see illustration)**. Hold the tensioner in this position and slip the drivebelt off the alternator and air conditioning compressor pulleys. Allow the tensioner to return to the released position.

15 Unbolt and remove the crankshaft TDC

sensor from the front of the engine (refer to Chapter 4A, Section 9).

16 Remove the drivebelt from the crankshaft pulley.

17 When renewing a drivebelt, ensure that the correct type is used.

18 Fit the belt around the pulleys, then rotate the tensioner until the belt can be slipped into place over the tensioner pulley.

19 Release the tensioner to allow the spring-loaded arm to automatically tension the belt.

20 Refit the crankshaft TDC sensor, then locate the drivebelt guard in position and secure with the two retaining bolts.

21 Refit the wheel arch liner panels and roadwheel, then lower the car to the ground.

Tensioning

22 Correct tensioning of the belt will ensure that it has a long life. A belt which is too slack will slip and perhaps squeal. Beware, however, of overtightening, as this can cause wear in the alternator bearings. On models equipped with air conditioning the correct belt tension is maintained automatically by means of the spring-loaded tensioning mechanism. On models without air conditioning, the tension must be adjusted manually as follows.

23 The belt should be tensioned so that, under firm thumb pressure, there is approximately 5.0 mm of free movement at the mid-point between the pulleys. To adjust the drivebelt, slacken the alternator pivot and adjustment bolts (if not already done) then swivel the alternator outwards until the belt tension is correct. Hold the alternator in this

position and fully-tighten the adjustment bolts followed by the pivot bolt.

24 Refit the wheel arch liner panels and roadwheel, then lower the car to the ground.

4 Hose and fluid leak check

1 Visually inspect the engine joint faces, gaskets and seals for any signs of water or oil leaks. Pay particular attention to the areas around the camshaft cover, cylinder head, oil filter and sump joint faces. Bear in mind that, over a period of time, some very slight seepage from these areas is to be expected – what you are really looking for is any indication of a serious leak. Should a leak be found, renew the offending gasket or oil seal by referring to the appropriate Chapters in this manual.

2 Also check the security and condition of all the engine-related pipes and hoses. Ensure that all cable-ties or securing clips are in place and in good condition. Clips which are broken or missing can lead to chafing of the hoses, pipes or wiring, which could cause more serious problems in the future.

3 Carefully check the radiator hoses and heater hoses along their entire length. Renew any hose which is cracked, swollen or deteriorated. Cracks will show up better if the hose is squeezed. Pay close attention to the hose clips that secure the hoses to the cooling system components. Hose clips can pinch and puncture hoses, resulting in cooling system leaks.

4 Inspect all the cooling system components (hoses, joint faces etc.) for leaks **(see Haynes Hint)**. Where any problems of this nature are found on system components, renew the component or gasket with reference to Chapter 3.

5 Where applicable, inspect the automatic transmission fluid cooler hoses for leaks or deterioration.

6 With the vehicle raised, inspect the fuel tank and filler neck for punctures, cracks and other damage. The connection between the filler neck and tank is especially critical. Sometimes a rubber filler neck or connecting hose will leak due to loose retaining clamps or deteriorated rubber.

7 Carefully check all rubber hoses and metal fuel lines leading away from the fuel tank. Check for loose connections, deteriorated hoses, crimped lines, and other damage. Pay particular attention to the vent pipes and hoses, which often loop up around the filler neck and can become blocked or crimped. Follow the lines to the front of the vehicle, carefully inspecting them all the way. Renew damaged sections as necessary.

8 From within the engine compartment, check the security of all fuel hose attachments and pipe unions, and inspect the fuel hoses and vacuum hoses for kinks, chafing and deterioration.

5 Front brake pad check

1 Firmly apply the handbrake, then jack up the front of the car and support it securely on axle stands (see *Jacking and vehicle support*). Remove the front roadwheels.

2 Using a steel rule, measure the thickness of the friction material of the brake pads on both front brakes. This must not be less than 1.5 mm **(see illustration)**.

3 For a comprehensive check, the brake pads should be removed and cleaned. The operation of the caliper can then also be checked, and the condition of the brake disc itself can be fully examined on both sides. Refer to Chapter 9 for further information.

4 If any pad's friction material is worn to the

A leak in the cooling system will usually show up as white or antifreeze-coloured deposits on the area adjoining the leak.

specified thickness or less, *all four pads must be renewed as a set*. Refer to Chapter 9.

5 On completion refit the roadwheels and lower the car to the ground.

6 Driveshaft gaiter check

1 With the car raised and securely supported on stands (see *Jacking and vehicle support*), turn the steering onto full lock, then slowly rotate the roadwheel. Inspect the condition of the outer constant velocity (CV) joint rubber gaiters, squeezing the gaiters to open out the folds. Check for signs of cracking, splits or deterioration of the rubber, which may allow the grease to escape, and lead to water and grit entry into the joint. Also check the security and condition of the retaining clips. Repeat these checks on the inner CV joints **(see illustration)**. If any damage or deterioration is found, the gaiters should be renewed (see Chapter 8).

2 At the same time, check the general condition of the CV joints themselves by first holding the driveshaft and attempting to rotate the wheel. Repeat this check by holding the inner joint and attempting to rotate the driveshaft. Any appreciable movement indicates wear in the joints, wear in the driveshaft splines, or a loose driveshaft retaining nut.

7 Steering and suspension check

Front suspension and steering

1 Firmly apply the handbrake, then jack up the front of the car and support it securely on axle stands (see *Jacking and vehicle support*).

2 Inspect the balljoint dust covers and the steering rack and pinion gaiters for splits, chafing or deterioration. Any wear of these will cause loss of lubricant, together with dirt and water entry, resulting in rapid deterioration of the balljoints or steering gear.

3 Grasp the roadwheel at the 12 o'clock and 6 o'clock positions, and try to rock it **(see illustration)**. Very slight free play may be felt, but if the movement is appreciable, further investigation is necessary to determine the source. Continue rocking the wheel while an assistant depresses the footbrake. If the movement is now eliminated or significantly reduced, it is likely that the hub bearings are at fault. If the free play is still evident with the footbrake depressed, then there is wear in the suspension joints or mountings.

4 Now grasp the wheel at the 9 o'clock and 3 o'clock positions, and try to rock it as before. Any movement felt now may again be caused by wear in the hub bearings or the steering track rod balljoints. If the inner or outer balljoint is worn, the visual movement will be obvious.

5 Using a large screwdriver or flat bar, check for wear in the suspension mounting bushes by levering between the relevant suspension component and its attachment point. Some movement is to be expected as the mountings are made of rubber, but excessive wear should be obvious. Also check the condition of any visible rubber bushes, looking for splits, cracks or contamination of the rubber.

6 With the car standing on its wheels, have an assistant turn the steering wheel back-and-forth about an eighth of a turn each way. There should be very little, if any, lost movement between the steering wheel and roadwheels. If this is not the case, closely observe the joints and mountings previously described, but in addition check the steering

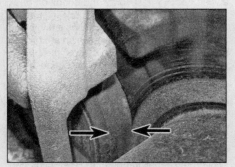

5.2 Measure the thickness of the friction material (arrowed)

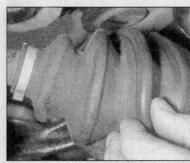

6.1 Check the condition of the driveshaft gaiters

7.3 Grasp the roadwheel at the 12 and 6 o'clock positions, and try to rock it

column universal joints for wear, and the rack and pinion steering gear itself.

Strut/shock absorber check

7 Check for any signs of fluid leakage around the suspension strut/shock absorber body, or from the rubber gaiter around the piston rod. Should any fluid be noticed, the suspension strut/shock absorber is defective internally, and should be renewed. **Note:** *Suspension struts/shock absorbers should always be renewed in pairs on the same axle.*

8 The efficiency of the suspension strut/shock absorber may be checked by bouncing the vehicle at each corner. Generally speaking, the body will return to its normal position and stop after being depressed. If it rises and returns on a rebound, the suspension strut/shock absorber is probably suspect. Examine also the suspension strut/shock absorber upper and lower mountings for any signs of wear.

8 Underbody sealant check

1 Jack up the front and rear of the car and support it securely on axle stands (see *Jacking and vehicle support*). Alternatively position the car over an inspection pit.

2 Check the underbody, wheel housings and side sills for rust and/or damage to the underbody sealant. If evident, repair as necessary.

9 Exhaust system check

1 With the engine cold (at least an hour after the vehicle has been driven), check the complete exhaust system from the engine to the end of the tailpipe. The exhaust system is most easily checked with the car raised on a hoist, or suitably supported on axle stands (see *Jacking and vehicle support*), so that the exhaust components are readily visible and accessible.

2 Check the exhaust pipes and connections for evidence of leaks, severe corrosion and damage. Make sure that all brackets and

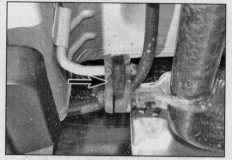

9.2 Check the condition of the rubber exhaust mountings (arrowed)

mountings are in good condition, and that all relevant nuts and bolts are tight **(see illustration)**. Leakage at any of the joints or in other parts of the system will usually show up as a black sooty stain in the vicinity of the leak.

3 Rattles and other noises can often be traced to the exhaust system, especially the brackets and mountings. Try to move the pipes and silencers. If the components are able to come into contact with the body or suspension parts, secure the system with new mountings. Otherwise separate the joints (if possible) and twist the pipes as necessary to provide additional clearance.

10 Handbrake check and adjustment

Apply the handbrake by pulling it through a maximum of five clicks of the ratchet mechanism and check that this locks the rear wheels, holding the vehicle stationary on an incline. In this position, there should be sufficient reserve travel in the handbrake lever to allow for brake shoe wear and cable stretching. If not, the handbrake mechanism should be adjusted as described in Chapter 9.

11 Pollen filter renewal

1 The pollen filter is located under the facia

on the driver's side, adjacent to the heater blower motor.

2 Undo the retaining screw(s) remove the footwell kickpanel adjacent to the heater air distribution housing **(see illustration)**.

3 Unclip the cover, and withdraw the filter from its housing **(see illustrations)**.

4 Wipe clean the filter housing then fit the new filter. Refit the cover and footwell panel.

12 Hinge and lock lubrication

1 Lubricate the hinges of the bonnet, doors and tailgate with a light general-purpose oil. Similarly, lubricate all latches, locks and lock strikers. At the same time, check the security and operation of all the locks, adjusting them if necessary (see Chapter 11).

2 Lightly lubricate the bonnet release mechanism and cable with a suitable grease.

13 Road test

Instruments and electrical equipment

1 Check the operation of all instruments and electrical equipment.

2 Make sure that all instruments read correctly, and switch on all electrical equipment in turn, to check that it functions properly.

Steering and suspension

3 Check for any abnormalities in the steering, suspension, handling or road feel.

4 Drive the vehicle, and check that there are no unusual vibrations or noises.

5 Check that the steering feels positive, with no excessive sloppiness, or roughness, and check for any suspension noises when cornering and driving over bumps.

Drivetrain

6 Check the performance of the engine, clutch, transmission and driveshafts.

7 Listen for any unusual noises from the engine, clutch and gearbox/transmission.

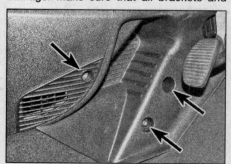

11.2 Undo the screws (arrowed)

11.3a Unclip the cover (arrowed)...

11.3b ...and withdraw the filter element

8 Make sure that the engine runs smoothly when idling, and that there is no hesitation when accelerating.
9 Check that the clutch action is smooth and progressive, that the drive is taken up smoothly, and that the pedal travel is not excessive. Also listen for any noises when the clutch pedal is depressed.
10 Check that all gears can be engaged smoothly without noise, and that the gear lever action is smooth and not abnormally vague or notchy.
11 Listen for a metallic clicking sound from the front of the vehicle, as the vehicle is driven slowly in a circle with the steering on full lock. Carry out this check in both directions. If a clicking noise is heard, this indicates wear in a driveshaft joint, in which case renew the joint if necessary.

Braking system

12 Make sure that the vehicle does not pull to one side when braking, and that the wheels do not lock when braking hard. **Note:** *Under heavy braking, vibration may be felt through the brake pedal. This is a normal feature of ABS operation, and does not constitute a fault.*
13 Check that there is no vibration through the steering when braking.
14 Check that the handbrake operates correctly without excessive movement of the lever, and that it holds the vehicle stationary on a slope.
15 Test the operation of the brake servo unit as follows. With the engine off, depress the footbrake four or five times to exhaust the vacuum. Hold the brake pedal depressed, then start the engine. As the engine starts, there should be a noticeable give in the brake pedal as vacuum builds-up. Allow the engine to run for at least two minutes, and then switch it off. If the brake pedal is depressed now, it should be possible to detect a hiss from the servo as the pedal is depressed. After about four or five applications, no further hissing should be heard, and the pedal should feel considerably harder.

Every 24 000 miles or 2 years – whichever comes first

14 Valve clearance check and adjustment

1 The importance of having the valve clearances correctly adjusted cannot be overstressed, as they vitally affect the performance of the engine. Adjustment should only be necessary when the valve gear has become noisy, after engine overhaul, or when trying to trace the cause of power loss. The clearances are checked as follows. The engine must be cold for the check to be accurate.
2 Apply the handbrake then jack up the right-hand front of the car and support on an axle stand (*see Jacking and vehicle support*). Engage 4th gear. The engine can now be rotated by turning the right-hand front roadwheel.
3 Remove all spark plugs as described in Section 15.
4 Remove the camshaft cover as described in Chapter 2A.
5 Each valve clearance must be checked when the high point of the cam lobe is pointing directly upward away from the cam follower.
6 Check the clearances in the firing order 1-3-4-2, No 1 cylinder being at the timing belt end of the engine. This will minimise the amount of crankshaft rotation required.
7 Insert the appropriate feeler blade between the heel of the cam and the cam follower shim of the first valve (**see illustration**). If necessary alter the thickness of the feeler blade until it is a stiff, sliding fit. Record the thickness, which will represent the valve clearance for this particular valve.
8 Turn the engine, check the second valve clearance and record it.
9 Repeat the operations on all the remaining valves, recording their respective clearances.
10 Remember that the clearance for intake and exhaust valves differs – see *Specifications*. Counting from the timing belt end of the engine, the valve sequence is:

Intake   2-4-5-7
Exhaust   1-3-6-8

11 Where clearances are incorrect, the particular shim will have to be changed. To remove the shim, turn the crankshaft until the high point of the cam is pointing directly upward. The cam follower will now have to be depressed so that the shim can be extracted. Special tools are commercially available to do the job, otherwise you will have to make up a forked lever to locate on the rim of the cam follower. This must allow room for the shim to be prised out by means of the cut-outs provided in the cam follower rim (**see illustration**).
12 Once the shim is extracted, establish its thickness and change it for a thicker or thinner one to bring the previously recorded clearance within specification. For example, if the measured valve clearance was 1.27 mm too great, a shim thicker by this amount will be required. Conversely, if the clearance was 1.27 mm too small, a shim thinner by this amount will be required.
13 Shims have their thickness (mm) engraved on them; although the engraved side should be fitted so as not to be visible, wear still occurs and often obliterates the number. In this case, measuring their thickness with a metric micrometer is the only method to establish their thickness (**see illustration**).
14 In practice, if several shims have to be changed, they can often be interchanged, between valves so avoiding the necessity of having to buy more new shims than is necessary, but do not turn the engine with any shims missing.
15 If more than two or three valve clearances are found to be incorrect, it may be more convenient to remove the camshaft for easier removal of the shims.
16 Where no clearance can be measured, even with the thinnest available shim in position, the valve will have to be removed and the end of its stem ground off squarely. This will reduce its overall length by the minimum amount to provide a clearance. This job should be entrusted to an engine reconditioning specialist as it is important to keep the end of the valve stem square.

14.7 Check the valve clearance with feeler gauge

14.11 Using a modified C-spanner and a screwdriver to remove a shim

14.13 Shim thickness is marked on the lower face

15.2 Pull the spark plug lead end fitting from the plug

15.4 Use a spark plug socket to unscrew the plug

It is often difficult to insert spark plugs into their holes without cross-threading them. To avoid this possibility, fit a short length of rubber or plastic hose over the end of the spark plug. The flexible hose acts as a universal joint, to help align the plug with the plug hole. Should the plug begin to cross-thread, the hose will slip on the spark plug, preventing thread damage to the cylinder head.

17 On completion, refit the camshaft cover as described in Chapter 2A, and the spark plugs as described in Section 15.

18 Lower the car to the ground.

15 Spark plug renewal

1 The correct functioning of the spark plugs is vital for the correct running and efficiency of the engine. It is essential that the plugs fitted are appropriate for the engine (a suitable type is specified at the beginning of this Chapter). If this type is used and the engine is in good condition, the spark plugs should not need attention between scheduled renewal intervals. Spark plug cleaning is rarely necessary, and should not be attempted unless specialised equipment is available, as damage can easily be caused to the firing ends.

2 To remove the plugs first remove the air cleaner assembly with reference to Chapter 4A. If the marks on the original-equipment spark plug (HT) leads cannot be seen, mark the leads 1 to 4, to correspond to the cylinder the lead serves (No 1 cylinder is at the timing belt end of the engine). Pull the leads from the plugs by gripping the end fitting, not the lead, otherwise the lead connection may be fractured **(see illustration)**.

3 It is advisable to remove the dirt from the spark plug recesses using a clean brush, vacuum cleaner or compressed air before removing the plugs, to prevent dirt dropping into the cylinders.

4 Unscrew the plugs using a spark plug box spanner or a deep socket and extension bar **(see illustration)**. Keep the socket aligned with the spark plug – if it is forcibly moved to one side, the ceramic insulator may be broken off. As each plug is removed, examine it as follows.

5 Examination of the spark plugs will give a good indication of the condition of the engine. If the insulator nose of the spark plug is clean and white, with no deposits, this is indicative of a weak mixture or too hot a plug (a hot plug transfers heat away from the electrode slowly, a cold plug transfers heat away quickly).

6 If the tip and insulator nose are covered with hard black-looking deposits, this indicates

that the mixture is too rich. If the plug is black and oily, then it is likely that the engine is fairly worn, as well as the mixture being too rich.

7 If the insulator nose is covered with light tan to greyish-brown deposits, then the mixture is correct and it is likely that the engine is in good condition.

8 The spark plug electrode gap is of considerable importance as, if it is too large or too small, the size of the spark and its efficiency will be seriously impaired. The gap should be the value given in the Specifications at the beginning of this Chapter. Note that if the recommended spark plugs are fitted, the electrode gap is pre-set by the manufacturer.

9 To check the gap measure it with a feeler blade. If the gap is not within specification, then replace the plugs. Do not attempt to adjust the gap.

11 Before fitting the spark plugs, check that the threaded connector sleeves are tight, and that the plug exterior surfaces and threads are clean **(see Haynes Hint)**.

12 Remove the rubber hose (if used), and tighten the plug to the specified torque using the spark plug socket and a torque wrench. Refit the remaining spark plugs in the same manner.

13 Connect the HT leads in their correct order, and refit the air cleaner assembly.

16 Ignition system check

⚠ *Warning: Due to the high voltages produced by the electronic ignition system, extreme care must be taken when working on the system with the ignition switched on. Persons with surgically-implanted cardiac pacemaker devices should keep well clear of the ignition circuits, components and test equipment.*

1 The spark plug (HT) leads should be checked whenever new spark plugs are fitted.

2 Remove the air cleaner assembly as described in Chapter 4A.

3 Pull the leads from the plugs by gripping the end fitting, not the lead, otherwise the lead connection may be fractured.

4 Check inside the end fitting for signs of corrosion, which will look like a white crusty powder. Push the end fitting back onto the spark plug, ensuring that it is a tight fit on the plug. If not, remove the lead again and use pliers to carefully crimp the metal connector inside the end fitting until it fits securely on the end of the spark plug.

5 Using a clean rag, wipe the entire length of the lead to remove any built-up dirt and grease. Once the lead is clean, check for burns, cracks and other damage. Do not bend the lead excessively, nor pull the lead lengthways – the conductor inside might break.

6 Disconnect the other end of the lead from the ignition coil. Again, pull only on the end fitting. Check for corrosion and a tight fit in the same manner as the spark plug end. Refit the lead securely on completion.

7 Check the remaining leads one at a time, in the same way.

8 If new spark plug (HT) leads are required, purchase a set for your specific car and engine.

9 Refit the air cleaner assembly on completion of the checks.

10 Even with the ignition system in first-class condition, some engines may still occasionally experience poor starting attributable to damp ignition components. To disperse moisture, a water-dispersant aerosol should be liberally applied.

17 Engine management system check

1 This check is part of the manufacturer's maintenance schedule, and involves testing the engine management system using special dedicated test equipment. Such testing will allow the test equipment to read any fault

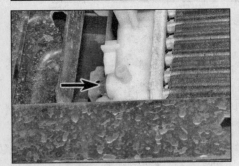

19.2 Slacken the radiator drain plug (arrowed)

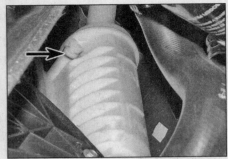

19.3a Radiator bleed screw (arrowed – viewed from beneath) and...

19.3b ...at the engine compartment bulkhead (arrowed)

codes stored in the electronic control unit memory.

2 Unless a fault is suspected, this test is not essential, although it should be noted that it is recommended by the manufacturers.

3 If access to suitable test equipment is not possible, make a thorough check of all ignition, fuel and emission control system components, hoses, and wiring, for security and obvious signs of damage. Further details of the fuel system, emission control system and ignition system can be found in the relevant parts of Chapters 4 and 5.

18 Brake fluid renewal

⚠️ **Warning: Brake hydraulic fluid can harm your eyes and damage painted surfaces, so use extreme caution when handling and pouring it. Do not use fluid that has been standing open for some time, as it absorbs moisture from the air. Excess moisture can cause a dangerous loss of braking effectiveness.**

1 The procedure is similar to that for the bleeding of the hydraulic system as described in Chapter 9, except that the brake fluid reservoir should be emptied by siphoning, using a clean poultry baster or similar before starting, and allowance should be made for the old fluid to be expelled when bleeding a section of the circuit.

2 Working as described in Chapter 9, open the first bleed screw in the sequence, and pump the brake pedal gently until nearly all the old fluid has been emptied from the master cylinder reservoir.

3 Top-up to the MAX level with new fluid, and continue pumping until only the new fluid remains in the reservoir, and new fluid can be seen emerging from the bleed screw. Tighten the screw, and top the reservoir level up to the MAX level line.

4 Work through all the remaining bleed screws in the sequence until new fluid can be seen at all of them. Be careful to keep the master cylinder reservoir topped-up to above the MIN level at all times, or air may enter the system and greatly increase the length of the task.

5 When the operation is complete, check that all bleed screws are securely tightened, and that their dust caps are refitted. Wash off all traces of spilt fluid, and recheck the master cylinder reservoir fluid level.

6 Check the operation of the brakes before taking the car on the road.

19 Coolant renewal

⚠️ **Warning: Wait until the engine is cold before starting this procedure. Do not allow antifreeze to come in contact with your skin, or with the painted surfaces of the vehicle. Rinse off spills immediately with plenty of water. Never leave antifreeze lying around in an open container, or in a puddle in the driveway or on the garage floor. Children and pets are attracted by its sweet smell, but antifreeze can be fatal if ingested.**

Cooling system draining

1 With the engine completely cold, cover the expansion tank cap with a wad of rag, and slowly turn the cap anti-clockwise to relieve the pressure in the cooling system (a hissing sound will normally be heard). Wait until any pressure remaining in the system is released, then continue to turn the cap until it can be removed.

2 A radiator drain plug is located at the lower left-hand end of the radiator. Position a suitable container beneath, then undo the drain plug and allow the coolant to escape **(see illustration)**.

3 The cooling system bleed screws should be opened to aid the draining process and help prevent airlocks. These are located on the top right-hand edge of the radiator, and on the heater inlet hose **(see illustrations)**. If the coolant has been drained for a reason other than renewal, then provided it is clean and less than two years old, it can be re-used, though this is not recommended.

4 Once all the coolant has drained, reconnect the hose to the radiator and secure it in position with the retaining clip, or tighten the drain plug as applicable.

Radiator flushing

5 Refer to Chapter 3.

Cooling system filling

6 Before attempting to fill the cooling system, make sure that all hoses and clips are in good condition, and that the clips are tight. Note that an antifreeze mixture must be used all year round, to prevent corrosion of the engine components (see below).

7 Remove the expansion tank filler cap, and fill the system by slowly pouring the coolant into the expansion tank to prevent airlocks from forming. Ensure that all bleed screws are open.

8 If the coolant is being renewed, begin by pouring in a couple of litres of water, followed by the correct quantity of antifreeze, then top-up with more water. Periodically squeeze the radiator top and bottom hoses to help expel any trapped air in the system.

9 Continue adding coolant until it is seen to emerge from the bleed screws. Close each bleed screw in turn as the coolant emerges.

10 Top-up the coolant level to the MAX mark and refit the expansion tank cap. Ensure that all bleed screws are closed.

11 Start the engine and run it at idling speed for two to three minutes. Allow the engine to continue running until the electric cooling fan operates, periodically increasing the engine speed gradually to 2000 to 3000 rpm.

12 Stop the engine and allow it to cool down completely.

13 Check for leaks, particularly around disturbed components. Check the coolant level in the expansion tank, and top-up if necessary. Note that the system must be cold before an accurate level is indicated in the expansion tank.

Antifreeze mixture

14 The antifreeze should always be renewed at the specified intervals. This is necessary not only to maintain the antifreeze properties, but also to prevent corrosion which would otherwise occur as the corrosion inhibitors become progressively less effective.

15 Always use a monoethylene-glycol based antifreeze of the specified type (see *Lubricants and fluids*). The quantity of antifreeze and

levels of protection are indicated in the *Specifications*.

16 Before adding antifreeze, the cooling system should be completely drained, preferably flushed, and all hoses checked for condition and security.

17 After filling with antifreeze, a label should be attached to the expansion tank, stating the type and concentration of antifreeze used, and the date installed. Any subsequent topping-up should be made with the same type and concentration of antifreeze.

Caution: Do not use engine antifreeze in the windscreen/tailgate washer system, as it will cause damage to the vehicle paintwork. A screenwash additive should be added to the washer system in the quantities stated on the bottle.

Every 36 000 miles or 3 years – whichever comes first

20 Air filter renewal

1 Undo the upper and lower bolts securing the front section of the air cleaner housing to main section of the housing (see illustration).
2 Separate the halves of the air cleaner assembly. Take out the filter element (see illustration).
3 Remove any debris that may have collected inside the air cleaner and wipe the inner surfaces clean.
4 Fit a new air filter element in position, ensuring that the edges are securely seated.
5 Refitting is a reversal of removal.

21 Timing belt inspection

1 The function of the timing belt is to drive the camshaft and coolant pump. Should the belt slip or break in service, the valve timing will be disturbed and piston-to-valve contact will occur, resulting in serious engine damage. It is therefore vitally important that the condition of the belt and surrounding components should be checked very carefully.
2 To gain access to the belt, remove the timing belt covers as described in Chapter 2A.
3 With the covers removed, inspect the timing belt for any signs of uneven wear, splitting, or oil contamination. Pay particular attention to the roots of the teeth. To enable the full length of the belt to be examined, turn the crankshaft using a spanner or socket on the crankshaft sprocket centre bolt.
4 Check for any signs of coolant leakage from the coolant pump or oil leakage from the crankshaft right-hand oil seal. If there is any doubt about the condition of the belt, it should be renewed as described in Chapter 2A. If any coolant or oil leakage is evident, trace the source of the leak and rectify it before fitting the new timing belt.
5 On completion of the inspection, refit the timing belt covers as described in Chapter 2A.

22 Manual transmission oil level check

1 Park the car on a level surface, if possible over an inspection pit or on a ramp as the filler/level plug is best reached from under the engine compartment. The oil level must be checked before the car is driven, or at least 5 minutes after the engine has been switched off. If the oil is checked immediately after driving the car, some of the oil will remain distributed around the transmission components, resulting in an inaccurate level reading.
2 Wipe clean the area around the filler/level plug, which is situated on the front of the transmission (see illustration). Using an Allen key, unscrew the plug and clean it.
3 The oil level should reach the lower edge of the filler/level hole. A certain amount of oil will have gathered behind the filler/level plug, and will trickle out when it is removed; this does **not** necessarily indicate that the level is correct. To ensure that a true level is established, wait until the initial trickle has stopped, then add oil as necessary until a trickle of new oil can be seen emerging. The level will be correct when the flow ceases; use only good-quality oil of the specified type. Make sure that the vehicle is completely level when checking the level and do not overfill.
4 When the level is correct refit and tighten the plug and wipe away any spilt oil.

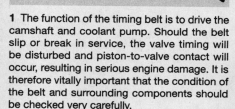

20.1 Remove the bolts (upper 3 shown, with 3 hidden below)

22.2 Transmission oil filler/level plug (arrowed)

23 Rear brake shoe check

1 Chock the front wheels then jack up the rear of the car and support it on axle stands (see *Jacking and vehicle support*). Remove the rear roadwheels.
2 Using the inspection hole at the edge of the brake drum, check that the linings are not worn below the minimum thickness given in the *Specifications* (see illustration). If necessary use an electric torch.
3 If the friction material on any shoe is worn down to the specified minimum thickness or less, all four shoes must be renewed as a set.
4 At the same time check for signs of brake fluid leakage.
5 For a comprehensive check, the brake drum should be removed and cleaned. This will allow the wheel cylinders to be checked, and the condition of the brake drum itself to be fully examined (see Chapter 9).
6 On completion of the check, lower the car to the ground.

20.2 Lift out the air filter element

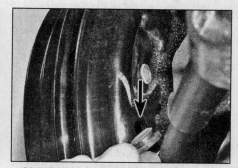
23.2 Pull the rubber grommet from the brake shoe inspection hole (arrowed)

27.1a Rotate the screw to the unlock position...

27.1b ...and remove the battery carrier

27.3 Fit the new battery

Every 48 000 miles or 4 years – whichever comes first

24 Timing belt renewal

Refer to Chapter 2A.

25 Evaporative loss system check

1 Refer to Chapter 4B, Section 2, and check that all wiring and hoses are correctly connected to the evaporative loss system components.

26 Emission control system check

1 Refer to Chapter 4B. A full check of the emissions control system must be made by a Ford dealer.

27 Remote control battery renewal

1 Press the button to release the key blade.

2 Rotate the screw to the 'unlock' position and remove the battery case from the side of the fob **(see illustrations)**.
3 Note the orientation of the battery, and remove it from the casing.
4 Insert the new battery into place, with the positive (+) side of the battery on the same side as the positive mark on the casing **(see illustration)**. Avoid touching the battery or the terminals with bare fingers.
5 Refit the battery case and rotate the screw to the 'locked' position.

Chapter 2 Part A:
Engine in-car repair procedures

Contents

Degrees of difficulty

Easy, suitable for
novice with little
experience

Fairly easy, suitable
for beginner with
some experience

Fairly difficult,
suitable for competent
DIY mechanic

Difficult, suitable
for experienced DIY
mechanic

Very difficult,
suitable for expert
DIY or professional

Specifications

General

Engine code	FP4 (Fiat 169A4000)
Capacity	1242cc
Bore	70.8 mm
Stroke:	78.86 mm
Compression ratio	11.1:1
Engine output:	
Power:	70 bhp (51 kW) @ 5500 rpm
Torque.	102 Nm @ 3000 rpm
Firing order	1-3-4-2
No 1 cylinder location.	Timing belt (right-hand) end of engine

* Note: *See 'Vehicle identification' for the location of code marking on the engine.*

Lubrication system

Oil pump type.	By-rotor driven from front of crankshaft
Outer rotor-to-housing clearance.	0.080 to 0.186 mm
Axial clearance	0.025 to 0.056 mm

Torque wrench settings

	Nm	lbf ft
Big-end bearing cap bolts:*		
Stage 1	20	15
Stage 2	Angle-tighten a further 40°	
Camshaft bearing cap bolts:		
M6	10	7
M8	23	17
Camshaft cover bolts	10	7
Camshaft sprocket bolt	70	52
Crankshaft oil seal housing bolts	10	7
Crankshaft pulley bolts	25	18
Crankshaft sprocket centre bolt:		
Stage 1	20	15
Stage 2	Angle-tighten a further 90°	
Cylinder head bolts:*		
Stage 1	30	22
Stage 2	Angle-tighten a further 90°	
Stage 3	Angle-tighten a further 90°	
Engine/transmission attachment bolts	80	59
Engine/transmission mountings:		
Left hand mounting-to-body nuts	50	37
Left-hand mounting bracket-to-transmission bolts	50	37
Left-hand mounting centre bolt	130	96
Rear mounting-to-subframe bolt	80	59
Rear mounting-to-transmission bolt/nut	80	59
Right-hand mounting lower bracket-to-cylinder head bolts	68	50
Right-hand mounting upper bracket-to-lower bracket nuts	60	44
Right-hand mounting-to-body nuts	60	44
Flywheel bolts:*		
Stage 1	15	11
Stage 2	Angle-tighten a further 40°	
Main bearing cap bolts:		
Stage 1	20	15
Stage 2	Angle-tighten a further 90°	
Oil pressure warning light switch	35	26
Oil pump retaining bolts	10	7
Subframe to body support bracket	50	37
Sump nuts/bolts:		
M6	10	7
M8	25	18
Timing belt tensioner nut	28	21

* Do not re-use.

1 General information

Using this Chapter

This Part of Chapter 2 is devoted to in-car repair procedures. Part B covers the removal of the engine/transmission as a unit, and describes the engine dismantling and overhaul procedures.

In Part A, the assumption is made that the engine is installed in the car, with all ancillaries connected. If the engine has been removed for overhaul, the preliminary dismantling information which precedes each operation may be ignored.

Engine description

The engine covered in this Part of Chapter 2 is a water-cooled, single overhead camshaft (SOHC), in-line four-cylinder unit, with cast iron cylinder block and aluminium-alloy cylinder head. The engine is mounted transversely at the front of the car, with the transmission bolted to the left-hand end.

The cylinder head carries the camshaft which is driven by a toothed timing belt and runs in three bearings. It also houses the intake and exhaust valves, which are closed by single coil springs, and which run in guides pressed into the cylinder head. The camshaft actuates the valves directly via cam followers mounted in the cylinder head. Adjustment of the valve clearances is by means of shims located on top of the followers. The cylinder head contains integral oilways which supply and lubricate the followers (tappets).

The crankshaft is supported by five main bearings, and endfloat is controlled by a thrust bearing fitted to the upper section of the centre main bearing.

Engine coolant is circulated by a pump, driven by the timing belt. For details of the cooling system, refer to Chapter 3.

Lubricant is circulated under pressure by a pump, driven from the front of the crankshaft. Oil is drawn from the sump through a strainer, and then forced through an externally-mounted, renewable screw-on filter. From there, it is distributed to the cylinder head, where it lubricates the camshaft journals and tappets, and also to the crankcase, where it lubricates the main bearings, connecting rod big- and small-ends, gudgeon pins and cylinder bores.

Operations with engine in car

The following work can be carried out with the engine in the vehicle:

a) Compression pressure – testing.
b) Valve clearances – checking and adjustment (see Chapter 1).
c) Camshaft cover – removal and refitting.
d) Timing belt covers – removal and refitting.
e) Timing belt – removal, refitting and adjustment.
f) Timing belt tensioner and sprockets – removal and refitting.
g) Camshaft and cam followers – removal and refitting.
h) Cylinder head – removal and refitting.
i) Camshaft oil seal – renewal.
j) Crankshaft oil seals – renewal.

2.5 Suitable tools like these from Auto Service Tools Limited are needed

2.9a Note that the slot in the camshaft (arrowed) is not horizontal

2.9b The locking tool (arrowed) fits into the slot and is secured to the upper surface of the cylinder head

k) *Flywheel – removal, inspection and refitting.*
l) *Engine mountings – inspection and renewal.*
m) *Sump – removal and refitting.*
n) *Oil pump and pick-up tube assembly – removal, inspection and refitting.*

2 Top dead centre (TDC) for No 1 piston – locating

General information

Note: *Ford special tools 303-1479 and 303-1480 (or alternatives, such as AST 4950) will be required for this procedure.*

1 The camshaft is driven by the crankshaft, by means of a timing belt and sprockets. Both sprockets rotate in phase with each other and this provides the correct valve timing as the engine rotates. When the timing belt is removed during servicing or repair, it is possible for the camshaft and crankshaft to rotate independently of each other and the correct valve timing is then lost.

2 The design of the engine is such that potentially damaging piston-to-valve contact may occur if the camshaft is rotated when any of the pistons are stationary at, or near, the top of their stroke.

3 For this reason it is important that the correct phasing between the camshaft and crankshaft is preserved whilst the timing belt is off the engine. This is achieved by setting the engine in a reference position (known as Top Dead Centre or TDC) before the timing belt is removed and then preventing the camshaft and crankshaft from rotating until the belt is refitted. Similarly, if the engine has been dismantled for overhaul, the engine can be set to the correct position during reassembly to ensure that the correct shaft phasing is restored.

4 TDC is the highest point in the cylinder that each piston reaches as the crankshaft turns. Each piston reaches TDC at the end of the compression stroke and again at the end of the exhaust stroke. However, for the purpose of timing the engine, TDC refers to the position of No 1 piston at the end of its compression

stroke. On all engines in this manual, No 1 piston (and cylinder) is at the timing belt end of the engine.

5 Conventional timing marks are not provided on the engine, and it is therefore necessary to use special tools **(see illustration)** to determine the correct position for No 1 piston, and the correct corresponding position for the camshaft.

6 Remove the camshaft cover as described in Section 7.

7 Remove the timing belt upper and lower covers as described in Section 4.

8 Remove the spark plugs as described in Chapter 1.

9 Turn the engine by means of the crankshaft sprocket until the Ford tool 303-1479 locates correctly in the slot at the left-hand end of the camshaft, and with the upper mating surface of the cylinder head. Secure the tool to the cylinder head using the bolt(s) provided **(see illustrations)**.

10 With the camshaft locked in place it must be possible to locate the crankshaft locking tool (303-1480) over the end of the crankshaft, and secure it to the engine block as shown **(see illustration)**.

3 Compression test – description and interpretation

1 When engine performance is down, or if misfiring occurs which cannot be attributed to the ignition or fuel systems, a compression

2.10 Lock the crankshaft with the special tool as shown (arrowed)

test can provide diagnostic clues as to the engine's condition. If the test is performed regularly, it can give warning of trouble before any other symptoms become apparent.

2 The engine must be fully warmed-up to normal operating temperature, the battery must be fully-charged, and all the spark plugs must be removed (see Chapter 1). The aid of an assistant will also be required.

3 Disable the ignition and fuel injection systems by disconnecting the wiring multiplug connectors at the engine management ECU, referring to Chapter 4A for further information.

4 Fit a compression tester to the No 1 cylinder spark plug hole – the type of tester which screws into the plug thread is to be preferred.

5 Have the assistant hold the throttle wide open, and crank the engine on the starter motor; after one or two revolutions, the compression pressure should build-up to a maximum figure, and then stabilise. Record the highest reading obtained.

6 Repeat the test on the remaining cylinders, recording the pressure in each.

7 All cylinders should produce very similar pressures; a difference of more than 2 bars between any two cylinders indicates a fault. Note that the compression should build-up quickly in a healthy engine; low compression on the first stroke, followed by gradually-increasing pressure on successive strokes, indicates worn piston rings. A low compression reading on the first stroke, which does not build-up during successive strokes, indicates leaking valves or a blown head gasket (a cracked head could also be the cause). Deposits on the undersides of the valve heads can also cause low compression.

8 Although Ford do not specify exact compression pressures, as a guide, any cylinder pressure of below 10 bars can be considered as less than healthy. Refer to a Ford dealer or other specialist if in doubt as to whether a particular pressure reading is acceptable.

9 If the pressure in any cylinder is low, carry out the following test to isolate the cause. Introduce a teaspoonful of clean oil into that cylinder through its spark plug hole, and repeat the test.

4.4a Remove the single rear bolt and...

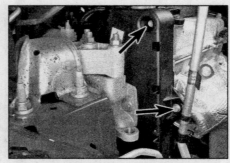

4.4b ...the 2 front bolts (arrowed)

4.4c Fully release the wiring loom as the cover is removed

10 If the addition of oil temporarily improves the compression pressure, this indicates that bore or piston wear is responsible for the pressure loss. No improvement suggests that leaking or burnt valves, or a blown head gasket, may be to blame.

11 A low reading from two adjacent cylinders is almost certainly due to the head gasket having blown between them; the presence of coolant in the engine oil will confirm this.

12 If the compression reading is unusually high, the combustion chambers are probably coated with carbon deposits. If this is the case, the cylinder head should be removed and decarbonised.

13 On completion of the test, refit the spark plugs and reconnect the engine management ECU wiring connectors.

4 Timing belt covers – removal and refitting

Removal

Upper cover

1 Disconnect the battery negative terminal as described in Chapter 5A.

2 Although not strictly necessary, to improve access, remove the air cleaner assembly as described in Chapter 4A.

3 Disconnect the wiring plug from the variable valve timing control solenoid. Release the wiring looms from the retaining clip.

4 Unbolt the upper cover and free the loom as the cover is removed **(see illustrations)**.

Lower cover

5 Jack up the front of the car and support it securely on axle stands (see *Jacking and vehicle support*). Remove the right-hand front roadwheel, then undo the fasteners and remove the engine undertray (where fitted).

6 Place a trolley jack beneath the right-hand side of the engine, with a block of wood on the jack head. Raise the jack until it is supporting the weight of the engine.

7 Unbolt and then remove the subframe support strut **(see illustration)**.

8 Release the wing liner and the protective engine crankshaft cover **(see illustration)**.

9 Undo the nuts securing the right-hand engine mounting to the body and the nuts securing the mounting upper bracket to the lower bracket on the engine. Lift the mounting and upper bracket assembly off the studs and remove it from the car **(see illustration)**.

10 Undo the bolts and remove the right-hand mounting lower bracket from the cylinder head **(see illustration)**. If necessary, raise the engine a little to facilitate removal of the bracket.

11 Release the wiring harness from the clip on the side of the cover.

12 Undo the retaining bolt and pull the crankshaft position sensor from the mounting bracket **(see illustration)**.

13 Remove the auxiliary drivebelt as described in Chapter 1.

14 Undo the bolts and remove the crankshaft pulley from the sprocket **(see illustration)**.

4.7 Remove the support strut

4.8 Remove the protective cover

4.9 Remove the engine mounting

4.10 Remove the bracket from the engine

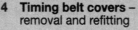

4.12 Remove the crankshaft position sensor (arrowed)

4.14 Use a strap wrench to hold the crankshaft stationary

5.5 Undo the nut (arrowed) and move the timing belt tensioner pulley away from the belt

5.11a Use right-angled circlip pliers to turn the tensioner pulley and fully-tension the timing belt

15 Undo the retaining bolt and remove the lower timing cover.

Refitting

16 Refitting is the reverse sequence to removal, bearing in mind the following points:
a) Tighten the engine mounting and crankshaft pulley retaining nuts/bolts to the specified torque.
b) Refit and adjust the auxiliary drivebelt as described in Chapter 1.
c) Refit the air cleaner assembly as described in Chapter 4A.

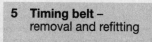

5 Timing belt – removal and refitting

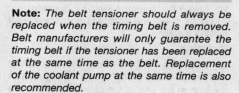

Note: The belt tensioner should always be replaced when the timing belt is removed. Belt manufacturers will only guarantee the timing belt if the tensioner has been replaced at the same time as the belt. Replacement of the coolant pump at the same time is also recommended.

General information

1 The function of the timing belt is to drive the camshaft and coolant pump. Should the belt slip or break in service, the valve timing will be disturbed and piston-to-valve contact will occur, resulting in serious engine damage.
2 The timing belt should be renewed at the specified intervals (see Chapter 1) or earlier if it is contaminated with oil, or if it is at all noisy in operation (a scraping noise due to uneven wear).
3 If the timing belt is being removed, always check the condition of the coolant pump at the same time. Replace it if in any doubt as to its condition.

Removal

4 Fit the timing tools and set the engine at the correct piston position as described in Section 2.
5 Release the nut on the timing belt tensioner, move the tensioner pulley away from the belt and retighten the nut to hold the pulley in the retracted position (see illustration).
6 If the timing belt is removed it must always

be replaced. Note that the crankshaft and camshaft must not be rotated whilst the belt is removed.
7 Check the timing belt carefully for any signs of uneven wear, splitting, or oil contamination. If signs of oil contamination are found, trace the source of the oil leak and rectify it. Wash down the engine timing belt area and all related components, to remove all traces of oil. The belt should always be replaced regardless of its condition.

Refitting

8 Before fitting the new belt, thoroughly clean the timing belt sprockets. Check that the tensioner pulley rotates freely, without any sign of roughness. Replacement of the tensioner pulley is considered best practise - see Section 6.
9 Referring to Section 2, make sure that the crankshaft and camshaft are locked in the correct positions using the special tools.
10 Engage the timing belt with the crankshaft sprocket first, then place it around the coolant pump sprocket and the camshaft sprocket. Finally slip the belt around the tensioner pulley.
11 Release the tensioner nut and insert the jaws of a pair of right-angled circlip pliers (or similar) into the two holes on the front face of

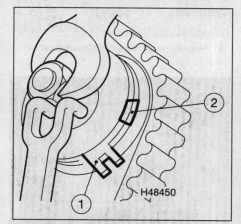

5.11b Rotate the tensioner anti-clockwise until the pointer (1) is in the maximum tension position (2)

the tensioner pulley. Rotate the pulley anti-clockwise to the stop – the pulley is now in the maximum tension position (see illustrations).
12 Turn the engine clockwise through two complete revolutions, then hold the tensioner pulley stationary, slacken the tensioner nut, and rotate the pulley until the tensioner front fork is aligned with the rear fork (see illustration). Tighten the tensioner nut to the specified torque.
13 With the engine positioned again as described in Section 2, check that the camshaft and crankshaft locking tools can be fitted. If not, repeat the complete tensioning procedure.
14 Refit the valve cover, the timing belt covers, the crankshaft pulley, auxiliary drivebelt, spark plugs and the air cleaner assembly, with reference to Chapter 1.
15 Refit the front wheel and lower the car to the ground.

6 Timing belt tensioner and sprockets – removal, inspection and refitting

Timing belt tensioner

Note: The tensioner should always be replaced whenever the timing belt is replaced.

Removal

1 Set the engine as described in Section 2.
2 Loosen the nut on the timing belt tensioner and move the tensioner pulley away from the belt. Keep the belt engaged with the sprockets using a cable-tie or string.

5.12 Align the front fork with the rear fork (arrowed) – viewed with a mirror

To make a camshaft sprocket holding tool, obtain two lengths of steel strip about 6 mm thick by 30 mm wide or similar, one 600 mm long, the other 200 mm long (all dimensions are approximate). Bolt the two strips together to form a forked end, leaving the bolt slack so that the shorter strip can pivot freely. At the end of the each 'prong' of the fork, secure a bolt with a nut and a lock nut, to act as the fulcrums; these will engage with the cut-outs in the sprocket and should protrude by about 30 mm.

3 Completely unscrew the nut and slide the tensioner off the mounting stud.

Inspection

4 Wipe the tensioner clean but do not use solvents that may contaminate the bearings. Spin the tensioner pulley on its hub by hand. Stiff movement or excessive free play is an indication of severe wear; the tensioner is not a serviceable component, and should be renewed.

Refitting

5 Slide the tensioner pulley over the mounting stud and fit the retaining nut.
6 Check and adjust the tension of the timing belt as described in Section 5.

A flywheel ring gear locking tool can be made from a short strip of steel bent to form a right-angle. Cut a slot in the upper part and bend this part up to engage with the ring gear teeth. File the edges to form a tooth profile. Drill a hole in the lower part to enable the tool to be bolted to the bellhousing flange.

6.9a Some timing tool kits will include a camshaft sprocket locking tool (arrowed)

7 Refitting of the remaining components is a reversal of removal.

Camshaft sprocket

Removal

8 Remove the timing belt as described in Section 5.
9 Slacken the camshaft sprocket retaining bolt while holding the sprocket stationary with a suitable tool (**see Tool Tip**). Unscrew the cap to access the camshaft bolt (**see illustrations**).
10 Unscrew and remove the retaining bolt and washer, then slide the sprocket from the end of the camshaft.

Inspection

11 With the sprocket removed, examine the camshaft oil seal for signs of leaking. If necessary, refer to Section 8 and renew it.
12 Check the sprocket teeth for damage.
13 Wipe clean the sprocket and camshaft mating surfaces.

Refitting

14 Locate the sprocket on the end of the camshaft, then refit the bolt and washer. Tighten the bolt to the specified torque while holding the camshaft stationary using the method described previously.
15 Refit the timing belt as described in Section 5.

Crankshaft sprocket

Removal

16 Remove the timing belt as described in Section 5.

7.4a Remove the wiring loom support bracket screws (arrowed)...

6.9b Remove the camshaft sprocket bolt cap

17 To prevent crankshaft rotation whilst the sprocket retaining bolt is being slackened, the flywheel ring gear must be locked using a suitable tool made from steel angle (**see Tool Tip**). Remove the cover plate from the base of the transmission bellhousing and bolt the tool to the lower bolt hole in the bellhousing flange so it engages with the ring gear teeth. Alternatively a strap wrench can be used to hold the crankshaft stationary (**see illustration 4.14**).
18 Using a suitable socket and extension bar, unscrew the crankshaft sprocket retaining bolt and slide the sprocket off the end of the crankshaft.

Inspection

19 With the sprocket removed, examine the crankshaft oil seal for signs of leaking. If necessary, refer to Section 9 and renew it.
20 Check the sprocket teeth for damage.
21 Wipe clean the sprocket and crankshaft mating surfaces.

Refitting

22 Slide the sprocket onto the crankshaft making sure the integral key engages with the slot on the end of the crankshaft. Refit the retaining bolt and tighten it to the specified torque. Hold the crankshaft stationary while the bolt is tightened using the method described in paragraph 19.
23 Refit the timing belt as described in Section 5.

7 Camshaft cover – removal and refitting

Note: *Ford Special tool 303-1478 will be required to correctly align the camshaft cover when refitting.*

Removal

1 Remove the air cleaner assembly as described in Chapter 4A.
2 Remove the battery and support tray as described in Chapter 5A.
3 Remove the engine management ECU as described in Chapter 4A.
4 Undo the screws and remove the wiring loom bracket, followed by the ECU support bracket (**see illustrations**).

7.4b ...and then undo the bolts and remove the ECU support bracket

7.6 Disconnect the breather hose from the camshaft cover

7.7 Camshaft position sensor retaining bolt (arrowed)

5 Disconnect the camshaft position sensor wiring plug.

6 Release the clamp and disconnect the engine breather hose from the camshaft cover **(see illustration)**.

7 Undo the retaining bolt and pull the camshaft position sensor from place **(see illustration)**.

8 Disconnect the variable valve timing solenoid wiring plug **(see illustration)**.

9 Undo the bolts securing the upper timing belt cover.

10 Remove the ignition coils as described in Chapter 5B and then remove the oxygen sensor wiring loom support bracket **(see illustration)**.

11 Where fitted, disconnect the earth lead from the camshaft cover **(see illustration)**.

12 Progressively unscrew the mounting bolts from the top of the camshaft cover and lift off

the cover – note the location of any supports on the bolts. If it sticks, do not attempt to lever it off – instead free it by working around the cover and tapping it lightly with a soft-faced mallet.

13 Recover the camshaft cover gasket. Inspect the gasket carefully, and renew it if damage or deterioration is evident.

14 Clean the mating surfaces of the cylinder head and camshaft cover thoroughly, removing all traces of oil and old gasket – take care to avoid damaging the surfaces as you do this. Check, and if necessary renew the O-rings on the underside of the camshaft cover **(see illustration)**.

Refitting

15 Locate a new gasket on the camshaft cover and make sure it is correctly seated **(see illustration)**.

16 Lower the cover onto the cylinder head, making sure the gasket is not displaced. Ensure the cover is flush with the cylinder head at the left-hand end by using Ford special tool 303-1478 or equivalent **(see illustration)**.

18 Insert the cover retaining bolts and tighten them progressively to the specified torque.

19 The remainder of refitting is the reverse sequence to removal.

8 Camshaft oil seal – renewal

1 Remove the timing belt and camshaft sprocket as described in Sections 5 and 6.
2 Undo the bolts and remove the camshaft bearing cap **(see illustration)**.
3 Punch or drill a small hole in the oil seal.

7.8 Variable valve timing solenoid wiring plug (arrowed)

7.10 Undo the bolts (arrowed) and remove the bracket

7.11 Disconnect the earth lead (arrowed)

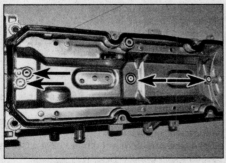

7.14 Note the O-ring seals (arrowed) on the underside of the cover

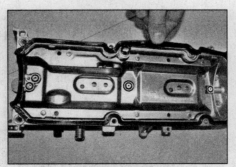

7.15 Fit the gasket into the groove

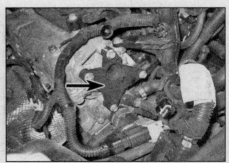

7.16 A special tool (arrowed) is available to ensure the camshaft cover is flush with the cylinder head

8.2 Undo the bolts (arrowed) and remove the bearing cap

Screw a self-tapping screw into the hole, and pull on the screw with pliers to extract the seal.

4 Clean the seal housing, and polish off any burrs or raised edges which may have caused the seal to fail in the first place.

5 Lubricate the lips of the new seal with clean engine oil, and drive it into position until it seats on its locating shoulder. Use a suitable tubular drift, such as a socket, which bears only on the hard outer edge of the seal. Take care not to damage the seal lips during fitting. Note that the seal lips should face inwards.

6 Refit the camshaft bearing cap, and tighten the bolts to the specified torque.

7 Refit the camshaft sprocket and timing belt as described in Sections 6 and 5.

9 Crankshaft oil seals – renewal

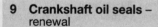

Right-hand side oil seal

1 The front oil seal is located in the oil pump casing on the front of the crankshaft. Remove the timing belt as described in Section 5 and the crankshaft sprocket as described in Section 6.

2 Using a small screwdriver, carefully prise the oil seal from the oil pump casing, taking care not to damage the surface of the crankshaft **(see illustration)**.

3 Clean the seating in the housing and the

9.2 Carefully prise the crankshaft right-hand oil seal from the oil pump housing

surface of the crankshaft. To prevent damage to the new oil seal as it is being fitted, wrap some adhesive tape around the end of the crankshaft and lightly oil it.

4 Lubricate the oil seal lip with clean engine oil then offer it up to the oil pump casing. Ensure that the sealing lip is facing inwards **(see illustration)**.

5 Using a suitable tubular drift, drive the oil seal squarely into the casing **(see illustration)**. Remove the adhesive tape.

6 Refit the crankshaft sprocket and timing belt as described in Sections 6 and 5.

Left-hand side oil seal

7 Remove the flywheel as described in Section 12.

8 Using a suitable hooked instrument, remove the oil seal from the oil seal housing, taking care not to damage the surface of the crankshaft.

9 Clean the seating in the housing and the surface of the crankshaft. Check the crankshaft for burrs which may damage the sealing lip of the new seal, and if necessary use a fine file to remove them.

10 Dip the new seal in clean engine oil and carefully locate it over the crankshaft flange, making sure that it is the correct way around.

11 Progressively tap the oil seal into the housing keeping it square to prevent distortion. A block of wood is useful for this purpose.

12 Refit the flywheel with reference to Section 12.

10 Camshaft and followers – removal, inspection and refitting

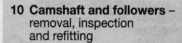

Removal

1 Remove the timing belt and camshaft sprocket as described in Sections 5 and 6.

2 Remove the camshaft cover as described in Section 7.

3 Mark the positions of the camshaft bearing caps **(see illustration)**, numbering them from the timing belt end.

4 Lift the camshaft carefully from the cylinder head, checking that the valve clearance shims and cam followers are not withdrawn by the adhesion of the oil. Recover the oil seal from the end of the camshaft.

5 Remove the shims and cam followers, but keep them in their originally fitted order.

Inspection

9 Inspect the camshaft for wear on the surfaces of the lobes and journals. Normally their surfaces should be smooth and have a dull shine; look for scoring and pitting. Accelerated wear will occur once the hardened exterior of the camshaft has been damaged.

10 Examine the bearing cap and journal surfaces for signs of wear.

11 To measure the camshaft endfloat, temporarily refit the camshaft then push the camshaft to one end of the cylinder head as far as it will travel. Attach a dial test indicator to the cylinder head and zero it, then push the camshaft as far as it will go to the other end of the cylinder head and record the gauge reading. Verify the reading by pushing the camshaft back to its original position and checking that the gauge indicates zero again.

12 Where the camshaft and bearings are worn excessively, consider renewing the complete cylinder head, together with camshaft and cam followers. A reconditioned head may be available from engine overhaul specialists.

Refitting

13 Lubricate the cam followers and locate them in their correct positions in the cylinder head. Locate the shims in the cam followers

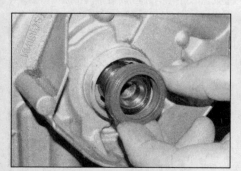

9.4 Locate the new oil seal on the oil pump housing with the sealing lips facing inwards

9.5 Use a suitable tubular drift to the drive the oil seal squarely in to the housing

10.3 When removing the camshaft bearing caps, note the position of the long and short locating dowels

making sure they are in their original positions.

14 Lubricate the journals then locate the camshaft in the cylinder head with the cam lobes of No 1 cylinder facing upwards (ie. No 1 piston at TDC).

15 Refit the bearing caps in their correct positions then locate the lubrication pipe (where fitted) over the bearing caps. Press in the oil feed stub then refit the bearing cap retaining bolts. Progressively tighten the bolts to the specified torque.

16 Lubricate the lips of the new seal with clean engine oil, and drive it into position until it seats on its locating shoulder. Use a suitable tubular drift, such as a socket, which bears only on the hard outer edge of the seal. Take care not to damage the seal lips during fitting. Note that the seal lips should face inwards. Where applicable, refit the oil retaining cap at the right-hand end of the camshaft **(see illustration 8.2)**.

17 Check the condition of the sealing O-ring on the ignition coil mounting bracket and renew the seal if necessary.

18 Unless the ignition coil mounting bracket was removed as part of the timing belt removal procedure, it can be refitted at this stage. Locate the bracket on the cylinder head and secure with the bolt and nuts tightened securely. Reconnect the HT leads and the LT wiring connectors.

19 Refit the camshaft sprocket and timing belt as described in Sections 6 and 5.

20 Check and if necessary adjust the valve clearances as described in Chapter 1, then refit the camshaft cover as described in Section 7.

11 Cylinder head – removal and refitting

Removal

1 Disconnect the battery, and battery tray as described in Chapter 5A.

2 Drain the cooling system as described in Chapter 1.

3 Remove the intake and exhaust manifolds as described in Chapter 4A.

4 Remove the timing belt as described in Section 5.

5 Remove the camshaft cover as described in Section 7.

6 Disconnect the radiator hose from the thermostat housing on the left-hand end of the cylinder head.

7 If not already done, disconnect the LT wiring connectors at the ignition coil pack.

8 Unscrew the cylinder head bolts half a turn at a time in the **reverse** order to that specified for tightening **(see illustration 11.21)**. When the bolts are free, remove them with their washers.

9 Lift the cylinder head from the block. If it is stuck tight, insert pieces of wood into the

exhaust or intake ports, and use them as levers to rock the head off the block. On no account drive levers into the gasket joint, or attempt to tap the head sideways, as it is located on positioning dowels.

10 Remove and discard the cylinder head gasket.

11 The cylinder head can be dismantled as described in Chapter 2B after removing the camshaft and cam followers as described in Section 10.

Preparation for refitting

12 The mating faces of the cylinder head and cylinder block must be perfectly clean before refitting the head. Use a hard plastic or wooden scraper to remove all traces of gasket and carbon; also clean the piston crowns. Take particular care when cleaning the piston crowns as the soft aluminium alloy is easily damaged. Make sure that the carbon is not allowed to enter the oil and water passages – this is particularly important for the lubrication system, as carbon could block the oil supply to the engine's components. Using adhesive tape and paper, seal the water, oil and bolt holes in the cylinder block. To prevent carbon entering the gap between the pistons and bores, smear a little grease in the gap. After cleaning each piston, use a small brush to remove all traces of grease and carbon from the gap, then wipe away the remainder with a clean rag. Clean all the pistons in the same way.

13 Check the mating surfaces of the cylinder block and the cylinder head for nicks, deep scratches and other damage. If slight, they may be removed carefully with a file, but if excessive, machining may be the only alternative to renewal. If warpage of the cylinder head gasket surface is suspected, use a straight-edge to check it for distortion. Refer to Part B of this Chapter if necessary.

14 Check the condition of the cylinder head bolts, and particularly their threads, whenever they are removed. Wash the bolts in a suitable solvent, and wipe them dry. Check each bolt for any sign of visible wear or damage, renewing them if necessary. Although Ford do not specify that the bolts must be renewed, it is strongly recommended that the bolts should be renewed as a complete set whenever they are disturbed.

15 Refit the camshaft and followers as described in Section 10, then adjust the valve clearances as described in Chapter 1 before refitting the cylinder head to the block.

Refitting

16 Before refitting the assembled cylinder head, make sure that the head and block mating surfaces are perfectly clean, and that the bolt holes in the cylinder block have been mopped out to clear any oil.

17 Referring to Section 2, make sure that the crankshaft and camshaft are still set at their correct TDC positions and, where applicable, the camshaft is locked in the correct position using the special tool.

11.19 Place the cylinder head gasket on the block so that the word ALTO can be read from above

18 The new gasket should not be removed from its nylon cover until required for use. Fit the gasket dry, and make sure that the mating surfaces on the head and block are perfectly clean.

19 Place the gasket on the cylinder block so that the word ALTO can be read from above **(see illustration)**.

20 Lower the cylinder head onto the block so that it locates on the positioning dowels.

21 The cylinder head bolt threads must be clean and lightly lubricated. Screw the bolts in finger-tight then working progressively and in the sequence shown, tighten all the cylinder head bolts to the Stage 1 torque setting given in the *Specifications*, using a torque wrench and a suitable socket **(see illustration)**. With all the bolts tightened to their Stage 1 setting, working again in the specified sequence, first angle-tighten the bolts through the specified Stage 2 angle, then again through the Stage 3 angle, using a socket and extension bar. It is recommended that an angle-measuring gauge is used during this stage of tightening, to ensure accuracy.

22 Refit the intake and exhaust manifolds as described in Chapter 4A.

23 Refit the camshaft cover as described in Section 7.

24 Refit the timing belt as described in Section 5.

25 Reconnect the LT wiring connectors at the ignition coil pack.

26 Reconnect the battery then fill and bleed the cooling system as described in Chapter 1.

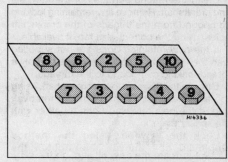

11.21 Cylinder head bolt tightening sequence

13.13 Left-hand mounting nuts and central bolt (arrowed)

13.20 Rear mounting bolts (arrowed)

12 Flywheel –
removal, inspection and refitting

Removal

1 Remove the transmission as described in Chapter 7, then remove the clutch assembly as described in Chapter 6. If you intend to refit the original clutch assembly, mark the cover plate in relation to the flywheel.

2 The flywheel must now be held stationary while the bolts are loosened. A home-made locking tool may be fabricated from a piece of scrap metal and used to lock the ring gear (see Tool Tip in Section 6). Bolt the tool to one of the transmission bellhousing mounting bolt holes on the cylinder block.

3 Mark the position of the flywheel with respect to the crankshaft using a dab of paint. Unscrew and remove the mounting bolts, together with the spacer plate, then lift off the flywheel. Discard the flywheel bolts; new ones must be used on refitting.

Inspection

4 If the flywheel's clutch mating surface is deeply scored, cracked or otherwise damaged, the flywheel must be renewed. However, it may be possible to have it surface-ground; seek the advice of a Ford dealer or engine reconditioning specialist.

5 If the ring gear is badly worn or has missing teeth, the flywheel must be renewed.

Refitting

6 Clean the mating surfaces of the flywheel and crankshaft. Remove any remaining locking compound from the threads of the crankshaft holes, using the correct-size tap, if available.

7 If the new retaining bolts are not supplied with their threads already pre-coated, apply a thread-locking compound to the threads.

8 Offer up the flywheel to the crankshaft, using the alignment marks made during removal, and fit the new retaining bolts together with the spacer plate.

9 Lock the flywheel using the method employed on removal, and tighten the retaining bolts to the specified torque.

10 Refit the clutch as described in Chapter 6, and the transmission as described in Chapter 7.

13 Engine mountings –
inspection and renewal

Inspection

1 Firmly apply the handbrake, then jack up the front of the car and support it securely on axle stands (see Jacking and vehicle support).

2 Check the mounting rubbers to see if they are cracked, hardened or separated from the metal at any point; renew the mounting if any such damage or deterioration is evident.

3 Check that all the mounting's fasteners are securely tightened; use a torque wrench to check if possible.

4 Using a large screwdriver or a crowbar, check for wear in the mounting by carefully levering against it to check for free play. Where this is not possible, enlist the aid of an assistant to move the engine/transmission back-and-forth, or from side-to-side, while you watch the mounting. While some free play is to be expected, even from new components, excessive wear should be obvious. If excessive free play is found, check first that the fasteners are correctly secured, then renew any worn components as described below.

Renewal

Right-hand mounting

5 Place a trolley jack beneath the right-hand side of the engine, with a block of wood on the jack head. Raise the jack until it is supporting the weight of the engine.

6 Undo the nuts securing the engine

14.2 Transmission-to-cylinder block bracket bolts (arrowed)

mounting to the body and the nuts securing the mounting upper bracket to the bracket on the engine (see illustration 4.9). Lift the mounting and upper bracket assembly off the studs and remove it from the car.

7 Undo the nut, withdraw the through-bolt and separate the mounting from the upper engine bracket.

8 Attach the new mounting to the upper engine bracket and secure with the nut and through-bolt. Do not fully-tighten the nut at this stage.

9 Locate the mounting assembly on the body and lower engine bracket, refit the nuts and tighten them to the specified torque.

10 Securely tighten the through-bolt and nut securing the mounting to the upper engine bracket, then remove the trolley jack.

Left-hand mounting

11 Remove the battery and battery tray as described in Chapter 5A.

12 Place a trolley jack beneath the transmission, with a block of wood on the jack head. Raise the jack until it is supporting the weight of the engine/transmission.

13 Unscrew the nuts securing the left-hand mounting to the body (see illustration).

14 Unscrew the bolt securing the mounting to the transmission bracket and lift the mounting off the transmission bracket stud.

15 Locate the new mounting in the transmission bracket, refit the bolt and tighten it to the specified torque.

16 Refit the mounting-to-body nuts and tighten them to the specified torque.

17 Remove the trolley jack, then refit the battery tray and battery as described in Chapter 5A.

Rear mounting

18 Firmly apply the handbrake, then jack up the front of the car and support it securely on axle stands (see Jacking and vehicle support).

19 Temporarily support the weight of the engine/transmission using a trolley jack.

20 Working beneath the vehicle, unscrew the bolt securing the rear mounting assembly to the subframe (see illustration).

21 Unbolt the rear mounting assembly from the transmission and withdraw from under the vehicle.

22 Fitting the new mounting is a reversal of the removal procedure, ensuring that all mounting bolts are tightened to the specified torque.

14 Sump –
removal and refitting

Removal

1 Firmly apply the handbrake, then jack up the front of the car and support it securely on axle stands (see Jacking and vehicle support). Drain the engine oil as described in Chapter 1.

2 Undo the bolts and remove the bracket joining the transmission to the cylinder block (see illustration).

3 Undo the bolts and remove the exhaust pipe support bracket **(see illustration)**.
4 Unbolt and remove the cover plate from the base of the transmission bellhousing.
5 Unscrew the sump securing bolts and nuts then cut through as much of the joint sealant as possible using a sharp knife. Pull the sump downwards to release it from the remaining sealant and remove it from under the car.
6 Thoroughly clean the sump and the cylinder block mating surfaces ensuring that all traces of old sealant are removed.

Refitting

7 Apply a 3.0 mm bead of RTV silicone sealant to the sump flange, then locate the sump in position. Refit the retaining bolts and nuts and tighten to the specified torque.
8 The remainder of refitting is a reversal of removal.
9 Lower the car to the ground and wait at least 1 hour before filling the engine with oil as described in Chapter 1.

15 Oil pump and pick-up tube – removal, inspection and refitting

Removal

1 Remove the timing belt and crankshaft sprocket as described in Sections 5 and 6.
2 Drain the engine oil and remove the oil filter as described in Chapter 1.
3 Remove the sump as described in Section 14.

14.3 Exhaust pipe support bracket (arrowed)

4 Remove the coolant pump as described in Chapter 3.
5 Disconnect the wiring connector from the oil pressure switch on the side of the pump casing.
6 Undo the oil pump retaining bolts, noting the location of the longer bolt, and withdraw the pump assembly from the front of the engine. Recover the gasket.

Inspection

7 With the pump on the bench, undo the two bolts and remove the pick-up tube. Using a small screwdriver or similar tool, hook out the pick-up tube sealing O-ring from the pump body.
8 The pressure relief valve components can be removed for examination by depressing the spring and pulling out the keeper plate **(see illustrations)**.

9 If pump wear is suspected, check the rotors in the following way. Extract the fixing screws and remove the rear cover plate. The screws are very tight, and will probably require the use of an impact screwdriver **(see illustration)**.
10 Inspect the pump rotors, pump casing and cover for any signs of wear or damage. If satisfactory, refit the rotors to the pump casing ensuring that the orientation marks are facing upwards.
11 Check the clearance between the outer rotor and the pump casing using feeler blades. Check the rotor endfloat by placing a straight-edge across the pump casing, and checking the gap between the straight-edge and rotor face **(see illustrations)**. If the clearances are outside the specified tolerance, renew the oil pump complete.
12 If the pump is unworn, lubricate the rotors with clean engine oil then place the cover plate in position. Apply thread-locking compound to the retaining screws and tighten the screws securely.
13 Locate a new O-ring in the pump casing then refit the pick-up tube. Secure the tube with the two bolts tightened securely.
14 Lubricate the pressure relief valve components then refit the valve, spring and end cap, securing the assembly with the keeper plate.
15 Lever out the crankshaft oil seal and drive a new one squarely into the oil pump casing **(see illustrations)**. Lubricate the oil seal lips with clean engine oil.
16 Prior to refitting, prime the pump by

15.8a Remove the oil pump pressure relief valve keeper plate

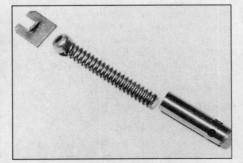

15.8b Oil pump pressure relief valve components

15.9 Use an impact driver to remove the oil pump rear cover plate screws

15.11a Measure the oil pump outer rotor-to-pump casing clearance

15.11b Measure the oil pump rotor clearance

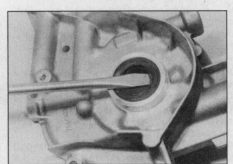

15.15a Prise out the oil pump seal

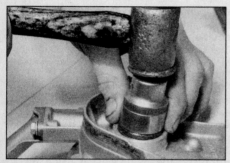

15.15b Use a suitable socket to fit the new oil seal

pouring clean engine oil into its inlet duct, while at the same time turning the oil pump inner rotor.

Refitting

17 Ensure that the oil pump and cylinder block mating faces are clean, then place a new gasket on the pump casing. Retain the

16.2 The oil pressure switch (arrowed) is located on the oil filter housing

gasket in position by inserting two of the pump retaining bolts.
18 Locate the pump on the cylinder block, insert the retaining bolts and tighten them progressively to the specified torque.
19 Refit the coolant pump as described in Chapter 3.
20 Refit the sump as described in Section 14.

21 Refit the crankshaft sprocket and timing belt as described in Sections 6 and 5.
22 Reconnect the oil pressure switch wiring connector.
23 Fit a new oil filter then fill the engine with oil and coolant as described in Chapter 1.

16 Oil pressure warning light switch – removal and refitting

1 Firmly apply the handbrake, then jack up the front of the car and support it securely on axle stands (see *Jacking and vehicle support*).
2 Disconnect the wiring plug from the switch, then unscrew it from the oil filter housing **(see illustration)**. Be prepared for oil spillage.
3 Screw the switch into the housing, and tighten it to the specified torque.
4 Reconnect the wiring plug and lower the vehicle to the ground. Check the engine oil level as described in *Weekly checks*.

Chapter 2 Part B:
Engine removal and overhaul procedures

Contents

Degrees of difficulty

Easy, suitable for novice with little experience	Fairly easy, suitable for beginner with some experience	Fairly difficult, suitable for competent DIY mechanic	Difficult, suitable for experienced DIY mechanic	Very difficult, suitable for expert DIY or professional

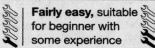

Specifications

Cylinder head
Maximum gasket face distortion . . . .   0.1 mm
Overall height of cylinder head (sealing surface-to-sealing surface) . . .   126.5 ± 0.35 mm

Valves and guides
Valve stem diameter. . . . .   6.982 to 7.000 mm
Valve face angle . . . .   45° 30' ± 5'
Valve stem-to-guide clearance. . . . .   0.022 to 0.058 mm

Cylinder block
Bore diameter (nominal size) . . . .   70.80 mm
Oversizes available. . . . .   0.4 mm

Pistons and piston rings
Piston diameter (nominal - measured 8.5 mm up from base of skirt) . .   70.76 to 70.77 mm
Piston-to-bore clearance . . . .   0.030 to 0.050 mm
Piston ring-to-groove clearance:
   Top compression ring. . . . .   0.040 to 0.080 mm
   2nd compression ring. . . . .   0.020 to 0.055 mm
   Oil scraper ring. . . . .   0.020 to 0.055 mm
Piston ring end gap:
   Top compression ring. . . . .   0.20 to 0.40 mm
   2nd compression ring. . . . .   0.25 to 0.45 mm
   Oil scraper ring . . . .   0.20 to 0.45 mm

Crankshaft and bearings
Bearing journal diameters (standard):
   Main bearings (nominal) . . . .   47.98 mm
   Big-end bearings (nominal). . . . .   41.98 mm
Endfloat . . . .   0.05 to 0.26 mm

Torque wrench settings
Refer to Chapter 2A Specifications

1 General information

Included in this Part of Chapter 2 are details of removing the engine/transmission from the car and general overhaul procedures for the cylinder head, cylinder block/crankcase and all other engine internal components.

The information given ranges from advice concerning preparation for an overhaul and the purchase of parts, to detailed step-by-step procedures covering removal, inspection, renovation and refitting of engine internal components.

After Section 5, all instructions are based on the assumption that the engine has been removed from the car. For information concerning in-car engine repair, as well as the removal and refitting of those external components necessary for full overhaul, refer to Part A of this Chapter (as applicable) and to Section 5. Ignore any preliminary dismantling operations described in Part A that are no longer relevant once the engine has been removed from the car.

Apart from torque wrench settings, which are given at the beginning of Part A, all specifications relating to engine overhaul are at the beginning of this Part of Chapter 2.

2 Engine overhaul – general information

It is not always easy to determine when, or if, an engine should be completely overhauled, as a number of factors must be considered.

High mileage is not necessarily an indication that an overhaul is needed, while low mileage does not preclude the need for an overhaul. Frequency of servicing is probably the most important consideration. An engine which has had regular and frequent oil and filter changes, as well as other required maintenance, should give many thousands of miles of reliable service. Conversely, a neglected engine may require an overhaul very early in its life.

Excessive oil consumption is an indication that piston rings, valve seals and/or valve guides are in need of attention. Make sure that oil leaks are not responsible before deciding that the rings and/or guides are worn. Perform a compression test, as described in Part A of this Chapter, to determine the likely cause of the problem.

Check the oil pressure with a gauge fitted in place of the oil pressure switch, and compare it with that specified. If it is extremely low, the main and big-end bearings, and/or the oil pump, are probably worn out.

Loss of power, rough running, knocking or metallic engine noises, excessive valve gear noise, and high fuel consumption may also point to the need for an overhaul, especially if they are all present at the same time. If a complete service does not cure the situation, major mechanical work is the only solution.

A full engine overhaul involves restoring all internal parts to the specification of a new engine. During a complete overhaul, the pistons and the piston rings are renewed, and the cylinder bores are reconditioned. New main and big-end bearings are generally fitted; if necessary, the crankshaft may be reground, to compensate for wear in the journals. The valves are also serviced as well, since they are usually in less-than-perfect condition at this point. Always pay careful attention to the condition of the oil pump when overhauling the engine, and renew it if there is any doubt as to its serviceability. The end result should be an as-new engine that will give many trouble-free miles.

Critical cooling system components such as the hoses, thermostat and coolant pump should be renewed when an engine is overhauled. The radiator should also be checked carefully, to ensure that it is not clogged or leaking.

Before beginning the engine overhaul, read through the entire procedure, to familiarise yourself with the scope and requirements of the job. Check on the availability of parts and make sure that any necessary special tools and equipment are obtained in advance. Most work can be done with typical hand tools, although a number of precision measuring tools are required for inspecting parts to determine if they must be renewed.

The services provided by an engineering machine shop or engine reconditioning specialist will almost certainly be required, particularly if major repairs such as crankshaft regrinding or cylinder reboring are necessary. Apart from carrying out machining operations, these establishments will normally handle the inspection of parts, offer advice concerning reconditioning or renewal and supply new components such as pistons, piston rings and bearing shells. It is recommended that the establishment used is a member of the Federation of Engine Re-Manufacturers, or a similar society.

Always wait until the engine has been completely dismantled, and until all components (especially the cylinder block/crankcase and the crankshaft) have been inspected, before deciding what service and repair operations must be performed by an engineering works. The condition of these components will be the major factor to consider when determining whether to overhaul the original engine, or to buy a reconditioned unit. Do not, therefore, purchase parts or have overhaul work done on other components until they have been thoroughly inspected. As a general rule, time is the primary cost of an overhaul, so it does not pay to fit worn or sub-standard parts.

As a final note, to ensure maximum life and minimum trouble from a reconditioned engine, everything must be assembled with care, in a spotlessly-clean environment.

3 Engine removal – methods and precautions

The engine must be removed complete with the transmission as an assembly. There is insufficient clearance in the engine compartment to remove the engine leaving the transmission in the vehicle. On all models the front panel is removed and the engine/transmission assembly is lowered slightly, then removed from the front of the vehicle.

If you have decided that the engine must be removed for overhaul or major repair work, several preliminary steps should be taken.

Locating a suitable place to work is extremely important. Adequate work space, along with storage space for the car, will be needed. If a workshop or garage is not available, at the very least, a flat, level, clean work surface is required.

Cleaning the engine compartment and engine/transmission before beginning the removal procedure will help keep tools clean and organised.

An engine hoist will also be necessary. Make sure the equipment is rated in excess of the combined weight of the engine and transmission. Safety is of primary importance, considering the potential hazards involved in removing the engine/transmission from the car.

The help of an assistant is essential. Apart from the safety aspects involved, there are many instances when one person cannot simultaneously perform all of the operations required during engine/transmission removal.

Plan the operation ahead of time. Before starting work, arrange for the hire of or obtain all of the tools and equipment you will need. Some of the equipment necessary to perform engine/transmission removal and installation safely (in addition to an engine hoist) is as follows: a heavy duty trolley jack, complete sets of spanners and sockets as described in the rear of this manual, wooden blocks, and plenty of rags and cleaning solvent for mopping-up spilled oil, coolant and fuel. If the hoist must be hired, make sure that you arrange for it in advance, and perform all of the operations possible without it beforehand. This will save you money and time.

Plan for the car to be out of use for quite a while. An engineering machine shop or engine reconditioning specialist will be required to perform some of the work which cannot be accomplished without special equipment. These places often have a busy schedule, so it would be a good idea to consult them before removing the engine, in order to accurately estimate the amount of time required to rebuild or repair components that may need work.

During the engine/transmission removal procedure, it is advisable to make notes of the locations of all brackets, cable ties,

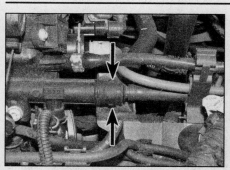

4.14 Squeeze together the sides (arrowed) and pull out the fuel pipe from the end of the fuel rail

4.22a Upper and lower crossmembers (arrowed)

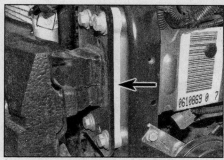

4.22b Where fitted, note the spacer (arrowed) fitted between the upper crossmember and the front panel

earthing points, etc, as well as how the wiring harnesses, hoses and electrical connections are attached and routed around the engine and engine compartment. An effective way of doing this is to take a series of photographs of the various components before they are disconnected or removed; the resulting photographs will prove invaluable when the engine/transmission is refitted.

Always be extremely careful when removing and refitting the engine/transmission. Serious injury can result from careless actions. Plan ahead and take your time, and a job of this nature, although major, can be accomplished successfully.

4 Engine and transmission unit – removal, separation and refitting

Note: *The following should be regarded as a guide to the work involved, rather than a step-by-step procedure. Where differences are encountered, or additional component disconnection or removal is necessary, make notes of the work involved as an aid to refitting.*

Removal

1 On models with air conditioning, have the refrigerant circuit evacuated by a Ford dealer or suitably-equipped repairer.
2 Position the steering with the front roadwheels straight-ahead, and lock the steering by removing the ignition key.
3 Apply the handbrake, then jack up the front of the vehicle and support it on axle stands (see *Jacking and vehicle support*). Remove both front roadwheels, and the right-hand inner wheel arch liner for access to the crankshaft pulley. Where fitted remove the engine compartment undertray and the engine top cover.
4 To improve access, remove the bonnet as described in Chapter 11.
5 Remove the engine management ECU as described in Chapter 4A.
6 Remove the battery and battery tray as described in Chapter 5A.
7 Drain the engine oil as described in Chapter 1.

8 Remove the air cleaner assembly as described in Chapter 4A.
9 Drain the cooling system as described in Chapter 1.
10 Disconnect the engine wiring loom wiring plug at the front, left-hand corner of the engine.
11 Disconnect the oxygen sensor(s) wiring plugs.
12 Prise the servo one-way valve from place, and move the vacuum pipe to one side.
13 Release the clamps and disconnect the heater hoses from the engine compartment bulkhead.
14 Depressurise the fuel system as described in Chapter 4A, then disconnect the fuel feed pipe **(see illustration)**. Be prepared for fuel spillage, and take adequate precautions. Clamp or plug the open unions, to minimise further fuel loss.
15 Remove the throttle body as described in Chapter 4A.
16 Release the clamp and disconnect the upper radiator coolant hose.
17 Remove the front bumper as described in Chapter 11.
18 Remove the head light units as described in Chapter 12.
19 Disconnect the wiring plugs from the horn, electric cooling fan, refrigerant pipe pressure sensor (where applicable) and the front impact sensor.
20 Disconnect the cable from the bonnet lock – see Chapter 11.
21 Undo the bolt and detach the refrigerant pipes from the condenser (where applicable). Plug the openings to prevent contamination,

and discard the pipe seals – new ones must be fitted.
22 Make alignment marks between the crossmembers, front panel, chassis legs, and retaining bolts each side, then undo the bolts and remove the upper and lower front crossmembers. Note that a spacer may be fitted behind the upper crossmember **(see illustrations)**.
23 Undo the retaining bolts, and with the help of as assistant, remove the front panel **(see illustration)**.
24 On models with air conditioning, remove the refrigerant pipe from the expansion valve to the compressor, from the expansion valve to the condenser, and the compressor to the condenser (where not already done so). Plug the openings to prevent contamination, and discard the pipe seals – new ones must be fitted.
25 Disconnect the earth lead and reversing light switch wiring plug from the transmission **(see illustration)**.
26 Remove the clutch slave cylinder and hydraulic hose from the transmission, with reference to Chapter 6.
27 Disconnect the gearchange cables from the levers on the transmission, then undo the bolts and detach the cables support bracket from the transmission. Refer to Chapter 7 if necessary.
28 Remove the centre exhaust pipe and rear silencer as described in Chapter 4A.
29 Undo the bolts and remove the exhaust manifold heat shield.
30 Remove the retaining clips and release the flexible brake pipes from the suspension strut each side.

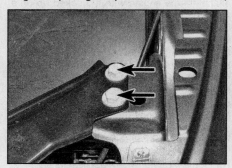

4.23 Undo the bolts (arrowed) securing the front panel to the wing each side

4.25 Disconnect the wiring plug (arrowed) from the reversing light switch

4.35 Undo the bolts (arrowed) and remove the front section of the subframe each side

31 Remove both driveshafts as described in Chapter 8.

32 Remove the lower/rear torque rod from under the engine/transmission as described in Chapter 2A.

33 Undo the retaining nuts and remove the exhaust manifold.

34 Attach a suitable hoist and lifting tackle to the engine lifting brackets on the cylinder head and transmission, and support the weight of the engine/transmission.

35 Undo the bolts and remove the front section of the subframe each side **(see illustration)**.

36 Unscrew the nuts securing the right-hand engine mounting to the engine lower mounting bracket and vehicle body, and remove the mounting assembly.

37 Slacken the two nuts securing the left-hand engine mounting to the vehicle body, then undo the central bolt securing the mounting to the transmission.

38 Make a final check to ensure that all relevant pipes, hoses, wires, etc, have been disconnected, and that they are positioned clear of the engine and transmission.

39 With the help of an assistant, carefully lower the engine/transmission slightly and then pull it forward. When the assembly is clear of the engine bay, lower it to the ground. Make sure that the surrounding components in the engine compartment are not damaged. Ideally, the assembly should be lowered onto a trolley jack or low platform with castors, so that it can easily be withdrawn from under the car.

40 Ensure that the assembly is adequately supported, then disconnect the engine hoist and lifting tackle, and withdraw the engine/

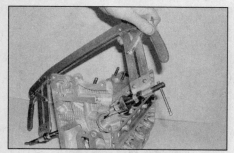

6.2 Fit a valve spring compressor tool, ensuring that the arms of the compressor are securely positioned

transmission assembly from under the front of the vehicle.

41 Clean away any external dirt using paraffin or a water-soluble solvent and a stiff brush.

42 With reference to Chapter 7, unbolt the transmission from the engine. Carefully withdraw the transmission from the engine. Ensure that its weight is not allowed to hang on the input shaft while engaged with the clutch friction disc. Note that the transmission locates on dowels positioned in the rear of the cylinder block.

Refitting

43 With reference to Chapter 7, refit the transmission to the engine and tighten the bolts to the specified torque.

44 With the front of the vehicle raised and supported on axle stands, move the engine/transmission assembly under the vehicle, ensuring that the assembly is adequately supported.

45 Reconnect the hoist and lifting tackle to the engine lifting brackets, and carefully raise the engine/transmission assembly up into the engine compartment with the help of an assistant.

46 Reconnect the right- and left-hand engine/transmission mountings and tighten the bolt/nuts to the specified torque given in Chapter 2A.

47 The reminder of refitting is a reversal of removal, noting the following points:

a) *Tighten all fasteners to their specified torque where given.*

b) *Fill the engine with fresh oil as described in Chapter 1.*

c) *Replenish the coolant as described in Chapter 1.*

d) *Check for leaks before venturing out onto the road.*

5 Engine overhaul – dismantling sequence

1 It is much easier to dismantle and work on the engine if it is mounted on a portable engine stand. These stands can often be hired from a tool hire shop. Before the engine is mounted on a stand, the flywheel should be removed, so that the stand bolts can be tightened into the end of the cylinder block/crankcase.

2 If a stand is not available, it is possible to dismantle the engine with it blocked up on a sturdy workbench, or on the floor. Be extra careful not to tip or drop the engine when working without a stand.

3 If you are going to obtain a reconditioned engine, all the external components must be removed first, to be transferred to the new engine (just as they will if you are doing a complete engine overhaul yourself). These components include the following:

a) *Engine wiring harness and supports.*

b) *Alternator and air conditioning compressor mounting brackets (as applicable).*

c) *Coolant pump (where applicable) and inlet/outlet housings.*

d) *Dipstick tube.*

e) *Fuel system components.*

f) *All electrical switches and sensors.*

g) *Intake and exhaust manifolds and, where fitted, the turbocharger.*

h) *Oil filter and oil cooler/heat exchanger.*

i) *Flywheel.*

Note: *When removing the external components from the engine, pay close attention to details that may be helpful or important during refitting. Note the fitted position of gaskets, seals, spacers, pins, washers, bolts, and other small items.*

4 If you are obtaining a 'short' engine (which consists of the engine cylinder block/crankcase, crankshaft, pistons and connecting rods all assembled), then the cylinder head, sump, oil pump, and timing chain/belt will have to be removed also.

5 Before beginning the dismantling and overhaul procedures, make sure that you have all of the correct tools necessary. See *Tools and working facilities* for further information.

6 If you are planning a complete overhaul, the engine can be dismantled, and the internal components removed, in the order given below.

a) *Intake and exhaust manifolds (see Chapter 4A).*

b) *Coolant pump (see Chapter 3).*

c) *Cylinder head (see Chapter 2A).*

d) *Flywheel (see Chapter 2A).*

e) *Sump (see Chapter 2A).*

f) *Oil pump (see Chapter 2A).*

g) *Timing belt and sprockets (see Chapter 2A).*

h) *Pistons/connecting rod assemblies (see Section 9).*

i) *Crankshaft (see Section 10).*

6 Cylinder head – dismantling

Note: *New and reconditioned cylinder heads may be available from the manufacturer, and from engine overhaul specialists. Due to the fact that some specialist tools are required for the dismantling and inspection procedures, and new components may not be readily available, it may be more practical and economical for the home mechanic to purchase a reconditioned head rather than to dismantle, inspect and recondition the original head. A valve spring compressor tool will be required for this operation.*

1 With the cylinder head removed as described in Chapter 2A, clean away all external dirt, and remove the following components as applicable, if not already done:

a) *Manifolds (see Chapter 4A).*

b) *Spark plugs (see Chapter 1).*

c) *Camshafts and followers (see Chapter 2A).*

d) *Engine lifting brackets.*

2 To remove a valve, fit a valve spring compressor tool. Ensure that the arms of the compressor tool are securely positioned on the head of the valve and the spring cap **(see illustration)**. The valves are deeply-

6.4 Extract the two split collets by hooking them out using a small screwdriver

6.5a Remove the valve spring cap...

6.5b ...and the spring...

6.5c ...then withdraw the valve through the combustion chamber

6.5d Remove the valve stem oil seal...

6.5e ...and the spring seat

recessed and a suitable extension piece may be required for the spring compressor.

3 Compress the valve spring to relieve the pressure of the spring cap acting on the collets.

4 Extract the two split collets by hooking them out using a small screwdriver, then slowly release the compressor tool **(see illustration)**.

5 Remove the valve spring cap and the spring, then withdraw the valve through the combustion chamber. Remove the valve stem oil seal (using long-nosed pliers if necessary), and the spring seat **(see illustrations)**.

6 Repeat the procedure for the remaining valves, keeping all components in strict order so that they can be refitted in their original positions, unless all the components are to be renewed. If the components are to be kept and used again, place each valve assembly in a labelled polythene bag or a similar small container **(see illustration)**. Note that as with cylinder numbering, the valves are normally numbered from the timing belt end of the engine. Make sure that the valve components are identified as intake and exhaust, as well as numbered.

7 Cylinder head and valve components – cleaning and inspection

1 Thorough cleaning of the cylinder head and valve components, followed by a detailed inspection, will enable a decision to be made on whether further work is necessary before reassembling the components.

Cleaning

2 Scrape away all traces of old gasket material and sealing compound from the cylinder head surfaces. Take care not to damage the cylinder head surfaces, as the head is made of light alloy.

3 Scrape away the carbon from the combustion chambers and ports, then wash the cylinder head thoroughly with paraffin or a suitable solvent.

4 Scrape off any heavy carbon deposits that may have formed on the valves, then use a power-operated wire brush to remove deposits from the valve heads and stems.

Inspection

Note: *Be sure to perform all the following inspection procedures before concluding that the services of a machine shop or engine overhaul specialist are required. Make a list of all items that require attention.*

6.6 Place each valve assembly in a labelled polythene bag or similar container

Cylinder head

5 Inspect the head very carefully for cracks, evidence of coolant leakage, and other damage. If cracks are found, a new cylinder head should be obtained.

6 Use a straight-edge and feeler blade to check that the cylinder head surface is not distorted **(see illustration)**. If the specified distortion limit is exceeded, it may be possible to have the cylinder head resurfaced, provided that the overall height of the head is not reduced to less than the specified minimum.

7 Examine the valve seats in each of the combustion chambers. If the seats are severely pitted, cracked or burned, then they will need to be recut or renewed by an engine overhaul specialist. If only slight pitting is evident, this can be removed by grinding the valve heads and seats together with coarse, then fine, grinding paste, as described later in this Section.

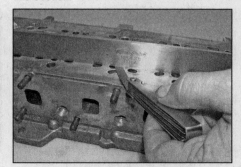

7.6 Check the cylinder head surface for distortion

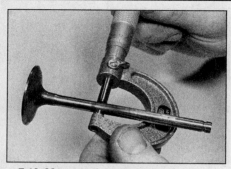

7.10 Measure the valve stem diameter using a micrometer

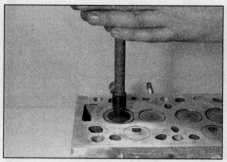

7.12 Grinding-in a valve

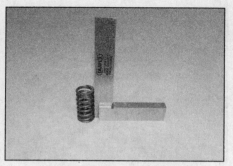

7.14 Check each valve spring for squareness

8 If the valve guides are worn, indicated by a side-to-side motion of the valve, oversize valve guides may be available, and valves with oversize stems can be fitted. This work is best carried out by an engine overhaul specialist. A dial gauge may be used to determine whether the amount of side play of a valve exceeds the specified maximum.

9 Check the tappet bores in the cylinder head for wear. If excessive wear is evident, the cylinder head must be renewed. Also check the tappet oil holes in the cylinder head for obstructions.

Valves

10 Examine the head of each valve for pitting, burning, cracks and general wear, and check the valve stem for scoring and wear ridges. Rotate the valve, and check for any obvious indication that it is bent. Look for pitting and excessive wear on the end of each valve stem. If the valve appears satisfactory at this stage, measure the valve stem diameter at several points using a micrometer **(see illustration)**. Any significant difference in the readings obtained indicates wear of the valve stem. Should any of these conditions be apparent, the valve(s) must be renewed. If the valves are in satisfactory condition, they should be ground (lapped) onto their respective seats to ensure a smooth gas-tight seal.

11 Valve grinding is carried out as follows. Place the cylinder head upside-down on a bench, with a block of wood at each end to give clearance for the valve stems.

12 Smear a trace of coarse carborundum paste on the seat face in the cylinder head, and press

a suction grinding tool onto the relevant valve head. With a semi-rotary action, grind the valve head to its seat, lifting the valve occasionally to redistribute the grinding paste **(see illustration)**. When a dull, matt, even surface is produced on the faces of both the valve seat and the valve, wipe off the paste and repeat the process with fine carborundum paste. When a smooth unbroken ring of light grey matt finish is produced on both the valve and seat faces, the grinding operation is complete. Carefully clean away every trace of grinding paste, taking great care to leave none in the ports or in the valve guides. Clean the valves and valve seats with a paraffin-soaked rag, then with a clean rag, and finally, if an airline is available, blow the valves, valve guides and cylinder head ports clean.

Valve springs

13 Check that all the valve springs are intact. If any one is broken, all should be renewed.

14 If possible, check the free height of the springs against new ones, then stand each spring on a flat surface and check it for squareness **(see illustration)**. If a spring is found to be too short, or damaged in any way, renew all the springs as a set. Springs suffer from fatigue, and it is a good idea to renew them even if they look serviceable.

Rocker arm components

15 Check the rocker arm thrust faces (the areas that contact the tappets and valve stems) for pits, wear, score-marks or any indication that the surface-hardening has worn through. Check the rocker arm camshaft roller in the same manner. Renew any rocker arms which appear suspect.

Note: *New valve stem oil seals should be used on reassembly. A valve spring compressor tool will be required for this operation.*

8 Cylinder head – reassembly

1 With all the components cleaned, starting at one end of the cylinder head, fit the valve components as follows.

2 Insert the appropriate valve into its guide (if new valves are being fitted, insert each valve into the location to which it has been ground), ensuring that the valve stem is well-lubricated with clean engine oil. If the original components are being refitted, all components must be refitted in their original positions.

3 Fit the spring seat.

4 New valve stem oil seals may be supplied with a fitting sleeve, which fits over the collet groove in the valve stem, to prevent damage to the oil seal as it is slid down the valve stem. If no sleeve is supplied, wind a short length of tape round the top of the valve stem to cover the collet groove.

5 Lubricate the valve stem oil seal with clean engine oil, then push the oil seal down the valve stem using a suitable tube or socket, until the seal is fully engaged with the valve guide **(see illustrations)**. Remove the fitting sleeve or the tape, as applicable, from the valve stem.

6 Fit the valve spring and the spring cap.

7 Fit the spring compressor tool, and compress the valve spring until the spring cap passes beyond the collet groove in the valve stem.

8 Refit the split collets to the groove in the valve stem, with the narrow ends nearest the spring.

9 Slowly release the compressor tool, ensuring that the collets are not dislodged from the groove. When the compressor is fully released, give the top of the valve assembly a tap with a soft-faced mallet to settle the components.

10 Repeat the procedure for the remaining valves, ensuring that if the original components are being used, they are all refitted in their original positions.

11 Refit the components removed in Section 6, paragraph 1.

8.5a Fit the new valve stem oil seal...

8.5b ...and push it down using a suitable tube or socket, until the seal is fully engaged with the spring seat

9 Piston/connecting rod assemblies – removal

Note: *New big-end cap bolts will be required for reassembly.*

1 Remove the sump and cylinder head as described in Part A of this Chapter.

2 Undo the two bolts and remove the oil pump pick-up tube.

3 If there is a pronounced wear ridge at the top of any bore, it may be necessary to remove it with a scraper or ridge reamer, to avoid piston damage during removal. Such a ridge indicates excess bore wear.

4 Check to see if the big-end caps and connecting rods are numbered **(see illustration)**. If no numbers are visible, use quick-drying paint, or similar, to mark each connecting rod and big-end cap with its respective cylinder number on the flat machined surface provided. Note that No 1 cylinder is at the timing belt end of the engine.

5 Turn the crankshaft to bring pistons 1 and 4 to BDC (bottom dead centre).

6 Unscrew the bolts from No 1 piston big-end bearing cap, and remove the big-end cap and bearing shell **(see illustration)**. If the bearing shells are to be re-used, tape the cap and the shell together.

7 Using a hammer handle, push the piston up through the bore, and remove it from the top of the cylinder block. Recover the bearing shell, and tape it to the connecting rod for safe-keeping.

8 Loosely refit the big-end cap to the connecting rod, and secure with the bolts – this will help to keep the components in their correct order.

9 Remove No 4 assembly in the same way.

10 Turn the crankshaft through 180° to bring pistons 2 and 3 to BDC (bottom dead centre), and remove them in the same way.

10 Crankshaft – removal

1 Remove the flywheel as described in Chapter 2A.

2 Remove the pistons and connecting rods, as described in Section 9.

3 Invert the engine so that the crankshaft is uppermost.

4 Before removing the crankshaft, check the endfloat using a dial gauge in contact with the end of the crankshaft. Push the crankshaft fully one way, and then zero the gauge. Push the crankshaft fully the other way, and check the endfloat **(see illustration)**. The result should be compared with the specified limit, and will give an indication as to the size of the main bearing shell thrust journal width which will be required for reassembly.

5 If a dial gauge is not available, a feeler

9.4 Connecting rod and big-end cap identification numbers

gauge can be used to measure crankshaft endfloat. Push the crankshaft fully towards one end of the crankcase, and insert a feeler gauge between the thrust flange of the main bearing shell and the machined surface of the crankshaft web **(see illustration)**. Before measuring, ensure that the crankshaft is fully forced towards one end of the crankcase, to give the widest possible gap at the measuring location. **Note:** *Measure at the bearing with the thrustwasher (see Section 17).*

6 Note the identification markings on the main bearing caps which should be as follows. One line on the cap nearest the timing belt end, two on the second cap, C on the centre cap, then three and four lines on the remaining caps **(see illustration)**. If no markings are visible, mark them using quick-drying paint.

7 Slacken and remove the main bearing cap retaining bolts, and lift off each bearing cap. Recover the lower bearing shells, and

10.4 Using a dial gauge to check the crankshaft endfloat

10.6 Main bearing cap identification markings

9.6 Unscrew the retaining bolts and remove the big-end cap and bearing shell

tape them to their respective caps for safe-keeping.

8 Lift the crankshaft from the crankcase and remove the upper bearing shells from the crankcase. Note that the centre main bearing shell incorporates thrustwashers to control crankshaft endfloat **(see illustration)**. If the shells are to be used again, keep them identified for position.

11 Cylinder block – cleaning and inspection

Cleaning

1 For complete cleaning, remove all external components (senders, sensors, brackets, oil pipes, coolant pipes, etc) from the cylinder block.

2 Scrape all traces of gasket and/or sealant

10.5 Checking the crankshaft endfloat with a feeler gauge

10.8 Thrustwashers located on the centre man bearing shell

from the cylinder block and cylinder block baseplate, taking particular care not to damage the cylinder head and sump mating faces.

3 Remove all oil gallery plugs, where fitted. The plugs are usually very tight – they may have to be drilled out and the holes retapped. Use new plugs when the engine is reassembled.

4 If the block and baseplate (where applicable) are extremely dirty, they should be steam-cleaned.

5 If the components have been steam-cleaned, clean all oil holes and oil galleries one more time on completion. Flush all internal passages with warm water until the water runs clear. Dry the block and, where necessary, the baseplate thoroughly and wipe all machined surfaces with a light oil. If you have access to compressed air, use it to speed-up the drying process, and to blow out all the oil holes and galleries.

 Warning: Wear eye protection when using compressed air.

6 If the block and baseplate are relatively clean, an adequate cleaning job can be achieved with hot soapy water and a stiff brush. Take plenty of time, and do a thorough job. Regardless of the cleaning method used, be sure to clean all oil holes and galleries very thoroughly, dry everything completely, and coat all cast-iron machined surfaces with light oil.

7 The threaded holes in the cylinder block and baseplate must be clean, to ensure accurate torque readings when tightening fixings during reassembly. Run the correct-size tap (which can be determined from the size of the relevant bolt) into each of the holes to remove rust, corrosion, thread sealant or other contamination, and to restore damaged threads. If possible, use compressed air to clear the holes of debris produced by this operation. Do not forget to clean the threads of all bolts and nuts which are to be re-used, as well.

8 Where applicable, apply suitable sealant to the new oil gallery plugs, and insert them into the relevant holes in the cylinder block. Tighten the plugs securely.

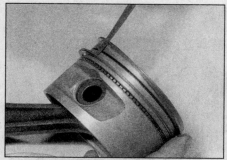
12.2 Use a feeler gauge to aid removal of a piston ring

9 If the engine is to be left dismantled for some time, cover the cylinder block with a large plastic bag to keep it clean and prevent corrosion. Where applicable, refit the baseplate and tighten the bolts finger-tight.

Inspection

10 Visually check the block for cracks, rust and corrosion. Look for stripped threads in the threaded holes. It's also a good idea to have the block checked for hidden cracks by an engine reconditioning specialist that has the equipment to do this type of work, especially if the vehicle had a history of overheating or using coolant. If defects are found, have the block repaired, if possible, or renewed.

11 If in any doubt as to the condition of the cylinder block, have it inspected and measured by an engine reconditioning specialist. If the bores are worn or damaged, they will be able to carry out any necessary reboring (where possible), and supply appropriate oversized pistons, etc.

12 Piston/connecting rod assemblies – inspection

1 Before the inspection process can begin, the piston/connecting rod assemblies must be cleaned, and the original piston rings removed from the pistons. **Note:** *Always use new piston rings when the engine is reassembled.*

2 Carefully expand the old rings over the top of the pistons. The use of two or three old feeler gauges will be helpful in preventing the rings dropping into empty grooves **(see illustration)**. Take care, however, as piston rings are sharp.

3 Scrape away all traces of carbon from the top of the piston. A hand-held wire brush, or a piece of fine emery cloth, can be used once the majority of the deposits have been scraped away.

4 Remove the carbon from the ring grooves in the piston, using an old ring. Break the ring in half to do this (be careful not to cut your fingers – piston rings are sharp). Be very careful to remove only the carbon deposits – do not remove any metal, and do not nick or scratch the sides of the ring grooves.

5 Once the deposits have been removed, clean the piston/connecting rod assembly with paraffin or a suitable solvent, and dry thoroughly. Make sure that the oil return holes in the ring grooves are clear.

6 If the pistons and cylinder bores are not damaged or worn excessively, and if the cylinder block does not need to be rebored, the original pistons can be refitted. Normal piston wear shows up as even vertical wear on the piston thrust surfaces, and slight looseness of the top ring in its groove. New piston rings should always be used when the engine is reassembled.

7 Carefully inspect each piston for cracks around the skirt, at the gudgeon pin bosses,

and at the piston ring lands (between the ring grooves).

8 Look for scoring and scuffing on the thrust faces of the piston skirt, holes in the piston crown, and burned areas at the edge of the crown. If the skirt is scored or scuffed, the engine may have been suffering from overheating, and/or abnormal combustion ('pinking') which caused excessively-high operating temperatures. The cooling and lubrication systems should be checked thoroughly. A hole in the piston crown, or burned areas at the edge of the piston crown indicates that abnormal combustion (pre-ignition, 'pinking', knocking or detonation) has been occurring. If any of the above problems exist, the causes must be investigated and corrected, or the damage will occur again.

9 Corrosion of the piston, in the form of pitting, indicates that coolant has been leaking into the combustion chamber and/or the crankcase. Again, the cause must be corrected, or the problem may persist in the rebuilt engine.

10 If in any doubt as to the condition of the pistons and connecting rods, have them inspected and measured by an engine reconditioning specialist. If new parts are required, they will be able to supply and fit appropriate-sized pistons/rings, and rebore (where possible) or hone the cylinder block.

13 Crankshaft – inspection

1 Clean the crankshaft using paraffin or a suitable solvent, and dry it, preferably with compressed air if available. Be sure to clean the oil holes with a pipe cleaner or similar probe, to ensure that they are not obstructed.

 Warning: Wear eye protection when using compressed air.

2 Check the main and big-end bearing journals for uneven wear, scoring, pitting and cracking.

3 Big-end bearing wear is accompanied by distinct metallic knocking when the engine is running (particularly noticeable when the engine is pulling from low revs), and some loss of oil pressure.

4 Main bearing wear is accompanied by severe engine vibration and rumble – getting progressively worse as engine revs increase – and again by loss of oil pressure.

5 Check the bearing journal for roughness by running a finger lightly over the bearing surface. Any roughness (which will be accompanied by obvious bearing wear) indicates that the crankshaft requires regrinding.

6 If the crankshaft has been reground, check for burrs around the crankshaft oil holes (the holes are usually chamfered, so burrs should not be a problem unless regrinding has been carried out carelessly). Remove any burrs with a fine file or scraper, and thoroughly clean the oil holes as described previously.

7 Have the crankshaft journals measured by an engine reconditioning specialist. If the crankshaft is worn or damaged, they may be able to regrind the journals and supply suitable undersize bearing shells. If no undersize shells are available and the crankshaft has worn beyond the specified limits, it will have to be renewed. Consult your Ford dealer or engine reconditioning specialist for further information on parts availability.

14 Main and big-end bearings – inspection

1 Even though the main and big-end bearings should be renewed during the engine overhaul, the old bearings should be retained for close examination, as they may reveal valuable information about the condition of the engine.
2 Bearing failure occurs because of lack of lubrication, the presence of dirt or other foreign particles, overloading the engine, or corrosion **(see illustration)**. If a bearing fails, the cause must be found and eliminated before the engine is reassembled, to prevent the failure from happening again.
3 To examine the bearing shells, remove them from the cylinder block, the cylinder block baseplate, the connecting rods and the big-end bearing caps, and lay them out on a clean surface in the same order as they were fitted to the engine. This will enable any bearing problems to be matched with the corresponding crankshaft journal.
4 Dirt and other foreign particles can enter the engine in a variety of ways. Contamination may be left in the engine during assembly, or it may pass through filters or the crankcase ventilation system. Normal engine wear produces small particles of metal, which can eventually cause problems. If particles find their way into the lubrication system, it is likely that they will eventually be carried to the bearings. Whatever the source, these foreign particles often end up embedded in the soft bearing material, and are easily recognised. Large particles will not embed in the bearing, and will score or gouge the bearing and journal. To prevent possible contamination, clean all parts thoroughly, and keep everything spotlessly-clean during engine assembly. Once the engine has been installed in the vehicle, ensure that engine oil and filter changes are carried out at the recommended intervals.
5 Lack of lubrication (or lubrication breakdown) has a number of interrelated causes. Excessive heat (which thins the oil), overloading (which squeezes the oil from the bearing face), and oil leakage (from excessive bearing clearances, worn oil pump or high engine speeds) all contribute to lubrication breakdown. Blocked oil passages, which may be the result of misaligned oil holes in a bearing shell, will also starve a bearing of oil and destroy it. When lack of lubrication is the cause of bearing failure, the bearing material

is wiped or extruded from the steel backing of the bearing. Temperatures may increase to the point where the steel backing turns blue from overheating.
6 Driving habits can have a definite effect on bearing life. Full-throttle, low-speed operation (labouring the engine) puts very high loads on bearings, which tends to squeeze out the oil film. These loads cause the bearings to flex, which produces fine cracks in the bearing face (fatigue failure). Eventually the bearing material will loosen in places, and tear away from the steel backing. Regular short journeys can lead to corrosion of bearings, because insufficient engine heat is produced to drive off the condensed water and corrosive gases which form inside the engine. These products collect in the engine oil, forming acid and sludge. As the oil is carried to the bearings, the acid attacks and corrodes the bearing material.
7 Incorrect bearing installation during engine assembly will also lead to bearing failure. Tight-fitting bearings leave insufficient bearing lubrication clearance, and will result in oil starvation. Dirt or foreign particles trapped behind a bearing shell results in high spots on the bearing which can lead to failure.
8 *Do not* touch any shell's bearing surface with your fingers during reassembly; there is a risk of scratching the delicate surface, or of depositing particles of dirt on it.
9 As mentioned at the beginning of this Section, the bearing shells should be renewed as a matter of course during engine overhaul; to do otherwise is false economy.

15 Engine overhaul – reassembly sequence

1 Before reassembly begins, ensure that all necessary new parts have been obtained (particularly gaskets, and various bolts which must be renewed), and that all the tools required are available. Read through the entire procedure to familiarise yourself with the work involved, and to ensure that all items necessary for reassembly of the engine are to hand. In addition to all normal tools and materials, a thread-locking compound will be required. A tube of suitable sealant will be required to seal certain joint faces which are not fitted with gaskets.
2 At this stage, all engine components should be absolutely clean and dry, with all faults repaired. The components should be laid out (or in individual containers) on a completely clean work surface.
3 In order to save time and avoid problems, engine reassembly can be carried out in the following order:
a) *Piston rings (see Section 16).*
b) *Crankshaft (see Section 17).*
c) *Piston/connecting rod assemblies (see Section 18).*
d) *Timing belt and sprockets (see Chapter 2A).*
e) *Oil pump (see Chapter 2A).*

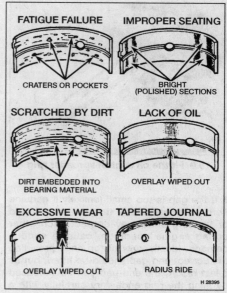

14.2 Typical bearing failures

f) *Sump (see Chapter 2A).*
g) *Flywheel (see Chapter 2A).*
h) *Cylinder head (see Chapter 2A).*
i) *Coolant pump (see Chapter 3).*
j) *Intake and exhaust manifolds (see Chapter 4A).*

16 Piston rings – refitting

1 Before refitting the new piston rings, the ring end gaps must be checked as follows.
2 Lay out the piston/connecting rod assemblies and the new piston ring sets, so that the ring sets will be matched with the same piston and cylinder during the end gap measurement and subsequent engine reassembly.
3 Insert the top ring into the first cylinder, and push it down the bore slightly using the top of the piston. This will ensure that the ring remains square with the cylinder walls.
4 Measure the end gap using feeler gauges, and compare the measurements with the figures given in the *Specifications* **(see illustration)**.

16.4 Measure the piston ring end gap using a feeler gauge

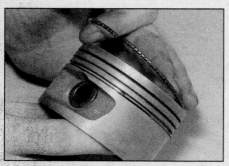

16.9 Fit the oil control spreader ring

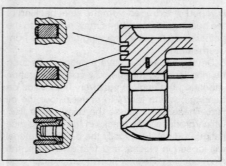

16.11 Sectional view showing correct orientation of piston rings

5 If the gap is too small (unlikely if genuine Ford parts are used), it must be enlarged or the ring ends may contact each other during engine operation, causing serious damage. Ideally, new piston rings providing the correct end gap should be fitted, but as a last resort, the end gap can be increased by filing the ring ends very carefully with a fine file. Mount the file in a vice equipped with soft jaws, slip the ring over the file with the ends contacting the file face, and slowly move the ring to remove material from the ends – take care, as piston rings are sharp, and are easily broken.

6 With new piston rings, it is unlikely that the end gap will be too large. If they are too large, check that you have the correct rings for your engine and for the particular cylinder bore size.

7 Repeat the checking procedure for each ring in the first cylinder, and then for the rings in the remaining cylinders. Remember to keep rings, pistons and cylinders matched up.

8 Once the ring end gaps have been checked and if necessary corrected, the rings can be fitted to the pistons.

9 The oil control ring (lowest one on the piston) should be installed first. Fit the lower steel ring, then the spreader ring, followed by the upper steel ring (see illustration).

10 With the oil control ring components installed, the second (middle) ring can be fitted. It is usually stamped with a mark (TOP) which must face up, towards the top of the piston. **Note:** *Always follow the instructions supplied with the new piston ring sets ñ different manufacturers may specify different procedures. Do not mix up the top and middle rings, as they have different cross-sections.* Using two or three old feeler blades, as for

removal of the old rings, carefully slip the ring into place in the middle groove.

11 Fit the top ring in the same manner, ensuring that, where applicable, the mark on the ring is facing up. If a stepped ring is being fitted, fit the ring with the smaller diameter of the step uppermost (see illustration).

12 Repeat the procedure for the remaining pistons and rings.

17 Crankshaft – refitting

1 Refitting the crankshaft is the first step in the engine reassembly procedure. It is assumed at this point that the cylinder block, baseplate and crankshaft have been cleaned, inspected and repaired or reconditioned as necessary.

2 Position the cylinder block with the baseplate mating face uppermost.

3 Clean the bearing shells and the bearing recesses in both the cylinder block and the baseplate. If new shells are being fitted, ensure that all traces of the protective grease are cleaned off using paraffin. Wipe the shells dry with a clean lint-free cloth.

4 Note that the crankshaft endfloat is controlled by thrustwashers located on the centre main bearing shells. The thrustwashers are incorporated into, or attached to, the bearing shells themselves.

5 If the original bearing shells are being re-used, they must be refitted to their original locations in the block and baseplate (see illustrations).

6 Fit the upper main bearing shells in place in the cylinder block.

7 Liberally lubricate each bearing shell in the cylinder block, and lower the crankshaft into position (see illustration).

8 If necessary, seat the crankshaft using light taps from a soft-faced mallet on the crankshaft balance webs.

9 Lubricate the lower bearing shells in the main bearing caps with clean engine oil.

10 Fit the main bearing caps to their correct locations, ensuring that they are fitted the correct way round (the bearing shell tab recesses in the block and caps must be on the same side). Insert the bolts loosely.

11 Tighten the main bearing cap bolts to the specified Stage 1 torque wrench setting. Once all the bolts have been tightened to the Stage 1 setting, angle-tighten the bolts through the specified Stage 2 angle, using a socket and extension bar. It is recommended that an angle-measuring gauge is used during this stage of the tightening, to ensure accuracy.

12 Check that the crankshaft rotates freely.

13 Prise out the crankshaft oil seal and fit a new seal to the housing (see illustrations).

14 Lubricate the oil seal lips then carefully locate the oil seal housing into position, using a new gasket. If the oil seal housing

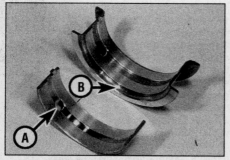

17.5a Main bearing shell (A) and central main bearing shell (B) with thrust flange

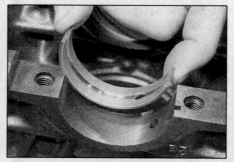

17.5b Fit the main bearing shell to the cylinder block

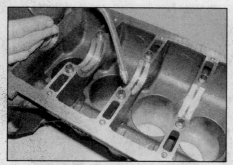

17.7 Liberally lubricate each bearing shell in the cylinder block then lower the crankshaft into position

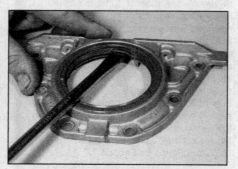

17.13a Use a screwdriver to prise out the oil seal...

17.13b ....locate the new oil seal in the housing...

17.13c ...and used a block of wood to drive it in

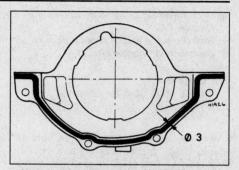

17.14 Application area for silicone sealant on the crankshaft oil seal housing

was originally fitted without a gasket, apply a 3.0 mm bead of RTV silicone sealant to the housing flange **(see illustration)**. Refit the retaining bolts and tighten them securely.

15 Continue with engine reassembly in the sequence given in Section 15.

16 Now rotate the crankshaft, and check that it turns freely, with no signs of binding or tight spots.

17 Check the crankshaft endfloat with reference to Section 10.

18 Refit the pistons and connecting rods as described in Section 18.

19 Refit the flywheel as described in Chapter 2A.

18 Pistons/connecting rods – refitting

1 Clean the backs of the big-end bearing shells and the recesses in the connecting rods and big-end caps. If new shells are being fitted, ensure that all traces of the protective grease are cleaned off using paraffin. Wipe the shells, caps and connecting rods dry with a lint-free cloth.

2 Press the bearing shells into the connecting rods and caps in their correct positions **(see illustration)**. **Note:** *When finally refitting the piston/connecting rod assemblies, new big-end bearing cap bolts must be used. Ensure that the mating faces of the connecting rods and big-end bearing caps are clean before refitting (refer to Section 9).*

3 Lubricate No 1 piston and piston rings,

and check that the ring gaps are correctly positioned. Where applicable, the gaps in the upper and lower steel rings of the oil control ring should be offset by 25 to 50 mm to the right and left of the spreader ring gap. The two upper compression ring gaps should be offset by 180° to each other.

4 Liberally lubricate the cylinder bore with clean engine oil.

5 Fit a ring compressor to No 1 piston, then insert the piston and connecting rod into the cylinder bore so that the base of the compressor stands on the block. With the crankshaft big-end bearing journal positioned at its lowest point, tap the piston carefully into the cylinder bore with the wooden handle of a hammer, and at the same time guide the connecting rod onto the bearing journal. Note that the arrow or notch (as applicable) on the piston crown must point towards

the timing chain/belt end of the engine **(see illustrations)**.

6 Fit the bearing shells to the bearing caps.

7 Liberally lubricate the bearing journals and bearing shells, and fit the bearing cap in its original location. Tighten the new bearing cap bolts to the Stage 1 torque setting, then tighten all bolts through the specified angles **(see illustrations)**.

8 After refitting each piston/connecting rod assembly, rotate the crankshaft, and check that it turns freely, with no signs of binding or tight spots.

9 Refit the following components.
a) *Refit the oil baffle plate and tighten the retaining bolts securely.*
b) *Refit the cylinder head as described in Chapter 2A.*
c) *Refit the timing belt, sprockets and tensioner as described in Chapter 2A.*

18.2 Press the bearing shells into the connecting rods and caps in their correct positions

18.5a Position the piston with the arrow or notch (as applicable) pointing towards the timing chain/belt end of the engine...

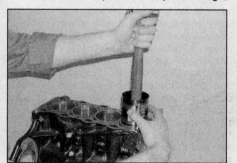

18.5b ...then tap the piston carefully into the cylinder bore

18.7a Tighten the big-end bearing cap bolts to the specified torque...

18.7b ...then through the specified angle

d) Refit the timing cover as described in Chapter 2A.

e) Refit the sump and oil pick-up pipe as described in Chapter 2A.

19 Engine – initial start-up after overhaul

1 With the engine refitted in the vehicle, double-check the engine oil and coolant levels. Make a final check that everything has been reconnected, and that there are no tools or rags left in the engine compartment.

2 Start the engine, noting that this may take a little longer than usual. Make sure that the oil pressure warning light goes out.

3 While the engine is idling, check for fuel, water and oil leaks. Don't be alarmed if there are some odd smells and smoke from parts getting hot and burning off oil deposits.

4 Assuming all is well, keep the engine idling until hot water is felt circulating through the top hose, then switch off the engine.

5 After a few minutes, recheck the oil and coolant levels as described in Weekly checks, and top-up as necessary.

6 Note that there is no need to retighten the cylinder head bolts once the engine has first run after reassembly.

7 If new pistons, rings or crankshaft bearings have been fitted, the engine must be treated as new, and run-in for the first 600 miles. Do not operate the engine at full-throttle, or allow it to labour at low engine speeds in any gear. It is recommended that the oil and filter be changed at the end of this period.

Chapter 3
Cooling, heating and ventilation systems

Contents

Degrees of difficulty

Easy, suitable for novice with little experience	Fairly easy, suitable for beginner with some experience	Fairly difficult, suitable for competent DIY mechanic	Difficult, suitable for experienced DIY mechanic	Very difficult, suitable for expert DIY or professional

Specifications

General

Expansion tank relief valve opening pressure	0.99 bar

Thermostat

Opening temperature	88 ± 2°C

Air conditioning

Lubricant capacity:	
Receiver/drier	15 cc
Pipes	5 cc
Evaporator	40 cc
Condenser	40 cc
Compressor	80 cc
Lubricant type	Synthetic PAG fluid WSS-M2C31-B2
Refrigerant capacity	500 ± 40g

Torque wrench settings

	Nm	lbf ft
Air conditioning compressor mounting bolts	25	18
Condenser supply pipes	20	25
Coolant pump bolts/nuts	8	6
Steering column lower pinch-bolt*	56	41
Thermostat housing bolts	10	7

Do not re-use

2.4 Lift the clip (arrowed) and pull the hose from the union

1 General information and precautions

The cooling system is of pressurised type, comprising a pump driven by the timing belt, an aluminium crossflow radiator, electric cooling fan, and a thermostat. The system functions as follows. Cold coolant from the radiator passes through the hose to the coolant pump, where it is pumped around the cylinder block and head passages. After cooling the cylinder bores, combustion surfaces and valve seats, the coolant reaches the underside of the thermostat, which is initially closed. The coolant passes through the heater, and is returned to the coolant pump.

When the engine is cold, the coolant circulates only through the cylinder block, cylinder head, expansion tank and heater. When the coolant reaches a predetermined temperature, the thermostat opens and the coolant passes through to the radiator. As the coolant circulates through the radiator, it is cooled by the inrush of air when the car is in forward motion. Airflow is supplemented by the action of the electric cooling fan when necessary. Once the coolant has passed through the radiator, and has cooled, the cycle is repeated.

The electric cooling fan, mounted on the rear of the radiator, is controlled by a thermostatic switch/sensor. At a predetermined coolant temperature, the fan is actuated.

An expansion tank is fitted into the engine compartment to accommodate expansion of

3.5 Cable ties (arrowed) can be used to support the condenser

the coolant when it gets hot. The expansion tank is connected to the top of the radiator by a small bore rubber hose.

⚠️ *Warning: Do not attempt to remove the expansion tank filler cap, or disturb any part of the cooling system, while the engine is hot; there is a high risk of scalding. If the expansion tank filler cap must be removed before the engine and radiator have fully cooled (even though this is not recommended) the pressure in the cooling system must first be relieved. Cover the cap with a thick layer of cloth, to avoid scalding, and slowly unscrew the filler cap until a hissing sound can be heard. When the hissing has stopped, indicating that the pressure has reduced, slowly unscrew the filler cap until it can be removed; if more hissing sounds are heard, wait until they have stopped before unscrewing the cap completely. At all times, keep well away from the filler cap opening.*
* *Do not allow antifreeze to come into contact with skin, or with the painted surfaces of the vehicle. Rinse off spills immediately, with plenty of water. Never leave antifreeze lying around in an open container, or in a puddle on the driveway or garage floor. Children and pets are attracted by its sweet smell, but antifreeze can be fatal if ingested.*
* *If the engine is hot, the electric cooling fan may start rotating even if the engine is not running; be careful to keep hands, hair and loose clothing well clear when working in the engine compartment.*
* *Refer to Section 10 for precautions to be observed when working on models equipped with air conditioning.*

2 Cooling system hoses – disconnection and renewal

Note: *Refer to the warnings given in Section 1 of this Chapter before proceeding. Do not attempt to disconnect any hose while the system is still hot.*

1 If the checks described in Chapter 1 reveal a faulty hose, it must be renewed as follows.

3.6a Disconnect the radiator lower hose (arrowed)...

2 First drain the cooling system (see Chapter 1). If the coolant is not due for renewal, it may be re-used if it is collected in a clean container.
3 Before disconnecting a hose, first note its routing in the engine compartment, and whether it is secured by any additional retaining clips or cable-ties. Use a pair of pliers to release the clamp-type clips, or a screwdriver to slacken the screw-type clips, then move the clips along the hose, clear of the relevant inlet/outlet union. Carefully work the hose free.
4 Some of the hose attachments may be of the quick-release type. Where this type of hose is encountered, lift the wire retaining clip, then withdraw the hose from the inlet/outlet union **(see illustration)**.
5 Note that the radiator inlet and outlet unions are fragile; do not use excessive force when attempting to remove the hoses. If a hose proves to be difficult to remove, try to release it by rotating the hose ends before attempting to free it.
6 When fitting a hose, first slide the clips onto the hose, then work the hose into position. If clamp-type clips were originally fitted, it is a good idea to use screw-type clips when refitting the hose. If the hose is stiff, use a little soapy water (washing-up liquid is ideal) as a lubricant, or soften the hose by soaking it in hot water.
7 Work the hose into position, checking that it is correctly routed and secured. Slide each clip along the hose until it passes over the flared end of the relevant inlet/outlet union, before tightening the clips securely.
8 Refill the cooling system with reference to Chapter 1.
9 Check thoroughly for leaks as soon as possible after disturbing any part of the cooling system.

3 Radiator – removal, inspection and refitting

Removal

1 Jack up and support the front of the vehicle (see *Jacking and vehicle support* in the reference section). The vehicle must be raised sufficiently to allow the radiator to be lowered from the engine bay.
2 Drain the cooling system as described in Chapter 1.
3 Remove the front bumper as described in Chapter 11.
4 Remove the cooling fan as described in Section 5 of this Chapter. Alternatively the cooling fan can be removed with the radiator.
5 Where fitted, support the AC condenser **(see illustration)** and then remove the condenser mounting bolts
6 Slacken the retaining clips, and disconnect the coolant top and bottom hoses from the radiator. If necessary, prise up the clip and disconnect the lower coolant pipe as the radiator is pulled forwards **(see illustrations)**.

3.6b ...and upper hose (arrowed)

3.7a Remove the support brackets (arrowed)...

3.7b ...and lower the radiator from the engine bay

Note that on some models the upper hose clip is a single use clip and will have to be cut to remove it. A new hose clip will be required for refitting

7 Support the radiator and then undo the radiator lower mounting bracket bolt on each side. Lower the radiator from the engine bay **(see illustrations)**.

Inspection

8 Clean dirt and debris from the radiator fins, using an airline (in which case, wear eye protection) or a soft brush.
Caution: Be careful, as the fins are easily damaged, and are sharp.
9 If necessary, a radiator specialist can perform a 'flow test' on the radiator, to establish whether an internal blockage exists.
10 In an emergency, minor leaks from the radiator can be cured by using a suitable radiator sealant (in accordance with its manufacturer's instructions) with the radiator *in situ*.

Flushing

11 Disconnect the top and bottom hoses and any other relevant hoses from the radiator.
12 Insert a garden hose into the radiator top inlet. Direct a flow of clean water through the radiator, and continue flushing until clean water emerges from the radiator bottom outlet.
13 If after a reasonable period, the water still does not run clear, the radiator can be flushed with a good proprietary cleaning agent. It is important that their manufacturer's instructions

are followed carefully. If the contamination is particularly bad, insert the hose in the radiator bottom outlet, and reverse-flush the radiator.

Refitting

14 Refitting is a reversal of removal, bearing in mind the following points:
a) *Ensure that all hoses are correctly reconnected, and their retaining clips securely tightened.*
b) *On completion, refill the cooling system as described in Chapter 1.*

---

4 Thermostat –
removal, testing and refitting

Removal

1 Remove the air filter (Chapter 4A), battery and battery tray as described in Chapter 5A.
2 Drain the cooling system (see Chapter 1).
3 Slacken the retaining clips, disconnect the coolant hoses and wiring plug from the thermostat housing located at the left-hand end of the cylinder head **(see illustration)**.
4 Slacken and remove the 2 retaining bolts **(see illustration)**. Remove the thermostat housing.
5 Note that the thermostat is an integral part of the housing, and cannot be renewed separately.
6 Remove the sealing ring from the housing and discard it **(see illustration)**. A new one should be used on refitting.

Testing

7 If there is any question about the operation of the thermostat, it's best to renew it. Testing involves heating in an open pan of boiling water, which carries with it the risk of scalding. A thermostat which has seen more than five years' service may well be past its best already.
8 The opening temperature maybe marked on the thermostat. If a thermometer is available, the precise opening temperature of the thermostat may be determined, and compared with the value marked on the thermostat.
9 A thermostat which fails to close as the water cools must also be renewed.

Refitting

10 Refitting is a reversal of removal, bearing in mind the following points:
a) *Fit the new sealing rings to all applicable mating faces.*
b) *Tighten the thermostat housing/cover bolts to the specified torque.*
c) *On completion, refill the cooling system as described in Chapter 1.*

---

5 Electric cooling fan –
removal and refitting

⚠ *Warning: If the engine is hot, the cooling fan may start up at any time. Take extra precautions when working in the vicinity of the fan.*

4.3 Disconnect the coolant hoses and wiring plug (arrowed) from the thermostat housing

4.4 Remove the bolts (arrowed)

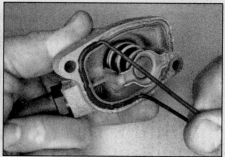

4.6 Remove the seal and discard it

5.4a Disconnect the cooling fan motor and resistor wiring plugs (arrowed)

1 Disconnect the battery negative terminal as described in Chapter 5A.
2 Firmly apply the handbrake, then jack up the front of the car and support it securely on axle stands (see *Jacking and vehicle support*).
3 Remove the air cleaner assembly as described in Chapter 4A.
4 Disconnect the cooling fan wiring plug and the fan speed control resistor. Undo the retaining bolts and lower the fan and shroud from place **(see illustrations)**.

Refitting

5 Refitting is a reversal of removal, bearing in mind the following points:
  a) *Ensure that the shroud is correctly located on the radiator.*
  b) *Use new cable-ties to secure all disturbed wiring harnesses.*
  c) *On completion, start the engine and run it until it reaches normal operating*

6.4 Coolant temperature sensor (arrowed)

7.6 A sharp blade can be used to clean the mounting surface

5.5a Remove the cooling fan shroud retaining bolts (arrowed)

temperature; continue to run the engine, and check that the cooling fan cuts in and functions correctly.

6 Coolant temperature sensor – testing, removal and refitting

Testing

1 Testing of the coolant temperature sensor circuit is best entrusted to a Ford dealer, who will have the necessary specialist diagnostic equipment.

Removal

2 Drain the cooling system as described in Chapter 1, to below the level of the sensor.
3 Remove the battery and battery tray as described in Chapter 5A.

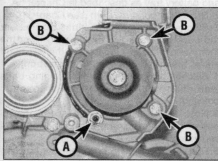

7.4 Coolant pump retaining nut (A) and bolts (B)

7.7 Apply a bead of RTV sealant to the coolant pump flange

4 The sensor is fitted to the thermostat housing at the left-hand end of the cylinder head. Disconnect the sensor wiring plug **(see illustration)**.
5 Unscrew the sensor from place. Be prepared for coolant spillage. Plug the openings to prevent contamination.

Refitting

6 Refitting is a reversal of removal, bearing in mind the following points:
  a) *Where applicable fit a new sealing O-ring to the sensor. Where the sensor is fitted without an O-ring, ensure the sensor threads are clean, and apply a smear of suitable sealant to them.*
  b) *On completion, top-up/refill the cooling system as described in Chapter 1.*

7 Coolant pump – removal and refitting

Removal

1 Disconnect the battery negative terminal as described in Chapter 5A.
2 Drain the cooling system and remove the auxiliary drivebelt as described in Chapter 1.
3 Remove the timing belt as described in Chapter 2A.
4 Unscrew the retaining nut and the three bolts and withdraw the coolant pump **(see illustration)**. If the pump is stuck, tap it gently using a soft-faced mallet – **do not** lever between the pump and cylinder block mating faces.

Inspection

5 Check the pump body and impeller for signs of excessive corrosion or evidence of coolant leakage. Turn the impeller, and check for stiffness due to corrosion, or roughness due to excessive end play. If any of these conditions are apparent, the pump must be renewed as a complete assembly.

Refitting

6 Commence refitting by thoroughly cleaning all traces of sealant from the mating faces of the pump and cylinder block **(see illustration)**.
7 Apply a continuous bead of RTV sealant to the cylinder block mating face of the pump, taking care not to apply excessive sealant, which may enter the pump itself **(see illustration)**.
8 Place the pump in position in the cylinder block, then refit and tighten the nut and bolts to the specified torque.
9 Refit the timing belt as described in Chapter 2A.
10 Refit the auxiliary drivebelt and refill the cooling system as described in Chapter 1.
11 Reconnect the battery negative terminal as described in Chapter 5A.

8 Heater/ventilation system – general information

The heater/ventilation system consists of a four-speed blower, face-level vents in the centre and at each end of the facia, and air ducts to the front footwells and windscreen.

The controls operate flap valves to deflect and mix the air flowing through the various parts of the heater/ventilation system. The flap valves are contained in the air distribution housing, which acts as a central distribution unit, passing air to the various ducts and vents.

Cold air enters the system through the grille at the rear of the engine compartment. A pollen filter is fitted to the ventilation intake, to filter out dust, soot, pollen and spores from the air entering the vehicle.

The air (boosted by the blower fan if required) then flows through the various ducts, according to the settings of the controls. Stale air is expelled through ducts behind the doors. If warm air is required, the cold air is passed through the heater matrix, which is heated by the engine coolant.

A recirculation lever enables the outside air supply to be closed off, while the air inside the vehicle is recirculated. This can be useful to prevent unpleasant odours entering from outside the vehicle, but should only be used briefly, as the recirculated air inside the vehicle will soon deteriorate.

9 Heater/ventilation system components – removal and refitting

Heater control unit

1 Disconnect the battery as described in Chapter 5A.

2 Remove the audio unit as described in Chapter 12 and then prise free the centre air vents (as described in Chapter 11).

3 Release the gear lever gaiter trim as described in Chapter 11.

4 Remove the 2 upper and 2 lower mounting screws and release the control panel trim.

5 At this point it is possible to remove the

9.5 Pull the heater control knobs from place

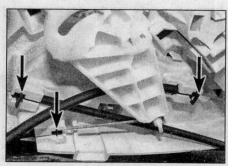

9.7b …remove the outer cable retaining clips (arrowed)

control unit switches, but not the main control panel. Remove the switch assemblies by prising them free from the control panel **(see illustration)**.

6 To remove the main section of the control panel the facia must be partially removed as described in Chapter 11. There is no requirement to remove the facia completely – the panel just needs the upper mounting screws loosening and the lower removing so that the panel can be lifted enough to release the heater control panel.

7 With the control panel free from the facia rotate it carefully to give access to the heater control cables. Disconnect the wiring plug. Note the position of the control cables and then remove them **(see illustrations)**. This is an awkward task with little room for manoeuvre.

8 Remove the micro switches and panel illumination bulb holders from the control panel **(see illustration)**.

9.7a Turn over the panel and…

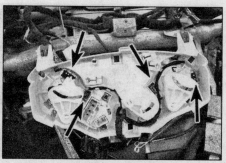

9.8 Remove the micros switches and bulb holders (arrowed)

9 Refitting is a reversal of removal.

Heater control assembly cables

10 Remove the complete facia as described in Chapter 11. Mark the position of the heater control cables in their respective retaining clips on the air distribution housing, then prise out the outer cable retaining clips and disconnect the inner cables from their attachments.

11 Note the orientation of the control cables, then release the outer cable retaining clips and disconnect the inner cable ends from the control levers **(see illustrations)**. Remove the control assembly from the facia. Alternatively, the control cables can be left attached to be removed complete with the control assembly.

12 Refitting is a reversal of removal. Ensure that the wiring connectors and control cables are correctly routed and reconnected to the control assembly, as noted before removal. Clip the outer cable(s) in position, and check

9.11a Disconnect the cables from the distribution flap lever…

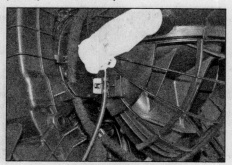

9.11b …the recirculation flap lever…

9.11c …and the temperature control lever

9.15 Disconnect the heater hoses (arrowed) at the engine compartment bulkhead

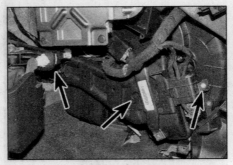

9.16a Remove the screws...

9.16b ...unclip the small cover...

9.16c ...and remove the main cover

9.17a Release and remove the locking clips

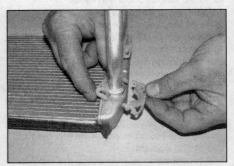

9.17b Note how the clips lock together (matrix removed for clarity)

the operation of each knob/lever before refitting the components removed for access.

Heater matrix

13 Drain the coolant and described in Chapter 1.
14 Remove the glovebox (as described in Chapter 11) and the left-hand lower centre side panel.
15 Release the clamps and disconnect the heater matrix hoses at the engine compartment bulkhead **(see illustration)**.
16 Undo the screws and remove the matrix/pipes cover from the air distribution housing **(see illustrations)**.
17 Release the clamps securing the pipes to the matrix. Note how the clamps lock together **(see illustrations)**.
18 Push the pipes forwards slightly and slide the matrix from the housing.
19 Refitting is a reversal of the removal

procedure, but fit new seals to the heater matrix pipes. On completion, top-up/refill the cooling system as described in Chapter 1.

Heater blower motor

Note: *It is theoretically possible to remove the blower motor with the facia in place, however we found this impossible.*
20 Disconnect the battery negative terminal as described in Chapter 5A.
21 Remove the passenger's side glovebox as described in Chapter 11.
22 Remove the complete facia as described in Chapter 11.
23 On models fitted with Stop/Start remove the control module **(see illustration)**.
24 Reach under the passenger's side of the facia, and disconnect the blower motor wiring plug **(see illustration)**.
25 Undo the retaining bolt (or lift up the locking tab). Rotate the blower motor clockwise and

remove it from the air distribution housing **(see illustration)**.
26 Refitting is a reversal of the removal procedure.

Heater blower motor resistor

27 The blower motor resistor pack is located on the bulkhead side of the heater housing.
28 Remove the facia as described in Chapter 11.
29 Drain the cooling system (as described in Chapter 1) and then disconnect the heater hoses at the bulkhead.
30 Where AC is fitted, have the AC system drained at a suitably equipped garage or automotive air conditioning specialist before proceeding. Disconnect the AC refrigerant lines at the bulkhead.
31 If not already done so, remove the steering wheel and unbolt the column pinch bolt from the steering rack. Unbolt the column from the

9.23 Remove the control unit

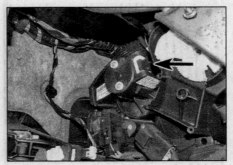

9.24 Disconnect the wiring plug (arrowed)

9.25 Remove the blower motor

Cooling, heating and ventilation systems 3•7

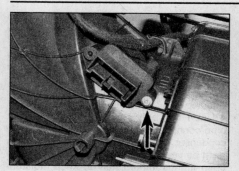

9.36a Remove the screw and...

9.36b ...then remove the resistor pack

9.43 Preparing to remove the complete air distribution housing

crossmember as described in Chapter 10 and remove it from the vehicle.

32 Remove both front doors and then mark the position of the crossmember.

33 Remove the bolts from the A-pillars and then slacken the upper crossmember bolts.

34 With the aid of an assistant lift up the crossmember (complete with the air distribution housing) sufficiently to gain access to the resistor. If necessary remove the crossmember complete with the air distribution housing.

35 Reach up and disconnect the wiring connector from the blower motor resistor. Note that access is still limited unless the complete housing is removed.

36 Undo the retaining screw and unclip the resistor from the blower motor housing **(see illustrations)**.

37 Refitting is the reverse of removal.

Air distribution housing

Note: *On models with air conditioning have the refrigerant discharged at a suitably equipped garage or by a mobile automotive air conditioning specialist before proceeding.*

38 Drain the cooling system as described in Chapter 1 and then disconnect the heater hoses at the bulkhead.

39 Remove the complete facia assembly and both front doors as described in Chapter 11.

40 Remove the fascia crossmember as described in Chapter 11.

41 Undo the retaining nuts and disconnect the refrigerant pipes from the engine compartment bulkhead. Plug the openings to prevent contamination.

42 Cover the carpet directly underneath the air distribution housing, to catch any coolant which may be spilt from the matrix as the housing assembly is removed.

43 On models with AC, disconnect the evaporator drain tube from the base of the housing. Release any wiring looms as necessary. Check that all electrical connections have been released and the pull the air distribution housing away from the bulkhead **(see illustration)**. Remove the housing from the vehicle.

44 Refitting is the reverse of removal. On completion, refill the cooling system as described in Chapter 1. Where necessary, have the air conditioning system evacuated,

charged and leak-tested by the specialist who discharged it.

10 Air conditioning system – general information and precautions

General information

1 Air conditioning is fitted to many models. It enables the temperature of the incoming air to be lowered, and also dehumidifies the air, which makes for rapid demisting and increased comfort.

2 The cooling side of the system works in the same way as a domestic refrigerator. Refrigerant gas is drawn into a belt-driven compressor, and passes into a condenser mounted in front of the radiator, where it loses heat and becomes liquid. The liquid passes through an expansion valve to an evaporator, where it changes from liquid under high pressure to gas under low pressure. This change is accompanied by a drop in temperature, which cools the evaporator. The refrigerant returns to the compressor, and the cycle begins again.

3 Air blown through the evaporator passes to the air distribution unit, where it is mixed with hot air blown through the heater matrix, to achieve the desired temperature in the passenger compartment.

4 The heating side of the system works in the same way as on models without air conditioning (see Section 8).

5 The operation of the system is controlled

10.6 Refrigerant circuit service ports (arrowed)

electronically. Any problems with the system should be referred to a Ford dealer or suitably equipped garage.

Air conditioning service ports

6 The low-pressure and high-pressure service ports are located above the air conditioning compressor **(see illustration)**.

Precautions

7 It is necessary to observe special precautions whenever dealing with any part of the system, its associated components, and any items which necessitate disconnection of the system.

⚠️ *Warning: The refrigeration circuit contains a liquid refrigerant. This refrigerant is potentially dangerous, and should only be handled by qualified persons. If it is splashed onto the skin, it can cause frostbite. It is not itself poisonous, but in the presence of a naked flame it forms a poisonous gas; inhalation of the vapour through a lighted cigarette could prove fatal. Uncontrolled discharging of the refrigerant is dangerous, and potentially damaging to the environment. It is therefore dangerous to disconnect any part of the system without specialised knowledge and equipment. If for any reason the system must be disconnected, entrust this task to your Ford dealer, suitably equipped garage or air conditioning specialist.*

11 Air conditioning system components – removal and refitting

⚠️ *Warning: The air conditioning system is under high pressure. Do not loosen any fittings or remove any components until after the system has been discharged. Air conditioning refrigerant should be properly discharged into an approved type of container at a dealer service department or an automotive air conditioning repair facility capable of handling R134a refrigerant. Cap or plug the pipe lines as soon as they are disconnected, to prevent the entry of moisture. Always wear eye protection when disconnecting air conditioning system fittings.*

11.4a Disconnect the refrigerant pipes

11.4b Recover the seals (arrowed)...

11.4c ...and immediately plug the openings

11.5 Remove the bolts (arrowed)

Note: *This Section refers to the components of the air conditioning system itself – refer to Section 9 for details of components common to the heating/ventilation system.*

Condenser

Note: *The receiver/drier is an integral part of the condenser and is not available as a separate item.*

11.10 Remove the cover and extract the pollen filter

11.11a Remove the lower cover...

11.11b ...and recover the temperature sensor

11.13 Remove the operating lever

11.14 Remove the evaporator

1 Have the refrigerant discharged at a suitably equipped garage or at an automotive air conditioning specialist.

2 Firmly apply the handbrake, then jack up the front of the car and support it securely on axle stands (see *Jacking and vehicle support*).

3 Remove the front bumper as described in Chapter 11.

4 Undo the bolt securing the refrigerant pipe connector to the right-hand side of the condenser. Discard the pipe seals – new ones must be used when refitting. Suitably cap the open fittings immediately to keep moisture and contamination out of the system **(see illustrations)**.

5 Undo the retaining bolts and manoeuvre the condenser from position **(see illustration)**. Note that the receiver/drier is integral with the condenser.

6 Refitting is the reverse of removal. Renew the O-rings and lubricate with refrigerant oil.

7 Have the system evacuated, charged and leak-tested by the specialist who discharged it.

Evaporator

8 Have the refrigerant discharged at a suitably equipped garage or at an automotive air conditioning specialist.

9 Remove the air distribution housing as described in Section 9.

10 Unclip the cover and remove the pollen filter from the right-hand side of the housing **(see illustration)**.

11 Disconnect the wiring plug, undo the screws and remove the lower half of the evaporator housing. Unclip the temperature probe as the housing is removed **(see illustrations)**.

12 Undo the bolt, release the clip and remove the blower motor **(see illustration 9.25)**.

13 The air distribution housing must now be split vertically. Disconnect the wiring loom as necessary and then note the position of the air distribution gear mechanism. Locate the 2 small index pegs on the smaller gear wheels and then remove the operating arm **(see illustration)**

14 Remove the screws and pull the halves apart in the area of the evaporator. Manoeuvre the evaporator from the housing **(see illustration)**.

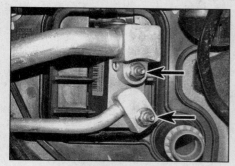
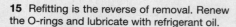

11.17a Undo the nuts (arrowed) and pull the refrigerant pipes from the expansion valve

11.17b Renew the refrigerant pipe seals (arrowed)

11.19 The expansion valve retaining screws (arrowed)

15 Refitting is the reverse of removal. Renew the O-rings and lubricate with refrigerant oil.

Expansion valve

16 Have the refrigerant discharged at a suitably equipped garage or at an automotive air conditioning specialist.

17 With the system discharged, undo the retaining nuts and disconnect the refrigerant pipe connector blocks. Discard the O-ring seals – new ones must be used when refitting **(see illustrations)**. Suitably cap the open fittings immediately to keep moisture and contamination out of the system.

18 Release the refrigerant pipes from the retaining clips on the engine compartment bulkhead, and pull the pipes away from the expansion valve.

19 Undo the screws and pull the expansion valve from the evaporator pipes **(see illustration)**. Renew the valve O-ring seals.

20 Refitting is the reverse of removal ensuring that all disturbed seals are renewed.

Compressor

21 Have the refrigerant discharged at a suitably equipped garage or at an automotive air conditioning specialist.

22 Disconnect the battery negative terminal as described in Chapter 5A.

23 Firmly apply the handbrake, then jack up the front of the car and support it securely on axle stands (see *Jacking and vehicle support*). Remove the right-hand front wheel.

24 Remove the air cleaner assembly as described in Chapter 4A.

25 Release the auxiliary drivebelt from the pulleys as described in Chapter 1.

26 With the system discharged, undo the retaining bolt and disconnect the refrigerant pipes from the compressor. Discard the O-ring seals – new ones must be used when refitting. Suitably cap the open fittings immediately to keep moisture and contamination out of the system.

27 Disconnect the compressor wiring connector.

28 Unbolt the compressor from the cylinder block/crankcase, then withdraw the compressor from place.

29 Refit the compressor in the reverse order of removal; renew all seals disturbed.

30 If you are installing a new compressor, refer to the compressor manufacturer's instructions for adding refrigerant oil to the system.

31 Have the system evacuated, charged and leak-tested by the specialist that discharged it.

Chapter 4 Part A:
Fuel and exhaust systems

Contents

Degrees of difficulty

Easy, suitable for novice with little experience 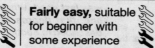	Fairly easy, suitable for beginner with some experience	Fairly difficult, suitable for competent DIY mechanic	Difficult, suitable for experienced DIY mechanic	Very difficult, suitable for expert DIY or professional

Specifications

System type
All models. . . . . Magneti-Marelli IAW sequential fuel injection/ignition system

Fuel system data
Engine idle speed*	900 ± 50 rpm
Fuel pump type	Electric, immersed in fuel tank
Fuel pump delivery rate	110 litres/hour
Regulated fuel pressure	3.5 bars
Crankshaft TDC sensor resistance at 20°C	1134 to 1386 ohms
Injector electrical resistance	13.8 to 15.2 ohms
Fuel level sensor:	
Full	33 ± 3 ohms
Empty	299 ± 3 ohms

* Not adjustable – controlled by ECU

Recommended fuel
Minimum octane rating. . . . . 95 RON unleaded

Torque wrench settings

	Nm	lbf ft
Camshaft position sensor	8	6
Exhaust manifold downpipe support bracket bolt	25	18
Exhaust manifold to cylinder head:		
Stage 1	10	7
Stage 2	Angle-tighten a further 60°	
Exhaust system flange joint	25	18
Exhaust system mounting bracket bolts	30	22
Intake manifold to cylinder head	27	20
Oxygen sensor	45	33

1 General information and precautions

The fuel supply system consists of a fuel tank (which is mounted under the centre of the car, with an electric fuel pump immersed in it) and fuel feed line. The fuel pump supplies fuel to the fuel rail, which acts as a reservoir for the four fuel injectors which inject fuel into the intake tracts.

The fuel injection and ignition functions are combined into a single engine management system. The system incorporates a closed-loop catalytic converter and an evaporative emission control system, and complies with the latest emission control standards. Refer to Chapter 5B for information on the ignition side of each system; the fuel side of the system operates as follows.

The fuel pump supplies fuel from the tank to the fuel rail (mounted directly above the fuel injectors) by means of a 'returnless' system. With this arrangement, the fuel filter and fuel pressure regulator are an integral part of the fuel pump assembly located in the fuel tank. The regulator maintains a constant fuel pressure in the supply line to the fuel rail and allows excess fuel to recirculate in the fuel tank, by means of a bypass channel, if the regulated fuel pressure is exceeded. As the fuel filter is an integral part of the pump assembly, fuel filter renewal is no longer necessary as part of the maintenance and servicing schedule.

The fuel injectors are electromagnetic pintle valves which spray atomised fuel into the combustion chambers under the control of the ECU. There are four injectors, one per cylinder, mounted in the intake manifold close to the cylinder head. Each injector is mounted at an angle that allows it to spray fuel directly onto the back of the intake valve(s). The ECU controls the volume of fuel injected by varying the length of time for which each injector is held open. The fuel injection systems are of the sequential type, whereby each injector operates individually in cylinder sequence.

The electrical control system consists of the ECU, along with the following sensors:

a) *Throttle potentiometer – informs the ECU of the throttle valve position, and the rate of throttle opening/closing – models with a throttle cable.*
b) *Engine coolant temperature sensor – informs the ECU of engine temperature (refer to Chapter 3).*
c) *Intake air temperature/pressure sensor – informs the ECU of intake air temperature and load on the engine (expressed in terms of intake manifold vacuum).*
d) *Lambda sensors – inform the ECU of the oxygen content of the exhaust gases.*
e) *Crankshaft TDC sensor – informs the ECU of engine speed and crankshaft angular position.*
f) *Vehicle speed sensor – informs the ECU of the vehicle speed.*
g) *Knock sensor – informs the ECU of pre-ignition (detonation) within the cylinders (refer to Chapter 5B).*
h) *Camshaft position sensor – informs the ECU of which cylinder is on the firing stroke.*
i) *Accelerator pedal potentiometer – informs the ECU of accelerator pedal position and rate of change.*

Signals from each of the sensors are compared by the ECU and, based on this information, the ECU selects the response appropriate to those values, and controls the fuel injectors (varying the pulse width – the length of time the injectors are held open – to provide a richer or weaker air/fuel mixture, as appropriate). The air/fuel mixture is constantly varied by the ECU, to provide the best settings for cranking, starting (with either a hot or cold engine) and engine warm-up, idle, cruising and acceleration.

The ECU also has full control over the engine idle speed, via a stepper motor or throttle valve actuator fitted to the throttle body. The accelerator pedal potentiometer informs the ECU of accelerator pedal position and from this data, the ECU controls the throttle valve actuator so that a corresponding throttle opening can be obtained. This arrangement is often termed 'drive-by-wire' as there is no direct accelerator cable connection between the accelerator pedal and throttle valve.

The evaporative loss emission control systems are described in more detail in Chapter 4B.

If there is any abnormality in any of the readings obtained from the main engine sensors, the ECU enters its 'back-up' mode. If this happens, the erroneous sensor signal is overridden, and the ECU assumes a pre-programmed 'back-up' value, which will allow the engine to continue running, albeit at reduced efficiency. If the ECU enters this mode, the warning lamp on the instrument panel will be illuminated, and the relevant fault code will be stored in the ECU memory.

If the warning light illuminates, the vehicle should be taken to a Ford dealer (or suitably equipped garage) at the earliest opportunity. Once there, a complete test of the engine management system can be carried out, using a special electronic diagnostic test unit which is plugged into the system's diagnostic connector – see Section 8.

⚠ *Warning: Many of the procedures in this Chapter require the removal of fuel lines and connections, which may result in some fuel spillage. Before carrying out any operation on the fuel system, refer to the precautions given in 'Safety first!' at the beginning of this manual, and follow them implicitly. Petrol is a highly dangerous and volatile liquid, and the precautions necessary when handling it cannot be overstressed. Note that residual pressure will remain in the fuel lines long after the vehicle was last used. When disconnecting any fuel line, first depressurise the fuel system as described in Section 4.*

2 Air cleaner assembly – removal and refitting

Removal

1 Unbolt the air intake hose from the front panel (see illustration). If required the hose can be removed from the main filter housing.
2 Undo the two retaining bolts, and pull the air cleaner assembly upwards from the mounting (see illustration).
3 Release the rear section of the assembly from the mounting stud by pulling it upwards from both the stud and the throttle body.
4 Invert the housing and then release the breather hose (see illustration).

2.1 Remove the bolt from the slam panel (arrowed)

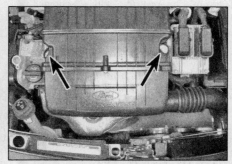

2.2 Remove the mounting bolts (arrowed)

2.4 Remove the breather hose retaining clip (arrowed)

Refitting

5 Refitting is a reversal of removal but renew the air cleaner filter element, as described in Chapter 1A, if necessary.

3 Accelerator pedal – removal and refitting

Removal

1 Remove the trim panel from above the pedal assembly as described in Chapter 11.
2 From under the facia inside the car, undo the nuts securing the pedal and potentiometer assembly to the mounting bracket (see illustration).
3 Withdraw the pedal from its location, disconnect the potentiometer wiring connector, and remove the assembly from the car.

Refitting

4 Refitting is a reversal of removal.

4 Fuel system – depressurisation

⚠ **Warning: The following procedure will merely relieve the pressure in the fuel system – remember that fuel will still be present in the system components and take precautions accordingly before disconnecting any of them.**

Note: Refer to the warning given in Section 1 before proceeding.

1 The fuel system referred to in this Section is defined as the tank-mounted fuel pump, the fuel rail, the fuel injectors, and the metal pipes and flexible hoses of the fuel lines between these components. All these contain fuel which will be under pressure while the engine is running and/or while the ignition is switched on. The pressure will remain for some time after the ignition has been switched off, and must be relieved before any of these components are disturbed for servicing work.
2 Disconnect the battery negative terminal as described in Chapter 5A.
3 Remove the air cleaner assembly as described in Section 2.
4 Locate the Schrader valve situated at the right-hand end of the fuel rail (see illustration). The Schrader valve works like a tyre valve whereby on depressing the central plunger, the system fuel pressure will be released.
5 Unscrew the protective plastic cap from the top of the valve.
6 Place an absorbent rag around the valve then, using a small screwdriver, slowly depress the central plunger to allow the pressure to be released. Ensure that the rag completely

3.2 Accelerator pedal assembly retaining nuts (arrowed) – facia removed for clarity

covers the valve to catch the fuel spray which will be expelled.
7 On completion of the operations for which system depressurisation was necessary, refit the Schrader valve cap and reconnect the battery negative terminal. Refit the air cleaner assembly as described in Section 2.

5 Fuel pipes and fittings - general information

1 Disconnect the cable from the negative battery terminal (see Chapter 5A) before proceeding.
2 The fuel supply pipe connects the fuel pump in the fuel tank to the fuel rail on the engine.
3 Whenever you're working under the vehicle, be sure to inspect all fuel and evaporative emission pipes for leaks, kinks, dents and other damage. Always replace a damaged fuel pipe immediately.
4 If you find signs of dirt in the pipes during disassembly, disconnect all pipes and blow them out with compressed air. Inspect the fuel strainer on the fuel pump pick-up unit for damage and deterioration.

Steel tubing

5 It is critical that the fuel pipes be replaced with pipes of equivalent type and specification.
6 Some steel fuel pipes have threaded fittings. When loosening these fittings, hold the stationary fitting with a spanner while turning the union nut.

Plastic tubing

⚠ **Warning: When removing or installing plastic fuel tubing, be careful not to bend or twist it too much, which can damage it. Also, plastic fuel tubing is NOT heat resistant, so keep it away from excessive heat.**

7 When replacing fuel system plastic tubing, use only original equipment replacement plastic tubing.

Flexible hoses

8 When replacing fuel system flexible hoses,

4.4 The fuel pressure relief valve (arrowed)

use original equipment replacements, or hose to the same specification.
9 Don't route fuel hoses (or metal pipes) within 100 mm of the exhaust system or within 280 mm of the catalytic converter. Make sure that no rubber hoses are installed directly against the vehicle, particularly in places where there is any vibration. If allowed to touch some vibrating part of the vehicle, a hose can easily become chafed and it might start leaking. A good rule of thumb is to maintain a minimum of 8.0 mm clearance around a hose (or metal pipe) to prevent contact with the vehicle underbody.

6 Fuel pump and fuel gauge sender unit – removal and refitting

Note 1: Refer to the warning given in Section 1 before proceeding.
Note 2: A new sealing O-ring will be required for refitting.

Removal

1 Disconnect the battery negative terminal as described in Chapter 5A.
2 Depressurise the fuel system as described in Section 4.
3 Remove the rear seat cushion as described in Chapter 11, then lift the floor covering for access to the fuel pump cover.
4 Remove the screws and lift off the cover (see illustration).
5 Release the locking catch and disconnect

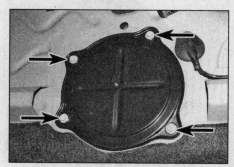

6.4 The cover is retained by screws (arrowed)

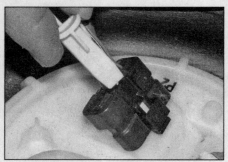

6.5 Slide out the locking catch and disconnect the wiring plug

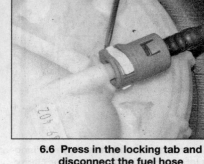

6.6 Press in the locking tab and disconnect the fuel hose

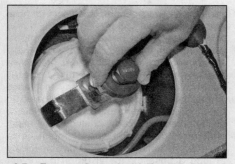

6.7a Engage the tool with the ribs on the locking ring . . .

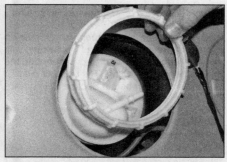

6.7b . . . then unscrew and remove it

the wiring connector from the top of the fuel pump **(see illustration)**.

6 Bearing in mind the warning given in Section 1, disconnect the fuel supply line

quick-release fitting from the pump unit by pressing the tabs **(see illustration)**. Plug the end of the supply line or cover it with adhesive tape.

6.8a Lift the fuel pump and sender unit from the tank . . .

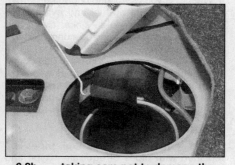

6.8b . . . taking care not to damage the float arm

6.8c Renew the sealing O-ring

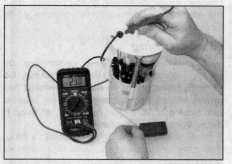

6.9 Check the resistance of the sender unit with the float at full, and zero deflection

7 Unscrew the large locking ring and remove it from the tank. Engage the tool with the ribs of the locking ring, and turn the ring anti-clockwise until it can be unscrewed by hand **(see illustrations)**.

8 Lift the fuel pump and sender unit assembly out of the fuel tank, taking great care not to damage the float arm. There will be fuel still present in the pump assembly and extreme caution should be exercised when removing the pump and sender assembly. Recover the sealing O-ring and discard it – a new one must be used on refitting **(see illustrations)**. To avoid any possibility of the fuel tank distorting, immediately refit the locking ring to the tank after removing the pump/sender unit.

9 If required the fuel pump and sender unit can be separated from the pump assembly – the sender is available as a separate part. The resistance of the fuel level sender unit can be checked by connecting a multimeter across the sender unit terminals at the plug socket **(see illustration)**. At full deflection (full tank) the resistance should be approximately 34 ohms, and zero deflection (empty tank) should be approximately 298 ohms. If the readings are significantly different than these, the unit may be faulty.

Refitting

10 Refitting is a reversal of the removal procedure using a new sealing ring, and aligning the arrow on the cover with the arrow on the tank **(see illustration)**. Prior to refitting the access cover, reconnect the battery, then start the engine and check the fuel line for signs of leakage.

7 Fuel tank –
   removal and refitting

Note: *Refer to the warning given in Section 1 before proceeding.*

Removal

1 Before removing the fuel tank, all fuel must be drained from the tank. Since a fuel tank drain plug is not provided, it is therefore preferable to carry out the removal operation when the tank is nearly empty. Before

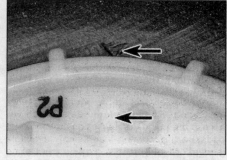

6.10 Align the arrow on the cover with the mark on the tank (arrowed)

proceeding, disconnect the battery negative terminal as described in Chapter 5A.

2 Working as described in Section 5, disconnect the fuel pump wiring connector and the fuel supply line from the top of the pump.

3 Chock the front wheels, then jack up the rear of the car and securely support it on axle stands (see *Jacking and vehicle support*). Remove the right-hand rear roadwheel.

4 Remove the exhaust system as described in Section 12.

5 Loosen the clips and disconnect the filler pipe, vent pipe and roll-over valve hoses from fuel tank **(see illustration)**.

6 Place a trolley jack with an interposed block of wood beneath the tank, then raise the jack until it is supporting the weight of the tank.

7 Undo the fuel tank mounting bolts, then carefully lower the tank from its location, unclipping any hoses from the top of the tank as it's lowered.

8 If the tank is contaminated with sediment or water, remove the fuel pump/fuel gauge sender unit as described in Section 6, and swill the tank out with clean fuel. The tank is injection-moulded from a synthetic material – if seriously damaged, it should be renewed. However, in certain cases, it may be possible to have small leaks or minor damage repaired. Seek the advice of a specialist before attempting to repair the fuel tank.

Refitting

9 Refitting is a reversal of the removal procedure, ensuring that all pipes/hoses are correctly routed and securely reconnected.

8 Engine management system – testing and adjustment

Testing

1 If a fault appears in the engine management system, first ensure that all the system wiring connectors are securely connected and free of corrosion. Ensure that the fault is not due to poor maintenance; ie, check that the air cleaner filter element is clean, the spark plugs are in good condition and correctly gapped, the valve clearances are correctly adjusted (where applicable), the cylinder compression pressures are correct, and that the engine breather hoses are clear and undamaged, referring to the relevant Parts of Chapters 1 and 2A for further information.

2 If these checks fail to reveal the cause of the problem, the vehicle should be taken to a Ford dealer or suitably-equipped garage for testing. Simple code readers (which will access the mandatory emissions related fault codes) are becoming increasingly available (and affordable) for the experienced home mechanic. It should be noted that these code readers will rarely access all the vehicles onboard systems, such as the ABS system

7.5 Disconnect the filler pipe, vent pipe, and the quick-release fittings (arrowed)

or the SRS components. A diagnostic socket is located on the right-hand side of the facia, into which a fault code reader or other suitable test equipment can be connected **(see illustration)**. By using the code reader or test equipment, the engine management ECU (and the various other vehicle system ECUs) can be interrogated, and any stored fault codes can be retrieved. This will allow the fault to be quickly and simply traced, alleviating the need to test all the system components individually, which is a time-consuming operation that carries a risk of damaging the ECU.

Adjustment

3 Experienced home mechanics with a considerable amount of skill and equipment (including a tachometer and an accurately calibrated exhaust gas analyser) may be able to check the exhaust CO level and the idle speed. However, if these are found to be outside the specified tolerance, the car must be taken to a suitably-equipped garage for further testing. Neither the mixture adjustment (exhaust gas CO level) nor the idle speed are adjustable, and should either be incorrect, a fault may be present in the engine management system.

9 Engine management components – removal and refitting

Note: Refer to the warning given in Section 1 before proceeding.

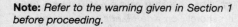

9.3 Slide out the yellow locking catch (arrowed) and disconnect the wiring plug

8.2 A suitable code reader can be connected to the diagnostic socket

Throttle body assembly

1 Disconnect the battery negative terminal as described in Chapter 5A.

2 Remove the air cleaner assembly as described in Section 2.

3 Disconnect the wiring plug from the throttle body, and unclip the wiring loom from the retaining clips **(see illustration)**.

4 Release the fuel supply, and vacuum/breather hoses from the clips on the throttle body.

5 Undo the retaining bolts, then remove the support bracket and throttle body from the manifold **(see illustration)**.

6 Refitting is a reversal of the removal procedure, bearing in mind the following points:

a) Ensure the throttle body and intake manifold mating surfaces are clean and dry.

b) Fit the throttle body with a new O-ring, and securely tighten the retaining bolts.

Fuel rail and injectors

7 Disconnect the battery negative terminal as described in Chapter 5A.

8 Remove the air cleaner assembly as described in Section 2.

9 Depressurise the fuel system as described in Section 4.

10 Disconnect the injector wiring plug **(see illustration)**. Release the wiring loom retaining clips.

11 Disconnect the fuel supply pipe at the

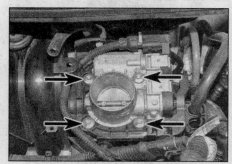

9.5 Throttle body retaining bolts (arrowed)

9.10 Disconnect the injector loom wiring plug (arrowed)

9.11 Squeeze together the clips (arrowed) and disconnect the fuel supply pipe

9.12 Fuel rail mounting bolts (arrowed)

quick-release connector on the end of the fuel rail **(see illustration)**.

12 Unscrew the two bolts securing the fuel rail assembly to the intake manifold, then carefully pull the injectors from their manifold locations **(see illustration)**. Remove the assembly from the engine and remove the injector lower O-ring seals.

13 The injectors can be removed individually from the fuel rail by extracting the relevant metal clip and easing the injector out of the rail. Remove the injector upper O-ring seals.

14 Check the electrical resistance of the injector using a multimeter and compare it with the *Specifications*. **Note:** *If a faulty injector is suspected, before condemning the injector it is worth trying the effect of one of the proprietary injector-cleaning treatments.*

15 Refitting is a reversal of the removal procedure, bearing in mind the following points:
  a) *Renew the injector O-ring seals, and smear them with a little petroleum jelly before assembling. Take care when fitting the injectors to the fuel rail and do not press them in further than required to fit the retaining clip otherwise the O-ring seal may be damaged.*
  b) *Ensure that the injector retaining clips are securely seated.*
  c) *On completion check the fuel rail and injectors for fuel leaks.*

Idle control stepper motor

16 The idle control stepper motor is an integral part of the throttle body and cannot be individually renewed.

Throttle potentiometer

17 The idle control stepper motor is an integral part of the throttle body and cannot be individually renewed.

Intake air temperature/ pressure sensor

18 Disconnect the battery negative terminal as described in Chapter 5A.

19 Remove the air cleaner assembly as described in Section 2.

20 Disconnect the wiring connector, undo the screw and remove the sensor from the end of the intake manifold **(see illustration)**.

21 Refitting is a reversal of the removal procedure.

Coolant temperature sensor

22 Refer to Chapter 3.

Front oxygen sensor

23 Refer to Chapter 4B, Section 2.

Rear oxygen sensor

24 Refer to Chapter 4B, Section 2.

Crankshaft TDC sensor

25 The crankshaft TDC sensor is located adjacent to the front facing side of the crankshaft pulley **(see illustration)**.

26 Disconnect the battery negative terminal as described in Chapter 5A.

27 Raise the front of the vehicle and support it securely on axle stands (see *Jacking and*

vehicle support).

28 Undo the bolt securing the sensor to the oil pump casing and remove the sensor from its location.

29 Locate the sensor in position and secure with the retaining bolt.

30 The remainder of refitting is a reversal of removal. If a new TDC sensor has been fitted, the following 'learning' procedure must be carried out if the MIL (engine management warning light) flashes after renewal:
  a) *Run the engine until it reaches normal operating temperature.*
  b) *Press the accelerator pedal at least 3 times, revving the engine to at least 6000 rpm each time, allowing the engine to return to idle speed between each press.*
  c) *If the MIL is still flashing, the procedure must be repeated.*
  d) *Once the MIL has stopped flashing, turn off the ignition and wait at least 1 minute to allow the ECU to permanently store the data.*

Knock sensor

31 Refer to Chapter 5B.

Camshaft position sensor

32 Disconnect the battery negative terminal as described in Chapter 5A.

33 Remove the battery and battery tray as described in Chapter 5A.

34 Move the engine wiring loom to one side, then disconnect the wiring plug, undo the retaining bolt and pull sensor from place **(see illustration)**.

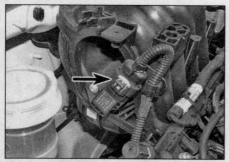

9.20 Intake air temperature/pressure sensor wiring plug (arrowed)

9.25 Crankshaft TDC sensor (arrowed)

9.34 The camshaft position sensor (arrowed) is located at the left-hand end of the cylinder head

35 Refitting is a reversal of the removal procedure.

Electronic control unit (ECU)

36 Disconnect the battery negative terminal as described in Chapter 5A.

37 Disconnect the two wiring connectors from the top of the ECU **(see illustration)**.

38 Undo the mounting nuts and remove the ECU **(see illustration)**.

39 Refitting is a reversal of removal. If a new ECU is fitted, it must be programmed using Ford diagnostic equipment. Entrust this task to a Ford dealer or suitably-equipped repairer.

Accelerator pedal potentiometer

40 The potentiometer is integral with the accelerator pedal assembly – see Section 4.

---

10 Intake manifold – removal and refitting

Note: Refer to the warning given in Section 1 before proceeding.

Removal

1 Remove the battery and battery tray as described in Chapter 5A.

2 Remove the air cleaner assembly as described in Section 2.

3 Disconnect the HT leads and remove the ignition coil pack.

4 Depressurise the fuel system as described in Section 4, then disconnect the fuel supply pipe from the fuel rail **(see illustration 9.11)**.

5 Unbolt and then remove the scuttle front panel.

6 Note their fitted positions, then disconnect the various wiring plugs from the throttle body and manifold.

7 Disconnect the vapour hose from the EVAP purge valve **(see illustration)**.

8 Prise the servo check valve (complete with hose) from the servo.

9 Release the wiring loom from the retaining clips on the underside of the intake manifold.

10 Remove the nuts/bolt securing the lower edge of the manifold to the cylinder head.

11 Undo the bolt/nuts securing the upper

9.37 Release the clip (arrowed), pivot up the locking catch and disconnect the ECU wiring plugs

edge of the intake manifold to the cylinder head **(see illustration)**.

Refitting

12 Refitting is a reverse of the removal procedure, noting the following points:
a) Ensure that the manifold and cylinder head mating surfaces are clean and dry, and fit new manifold sealing rings. Refit the manifold and securely tighten its retaining nuts/bolts.
b) Ensure all relevant hoses and wiring are reconnected to their original positions and are securely held (where necessary) by the retaining clips.

---

11 Exhaust manifold – removal and refitting

Removal

1 Disconnect the battery negative terminal as described in Chapter 5A.

2 Remove the air cleaner assembly as described in Section 2.

3 Remove the exhaust system as described in Section 12.

4 Disconnect the oxygen sensors' wiring plugs as described in Section 9.

5 Soak the fasteners in releasing fluid, then undo the bolts/nuts and remove the heat shield from the manifold **(see illustration)**.

6 Undo the upper and lower mounting bolt/nuts and manoeuvre the manifold from place.

9.38 ECU mounting nuts (arrowed)

Refitting

7 Refitting is a reversal of the removal procedure but use a new manifold gasket, and new front pipe flange gasket. Tighten all mounting and attachment nuts/bolts to the specified torque.

---

12 Exhaust system – general information and component renewal

General information

1 A 3-piece exhaust system is fitted comprising a centre pipe, catalytic converter and rear silencer. The centre pipe is connected to the exhaust manifold downpipe by means of a flange joint, and contains a flexible section to cater for engine movement. A catalytic converter is fitted to all models, and is an integral part of the exhaust manifold.

2 The system is suspended throughout its entire length by rubber mountings.

Component renewal

Exhaust manifold and catalytic converter

3 Refer to Section 11.

Rear silencer

4 Firmly apply the handbrake, then jack up the front and rear of the car and support it securely on axle stands (see *Jacking and vehicle support*).

10.7 Pull back the collar (arrowed) and disconnect the EVAP pipe from the purge valve

10.11 Undo the nuts (arrowed) at the top edge of the manifold

11.5 Remove the heat shield (arrowed) from the exhaust manifold

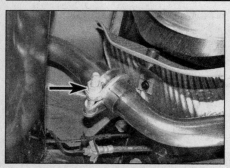

12.5 Undo the clamp (arrowed) securing the rear silencer to the pipe

5 Undo the clamp securing the rear silencer to the centre pipe, and spray releasing fluid around the joint **(see illustration)**.
6 Free the silencer from the rubber mountings, and manoeuvre it from position.

Centre pipe

7 Remove the rear silencer as previously described.

8 Slacken the clamp securing the catalytic converter to the centre pipe, and spray releasing fluid around the joint.
9 Free the centre pipe from the rubber mounting and separate it from the catalytic converter.

Chapter 4 Part B:
Emissions control systems

Contents

Degrees of difficulty

Easy, suitable for novice with little experience	Fairly easy, suitable for beginner with some experience	Fairly difficult, suitable for competent DIY mechanic	Difficult, suitable for experienced DIY mechanic	Very difficult, suitable for expert DIY or professional

Specifications

Torque wrench setting	Nm	lbf ft
Oxygen sensor	45	33

1 General information and precautions

1 All models use unleaded petrol and also have various other features built into the fuel/exhaust system to help minimise harmful emissions. All models are equipped with a crankcase emission control system, a catalytic converter and an evaporative emission control system to keep fuel vapour/exhaust gas emissions down to a minimum.

2 The emission control systems function as follows.

Crankcase emissions control

3 To reduce the emission of unburned hydrocarbons from the crankcase into the atmosphere, the engine is sealed and the blow-by gases and oil vapour are drawn from the camshaft cover into the intake manifold to be burned by the engine during normal combustion.

4 The gases are forced out of the crankcase by the relatively higher crankcase pressure; if the engine is worn, the raised crankcase pressure (due to increased blow-by) will cause some of the flow to return under all manifold conditions.

Exhaust emission control

5 To minimise the amount of pollutants which escape into the atmosphere, all models are fitted with a catalytic converter which is integral with the exhaust manifold. The system is of the closed-loop type, in which oxygen sensors in the exhaust system provide the fuel injection/ignition system ECU with constant feedback, enabling the ECU to

adjust the mixture to provide the best possible conditions for the converter to operate.

6 On all engines covered by this manual, there are two heated oxygen sensors fitted to the exhaust system. The sensor on the top of the exhaust manifold/catalytic converter determines the residual oxygen content of the exhaust gases for mixture correction. The sensor in the exhaust front pipe (after the catalytic converter) monitors the function of the catalytic converter to give the driver a warning signal if there is a fault.

7 The oxygen sensor's tip is sensitive to oxygen and sends the ECU a varying voltage depending on the amount of oxygen in the exhaust gases. Peak conversion efficiency of all major pollutants occurs if the intake air/fuel mixture is maintained at the chemically-correct ratio for the complete combustion of petrol of 14.7 parts (by weight) of air to 1 part of fuel (the 'stoichiometric' ratio). The sensor output voltage alters in a large step at this point, the ECU using the signal change as a reference point and correcting the intake air/fuel mixture accordingly by altering the fuel injector pulse width.

Fuel evaporation emission control

8 To minimise the escape into the atmosphere of unburned hydrocarbons, a fuel evaporation emission control system is fitted. The fuel tank filler cap is sealed and a charcoal canister is mounted behind the wheel arch liner under the right-hand rear wing. The canister collects the petrol vapours generated in the tank when the car is parked and stores them until they can be cleared from the canister (under the control of the fuel injection/ignition system ECU) via the purge valve into the intake manifold to be burned by the engine during normal combustion.

9 To ensure that the engine runs correctly when it is cold and/or idling and to protect the catalytic converter from the effects of an over-rich mixture, the purge control valve is not opened by the ECU until the engine has warmed-up, and the engine is under load; the valve solenoid is then modulated on and off to allow the stored vapour to pass into the intake manifold.

2 Emissions control systems – testing and component renewal

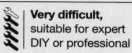

Crankcase emission control

1 The components of this system require no attention other than to check that the hose(s) are clear and undamaged at regular intervals.

Evaporative emission control

2 If the system is thought to be faulty, disconnect the hoses from the charcoal canister and purge control valve and check that they are clear by blowing through them. Full testing of the system can only be carried out using specialist electronic equipment which is connected to the engine management system diagnostic connector. If the purge control valve or charcoal canister are thought to be faulty, they must be renewed.

Charcoal canister

3 Chock the front wheels then jack up the rear of the vehicle and support on axle stands (see *Jacking and vehicle support*). Remove the right-hand rear wheel.

4 Undo the fasteners and remove the right-hand rear wheel arch liner for access to the charcoal canister.

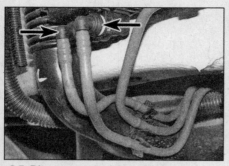

2.5 Disconnect the hoses (arrowed) from the charcoal canister

2.7 Charcoal canister retaining nuts (arrowed)

8 Refitting is a reversal of the removal procedure. Make sure the hoses are correctly and securely reconnected.

Purge valve

9 The purge valve is mounted in the intake manifold, below the throttle body.

10 Remove the air cleaner assembly as described in Chapter 4A.

11 Reach beneath the throttle body or alternatively remove the throttle body, described in Chapter 4A.

12 Disconnect the wiring connector and vapour hose from the purge valve.

13 Extract the retaining spring clip, and remove the solenoid from the manifold **(see illustration)**.

14 Refitting is a reversal of the removal procedure.

Exhaust emission control

15 The performance of the catalytic converter can be checked only by measuring the exhaust gases using a good-quality, carefully-calibrated exhaust gas analyser.

16 If the CO level at the tailpipe is too high, the vehicle should be taken to a Ford dealer or suitably-equipped repairer so that the complete fuel injection and ignition systems, including the oxygen sensors, can be thoroughly checked using the special diagnostic equipment. Once these have been checked and are known to be free from faults, the fault must be in the catalytic converter, which must be renewed.

Catalytic converter

17 The catalytic converter is welded to the exhaust manifold, and the removal and refitting procedure is described in Chapter 4A.

Oxygen sensors

18 The pre-catalytic convertor sensor is mounted in the exhaust manifold, the post-catalytic convertor is mounted in the exhaust down pipe **(see illustrations)**.

19 If working on the pre-catalytic convertor, remove the air filter housing as described in Chapter 4A.

20 Disconnect the wiring plug from the appropriate sensor **(see illustration)**.

21 A special socket with a slot in it will be

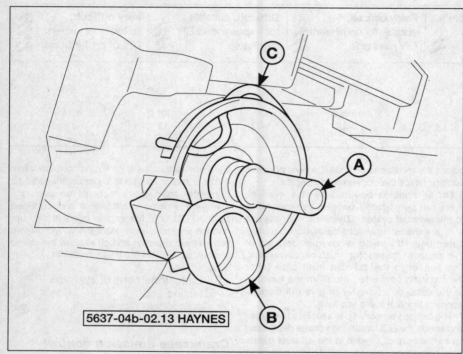

5637-04b-02.13 HAYNES

2.13 Remove the vapour hose (A), disconnect the wiring plug (B) and prise free the spring clip (C)

5 Disconnect the two vent hoses at the quick-release connectors on the charcoal canister **(see illustration)**. Suitably seal the vent hoses and canister unions to prevent dirt ingress.

6 Release the two disconnected vent hoses

from the retaining clips around the charcoal canister.

7 Unscrew the retaining nuts and remove the canister from under the wheel arch **(see illustration)**.

2.18a The pre-catalytic convertor sensor and...

2.18b ...the post catalytic convertor sensor

2.20 Disconnect the wiring plug (arrowed) - pre-catalytic convertor sensor shown

required to remove the sensor. Alternatively a flare nut spanner can be used **(see illustrations)**.
22 Refitting is a reversal of removal.

3 Catalytic converter – general information and precautions

The catalytic converter is a reliable and simple device which needs no maintenance in itself, but there are some facts of which an owner should be aware if the converter is to function properly for its full service life.

a) *DO NOT use leaded petrol or LRP in a car equipped with a catalytic converter – the lead will coat the precious metals, reducing their converting efficiency and will eventually destroy the converter.*

b) *Always keep the ignition and fuel systems well-maintained in accordance with the manufacturer's schedule.*

c) *If the engine develops a misfire, do not drive the car at all (or at least as little as possible) until the fault is cured.*

d) *DO NOT push- or tow-start the car – this will soak the catalytic converter in unburned fuel, causing it to overheat when the engine does start.*

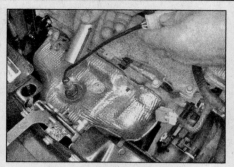

2.21a A special socket or...

e) *DO NOT switch off the ignition at high engine speeds.*

f) *DO NOT use fuel or engine oil additives – these may contain substances harmful to the catalytic converter.*

g) *DO NOT continue to use the car if the engine burns oil to the extent of leaving a visible trail of blue smoke.*

h) *Remember that the catalytic converter operates at very high temperatures. DO NOT, therefore, park the car in dry undergrowth, over long grass or piles of dead leaves after a long run.*

i) *Remember that the catalytic converter*

2.21b ...flare nut spanner will be require to remove the sensor

is FRAGILE – do not strike it with tools during servicing work.

j) *In some cases a sulphurous smell (like that of rotten eggs) may be noticed from the exhaust. This is common to many catalytic converter-equipped cars and once the car has covered a few thousand miles the problem should disappear.*

k) *The catalytic converter, used on a well-maintained and well-driven car, should last for between 50 000 and 100 000 miles – if the converter is no longer effective it must be renewed.*

Chapter 5 Part A:
Starting and charging systems

Contents

Degrees of difficulty

Easy, suitable for novice with little experience	Fairly easy, suitable for beginner with some experience	Fairly difficult, suitable for competent DIY mechanic	Difficult, suitable for experienced DIY mechanic	Very difficult, suitable for expert DIY or professional

Specifications

General

Electrical system type . . . . 12 volt negative earth

Battery

Type . . . . Lead-acid, 'maintenance-free' (sealed for life)
Battery capacity . . . . 30, 40 or 50 Ah (depending on model)

Alternator

Type . . . . Bosch or Magneti-Marelli
Regulated voltage . . . . 13.7 to 14.7 volts (approximately)

Starter motor

Type . . . . Pre-engaged, Hitachi or Valeo

Torque wrench settings	Nm	lbf ft
Alternator	55	41
Starter motor	25	18

1 General information and precautions

General information

The engine electrical system consists mainly of the charging and starting systems. Because of their engine-related functions, these components are covered separately from the body electrical devices such as the lights, instruments, etc (which are covered in Chapter 12).

The electrical system is of 12 volt negative earth type.

The battery is of the maintenance-free (sealed for life) type, and is charged by the alternator, which is belt-driven from the crankshaft pulley.

The starter motor is of pre-engaged type incorporating an integral solenoid. On starting, the solenoid moves the drive pinion into engagement with the flywheel ring gear before the starter motor is energised. Once the engine has started, a one-way clutch prevents the motor armature being driven by the engine until the pinion disengages.

Further details of the various systems are given in the relevant Sections of this Chapter. While some repair procedures are given, the usual course of action is to renew the component concerned.

Precautions

It is necessary to take extra care when working on the electrical system to avoid damage to semi-conductor devices (diodes and transistors), and to avoid the risk of personal injury. In addition to the precautions given in *Safety first!* at the beginning of this manual, observe the following when working on the system:

• *Always remove rings, watches, etc, before working on the electrical system. Even with the battery disconnected, capacitive discharge could occur if a component's live terminal is earthed through a metal object. This could cause a shock or nasty burn.*

• *Do not reverse the battery connections. Components such as the alternator,*

3.5 Battery condition indicator (arrowed)

electronic control units, or any other components having semi-conductor circuitry could be irreparably damaged.

• *If the engine is being started using jump leads and a slave battery, connect the batteries positive-to-positive and negative-to-negative (see 'Jump starting'). This also applies when connecting a battery charger but in this case both of the battery terminals should first be disconnected.*

• *Never disconnect the battery terminals, the alternator, any electrical wiring or any test instruments when the engine is running.*

• *Do not allow the engine to turn the alternator when the alternator is not connected.*

• *Never test for alternator output by flashing the output lead to earth.*

• *Never use an ohmmeter of the type incorporating a hand-cranked generator for circuit or continuity testing.*

• *Always ensure that the battery negative lead is disconnected when working on the electrical system.*

• *Before using electric-arc welding equipment on the car, disconnect the battery, alternator and components such as the fuel injection/ignition electronic control unit to protect them from the risk of damage.*

2 Electrical fault finding – general information

Refer to Chapter 12.

3 Battery – testing and charging

Testing

Traditional and low maintenance battery

1 If the vehicle covers a small annual mileage, it is worthwhile checking the specific gravity of the electrolyte every three months to determine the state of charge of the battery. Use a hydrometer to make the check and compare the results with the following table. Note that the specific gravity readings assume an electrolyte temperature of 15°C; for every 10°C below 15°C subtract 0.007. For every 10°C above 15°C add 0.007.

	Ambient temperature	
	above 25°C	below 25°C
Fully-charged	1.210 to 1.230	1.270 to 1.290
70% charged	1.170 to 1.190	1.230 to 1.250
Discharged	1.050 to 1.070	1.110 to 1.130

2 If the battery condition is suspect, first check the specific gravity of electrolyte in each cell. A variation of 0.040 or more between any cells indicates loss of electrolyte or deterioration of the internal plates.

3 If the specific gravity variation is 0.040 or more, the battery should be renewed. If the cell variation is satisfactory but the battery is discharged, it should be charged as described later in this Section.

Maintenance-free battery

4 Where a 'sealed for life' maintenance-free battery is fitted, topping-up and testing of the electrolyte in each cell is not possible. The condition of the battery can therefore only be tested using a battery condition indicator or a voltmeter.

5 Later models are fitted with a maintenance-free battery with a built-in 'magic-eye' charge condition indicator. The indicator is located in the top of the battery casing, and indicates the condition of the battery from its colour **(see illustration)**. If the indicator shows green, then the battery is in a good state of charge. If the indicator turns darker, eventually to black, then the battery requires charging, as described later in this Section. If the indicator shows clear/yellow, then the electrolyte level in the battery is too low to allow further use, and the battery should be renewed. Do not attempt to charge, load or jump start a battery when the indicator shows clear/yellow.

All battery types

6 If testing the battery using a voltmeter, connect the voltmeter across the battery. The test is only accurate if the battery has not been subjected to any kind of charge for the previous six hours. If this is not the case, switch on the headlights for 30 seconds, then wait four to five minutes before testing the battery after switching off the headlights. All other electrical circuits must be switched off, so check that the doors and tailgate are fully shut when making the test.

7 If the voltage reading is less than 12.2 volts, then the battery is discharged, whilst a reading of 12.2 to 12.4 volts indicates a partially-discharged condition.

8 If the battery is to be charged, remove it from the vehicle (Section 4) and charge it as described later in this Section.

Charging

Note: *The following is intended as a guide only. Always refer to the manufacturer's recommendations (often printed on a label attached to the battery) before charging a battery.*

Traditional and low maintenance battery

9 Charge the battery at a rate of 3.5 to 4 amps and continue to charge the battery at this rate until no further rise in specific gravity is noted over a four hour period.

10 Alternatively, a trickle charger charging at the rate of 1.5 amps can safely be used overnight.

11 Specially rapid 'boost' charges which are claimed to restore the power of the battery in 1 to 2 hours are not recommended, as they can cause serious damage to the battery plates through overheating.

4.1 Depress the clip (arrowed) and lift the earth terminal (-) from the 'false pole'

4.2 Disconnect the wiring plug (arrowed) from the battery monitor sensor

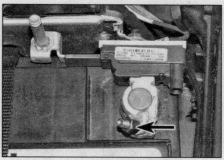

4.3 Slacken the negative terminal clamp nut (arrowed)

12 While charging the battery, note that the temperature of the electrolyte should never exceed 38ºC.

Maintenance-free battery

13 This battery type takes considerably longer to fully recharge than the standard type, the time taken being dependent on the extent of discharge, but it will take anything up to three days.

14 A constant voltage type charger is required, to be set, when connected, to 13.9 to 14.9 volts with a charger current below 25 amps. Using this method, the battery should be usable within three hours, giving a voltage reading of 12.5 volts, but this is for a partially-discharged battery and, as mentioned, full charging can take considerably longer.

15 If the battery is to be charged from a fully-discharged state (condition reading less than 12.2 volts), have it recharged by your Fiat dealer or local automotive electrician, as the charge rate is higher and constant supervision during charging is necessary.

4	Battery and battery tray – removal, disconnection and refitting

Battery disconnection

1 Depress the clip and disconnect the earth lead from the 'false pole' **(see illustration)**.
2 Depress the clip and disconnect the wiring plug from the battery monitor sensor **(see illustration)**.

3 Slacken the negative terminal clamp nut, rotate the clamp back and forth a little, to release it from the terminal post, and pull it upwards from place **(see illustration)**. Cover the terminal post, and position the clamp away from the battery to prevent accidental reconnection.

Removal

4 Disconnect the battery negative lead clamp as previously described.
5 Remove the plastic cover over the positive (+) terminal lead clamp, then disconnect the lead at the battery positive (+) terminal by slackening the retaining nut and removing the terminal clamp **(see illustrations)**.
6 Undo the retaining nut, and remove the battery securing strap **(see illustration)**.
7 Carefully lift the battery from its location and remove from the car. Make sure the battery is kept upright at all times.

Refitting

Note: *As a precaution, before refitting the battery check that all doors are unlocked.*
8 Refitting is a reversal of removal, but smear petroleum jelly on the terminals after reconnecting the leads to reduce corrosion, and always reconnect the positive lead first, followed by the negative lead.

Battery tray

9 Remove the battery as described previously.
10 Pull the battery tray cover upwards from place **(see illustration)**. Note the drain tube.
11 Release the locking catches, and disconnect the wiring loom from the rear of the tray.
12 Where applicable, undo the bolt/nut securing the earth lead to the ECU.
13 Undo the retaining bolts/nut **(see illustration)**, lift up the battery tray and unclip

4.5a Pull up the plastic cover…

4.5b …then slacken the positive (+) terminal clamp nut (arrowed)

4.6 Undo the battery retaining strap nut

4.10 Pull the battery tray cover upwards, noting the drain hose routing

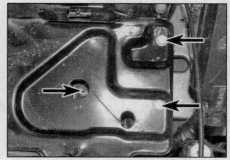

4.13 Battery tray retaining bolts/nut (arrowed)

any remaining cables. Manoeuvre the battery tray from place.

14 Refitting is a reversal of removal.

5 Charging system – testing

Note: *Refer to the precautions given in 'Safety first!' and in Section 1 of this Chapter before starting work.*

1 If the ignition no-charge warning light fails to illuminate when the ignition is switched on, first check the alternator wiring connections for security. If all is satisfactory, the alternator is at fault, and should be renewed, or taken to an auto-electrician for testing and repair.

2 If the ignition warning light illuminates when the engine is running, stop the engine and check the condition of the auxiliary drivebelt (see Chapter 1) and that the alternator connections are secure. If all is so far satisfactory, have the alternator checked by an auto-electrician for testing and repair.

3 If the alternator output is suspect even though the warning light functions correctly, the regulated voltage may be checked as follows.

4 Connect a voltmeter across the battery terminals, and start the engine.

5 Increase the engine speed until the voltmeter reading remains steady; the reading should be approximately 12 to 13 volts, and no more than 14 volts.

6 Switch on as many electrical accessories (eg, the headlights, heated rear window and heater blower) as possible, and check that the alternator maintains the regulated voltage at around 13.5 to 14.5 volts.

7 If the regulated voltage is not as stated, the fault may be due to worn brushes, weak brush springs, a faulty voltage regulator, a faulty diode, a severed phase winding, or worn or damaged slip-rings. The alternator should be renewed or taken to an auto-electrician for testing and repair.

6 Auxiliary drivebelt – removal and refitting

Refer to Chapter 1.

7 Alternator – removal and refitting

Removal

1 Disconnect the battery negative terminal as described in Section 4.

2 Remove the air cleaner assembly as described in Chapter 4A.

3 Remove the auxiliary drivebelt as described in Chapter 1.

4 Remove the right-hand driveshaft as described in Chapter 8.

7.6 Disconnect the wiring (arrowed) from the rear of the alternator

5 Unscrew the bolt securing the rear engine mounting assembly to the subframe.

6 Undo the retaining nuts and disconnect the cables from the rear of the alternator **(see illustration)**.

7 Unscrew the alternator upper and lower mounting bolts and withdraw the alternator from the engine **(see illustration)**. Note that it may be necessary to tip the engine forward slightly to gain access to the upper mounting bolt.

Refitting

8 Refitting is a reversal of removal, but tighten the mounting bolts to the specified torque. Refit the auxiliary drivebelt as described in Chapter 1.

8 Alternator – testing and overhaul

If the alternator is thought to be suspect, it should be removed from the vehicle and taken to an auto-electrician for testing. Most auto-electricians will be able to supply and fit brushes at a reasonable cost. However, check on the cost of repairs before proceeding as it may prove more economical to obtain a new or exchange alternator.

9 Starting system – testing

Note: *Refer to the precautions given in 'Safety*

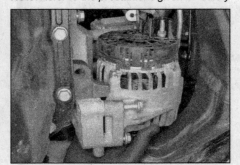

7.7 Lower the alternator to remove it

first!' and in Section 1 of this Chapter before starting work.

1 If the starter motor fails to operate when the ignition key is turned to the appropriate position, the possible causes are as follows:
   a) *The engine immobiliser is faulty.*
   b) *The battery is faulty.*
   c) *The electrical connections between the switch, solenoid, battery and starter motor are somewhere failing to pass the necessary current from the battery through the starter to earth.*
   d) *The solenoid is faulty.*
   e) *The starter motor is mechanically or electrically defective.*

2 To check the battery, switch on the headlights. If they dim after a few seconds, this indicates that the battery is discharged – recharge (see Section 3) or renew the battery. If the headlights glow brightly, operate the starter switch while watching the headlights. If they dim, then this indicates that current is reaching the starter motor, therefore the fault must lie in the starter motor. If the lights continue to glow brightly (and no clicking sound can be heard from the starter motor solenoid), this indicates that there is a fault in the circuit or solenoid – see the following paragraphs. If the starter motor turns slowly when operated, but the battery is in good condition, then this indicates either that the starter motor is faulty, or there is considerable resistance somewhere in the circuit.

3 If a fault in the circuit is suspected, disconnect the battery leads (including the earth connection to the body), the starter/solenoid wiring and the engine/transmission earth strap – see Chapter 12. Thoroughly clean the connections, and reconnect the leads and wiring. Use a voltmeter or test light to check that full battery voltage is available at the battery positive lead connection to the solenoid. Smear petroleum jelly around the battery terminals to prevent corrosion – corroded connections are among the most frequent causes of electrical system faults.

4 If the battery and all connections are in good condition, check the circuit by disconnecting the switched feed wire from the solenoid (the thinner wire). Connect a voltmeter or test light between the wire end and a good earth (such as the battery negative terminal), and check that the wire is live when the ignition switch is turned to the 'start' position. If it is, then the circuit is sound – if not, there is a fault in the ignition/starter switch or wiring.

5 The solenoid contacts can be checked by connecting a voltmeter or test light between the battery positive feed connection on the starter side of the solenoid and earth. When the ignition switch is turned to the 'start' position, there should be a reading or lighted bulb, as applicable. If there is no reading or lighted bulb, the solenoid is faulty and should be renewed.

10.5 Starter motor upper mounting bolt

10.6 Raise the plastic cover over the starter motor terminals

10.7 Disconnect the wiring from the terminal studs

6 If the circuit and solenoid are proved sound, the fault must lie in the starter motor. In this event, it may be possible to have the starter motor overhauled by a specialist, but check on the cost of spares before proceeding, as it may prove more economical to obtain a new or exchange motor.

10 Starter motor – removal and refitting

1 Disconnect the battery negative terminal as described in Section 4.
2 Firmly apply the handbrake, then jack up the front of the car and support it securely on axle stands (see *Jacking and vehicle support*).
3 Remove the battery and battery tray as described in Section 4.
4 With reference to Chapter 8, remove the right-hand driveshaft.
5 Unscrew and remove the starter motor upper mounting bolt located at the top of the transmission bellhousing (see illustration).
6 From under the car, raise the plastic cover over the starter solenoid wiring terminals (see illustration).
7 Unscrew the two nuts and disconnect the wiring from the solenoid terminal studs (see illustration).
8 Unscrew the lower mounting bolt(s), then withdraw the starter motor from the transmission (see illustrations).
9 Refitting is a reversal of removal.

11 Starter motor – testing and overhaul

If the starter motor is thought to be suspect, it should be removed from the vehicle and taken to an auto-electrician for testing. Most auto-electricians will be able to supply and fit brushes at a reasonable cost. However, check on the cost of repairs before proceeding as it may prove more economical to obtain a new or exchange motor.

10.8a Starter motor lower mounting bolt (arrowed)

12 Ignition switch/steering lock – removal and refitting

Removal
Switch
1 Remove the steering column combination switch assembly as described in Chapter 12.
2 Disconnect the ignition switch wiring plug.
3 Drill out the shear bolts, and remove the ignition switch/steering lock assembly (see illustration).
Lock barrel
4 Insert the ignition key, and turn it to the 1st position.
5 Press in the retaining pin and pull the barrel from the switch (see illustration).
6 Remove the circlip from the end of the barrel,

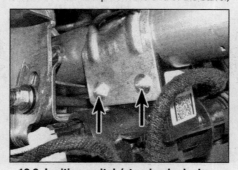

12.3 Ignition switch/steering lock shear bolts (arrowed)

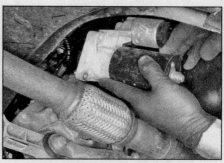

10.8b Lower the starter motor

press in the lever, rotate the barrel to align the lug and slot, then pull the tumbler assembly.
7 Refitting is a reversal of removal.

Refitting
8 Position the ignition switch/steering lock assembly, insert the new shear bolts, and tighten them until the heads shear off.
9 Reconnect the ignition switch wiring plug.
10 Refit the steering column combination switch assembly as described in Chapter 12.

13 Stop/start system – component renewal

1 Some models are equipped with a stop/start fuel saving system, where the engine is turned off when neutral is selected in a traffic jam. The engine is restarted when the clutch is depressed, prior to selecting 1st gear.

12.5 Depress the pin and remove the barrel assembly

13.3 Prise the neutral sensor linkage rod from the gearchange cable (arrowed)

13.6 Brake servo vacuum sensor (arrowed)

13.9 Remove the control unit (shown with facia removed for clarity)

Gear lever neutral sensor

2 Remove the centre console covers as described in Chapter 11.

3 Disconnect the wiring plug, prise the linkage rod from the gear lever, then remove the retaining clips and manoeuvre the sensor assembly from place (see illustration).

4 Refitting is a reversal of removal. Note that if a new sensor has been fitted, it must be initialised using Fiat diagnostic equipment. Entrust this task to a suitably-equipped specialist.

Brake servo vacuum sensor

5 Remove the throttle body as described in Chapter 4B.

6 Disconnect the sensor wiring plug, then carefully prise the sensor from the servo (see illustration).

7 Refitting is a reversal of removal.

Control unit

8 Remove the glovebox and the facia side panels as described in Chapter 11.

9 Reach up behind the facia panel and remove the single bolt. Disconnect the wiring plug as the control unit is lowered from the facia (see illustration).

Chapter 5 Part B:
Ignition system

Contents

Degrees of difficulty

Easy, suitable for novice with little experience	Fairly easy, suitable for beginner with some experience	Fairly difficult, suitable for competent DIY mechanic	Difficult, suitable for experienced DIY mechanic	Very difficult, suitable for expert DIY or professional

Specifications

General

System type	Static (distributorless) ignition system controlled by engine management ECU
Firing order	1–3–4–2 (No 1 cylinder at timing belt end of engine)
Spark plugs	See Chapter 1 Specifications
Ignition timing.	Controlled by engine management ECU

Torque wrench setting

	Nm	lbf ft
Knock sensor securing bolt	25	18

1 General information

The ignition system is integrated with the fuel injection system to form a combined engine management system under the control of one ECU (see Chapter 4A for further information).

The ignition side of the system is of the static (distributorless) type with 4 separate ignition coils (one per cylinder) located in an assembly bolted to the cylinder head cover.

The ECU uses its inputs from the various sensors to calculate the required ignition advance setting and coil charging time depending on engine temperature, load and speed.

A knock sensor is also incorporated into the ignition system. Mounted onto the cylinder block, the sensor detects the high-frequency vibrations caused when the engine starts to pre-ignite, or 'pink'. Under these conditions, the knock sensor sends an electrical signal to the ECU which in turn retards the ignition advance setting in small steps until the 'pinking' ceases.

2 Ignition system – testing

⚠️ **Warning: Due to the high voltages produced by the electronic ignition system, extreme care must be taken when working on the system with the ignition switched on. Persons with surgically-implanted cardiac pacemaker devices should keep well clear of the ignition circuits, components and test equipment.**

1 If a fault appears in the engine management (fuel injection/ignition) system first ensure that the fault is not due to a poor electrical connection or poor maintenance; ie, check that the air cleaner filter element is clean, the spark plugs are in good condition and correctly gapped, that the engine breather hoses are clear and undamaged, referring to Chapter 1 for further information. If the engine is running very roughly, check the compression pressures and the valve clearances as described in Chapter 2.

2 If these checks fail to reveal the cause of the problem, the vehicle should be taken to a suitably equipped garage or Ford dealer for testing. A diagnostic connector, often referred to as the Data Link Connector (DLC), is incorporated in the engine management wiring circuit into which a special electronic diagnostic tester can be plugged. The tester will help an experienced technician locate the fault and alleviating the need to test all the system components individually.

3 The only ignition system checks which can be carried out by the home mechanic are those described in Chapter 1, relating to the spark plugs, and the ignition coil test described in this Chapter. If necessary, the system wiring and wiring connectors can be checked as described in Chapter 12, ensuring that the ECU wiring connectors have first been disconnected.

3 Ignition HT coils – removal, testing and refitting

Removal

1 Remove the air cleaner assembly as described in Chapter 4A.
2 Disconnect the LT wiring plug from the ignition coil **(see illustration)**.
3 Identify the HT leads for position then disconnect them from the coil HT terminals.
4 Unscrew the mounting bolts and remove the ignition coil from the cylinder head cover **(see illustration)**.

Testing

5 Testing of the coil consists of using a multimeter set to its resistance function, to check the primary and secondary windings for continuity and resistance. Test figures are not given for the individual coils incorporated in the coil pack, but they should be all similar. Note the resistance of the coil windings varies slightly according to the coil temperature.
6 Check that there is no continuity between the HT lead terminals and the coil body/mounting bracket.

7 Note that with the ignition switched on and the engine stationary, voltage will only be supplied to the ignition coils for approximately 2 seconds. However, when the engine is being cranked or running, voltage will be continually supplied.
8 If faulty, the coil should be renewed.

Refitting

9 Refitting is a reversal of the removal procedure ensuring that the wiring and HT leads are correctly reconnected.

4 Ignition timing – checking and adjustment

1 The ignition timing is constantly being monitored and adjusted by the engine management ECU, and nominal values cannot be given. Therefore, it is not possible for the home mechanic to check the ignition timing.
2 The only way in which the timing can be checked is using special electronic test equipment, connected to the engine management system diagnostic connector (refer to Chapter 4A for further information).

5 Knock sensor – removal and refitting

Removal

1 The knock sensor is screwed into the rear face of the cylinder block, under the intake manifold.
2 Firmly apply the handbrake, then jack up the front of the car and support it securely on axle stands (see *Jacking and vehicle support*).
3 Trace the wiring back from the sensor to its wiring connector, and disconnect it from the main loom.
4 From under the car, disconnect the knock sensor wiring connector.
5 Undo the sensor securing bolt and remove the sensor from the cylinder block.

Refitting

6 Refitting is a reversal of the removal procedure, ensuring that the sensor securing bolt is tightened to the specified torque.

3.2 Disconnect the LT wiring plug from the coil pack (arrowed)

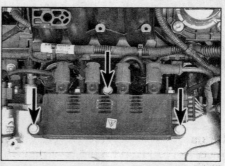

3.4 Ignition coil mounting bolts (arrowed)

Chapter 6
Clutch

Contents

Degrees of difficulty

Easy, suitable for novice with little experience	Fairly easy, suitable for beginner with some experience	Fairly difficult, suitable for competent DIY mechanic	Difficult, suitable for experienced DIY mechanic	Very difficult, suitable for expert DIY or professional

Specifications

Type . . . . Single dry plate with diaphragm spring, hydraulically-operated

Friction disc
Diameter . . . . 200 mm
New lining thickness . . . . 7.7 mm

Torque wrench settings	Nm	lbf ft
Master cylinder retaining nuts	15	10
Pressure plate retaining bolts*	15	10
Slave cylinder mounting bolts	15	11

* Do not re-use

1 General information

The clutch consists of a friction disc, a pressure plate assembly, and the clutch release bearing. All of these components are contained in a large cast-aluminium alloy bellhousing, sandwiched between the engine and the transmission.

The friction disc is fitted between the engine flywheel and the clutch pressure plate, and is allowed to slide on the transmission input shaft splines.

The pressure plate assembly is bolted to the engine flywheel. When the engine is running, drive is transmitted from the crankshaft, via the flywheel, to the friction disc (these components being clamped securely together by the pressure plate assembly) and from the friction disc to the transmission input shaft.

To interrupt the drive, the spring pressure must be relaxed. This is achieved using a hydraulic release mechanism which consists of the master cylinder, the externally mounted slave cylinder and the pipe/hose linking the two components. Depressing the pedal pushes on the master cylinder pushrod which hydraulically forces the slave cylinder piston push rod against the clutch release fork. This in turn pushes the release bearing against the pressure plate spring fingers. This causes the springs to deform and releases the clamping force on the friction disc.

The clutch is self-adjusting and requires no manual adjustment.

2 Clutch hydraulic system – bleeding

Warning: Hydraulic fluid is poisonous; thoroughly wash off spills from bare skin without delay. Seek immediate medical advice if any fluid is swallowed or gets into the eyes. Certain types of hydraulic fluid are inflammable and may ignite when brought into contact with hot components; when servicing any hydraulic system, it is safest

2.4 Bleed nipple (arrowed)

to assume that the fluid IS inflammable, and to take precautions against the risk of fire as though it were petrol that was being handled. Hydraulic fluid is an effective paint stripper and will also attack many plastics. If spillage occurs onto painted bodywork or fittings it should be washed off immediately, using copious quantities of fresh water. It is also hygroscopic – it can absorb moisture from the air, which then renders it useless. Old fluid may have suffered contamination, and should never be re-used. When topping-up or renewing the fluid, always use the recommended grade, and ensure that it comes from a new sealed container.

General information

1 Whenever the clutch hydraulic lines are disconnected for service or repair, a certain amount of air will enter the system. The presence of air in any hydraulic system will introduce a degree of elasticity, and in the clutch system this will translate into poor pedal feel and reduced travel, leading to inefficient gearchanges and even clutch system failure. For this reason, after reconnection of the hydraulic lines, the system must be topped-up and bled to remove any air bubbles.
2 The most effective way of bleeding the clutch hydraulic system is to use a pressure brake bleeding kit. These are readily available in motor accessories shops and are extremely effective. The following procedure describes bleeding the clutch system using such a kit. The alternative method is to bleed the system by depressing the clutch pedal – refer to the brake hydraulic system bleeding procedures contained in Chapter 9 for details of this method.
3 Remove the battery and battery tray as described in Chapter 5A, then observe if the release cylinder which is located on the top of the transmission housing. On models without a visible slave cylinder, the cylinder is in fact concentric with the transmission input shaft, within the gearbox bellhousing. On both types, a bleed nipple should be visible either on the slave cylinder itself, or on the plastic connecting piece.

Bleeding

4 Remove the protective cap from the slave cylinder bleed nipple **(see illustration)**. Connect a length of clear plastic hose over the nipple or outlet and insert the other end into a clean container. Pour hydraulic fluid into the container, such that the end of the hose is covered.
5 Following the manufacturer's instructions, pour hydraulic fluid into the bleeding kit vessel.
6 Unscrew the brake or clutch fluid reservoir filler cap, then connect the bleeding kit fluid supply hose to the reservoir.
7 Connect the pressure hose to a supply of compressed air – a spare tyre is a convenient source.

Caution: Check that the pressure in the tyre does not exceed the maximum supply pressure quoted by the kit manufacturer, let some air escape to reduce the pressure, if necessary. Gently open the air valve and allow the air and fluid pressures to equalise. Check that there are no leaks before proceeding.
8 Slacken the nipple approximately half a turn.
9 Allow the hydraulic fluid to flow from the slave cylinder, through the plastic hose and into the container. Maintain a steady flow until the emerging fluid is free of air bubbles; keep a watchful eye on the level of fluid in the bleeding kit vessel and the fluid reservoir – if it is allowed to drop too low, air may be forced into the system, defeating the object of the exercise. To refill the vessel, turn off the compressed air supply, remove the lid and pour in an appropriate quantity of fresh fluid – do not re-use the fluid collected in the receiving container. Repeat as necessary until the ejected fluid is bubble-free.
10 When clean hydraulic fluid, free from air bubbles, emerges from the plastic hose, tighten the bleed nipple, or press the pipe fully into the connector as applicable.
11 Pump the clutch pedal several times to assess its feel and travel. If firm, constant pedal resistance is not felt throughout the pedal stroke, it is probable that air is still present in the system – repeat the bleeding procedure until the pedal feel is restored.
12 Depressurise the bleeding kit and remove the kit, plastic hose and receiving container from the vehicle. Refit the protective cap to the bleed nipple. Discard the fluid expelled from the hydraulic system as it will be contaminated with moisture, air and dirt, making it unfit for further use.
13 Check the fluid level in the reservoir. At this point, the reservoir may be over-full; the excess should be removed using a clean pipette to reduce the level to the MAX mark.
14 Refit the battery and tray with reference to Chapter 5A.
15 Finally, road test the vehicle and check the operation of the clutch system whilst changing up and down through the gears, whilst pulling away from a standstill and from a hill start.

3 Master cylinder – removal and refitting

Removal

1 Unscrew the brake/clutch hydraulic fluid reservoir filler cap, and top-up the reservoir to the MAX mark (see *Weekly checks*). Place a piece of polythene over the filler neck, and secure the polythene with the filler cap. This will minimise fluid loss during subsequent operations. Alternatively, position a hose clamp on the fluid supply pipe above the master cylinder **(see illustration 3.4)**.

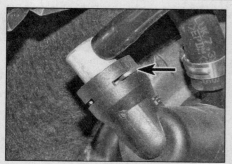

3.3 Prise out the fluid pipe retaining clip (arrowed)

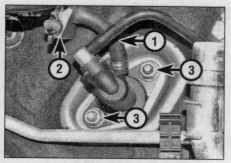

3.4 Clutch fluid supply hose (1), hose clamp (2) and master cylinder mounting nuts (3)

3.5 Working under the facia, prise the clutch master cylinder pushrod (arrowed) from the pedal

2 Remove all traces of dirt from the outside of the master cylinder, then position some cloth beneath the cylinder to catch any spilt fluid.
3 Extract the retaining clip (or on some models unbolt the 'banjo' bolt) and then disconnect the hydraulic pipe from the connector on the end of the master cylinder (see illustration). Plug the pipe end and master cylinder port to minimise fluid loss and prevent the entry of dirt.
4 Disconnect the fluid supply hose from the clutch master cylinder (see illustration).
5 Working inside the vehicle, carefully prise the master cylinder pushrod from the clutch pedal (see illustration).
6 Unscrew the two nuts securing the master cylinder to the engine compartment bulkhead and manoeuvre it from position. Be prepared for fluid spillage.
7 If the master cylinder is faulty it must be renewed; overhaul of the unit is not possible.

Refitting

8 Manoeuvre the master cylinder into position and refit the two retaining nuts. Tighten the nuts to the specified torque.
9 Press the end of the pushrod onto the pedal balljoint.
10 Connect the fluid supply hose to the master cylinder.
11 Press the hydraulic pipe back into the connector on the end of the master cylinder and secure with the clip.
12 Bleed the clutch hydraulic system as described in Section 2.

4 Slave cylinder –
removal and refitting

Note: Refer to the warning at the beginning of Section 2 regarding the hazards of working with hydraulic fluid.

Removal

1 Remove the battery and battery tray as described in Chapter 5A.
2 Remove the air cleaner assembly as described in Chapter 4A.
3 To minimise hydraulic fluid loss, remove the clutch master cylinder reservoir filler cap, then

tighten it down onto a piece of polythene to obtain an airtight seal.
4 Place absorbent rags around the slave cylinder, and be prepared for hydraulic fluid loss.
5 Extract the retaining clip and disconnect the hydraulic hose from the slave cylinder.
6 Unscrew the slave cylinder mounting bolts, release the cylinder pushrod from the release arm on the transmission, then remove the unit from the engine compartment (see illustration).
7 Repair of the slave cylinder is not possible. If the cylinder is faulty or leaking it must be replaced.

Refitting

8 Refitting is the reverse of the removal procedure, but bleed the clutch hydraulic system as described in Section 2 on completion.

5 Clutch pedal –
removal and refitting

1 Carefully prise the clutch master cylinder pushrod end fitting from the balljoint on the clutch pedal (see illustration 3.5).
2 Remove the circlip from the left-hand end of the pivot pin (see illustration).
3 Remove the clutch pedal position sensor (where fitted) as described in Chapter 12.
4 Slide the pivot to the right and remove the pedal.
5 Refitting is a reversal of removal.

4.6 Slave cylinder mounting bolts (arrowed)

6 Clutch assembly –
removal, inspection and refitting

⚠ *Warning: Dust created by clutch wear and deposited on the clutch components may contain asbestos, which is a health hazard. DO NOT blow it out with compressed air, or inhale any of it. DO NOT use petrol or petroleum-based solvents to clean off the dust. Brake system cleaner or methylated spirit should be used to flush the dust into a suitable receptacle. After the clutch components are wiped clean with rags, dispose of the contaminated rags and cleaner in a sealed, marked container.*

Removal

1 Unless the complete engine/transmission unit is to be removed from the car and separated for major overhaul (see Chapter 2B), the clutch can be reached by removing the transmission as described in Chapter 7.
2 Before disturbing the clutch, use chalk or a marker pen to mark the relationship of the pressure plate assembly to the flywheel.
3 Progressively unscrew the pressure plate retaining bolts in diagonal sequence by half a turn at a time, until spring pressure is released and the bolts can be unscrewed by hand.
4 Remove the pressure plate assembly and collect the friction disc, noting which way round the disc is fitted. It is recommended

5.2 Clutch pedal pivot pin retaining circlip (arrowed)

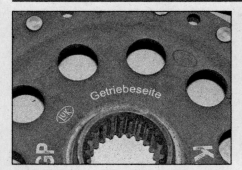

6.13 The side marked 'transmission side' or 'Getriebeseite' must point towards the transmission

6.14 Fit the pressure plate assembly over the friction disc

6.16 Centralise the friction disc using a clutch aligning tool or similar

that new pressure plate retaining bolts are obtained.

Inspection

Note: *Due to the amount of work necessary to remove and refit clutch components, it is usually considered good practice to renew the clutch friction disc, pressure plate assembly and release bearing as a matched set, even if only one of these is actually worn enough to require renewal. It is also worth considering the renewal of the clutch components on a preventive basis if the engine and/or transmission have been removed for some other reason.*

5 When cleaning clutch components, read first the warning at the beginning of this Section; remove dust using a clean, dry cloth, and working in a well-ventilated atmosphere.

6 Check the friction disc facings for signs of wear, damage or oil contamination. If the friction material is cracked, burnt, scored or damaged, or if it is contaminated with oil or grease (shown by shiny black patches), the friction disc must be renewed.

7 If the friction material is still serviceable, check that the centre boss splines are unworn, that the torsion springs are in good condition and securely fastened, and that all the rivets are tight. If any wear or damage is found, the friction disc must be renewed.

8 If the friction material is fouled with oil, this must be due to an oil leak from the crankshaft oil seal, from the sump-to-cylinder block joint, or from the release cylinder assembly (either

the main seal or the sealing ring). Renew the crankshaft oil seal or repair the sump joint as described in the appropriate Part of Chapter 2, before installing the new friction disc. The clutch slave cylinder is covered in Section 4.

9 Check the pressure plate assembly for obvious signs of wear or damage; shake it to check for loose rivets, or worn or damaged fulcrum rings, and check that the drive straps securing the pressure plate to the cover do not show signs of overheating (such as a deep yellow or blue discoloration). If the diaphragm spring is worn or damaged, or if its pressure is in any way suspect, the pressure plate assembly should be renewed.

10 Examine the machined bearing surfaces of the pressure plate and of the flywheel; they should be clean, completely flat, and free from scratches or scoring. If either is discoloured from excessive heat, or shows signs of cracks, it should be renewed – although minor damage of this nature can sometimes be polished away using emery paper.

11 Check that the release bearing rotates smoothly and easily, with no sign of noise or roughness. Also check that the surface itself is smooth and unworn, with no signs of cracks, pitting or scoring. If there is any doubt about its condition, the clutch release bearing or slave cylinder (as applicable) should be renewed.

Refitting

12 Lightly oil the teeth of the friction disc

hub. Do not apply too much, otherwise it may eventually contaminate the friction disc linings. Note that some replacement clutch kits will be supplied with a specialist lubricant for this purpose.

13 Locate the friction disc on the flywheel, making sure that the lettering 'transmission side' or 'Getriebeseite' points towards the transmission **(see illustration)**.

14 Refit the pressure plate assembly, aligning the marks made on dismantling (if the original pressure plate is re-used). Fit new pressure plate bolts, but tighten them only finger-tight so that the friction disc can still be moved **(see illustration)**.

15 The friction disc must now be centralised so that, when the transmission is refitted, its input shaft will pass through the splines at the centre of the friction disc.

16 Centralisation can be achieved by passing a screwdriver or other long bar through the friction disc and into the hole in the crankshaft. The friction disc can then be moved around until it is centred on the crankshaft hole. Alternatively, a clutch-aligning tool can be used to eliminate the guesswork; these can be obtained from most accessory shops **(see illustration)**.

17 When the friction disc is centralised, tighten the pressure plate bolts evenly and in a diagonal sequence to the specified torque setting.

18 Refit the transmission as described in Chapter 7.

Chapter 7
Manual transmission

Contents

Degrees of difficulty

Easy, suitable for novice with little experience	Fairly easy, suitable for beginner with some experience	Fairly difficult, suitable for competent DIY mechanic	Difficult, suitable for experienced DIY mechanic	Very difficult, suitable for expert DIY or professional

Specifications

General

Type	Transversely-mounted, front wheel drive layout with integral transaxle differential/final drive. 5 forward speeds, 1 reverse speed
Designation	C.514

Lubrication

Recommended oil type	Refer to *Lubricants and fluids*
Capacity	1.65 litres

Torque wrench settings

	Nm	lbf ft
Engine/transmission attachment bolts	60	44
Engine/transmission mountings:		
Left-hand mounting bracket-to-transmission bolt	50	37
Left hand mounting-to-body nuts/bolt	50	37
Transmission oil drain plug	25	18
Transmission oil filler plug	20	15

1 General information

The transmission is contained in a cast-aluminium alloy casing bolted to the engine's left-hand end, and consists of the gearbox and final drive differential.

Drive is transmitted from the crankshaft via the clutch to the input shaft, which has a splined extension to accept the clutch friction plate and rotates in roller bearings at its right-hand end and ball-bearings at its left-hand end. From the input shaft, drive is transmitted to the output shaft which rotates in roller bearings at its right-hand end and ball-bearings at its left-hand end. From the output shaft, the drive is transmitted to the differential crownwheel which rotates with the differential case and gears in taper roller bearings, thus driving the sun gears and driveshafts. The rotation of the differential gears on their shaft allows the inner roadwheel to rotate at a slower speed than the outer roadwheel when the car is cornering.

The input and output shafts are arranged side-by-side, parallel to the crankshaft and driveshafts, so that their gear pinion teeth are in constant mesh. In the neutral position, the relevant input shaft and output shaft gear pinions rotate freely, so that drive cannot be transmitted to the output shaft and crownwheel.

Gear selection is via a floor-mounted lever and twin selector cable mechanism. The selector cables cause the appropriate selector fork to move its respective synchro-sleeve along the shaft, to lock the gear to the synchro-hub. Since the synchro-hubs are splined to the input and output shafts, this locks the gear to the shaft so that drive can be transmitted. To ensure that gearchanging can be made quickly and quietly, a synchromesh system is fitted to all forward gears.

2 Manual transmission oil – draining and refilling

1 Park the vehicle on a level surface, if possible over an inspection pit or on a ramp as the filler/level and drain plugs are accessed from under the engine compartment. If necessary jack up the vehicle and support on axle stands (see *Jacking and vehicle support*).

2.2a Transmission oil filler plug (arrowed) . . .

2.2b . . . and drain plug (arrowed) – C.514 and C.514R transmissions

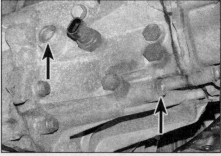

2.2c Transmission oil filler and drain plugs (arrowed) – C.510 transmission

2 Wipe clean the area around the filler/level and drain plugs, which are on the front and bottom of the transmission **(see illustrations)**.

3 Using an Allen key, unscrew the filler/level plug and clean it.

4 Position a suitable container beneath the transmission, then use the Allen key to unscrew the drain plug. Allow the oil to completely drain.

5 Wipe clean the drain plug then refit and tighten it to the specified torque.

6 Fill the transmission with the correct grade and quantity of oil, referring to Chapter 1 when checking the level. The oil level should be up to the lower edge of the filler plug opening. Refit and tighten the filler/level plug.

7 Where applicable lower the vehicle to the ground.

3 Gearchange selector cables – removal and refitting

Removal

1 Prise up the gear lever gaiter from the gear lever surround panel **(see illustration)**.

2 Remove the battery and air cleaner assembly as described in Chapter 5A and Chapter 4A.

3 Remove the centre console and the lower centre facia panel as described in Chapter 11.

4 At the base of the facia, undo the bolts and remove the support bracket between the facia crossmember and the floor **(see illustration)**.

5 Remove the glovebox and then remove the left-hand side lower air duct.

6 Disconnect the selector cable end fittings from their attachments at the gear lever linkage **(see illustration)**.

7 Where fitted gently remove the neutral position sensor **(see illustration)**.

8 Extract the two retaining clips securing the selector cables to the gear lever housing **(see illustration)**.

9 Disconnect the selector cable end fittings from their attachments at the transmission selector levers **(see illustration)**.

10 Pull back the collars, and pull the outer cables from the transmission support bracket **(see illustration)**.

11 Firmly apply the handbrake, then jack up the front of the car and support it securely on axle stands (see *Jacking and vehicle support*).

12 Release the gearchange cables from the bracket on the vehicle underside.

3.1 Prise up the gearchange lever gaiter

3.4 Remove the support bracket (arrowed) between the floor and the crossmember

3.6 Prise the selector cable end fittings from the lever attachments

3.7 Gently prise the neutral sensor linkage from the cable casing

3.8 Slide out the cable retaining clips

3.9 Use an open-ended spanner to prise the end of the cables from the lever balljoints

13 Release the rubber grommet from the vehicle floor, and manoeuvre the cables from position **(see illustration)**.

Refitting

14 Refitting is a reversal of removal, but before refitting the gear lever control panel, adjust the selector cable as follows:

a) *With the transmission in Neutral, depress the selector cable locking clip, then press in the locking catch. This allows the end fitting to slide on the cable* **(see illustration)**.

b) *Place the gear lever in neutral and fit an 8.5mm thick spacer between the sleeve and barrier* **(see illustration)**.

c) *Hold the lever against the tool, then release the locking clip.*

d) *Check that all gears can be selected without stiffness or binding. If necessary, repeat the adjustment procedure.*

4 Gearchange lever assembly – removal and refitting

Removal

1 Disconnect the gearchange cables from the lever assembly as described in Section 3.

2 Undo the retaining bolts/nuts and remove the lever and bracket assembly **(see illustration)**.

Refitting

3 Refitting is a reversal of removal.

5 Manual transmission – removal and refitting

Removal

1 Firmly apply the handbrake, then jack up the front of the car and support it securely on axle stands (see *Jacking and vehicle support*).

2 Remove both front wheels, then remove the left-hand wheel arch liner main and centre panels.

3 Remove the air cleaner assembly as described in Chapter 4A.

4 Remove the battery, battery tray and starter motor as described in Chapter 5A.

5 Disconnect the wiring connector from the reversing light switch on the front of the transmission, then unscrew the nut and disconnect the transmission earth lead from the top of the unit.

6 Disconnect the gearchange selector cable end fittings from the transmission lever ball-studs. Undo the bolts securing the selector cable support bracket to the transmission and move the bracket and cables to one side.

7 Unbolt the clutch slave cylinder from the top of the transmission then fit a cable-tie around it to prevent the piston from being ejected. Position the cylinder to one side.

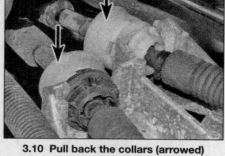

3.10 Pull back the collars (arrowed) and detach the outer cables from the transmission bracket

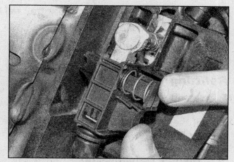

3.14a Depress the locking clip, then press in the locking catch

8 Remove the front bumper as described in Chapter 11.

9 Drain the transmission (Section 2 of this Chapter) and then remove both driveshafts as described in Chapter 8.

10 Detach the exhaust pipe support bracket, then undo the bolts and remove the cover plate (where fitted) from the base of the transmission bellhousing.

11 Working beneath the car, unscrew the bolts and nuts securing the rear engine mounting to the subframe and transmission, and withdraw the mounting.

12 Undo the bolts and remove the transmission-to-engine support bracket above the right-hand driveshaft location.

13 Support the weight of the engine using a hoist attached to home-made brackets secured to suitable positions at the left-hand end of the engine.

4.2 Gearchange lever/bracket assembly retaining bolt/nuts (arrowed)

3.13 Prise up the rubber gaiter from the floor – heater housing removed for clarity

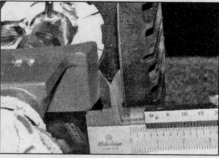

3.14b There must be a gap of 8.5 mm between the reverse inhibitor sleeve and the support barrier

14 Support the weight of the transmission on a trolley jack then unscrew the engine-to-transmission retaining bolts. Move aside all wiring and support brackets secured by the retaining bolts.

15 Unscrew the central bolt, and slacken the nuts securing the left-hand engine/transmission mounting to the body.

16 Undo the bolts securing the mounting bracket to the end of the transmission casing **(see illustration)**.

17 Check that all pipes, hoses and wiring are moved clear then carefully pull the transmission away from the engine. Lower the trolley jack and remove the transmission from under the car.

⚠ *Warning: Support the transmission to ensure that it remains steady on the jack head. Keep the transmission level until the input shaft is*

5.16 Undo the bolt (arrowed) securing the mounting to the transmission/bracket

fully withdrawn from the clutch friction plate.

Refitting

18 Refitting is a reversal of the removal procedure, bearing in mind the following points.
  a) *Apply a smear of high-melting-point grease to the clutch friction plate splines; take care to avoid contaminating the friction surfaces.*
  b) *Tighten all bolts to the specified torque, referring to the Chapters indicated for components not covered in this Chapter.*

6 Reversing light switch – testing, removal and refitting

Testing

1 The reversing light circuit is controlled by a plunger-type switch screwed into the front of the transmission casing **(see illustration)**. If a fault develops, first ensure that the circuit fuse has not blown.
2 To test the switch, disconnect the wiring connector, and use a multimeter (set to the resistance function) or a battery-and-bulb test circuit to check that there is continuity between the switch terminals only when reverse gear is selected. If this is not the case, and there are no obvious breaks or other damage to the wires, the switch is faulty, and must be renewed.

6.1 Reversing light switch (arrowed)

Removal

3 Remove the battery and battery tray as described in Chapter 5A.
4 Disconnect the wiring connector, then unscrew the switch from the transmission casing.

Refitting

5 Refit and securely tighten the switch, then reconnect the wiring.
6 Refit the battery and tray as described in Chapter 5A.

7 Manual transmission overhaul – general information

Overhauling a manual transmission is a difficult and involved job for the DIY home mechanic. In addition to dismantling and reassembling many small parts, clearances must be precisely measured and, if necessary, changed by selecting shims and spacers. Internal transmission components are also often difficult to obtain, and in many instances, extremely expensive. Because of this, if the transmission develops a fault or becomes noisy, the best course of action is to have the unit overhauled by a specialist repairer, or to obtain an exchange reconditioned unit.

Nevertheless, it is not impossible for the more experienced mechanic to overhaul the transmission, provided the special tools are available, and the job is done in a deliberate step-by-step manner, so that nothing is overlooked.

The tools necessary for an overhaul include internal and external circlip pliers, bearing pullers, a slide hammer, a set of pin punches, a dial test indicator, and possibly a hydraulic press. In addition, a large, sturdy workbench and a vice will be required.

During dismantling of the transmission, make careful notes of how each component is fitted, to make reassembly easier and more accurate.

Before dismantling the transmission, it will help if you have some idea what area is malfunctioning. Certain problems can be closely related to specific areas in the transmission, which can make component examination and renewal easier. Refer to the *Fault finding* in the Reference Chapter for more information.

Chapter 8
Driveshafts

Contents

Degrees of difficulty

Easy, suitable for novice with little experience	**Fairly easy,** suitable for beginner with some experience	**Fairly difficult,** suitable for competent DIY mechanic	**Difficult,** suitable for experienced DIY mechanic	**Very difficult,** suitable for expert DIY or professional

Specifications

General

Type	Unequal-length, solid steel shafts, splined to inner and outer constant velocity joints

Lubrication

Lubricant type	Ford specification grease (WSD-M1C230A) or equivalent
Quantities (approximate):	
Wheel side joint	80g
Differential side joint	100g

Torque wrench settings

	Nm	lbf ft
Driveshaft nut:*		
Stage 1	70	52
Stage 2	Angle-tighten a further 55°	
Stage 3	275	203
Roadwheel bolts:		
Steel wheel	85	63
Aluminium wheel	110	81
Suspension strut-to-swivel hub bolts	75	55
Track rod end-to-swivel hub nut*	40	30

* Use a new nut.

1 General information

Power is transmitted from the differential to the roadwheels by the driveshafts, via inner and outer constant velocity (CV) joints.

The outer ball-and-cage type CV joints allow smooth transmission of drive to the wheels at all steering and suspension angles. Drive is transmitted by means of a number of radially static steel balls that run in grooves between the two halves of the joint.

The inner CV joints are of the tripod type. Drive is transmitted across the joint by means of three rollers, mounted on the driveshaft in a tripod arrangement, that are radially static but are free to slide in the grooved joint body.

The joints are protected by rubber gaiters, and are packed with grease to provide permanent lubrication. If wear is detected in the joint, it can be detached from the driveshaft and renewed. Normally, the CV joints do not require additional lubrication, unless they have been overhauled or the rubber gaiters have been damaged, allowing the grease to become contaminated. Refer to Chapter 1 for guidance in checking the condition of the driveshaft gaiters.

Both driveshafts are splined at their outer ends, to accept the wheel hubs, and are threaded so that the hubs can be fastened to the driveshafts by means of a staked nut.

2 Driveshafts – removal and refitting

Note: *A balljoint separator tool will be required for this operation.*

Removal

1 Firmly apply the handbrake, then jack up the front of the car and support it securely on axle stands (see *Jacking and vehicle support*). Remove the appropriate roadwheel(s).

2.2 Tap up the staking securing the driveshaft retaining nut in position

2 Using a hammer and chisel or similar tool, tap up the staking securing the driveshaft retaining nut in position **(see illustration)**.

3 The front wheel hub must be held stationary in order to loosen the driveshaft nut. Ideally, the hub should be held by a suitable tool bolted into place using two of the roadwheel bolts **(see Tool Tip)**. Alternatively, have an assistant firmly apply the footbrake to prevent the hub from rotating. Using a socket and extension bar, slacken and remove the driveshaft retaining nut.

 Warning: The nut is extremely tight. Discard the nut – a new one must be used on refitting.

4 Release the brake caliper hydraulic hose, the ABS wheel speed sensor cable and (where applicable) the pad wear indicator sensor cable from the brackets at the base of the suspension strut.

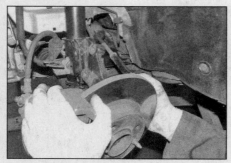

2.7a Pull the swivel hub outwards at the top . . .

2.8 Lever between the inner joint and the differential casing

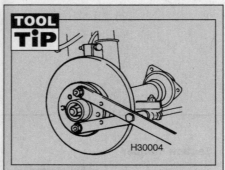

A tool to hold the front hub stationary whilst the driveshaft nut is slackened can be fabricated from two lengths of steel strip (one long, one short) and a nut and bolt; the nut and bolt forming the pivot of a forked tool.

5 Unscrew the nut securing the track rod end to the swivel hub. Release the track rod end tapered shank using a balljoint separator tool.

6 Unscrew the two nuts and remove the bolts securing the top of the swivel hub to the base of the suspension strut. Note that the bolts are inserted from the rear.

7 Pull the swivel hub outwards at the top and withdraw the driveshaft outer constant velocity joint from the hub assembly **(see illustrations)**. If necessary, the joint can be tapped out of the hub using a soft-faced mallet. Support the end of the driveshaft – do not allow the end of the driveshaft to hang

2.7b . . . and withdraw the driveshaft outer constant velocity joint from the hub assembly

2.17 Stake the nut using a hammer and chisel

down as this will strain the joint components and gaiters.

8 Insert a lever between the inner joint and the differential casing, and prise the driveshaft from place **(see illustration)**. Be prepared for oil spillage.

9 Remove the driveshaft from under the vehicle.

10 Loosely refit one of the strut lower mounting bolts to support the swivel hub while the driveshaft is removed.

Refitting

11 After removing the temporarily-fitted bolt from the strut mounting, pivot the swivel hub away from the car and engage the inner joint with the differential and the outer CV joint into the hub.

12 Screw on the new driveshaft retaining nut, but do not tighten it at this stage.

13 Refit and tighten the intermediate bearing bolts where applicable.

14 Refit the suspension strut-to-swivel hub bolts and tighten them to the specified torque.

15 Engage the track rod end with the swivel hub, refit the retaining nut and tighten the nut to the specified torque.

16 Refit the brake caliper hydraulic hose, the ABS wheel speed sensor cable (and where applicable) the brake pad wear sensor to the bracket on the base of the suspension strut.

17 Using the method employed on removal to prevent rotation of the hub, tighten the driveshaft retaining nut to the specified torque. Secure the nut by tapping the staking into the grooves in the end of the CV joint using a hammer and chisel. Note that the staking should be done so that the tang bites into the left-hand side of the slot in the driveshaft **(see illustration)**.

18 Check and top up the transmission fluid oil level as described in Chapter 1 and Chapter 7.

19 Refit the roadwheel and lower the car to the ground.

| 3 | Driveshaft overhaul and rubber gaiter renewal | |

Outer joint

1 Remove the driveshaft as described in Section 2.

2 Release the rubber gaiter retaining clips by cutting them off with a pair of side-cutters **(see illustration)**. Remove the clips and slide the gaiter down the driveshaft away from the CV joint.

3 The outer joint is secured to the driveshaft by an external circlip. Use a soft metal drift to drive the inner spider from the end of the driveshaft **(see illustration)**.

4 Slide the old gaiter off the end of the driveshaft.

5 With the constant velocity joint removed from the driveshaft, thoroughly clean the joint

3.2 Cut-through the clips securing the old rubber gaiter

3.3 Drive the inner spider from the end of the driveshaft

3.9a Slide the small clip onto the driveshaft, followed by the new gaiter...

3.9b ...and the large clip

3.10 Renew the circlip on the end of the driveshaft

3.11 Pack the joint with the specified grease

using paraffin, or a suitable solvent, and dry it thoroughly. Carry out a visual inspection of the joint.

6 Move the inner splined driving member from side-to-side, to expose each ball in turn at the top of its track. Examine the balls for cracks, flat spots, or signs of surface pitting.

7 Inspect the ball tracks on the inner and outer members. If the tracks have widened, the balls will no longer be a tight fit. At the same time, check the ball cage windows for wear or cracking between the windows.

8 If any of the constant velocity joint components are found to be worn or damaged, it will be necessary to renew the complete joint assembly as the internal parts are not available separately. If the joint is in satisfactory condition, obtain a new gaiter, retaining clips, circlip, and the correct type of grease. These components are all available

individually from Ford dealers, but may be supplied as a complete repair kit from other sources.

9 Slide the smaller gaiter securing clip onto the driveshaft, followed by the gaiter and the large securing clip **(see illustrations)**. Note that the closed end of the clips must point in the direction of rotation (when the vehicle moves forwards).

10 Renew the circlip on the end of the shaft **(see illustration)**.

11 Pack the CV joint with the specified grease, then twist the joint to ensure that all the recesses are filled **(see illustration)**.

12 Fit the CV joint to the driveshaft, and engage it with the shaft splines. Use a mallet to tap the joint onto the shaft until the circlip engages correctly.

13 Fill the gaiter with any remaining grease then slide the large end of the gaiter into position over the joint, ensuring that it is seated squarely over the joint body.

14 Locate the large securing clip over the gaiter and secure the clip in place by compressing the raised portion **(see illustration)**.

15 Check that the smaller end of the gaiter is located in the driveshaft groove then, using a small screwdriver, lift the lip of the gaiter to expel any air trapped inside **(see illustration)**.

16 Slide the smaller securing clip over the gaiter, and secure it as described previously **(see illustration)**.

17 Refit the driveshaft as described in Section 2.

Inner joint

18 Remove the driveshaft as described in Section 2.

19 Release the gaiter smaller and larger clips by cutting them off with a pair of side-cutters **(see illustration 3.2)**.

3.14 Pliers are available specifically to fit/compress driveshaft boot clips

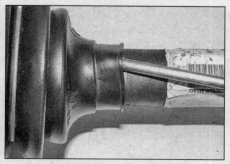

3.15 Lift the inner lip to equalise air pressure in the boot

3.16 Fit and compress the smaller gaiter retaining clip

3.20a Pull back the gaiter...

3.20b ...and slide the tripod from the end
of the driveshaft

3.22 Remove the circlip (arrowed)

3.23 Make alignment marks between the
tripod and shaft

3.27 The side of the tripod with the
chamfer (arrowed) must fit against the
driveshaft – not the circlip

3.28 Pack the joint with the specified
grease

20 Pull back the gaiter and slide the outer housing from the tripod joint **(see illustrations)**.
21 Wipe off the excess grease from the tripod and the end of the driveshaft.
22 Using circlip pliers, remove the circlip securing the tripod to the end of the driveshaft **(see illustration)**. Discard the circlip – a new one should be used on refitting.
23 Make alignment marks between the tripod and the shaft, then withdraw the tripod and the gaiter from the end of the driveshaft **(see illustration)**.
24 Thoroughly clean the tripod and rollers, and the end of the driveshaft using paraffin, or

a suitable solvent, and dry thoroughly. Carry out a visual inspection of the joint and renew any components as necessary. If the joint is in satisfactory condition, obtain a new gaiter, circlip, retaining clips, and the correct type of grease. These components are all available individually from Ford dealers, but may be supplied as a complete repair kit from other sources.
25 Commence reassembly by sliding the smaller gaiter securing clip onto the driveshaft, followed by the gaiter.
26 Check that the gaiter is located in the driveshaft groove, then fit the securing clip

over the gaiter and secure the clip in place by compressing the raised portion.
27 Refit the tripod and fit a new circlip to secure the tripod to the driveshaft. Note the slight chamfer on the driveshaft side of the tripod **(see illustration)**.
28 Pack the specified grease around the tripod rollers and into the joint body **(see illustration)**.
29 Slide on the outer housing, position the gaiter and secure the outer clip in place by compressing the raised portion **(see illustration 3.14)**.
30 Refit the driveshaft as described in Section 2.

Chapter 9
Braking system

Contents

Degrees of difficulty

Easy, suitable for novice with little experience ![spanner]	**Fairly easy,** suitable for beginner with some experience ![spanner]	**Fairly difficult,** suitable for competent DIY mechanic ![spanner]	**Difficult,** suitable for experienced DIY mechanic ![spanner]	**Very difficult,** suitable for expert DIY or professional ![spanner]

Specifications

Front disc brakes

Type	Solid disc with single-piston sliding calipers
Disc diameter	240.0 mm
Disc thickness (new)	10.8 to 11.1 mm
Minimum disc thickness (wear limit)	9.2 mm
Maximum disc runout	0.15 mm
Brake pad friction material minimum thickness	1.5 mm

Rear drum brakes

Drum inner diameter (new)	180.0 to 180.2 mm
Maximum drum diameter (wear limit)	181.3 mm
Minimum brake shoe lining thickness	2.0 mm

Torque wrench settings

	Nm	lbf ft
Bleed screw	6	4
Brake disc screw	10	7
Brake drum locating studs	12	9
Brake pipe and hose unions	14	10
Front caliper:		
Guide pin bolts	27	20
Mounting bracket-to-swivel hub bolts:		
M10	60	44
M12	100	74
Rear wheel cylinder mounting bolts	10	7
Roadwheel bolts:		
Steel wheel	85	63
Aluminium wheel	110	81

1 General information

The braking system is of the vacuum servo-assisted, dual-circuit hydraulic type. The arrangement of the hydraulic system is such that each circuit operates one front and one rear brake from a tandem master cylinder. Under normal circumstances, both circuits operate in unison. However, in the event of hydraulic failure in one circuit, full braking force will still be available at two diagonally-opposite wheels.

All models covered in this manual are fitted with front disc brakes and rear drum brakes. An anti-lock braking system (ABS) is fitted as standard on all models.

The front disc brakes are actuated by single-piston sliding type calipers, which ensure that equal pressure is applied to each brake pad.

The rear drum brakes incorporate leading and trailing shoes, which are actuated by twin-piston wheel cylinders. A self-adjust mechanism is incorporated, to automatically compensate for brake shoe wear. As the brake shoe linings wear, the footbrake operation automatically operates the adjuster mechanism to reduce the lining-to-drum clearance.

The mechanical handbrake linkage operates the brake shoes via a lever attached to the trailing brake shoe.

Note: *When servicing any part of the system, work carefully and methodically; also observe scrupulous cleanliness when overhauling any part of the hydraulic system. Always renew components (in axle sets, where applicable) if in doubt about their condition, and use only genuine Ford parts, or at least those of known good quality. Note the warnings given in 'Safety first!' and at relevant points in this Chapter concerning the dangers of asbestos dust and hydraulic fluid.*

2 Hydraulic system – bleeding

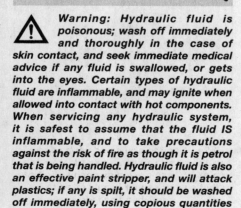

⚠ **Warning: Hydraulic fluid is poisonous; wash off immediately and thoroughly in the case of skin contact, and seek immediate medical advice if any fluid is swallowed, or gets into the eyes. Certain types of hydraulic fluid are inflammable, and may ignite when allowed into contact with hot components. When servicing any hydraulic system, it is safest to assume that the fluid IS inflammable, and to take precautions against the risk of fire as though it is petrol that is being handled. Hydraulic fluid is also an effective paint stripper, and will attack plastics; if any is spilt, it should be washed off immediately, using copious quantities**

of fresh water. Finally, it is hygroscopic (it absorbs moisture from the air) – old fluid may be contaminated and unfit for further use. When topping-up or renewing the fluid, always use the recommended type, and ensure that it comes from a freshly-opened sealed container.

⚠ **Warning: Ensure that the ignition is switched off before starting the bleeding procedure, to avoid any possibility of voltage being applied to the hydraulic modulator before the bleeding procedure is completed. Ideally, the battery should be disconnected. If voltage is applied to the modulator before the bleeding procedure is complete, this will effectively drain the hydraulic fluid in the modulator, rendering the unit unserviceable. Do not, therefore, attempt to 'run' the modulator in order to bleed the brakes.**

Note: *Ford recommend the use of a pressure bleeding kit, however unless major work has been undertaken to the brake hydraulics, it is possible to bleed the brakes using conventional methods.*

1 The correct operation of any hydraulic system is only possible after removing all air from the components and circuit; and this is achieved by bleeding the system.

2 During the bleeding procedure, add only clean, unused hydraulic fluid of the recommended type; never re-use fluid that has already been bled from the system. Ensure that sufficient fluid is available before starting work.

3 If there is any possibility of incorrect fluid being already in the system, the brake components and circuit must be flushed completely with uncontaminated, correct fluid, and new seals should be fitted throughout the system.

4 If hydraulic fluid has been lost from the system, or air has entered because of a leak, ensure that the fault is cured before proceeding further.

5 Park the car on level ground, switch off the engine and select first or reverse gear, then chock the wheels and release the handbrake.

6 Check that all pipes and hoses are secure, unions tight and bleed screws closed. Remove the dust caps (where applicable), and clean any dirt from around the bleed screws.

7 Unscrew the master cylinder reservoir cap, and top the master cylinder reservoir up to the MAX level line; refit the cap loosely. Remember to maintain the fluid level at least above the MIN level line throughout the procedure, otherwise there is a risk of further air entering the system.

8 There are a number of one-man, do-it-yourself brake bleeding kits currently available from motor accessory shops. It is recommended that one of these kits is used whenever possible, as they greatly simplify the bleeding operation, and also reduce the risk of expelled air and fluid being drawn back into the system. If such a kit is not available, the basic (two-man) method must be used, which is described in detail below.

9 If a kit is to be used, prepare the vehicle as described previously, and follow the kit manufacturer's instructions, as the procedure may vary slightly according to the type being used; generally, they are as outlined below in the relevant sub-section.

10 Whichever method is used, the same sequence must be followed (paragraphs 11 and 12) to ensure the removal of all air from the system.

Bleeding sequence

11 If the system has been only partially disconnected, and suitable precautions were taken to minimise fluid loss, it should be necessary to bleed only that part of the system (ie, the primary or secondary circuit).

12 If the complete system is to be bled, then it should be done working in the following sequence:

a) Left-hand rear wheel.
b) Right-hand front wheel.
c) Right-hand rear wheel.
d) Left-hand front wheel.

Basic (two-man) bleeding method

13 Collect a clean glass jar, a suitable length of plastic or rubber tubing which is a tight fit over the bleed screw, and a ring spanner to fit the screw. The help of an assistant will also be required.

14 Remove the dust cap from the first screw in the sequence if not already done. Fit a suitable spanner and tube to the screw, place the other end of the tube in the jar, and pour in sufficient fluid to cover the end of the tube.

15 Ensure that the master cylinder reservoir fluid level is maintained at least above the MIN level line throughout the procedure.

16 Have the assistant fully depress the brake pedal several times to build-up pressure, then maintain it on the final downstroke.

17 While pedal pressure is maintained, unscrew the bleed screw (approximately one turn) and allow the compressed fluid and air to flow into the jar. The assistant should maintain pedal pressure, following the pedal down to the floor if necessary, and should not release the pedal until instructed to do so. When the flow stops, tighten the bleed screw again, have the assistant release the pedal slowly, and recheck the reservoir fluid level.

18 Repeat the steps given in paragraphs 16 and 17 until the fluid emerging from the bleed screw is free from air bubbles. If the master cylinder has been drained and refilled, and air is being bled from the first screw in the sequence, allow approximately five seconds between cycles for the master cylinder passages to refill.

19 When no more air bubbles appear, tighten the bleed screw securely, remove the tube and spanner, and refit the dust cap (where applicable). Do not overtighten the bleed screw.

20 Repeat the procedure on the remaining screws in the sequence, until all air is removed from the system, and the brake pedal feels firm again.

Bleeding using a one-way valve kit

21 As their name implies, these kits consist of a length of tubing with a one-way valve fitted to prevent expelled air and fluid being drawn back into the system; some kits include a translucent container, which can be positioned so that the air bubbles can be more easily seen flowing from the end of the tube.

22 The kit is connected to the bleed screw, which is then opened **(see illustration)**. The user returns to the driver's seat, depresses the brake pedal with a smooth, steady stroke, and slowly releases it; this is repeated until the expelled fluid is clear of air bubbles.

23 Note that these kits simplify work so much that it is easy to forget the master cylinder reservoir fluid level; ensure that this is maintained at least above the MIN level line at all times.

Bleeding using a pressure-bleeding kit

24 These kits are usually operated by the reservoir of pressurised air contained in the spare tyre. However, note that it will probably be necessary to reduce the pressure to a lower level than normal; refer to the instructions supplied with the kit.

25 By connecting a pressurised, fluid-filled container to the master cylinder reservoir, bleeding can be carried out simply by opening each screw in turn (in the specified sequence), and allowing the fluid to flow out until no more air bubbles can be seen in the expelled fluid.

26 This method has the advantage that the large reservoir of fluid provides an additional safeguard against air being drawn into the system during bleeding.

27 Pressure-bleeding is particularly effective when bleeding 'difficult' systems, or when bleeding the complete system at the time of routine fluid renewal.

All methods

28 When bleeding is complete, and firm pedal feel is restored, wash off any spilt fluid, tighten the bleed screws securely, and refit their dust caps (where applicable).

29 Check the hydraulic fluid level in the master cylinder reservoir, and top-up if necessary.

30 Discard any hydraulic fluid that has been bled from the system; it will not be fit for re-use.

31 Check the feel of the brake pedal. If it feels at all spongy, air must still be present in the system, and further bleeding is required. Failure to bleed satisfactorily after a reasonable repetition of the bleeding procedure may be due to worn master cylinder seals.

⚠ *Warning: Do not operate the vehicle if you are in doubt about the effectiveness of the braking system. If considerable air was present in the system prior to bleeding, it is possible for some of this air to remain trapped in the hydraulic modulator. If the pedal continues* to feel spongy after repeated bleedings, or if any of the brake system warning lights remain on, have the vehicle towed to a Ford dealer to be bled with the use of Ford diagnostic equipment.

3 Hydraulic pipes and hoses – renewal

⚠ *Warning: Before starting work, refer to the warning at the beginning of Section 2 concerning the dangers of hydraulic fluid.*

1 If any pipe or hose is to be renewed, minimise fluid loss by first removing the master cylinder reservoir cap, then tighten the cap down onto a piece of polythene to obtain an airtight seal. Alternatively, flexible hoses can be sealed, if required, using a proprietary brake hose clamp; metal brake pipe unions can be plugged (if care is taken not to allow dirt into the system) or capped immediately they are disconnected. Place a wad of rag under any union that is to be disconnected, to catch any spilt fluid.

2 If a flexible hose is to be disconnected, unscrew the brake pipe union nut before removing the spring clip which secures the hose to its mounting bracket.

3 To unscrew the union nuts, it is preferable to obtain a brake pipe spanner of the correct size; these are available from most large motor accessory shops. Failing this, a close-fitting open-ended spanner will be required, though if the nuts are tight or corroded, their flats may be rounded-off if the spanner slips. In such a case, a self-locking wrench is often the only way to unscrew a stubborn union, but it follows that the pipe and the damaged nuts must be renewed on reassembly. Always clean a union and surrounding area before disconnecting it. If disconnecting a component with more than one union, make a careful note of the connections before disturbing any of them.

4 If a brake pipe is to be renewed, it can be obtained, cut to length and with the union nuts and end flares in place, from Ford dealers. All that is then necessary is to bend it to shape, following the line of the original, before fitting it to the vehicle. Alternatively, most motor accessory shops can make up brake pipes from kits, but this requires very careful measurement of the original, to ensure that the new one is of the correct length. The safest answer is usually to take the original to the shop as a pattern.

5 On refitting, do not overtighten the union nuts. It is not necessary to exercise brute force to obtain a sound joint.

6 Ensure that the pipes and hoses are correctly routed, with no kinks, and that they are secured in the clips or brackets provided. After fitting, remove the polythene from the reservoir, and bleed the hydraulic system as described in Section 2. Wash off any spilt fluid, and check carefully for fluid leaks.

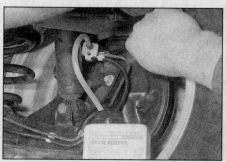
2.22 Using a one-way valve kit to bleed the rear brake

4 Front brake pads – renewal

⚠ *Warning: Renew both sets of front brake pads at the same time – never renew the pads on only one wheel, as uneven braking may result. Note that the dust created by wear of the pads may contain asbestos, which is a health hazard. Never blow it out with compressed air, and don't inhale any of it. An approved filtering mask should be worn when working on the brakes. DO NOT use petrol or petroleum-based solvents to clean brake parts; use brake cleaner or methylated spirit only.*

1 Apply the handbrake, then slacken the front roadwheel bolts. Jack up the front of the vehicle and support it on axle stands (see *Jacking and vehicle support*). Remove both front roadwheels.

2 Follow the relevant accompanying photos for the actual pad renewal procedure **(see illustrations 4.2a to 4.2u)**. Be sure to stay in order and read the caption under each illustration, and note the following points:

a) New pads may have an adhesive foil on the backplates. Remove this foil prior to installation.

b) Gently clean the caliper guide surfaces, and apply a little brake assembly grease.

c) When pushing the caliper piston back

4.2a Slide the brake pad wear sensor wiring plug (arrowed) upwards from the mounting bracket and disconnect it. Note that a wear sensor is only fitted to the left-hand caliper

4.2b Unclip the wear sensor wiring from the bracket

4.2c Pull out the retaining clip…

4.2d …and slide out the lower mounting pin

4.2e Pivot the caliper upwards…

4.2f …and secure it to the suspension spring to prevent straining the hose

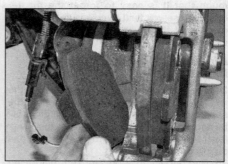

4.2g Remove the inner brake pad…

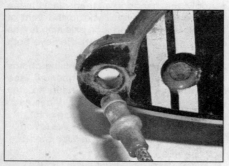

4.2h …and pull out the wear sensor

4.2i Remove the outer brake pad

4.2j Measure the thickness of the friction material. If it's less than 1.5 mm, renew all 4 pads

4.2k Clean the caliper guide surfaces with a soft brush and some brake cleaner

4.2l Fit the outer brake pad. Ensure the fiction material is against the disc surface…

4.2m …followed by the inner pad

4.2n Fit the wear sensor (arrowed) to the inner brake pad

4.2o Use a piston retraction tool to force the piston back into the caliper body. Keep an eye on the fluid level in the master cylinder reservoir

4.2p Lower the caliper over the pads

4.2q Apply a little anti-seize grease to the pin, then slide it through the holes in the bracket and caliper...

4.2r ...and secure it with the retaining clip (arrowed)

4.2s Fit the wiring retaining clip to the bracket...

to accommodate new pads, keep a close eye on the fluid level in the reservoir.

d) Early models have a single brake wear sensor fitted, later models have a brake wear sensor fitted to both sides.

3 Depress the brake pedal repeatedly, until the pads are pressed into firm contact with the brake disc, and normal (non-assisted) pedal pressure is restored.

4 Repeat the above procedure on the remaining front brake caliper.

5 Apply the little anti-seize grease to the hub surface, then refit the roadwheels, lower the vehicle to the ground and tighten the roadwheel bolts to the specified torque.

6 Check the hydraulic fluid level as described in *Weekly checks*.

Caution: New pads will not give full braking efficiency until they have bedded-in. Be prepared for this, and avoid hard braking as far as possible for the first hundred miles or so after pad renewal.

5 Front brake caliper – removal and refitting

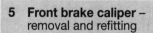

⚠️ *Warning: Before starting work, refer to the warnings at the beginning of Sections 2 and 4 concerning the dangers of hydraulic fluid and asbestos dust.*

4.2t ...reconnect the wiring plug...

4.2u ...and slide it onto the bracket

Removal

1 Firmly apply the handbrake, then jack up the front of the car and support it securely on axle stands (see *Jacking and vehicle support*). Remove the appropriate front roadwheel.

2 Remove the brake pads as described in Section 4.

3 To minimise fluid loss during the following operations, remove the master cylinder reservoir filler cap, then tighten it down onto a piece of polythene, to obtain an airtight seal. Alternatively, use a brake hose clamp to seal off the flexible hydraulic hose running to the caliper.

⚠️ *Warning: Do not use an ordinary G-clamp or mole grips for this purpose, as these can easily*

damage the hydraulic hose internally, possibly leading to failure.

4 Clean the area surrounding the brake hose union, then slacken the union half a turn. It won't be possible to separate the union completely without twisting the hose at this stage.

5 Unscrew the caliper upper guide pin bolt, or slide out the upper pin, and remove the caliper body from the mounting bracket.

6 Hold the brake hose and rotate the caliper to unscrew the hose union from the caliper body. Cover the open ends of the union and the caliper fluid inlet, to prevent dirt ingress. Alternatively, the flexible brake hose may be separated from the rigid brake pipe at the bracket mounted on the inner wheel arch.

5.7 Brake caliper mounting bracket bolts (arrowed)

7 If desired, the caliper mounting bracket can be removed from the swivel hub after unscrewing the two securing bolts (see illustration).

Refitting

8 Where applicable, refit the caliper mounting bracket to the hub carrier. Coat the threads of the mounting bolts with thread-locking compound, then tighten them to the specified torque.

9 Hold the brake hose and rotate the caliper to screw the hose union back into the caliper body.

10 Place the caliper in position on the mounting bracket and tighten the caliper upper guide pin bolt to the specified torque, where applicable.

11 Refit the brake pads as described in Section 4.

12 On all models, tighten the brake hose-to-caliper union securely.

13 Check that the caliper slides smoothly on its guide pins.

14 Remove the polythene from the master cylinder reservoir filler cap, or remove the clamp from the fluid hose, as applicable.

15 Bleed the hydraulic fluid circuit as described in Section 2. Note that if no other part of the system has been disturbed, it should only be necessary to bleed the relevant front circuit.

16 Depress the brake pedal repeatedly to bring the pads into contact with the brake disc, and ensure that normal pedal pressure is restored.

17 Refit the roadwheel, and lower the car to the ground.

6 Brake disc –
inspection, removal and refitting

Inspection

1 Firmly apply the handbrake, then jack up the front of the car and support it securely on axle stands (see Jacking and vehicle support). Remove the front roadwheels.

2 Rotate the brake disc by hand and examine the whole of the surface area swept by the brake pads, on both sides of the disc. Note: It will be necessary to remove the front brake pads to allow an adequate inspection of the disc's inner surface; refer to Section 4 for details.

3 Typically, the disc surface will have a polished appearance and should be free from heavy scoring. Smooth rippling is produced by normal operation and does not indicate excessive wear. Deep scoring and cracks, however, are indications of more serious damage in need of correction.

4 If deep scoring is discovered, it may be possible to have the disc reground to restore the surface, depending on the extent of the damage. To determine whether this is a feasible course of action, it will be necessary to measure the thickness of the disc, as described later.

5 Check the whole surface of the disc for cracks, particularly around the roadwheel bolt holes. A cracked disc must be renewed.

6 A ridge of rust and brake dust at the inner and outer edges of the disc, beyond the pad contact area, is normal – this can be scraped away quite easily.

7 Raised ridges caused by the brake pads eroding the disc material, however, are an indication of excessive wear. If close examination reveals such ridges, the thickness of the disc must be measured, to assess whether it is still fit for use.

8 To measure the thickness of the disc, take readings at several points on the surface using a micrometer, in the area swept by the brake pads (see illustration). Include any points where the disc has been scored; align the jaws of the micrometer with the deepest area of scoring, to get a true indication

of the extent of the wear. Compare these measurements with the limits listed in the Specifications. If the disc has worn below its minimum thickness, at any point, it must be renewed.

9 If the discs are suspected of causing brake judder, check the disc runout, using one of the following methods:

DTI gauge runout measurement

10 Refit the four roadwheel bolts, together with one M14 plain washer per bolt – this will ensure adequate disc-to-hub contact. Tighten the bolts securely.

11 Clamp the DTI gauge to a stand and attach the stand, preferably via a magnetic base, to the strut mounting bracket. Align the gauge so that its pointer rests upon the area of the disc swept by the brake pads, on an arc 2.0 mm from the outer edge of the disc (see illustration).

12 Zero the gauge and slowly rotate the disc through one revolution, observing the pointer movement. Note the maximum deflection recorded and compare the figure with that listed in Specifications.

Feeler blade runout measurement

13 Use the feeler blades to measure the clearance between the disc and a convenient fixed point, such as the caliper mounting bracket. Rotate the disc and measure the variation in clearance at several points around the disc. Compare the maximum figure with that listed in Specifications.

14 If the disc runout is outside of its specified tolerance, first check that the hub is not worn (see Steering and suspension check in Chapter 1). If the hub is in good condition, remove the disc (as described later in this Section), rotate it through 180° and refit it. This may improve the seating and eradicate the excessive runout.

15 If the runout is still unacceptable, then it may be possible to restore the disc by regrinding; consult your Ford dealer or a machine shop for a professional opinion – it may prove more economical to purchase a new disc. If the disc cannot be reground, then it must be renewed.

Removal

16 Mark the relationship between the disc and the hub with chalk or a marker pen, to allow correct refitting.

17 To allow the disc to be removed, undo the two bolts securing the brake caliper mounting bracket to the swivel hub (see illustration 5.7). Withdraw the brake caliper and mounting bracket assembly, complete with brake pads, from the swivel hub, and suspend it from a rigid point on the suspension, using wire or a cable-tie. Do not allow it to hang unsupported as this will strain the brake hose.

18 Slacken and remove the disc locating studs. Support the disc as you do this and lift it off as it becomes free (see illustration).

19 Remove the polished glaze from the surface of the disc with sand/emery paper.

6.8 Measure the thickness of the disc using a micrometer

6.11 Use a dial test indicator (DTI) to measure brake disc runout

Use small, circular motions to avoid producing a directional finish on the surface.

Refitting

20 If a new disc is being fitted, remove the protective coating from the surface using an appropriate solvent.

21 Locate the disc on the hub so that the roadwheel bolt and locating stud holes are all correctly lined up; use the alignment marks made during removal. If the disc is being removed in an attempt to improve seating and hence runout, turn the disc through 180° and then refit it.

22 Refit the locating studs and tighten them securely.

23 Recheck the disc runout, using one of the methods described earlier in this Section.

24 Refit the brake caliper and mounting bracket assembly to the swivel hub. Coat the threads of the mounting bolts with thread-locking compound, then tighten them to the specified torque.

25 Depress the brake pedal several times to bring the brake pads into contact with the disc.

26 Refit the roadwheel and lower the car to the ground.

27 Check the hydraulic fluid level as described in *Weekly checks*.

7 Rear brake drums – removal, inspection and refitting

⚠ *Warning: Before starting work, refer to the warning at the beginning of Section 4 concerning the dangers of asbestos dust.*

Removal

1 Chock the front wheels then jack up the rear of the car and securely support it on axle stands (see *Jacking and vehicle support*). Remove the appropriate rear roadwheel and fully release the handbrake.

2 If the original drum is to be refitted, mark the relationship between the drum and the hub. Slacken and remove the two locating studs and pull the drum from the hub **(see illustration)**.

3 If the drum is binding on the brake shoes, screw two M10 bolts into the locating stud threaded holes in the drum **(see illustration)**, and progressively tighten them against the hub flange to push the drum from the hub.

Inspection

Note: *If either drum requires renewal, BOTH should be renewed at the same time, to ensure even and consistent braking. New brake shoes should also be fitted.*

4 Working carefully, remove all traces of brake dust from the drum, but *avoid inhaling the dust, as it is a health hazard.*

5 Clean the outside of the drum, and check it for obvious signs of wear or damage, such as cracks around the roadwheel stud holes; renew the drum if necessary.

6.18 Undo the studs (arrowed) and remove the disc

6 Carefully examine the inside of the drum. Light scoring of the friction surface is normal, but if heavy scoring is found, the drum must be renewed.

7 It is usual to find a lip on the drum's inboard edge which consists of a mixture of rust and brake dust; this should be carefully scraped away, to leave a smooth surface which can be polished with fine (120- to 150-grade) emery paper. If, however, the lip is due to the friction surface being recessed by excessive wear, then the drum must be renewed.

8 If the drum is thought to be excessively worn, or oval, its internal diameter must be measured at several points using an internal micrometer. Take measurements in pairs, the second at right-angles to the first, and compare the two, to check for signs of ovality. Provided that it does not enlarge the drum to beyond the specified maximum diameter, it may be possible to have the drum refinished by skimming or grinding; if this is not possible, the drums on both sides must be renewed. Note that if the drum is to be skimmed, BOTH drums must be refinished, to maintain a consistent internal diameter on both sides.

Refitting

9 If a new brake drum is to be installed, use a suitable solvent to remove any preservative coating that may have been applied to its internal friction surfaces. Note that it may also be necessary to shorten the adjuster strut length, by rotating the serrated strut wheel, to

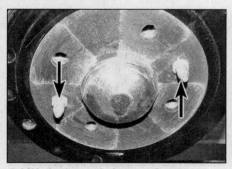

7.2 Undo the studs (arrowed) and remove the drum

allow the drum to pass over the brake shoes – see Section 8 for details.

10 If the original drum is being refitted, align the marks made on the drum and hub before removal, then fit the drum over the hub. Refit the locating studs and tighten them to the specified torque.

11 Depress the footbrake repeatedly to expand the brake shoes against the drum, and ensure that normal pedal pressure is restored.

12 Check and if necessary adjust the handbrake as described in Section 12.

13 Refit the roadwheels, and lower the car to the ground.

8 Rear brake shoes – renewal

⚠ *Warning: Renew BOTH sets of rear brake shoes at the same time – NEVER renew the shoes on only one wheel, as uneven braking may result. Before starting work, refer to the warning given at the beginning of Section 4, concerning the dangers of asbestos dust.*

1 Remove the rear brake drums, as described in Section 7.

2 Working carefully, and taking the necessary precautions, remove all traces of brake dust from the brake drum, backplate and shoes.

3 Measure the thickness of the friction material of each brake shoe at several points; if either shoe is worn at any point to the specified minimum thickness or less, all four shoes must be renewed as a set. The shoes should also be renewed if any are fouled with hydraulic fluid, oil or grease; there is no satisfactory way of degreasing friction material, once contaminated.

4 If any of the brake shoes are worn unevenly, or contaminated, trace and rectify the cause before reassembly.

5 Note the position of each shoe, and the location of the return springs and self-adjuster mechanism to aid refitting later **(see illustrations)**.

6 Depress the leading brake shoe hold-down spring clip and slide the clip out from under the pin head, while holding the pin from the

7.3 Screw 2 M10 bolts into the threaded holes, and push the drum from the hub

8.5a Correct fitted position of the brake shoe upper return spring...

8.5b...and lower return spring

8.6 Depress the shoe hold-down spring clip and slide it from under the pin head

8.7 Pull out the lower end of the shoe and detach the lower return spring

8.8 Depress the remaining clip and remove the pin

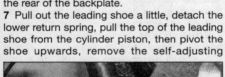

8.9a Slide the handbrake cable end from the lever...

8.9b ...on the trailing shoe – right-hand side brake assembly shown

rear (see illustration). Remove the pin from the rear of the backplate.

7 Pull out the leading shoe a little, detach the lower return spring, pull the top of the leading shoe from the cylinder piston, then pivot the shoe upwards, remove the self-adjusting mechanism, and detach the upper return spring (see illustration).

8 Remove the hold-down spring clip and pin from the trailing brake shoe, then withdraw the shoe from the backplate (see illustration).

9 Slide the handbrake cable end out of the lever on the trailing shoe (see illustrations). Remove the trailing brake shoe.

10 Retain the wheel cylinder pistons in the wheel cylinder using a cable-tie or a strong elastic band. Do not depress the brake pedal until the brakes are reassembled.

11 Carefully examine the self-adjuster mechanism for signs of wear or damage. Pay particular attention to the threads and the toothed adjuster wheel, and renew if necessary.

12 Check the condition of all return springs and renew any that show signs of distortion or other damage.

13 Peel back the rubber protective caps, and check the wheel cylinder for fluid leaks or other damage; check that both cylinder pistons are free to move easily. Refer to Section 9, if necessary, for information on wheel cylinder overhaul.

14 Prior to installation, clean the backplate, and apply a thin smear of high-temperature brake grease or anti-seize compound to all those surfaces of the backplate which bear on the shoes, particularly the wheel cylinder pistons and lower pivot point. Do not allow the lubricant to foul the friction material.

15 Connect the handbrake cable to the lever on the trailing brake shoe, locate the trailing shoe on the backplate and secure in position with the pin and hold-down spring clip (see illustration 8.8).

16 Fit upper brake shoe return spring, and the self-adjuster mechanism into the recess in the trailing brake shoe, then engage the leading shoe with the other end of the adjuster mechanism (see illustrations).

17 Fit the lower brake shoe return spring,

8.16a Engage the upper return spring with the slots in the brake shoes...

8.16b ...then engage the self-adjuster mechanism into the recess in the trailing shoe...

8.16c...and the other end with the leading shoe

engaging it with the slots in the shoes **(see illustration)**. Remove the elastic band or cable-tie from the wheel cylinder.

18 Manoeuvre the leading shoe into position and secure it with the hold-down pin and spring clip.

19 Turn the serrated wheel at the end of the self-adjuster mechanism, to retract the brake shoes – this will give additional clearance to allow the drum to pass over the shoes during refitting.

20 Refit the brake drum as described in Section 7.

21 Repeat the above procedure on the remaining rear brake.

22 Apply the brake pedal and handbrake lever several times to settle the self-adjusting mechanism. With both rear roadwheels refitted and the rear of the car still raised, turn the wheels by hand to check that the brake shoes are not binding. Check and if necessary adjust the operation of the handbrake, as described in Section 12.

23 On completion, check the brake hydraulic fluid level in the master cylinder reservoir as described in *Weekly checks*.

24 Note that new shoes will not give full braking efficiency until they have bedded-in. Be prepared for this, and avoid hard braking as far as possible for the first hundred miles or so after shoe renewal.

9 Rear wheel cylinder – removal, overhaul and refitting

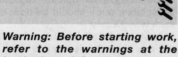

⚠️ *Warning: Before starting work, refer to the warnings at the beginning of Sections 2 and 4 concerning the dangers of hydraulic fluid and asbestos dust.*

Removal

1 Remove the brake drum as described in Section 7.

2 Remove the brake shoes as described in Section 8.

3 To minimise fluid loss during the following operations, remove the master cylinder reservoir filler cap, then tighten it down onto a piece of polythene, to obtain an airtight seal.

4 Clean the brake backplate around the wheel cylinder mounting bolts and the hydraulic pipe union, then unscrew the union nut and disconnect the hydraulic pipe **(see illustration)**. Cover the open ends of the pipe and the wheel cylinder to prevent dirt ingress.

5 Remove the two securing bolts, then withdraw the wheel cylinder from the backplate.

Overhaul

Note: *Before commencing work, ensure that the appropriate wheel cylinder overhaul kit is obtained.*

6 Clean the assembly thoroughly, using only methylated spirit or clean brake fluid.

7 Peel off both rubber dust covers, then use paint or similar to mark one of the pistons so that the pistons are not interchanged on reassembly.

8.17 Refit the lower return spring

8 Withdraw both pistons and the spring.

9 Discard the rubber piston cups and the dust covers. These components should be renewed as a matter of course, and are available as part of an overhaul kit, which also includes the bleed screw dust cap.

10 Check the condition of the cylinder bore and the pistons – the surfaces must be perfect and free from scratches, scoring and corrosion. It is advisable to renew the complete wheel cylinder if there is any doubt as to the condition of the cylinder bore or pistons.

11 Ensure that all components are clean and dry. The pistons, spring and cups should be fitted wet, using hydraulic fluid as a lubricant – soak them in clean fluid before installation.

12 Fit the cups to the pistons, ensuring that they are the correct way round. Use only your fingers (no tools) to manipulate the cups into position.

13 Fit the first piston to the cylinder, taking care not to distort the cup. If the original pistons are being re-used, the marks made on dismantling should be used to ensure that the pistons are refitted to their original bores.

14 Refit the spring and the second piston.

15 Apply a smear of rubber grease to the exposed end of each piston and to the dust cover sealing lips, then fit the dust covers to each end of the wheel cylinder.

Refitting

16 Refitting is a reversal of removal, bearing in mind the following points:

a) *Tighten the mounting bolts to the specified torque.*

b) *Refit the brake shoes as described*

9.4 Rear wheel cylinder hydraulic pipe union and securing bolts (arrowed)

in Section 8, and the brake drum as described in Section 7.

c) *Before refitting the roadwheel and lowering the car to the ground, remove the polythene from the fluid reservoir, and bleed the hydraulic system as described in Section 2. Note that if no other part of the system has been disturbed, it should only be necessary to bleed the relevant rear circuit.*

10 Master cylinder – removal and refitting

⚠️ *Warning: Before starting work, refer to the warning at the beginning of Section 2 concerning the dangers of hydraulic fluid.*

Removal

1 Remove the battery and battery tray as described in Chapter 5A.

2 Remove the air cleaner assembly as described in Chapter 4A.

3 Remove the master cylinder fluid reservoir filler cap, and siphon the hydraulic fluid from the reservoir. **Note:** *Do not siphon the fluid by mouth, as it is poisonous; use a syringe or an old poultry baster.* Alternatively, open any convenient bleed screw in the system, and gently pump the brake pedal to expel the fluid through a tube connected to the screw (see Section 2).

4 Disconnect the wiring connector from the brake fluid level sender unit, and, where applicable, the fluid supply pipe for the clutch master cylinder **(see illustrations)**.

10.4a Disconnect the fluid level sender wiring plug (arrowed)...

10.4b ...and the clutch fluid supply pipe (arrowed)

10.6 Brake master cylinder securing nuts (arrowed)

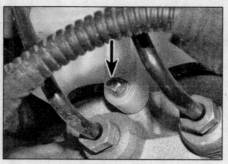

10.7 Master cylinder reservoir retaining pin (arrowed)

5 Wipe clean the area around the brake pipe unions on the side of the master cylinder, and place absorbent rags beneath the pipe unions to catch any surplus fluid. Make a note of the correct fitted positions of the unions, then unscrew the union nuts and carefully withdraw the pipes. Plug or tape over the pipe ends and master cylinder orifices to minimise the loss of brake fluid, and to prevent the entry of dirt into the system. Wash off any spilt fluid immediately with cold water.

6 Slacken and remove the two nuts securing the master cylinder to the vacuum servo unit, then withdraw the unit from the engine compartment **(see illustration)**.

7 If required, pull out the retaining pin and separate the fluid reservoir from the master cylinder **(see illustration)**.

Refitting

8 Remove all traces of dirt from the master cylinder and servo unit mating surfaces and, where applicable, fit a new seal between the master cylinder body and the servo.

9 Refit the reservoir to the master cylinder using new rubber grommets where necessary. Securely refit the retaining pin.

10 Fit the master cylinder to the servo unit, ensuring that the servo unit pushrod enters the master cylinder bore centrally. Refit the master cylinder mounting nuts, and tighten them securely.

11 Wipe clean the brake pipe unions, then refit them to the correct master cylinder ports, as noted before removal, and tighten the union nuts securely.

12 Reconnect the clutch master cylinder

supply hose and the level warning sender wiring plug.

13 Refill the master cylinder reservoir with fresh hydraulic fluid of the specified type (see *Lubricants and fluids*), and bleed the complete hydraulic system as described in Section 2. Note that it may also be necessary to bleed the clutch hydraulic system as described in Chapter 6.

14 Refit the air cleaner assembly, battery and battery tray.

15 On completion, thoroughly check the operation of the brake and clutch systems.

11 Brake light switch – removal and refitting

Note: *Ford insist that if the switch is removed, it must be renewed.*

Removal

1 Disconnect the battery negative lead as described in Chapter 5A.

2 Reach up under the facia on the passenger's side, and disconnect the wiring connector from the switch **(see illustration)**.

3 Twist the switch anti-clockwise through about half a turn, and withdraw the switch from the pedal bracket.

Refitting

4 Depress the brake pedal and hold it in this position.

5 Insert the switch into its mounting bracket. Rotate the switch body clockwise through 90°

until the locating lug is felt to engage in its recess.

6 Release the brake pedal and allow it to rest against the switch plunger – this adjusts the position of the switch body inside the bush.

7 Reconnect the wiring connector, then reconnect the battery lead and test the operation of the brake lights.

12 Handbrake – checking and adjustment

Checking

1 The handbrake should be capable of holding the parked vehicle stationary, even on steep slopes, when applied with moderate force. The mechanism should be firm and positive in feel, with no trace of stiffness or sponginess from the cables, and the mechanism should release immediately the handbrake lever is released. If the mechanism does not operate satisfactorily, it should be checked immediately.

2 To check the operation of the handbrake, chock the front wheels then jack up the rear of the car and securely support it on axle stands (see *Jacking and vehicle support*). Release the handbrake lever.

3 Depress the brake pedal several times to establish the correct shoe-to-drum clearance.

4 With the pedal released, check that the rear roadwheels can be rotated – slight dragging is acceptable, but it should be possible to turn each wheel easily.

5 Apply the handbrake lever and check that the rear roadwheels start to drag after one click of the ratchet mechanism, and are fully locked within 5 clicks of the ratchet.

6 Fully release the handbrake, and check that the rear roadwheels can again be rotated by hand.

7 If the handbrake does not operate as described, carry out the adjustment procedure as follows.

Adjustment

8 Remove the rear section of the centre console as described in Chapter 11 **(see illustration)**.

9 Using a spanner or suitable socket, turn the adjuster nut clockwise to apply tension to the cables, or anti-clockwise to release the tension on the cables, as necessary **(see illustration)**.

11.2 Disconnect the brake light switch wiring plug (arrowed)

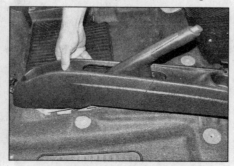

12.8 Remove the centre console

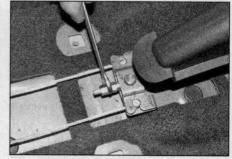

12.9 Adjust the cable tension as required

Check the operation of the handbrake as described previously and repeat the adjustment procedure as required.
10 On completion, refit the rear section of the centre console and lower the car to the ground.

13 Handbrake cables – removal and refitting

Removal

1 There are two rear handbrake cables, one on each side of the car. To renew either rear cable, proceed as follows.
2 Remove the rear section of the centre console as described in Chapter 11.
3 At the base of the handbrake lever, fully slacken the handbrake adjuster nut to remove all tension from the cable draw bar, then disconnect the relevant handbrake inner cable from the draw bar.
4 Depress the retaining tabs and release the outer cables from the floorpan **(see illustration)**.
5 Chock the front wheels then jack up the rear of the car and securely support it on axle stands (see *Jacking and vehicle support*).
6 Remove the rear brake shoes and disconnect the end of the handbrake cable from the lever on the trailing shoe as described in Section 8. Withdraw the cable from the brake backplate.
7 Release the handbrake cable from the retaining clips on the rear axle mounting, exhaust heat shield, fuel tank support bracket and fuel tank, then remove the cable from under the car.

Refitting

8 Refitting is a reversal of removal, bearing in mind the following points:
a) *Ensure that the cable is securely fastened to the clips on the rear axle, heat shield, fuel tank and support bracket.*
b) *Connect the cable to the trailing brake shoe then refit the brake shoes as described in Section 8.*

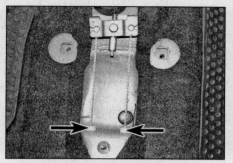
13.4 Depress the tabs (arrowed) and release the outer cables

c) *Refit the centre console as described in Chapter 11.*
d) *On completion, adjust the handbrake as described in Section 12.*

14 Handbrake lever – removal and refitting

Removal

1 Remove the rear section of the centre console as described in Chapter 11, then release the handbrake lever.
2 At the base of the handbrake lever, fully slacken the handbrake adjuster bolt, to remove all tension from the cable draw bar, then disconnect both handbrake inner cables from the draw bar.
3 Disconnect the wiring connector from the handbrake 'on' warning light switch located at the front of the handbrake lever base.
4 Undo the bolts securing the handbrake lever to the floor and remove the lever from the car **(see illustration)**.

Refitting

5 Refitting is a reversal of removal, bearing in mind the following points:
a) *Refit the centre console as described in Chapter 11.*
b) *On completion, adjust the handbrake as described in Section 12.*

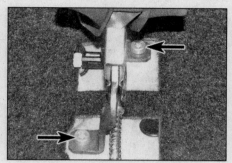
14.4 Handbrake lever securing bolts (arrowed)

15 Handbrake 'on' warning light switch – removal and refitting

Removal

1 Remove the centre console as described in Chapter 11.
2 Disconnect the wiring connector from the switch located at the front of the handbrake lever base **(see illustration)**.
3 Release the retaining clip and remove the switch from its location.

Refitting

4 Refitting is a reversal of removal.

16 Vacuum servo unit – removal and refitting

Removal

1 Remove the master cylinder as described in Section 10.
2 Prise out the grommet and disconnect the vacuum hose from the front of the servo unit.
3 From inside the car, remove the plastic cover, then release the retaining clip securing the brake pedal reaction link to the servo unit pushrod **(see illustrations)**.
4 Undo the nuts securing the servo unit to the

15.2 Handbrake 'on' warning switch wiring plug and retaining clip (arrowed)

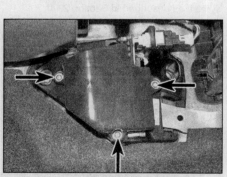
16.3a Undo the screws (arrowed) and remove the plastic cover

16.3b Release the clips (arrowed) and disengage the servo unit pushrod from the reaction link

16.4 Servo unit securing nuts (arrowed)

bulkhead and withdraw the unit from within the engine compartment **(see illustration)**.

Refitting

5 Refitting is a reversal of removal.

17 Anti-lock braking system (ABS) – general information

ABS is fitted as standard equipment on all models. The purpose of the system is to prevent the wheels locking during heavy braking. This is achieved by automatic release of the brake on the relevant wheel, followed by modulated re-application of the brake. The system comprises an electronic control unit, a hydraulic modulator, hydraulic solenoid valves (located in the modulator unit), an electrically-driven fluid return pump, and four wheel speed sensors.

The solenoids (which control the fluid pressure to the calipers/wheel cylinders) are controlled by the electronic control unit, which itself receives signals from the wheel speed sensors. The wheel speed sensors monitor the speed of rotation of each wheel. By comparing the speed signals from the four wheels, the control unit can determine when a wheel is decelerating at an abnormal rate, compared to the speed of the of the other wheels. Using this information, the control unit can predict when a wheel is about to lock, and is able to reduce the fluid pressure to the brake on the relevant wheel to prevent it locking. Once the rotational speed of the monitored wheel returns to approximately that of the other wheels, the hydraulic fluid pressure is increased in stages, to enable braking to continue.

During normal operation, the system functions in the same way as a conventional non-ABS braking system.

18 Anti-lock braking system (ABS) components – removal and refitting

Hydraulic modulator

 Warning: Before starting work, refer to the warning at the beginning of Section 2 concerning the dangers of hydraulic fluid.

Removal

1 Remove the battery and battery tray as described in Chapter 5A.
2 Release the locking clip and disconnect the ECU wiring harness connector.
3 Wipe clean the area around the brake pipe unions on the side of the modulator, and place absorbent rags beneath the pipe unions to catch any surplus fluid. Make a note of the correct fitted positions of the unions, then unscrew the union nuts and carefully withdraw the pipes. Plug or tape over the pipe ends and modulator orifices to minimise the loss of fluid, and to prevent the entry of dirt into the system.
4 Undo the retaining nuts/bolts, and remove the unit from the engine compartment.

Refitting

5 If a new modulator assembly is being fitted, it will be supplied prefilled with hydraulic fluid, and sealed with blanking plugs. Leave the plugs in position until just before connecting the brake pipes.
6 Locate the modulator in position and refit the retaining nuts/bolts.
7 Reconnect the brake pipes to their correct locations as noted during removal and tighten the union nuts securely.
8 Reconnect the ECU wiring connector.
9 Refit the battery and tray as described in Chapter 5A.
10 Bleed the complete brake hydraulic system as described in Section 2.

Electronic control unit

11 The electronic control unit is removed with the modulator assembly as described previously. The ECU is part of the modulator and the two components cannot be separated.

Front wheel speed sensor

Removal

12 Firmly apply the handbrake, then jack up the front of the car and support it securely on axle stands (see *Jacking and vehicle support*). Remove the relevant front roadwheel and wheel arch liner.
13 Trace the wiring back from the sensor, and separate the two halves of the wiring connector. Note the routing of the wiring to aid correct refitting.
14 Unclip the wheel speed sensor wiring from the brackets on the suspension strut **(see illustration)**.
15 Unscrew the retaining bolt and withdraw the sensor from the swivel hub **(see illustrations)**.

Refitting

16 Refitting is a reversal of removal, noting the following points:
  a) *Ensure that the mating faces of the sensor and the swivel hub are clean, and apply a smear of high melting-point brake grease to the sensor location in the swivel hub before refitting.*
  b) *Ensure that the end face of the sensor is clean.*
  c) *Route the wiring as noted before removal.*

Rear wheel speed sensor

Removal

17 Chock the front wheels then jack up the rear of the car and securely support it on axle stands (see *Jacking and vehicle support*). Remove the appropriate rear roadwheel.
18 Trace the wiring back from the sensor to its wiring connector. Free the connector from its retaining clip, and disconnect the wiring from the main wiring loom.
19 Work back along the sensor wiring, and release it from the retaining clips. Note the routing of the wiring to aid correct refitting.

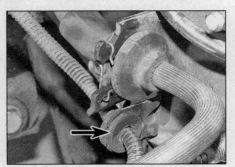

18.14 Unclip the wheel speed sensor wiring (arrowed)

18.15a Undo the retaining bolt (arrowed)...

18.15b ...and withdraw the wheel speed sensor

20 Slacken and remove the bolt securing the sensor unit to the rear stub axle, and remove the sensor and lead assembly **(see illustration)**.

Refitting

21 Refitting is a reversal of removal, noting the following points:

a) *Ensure that the mating faces of the sensor and the stub axle are clean, and apply a smear of high melting-point brake grease to the sensor location in the stub axle before refitting.*

b) *Ensure that the end face of the sensor is clean.*

c) *Route the wiring as noted before removal.*

Yaw/Acceleration sensor

Note: *Only fitted to models with traction control.*

22 Remove the rear cover of the centre console as described in Chapter 11.

23 Disconnect the wiring plug and then remove the mounting bolts.

24 Refitting is a reversal of removal, noting that the sensor must be fitted with the direction arrow pointing to the front of the vehicle.

18.20 Rear wheel speed sensor retaining bolt (arrowed)

Chapter 10
Suspension and steering

Contents

Degrees of difficulty

Easy, suitable for novice with little experience	Fairly easy, suitable for beginner with some experience	Fairly difficult, suitable for competent DIY mechanic	Difficult, suitable for experienced DIY mechanic	Very difficult, suitable for expert DIY or professional

Specifications

Front suspension

Type . . . . Independent, with MacPherson struts and transverse lower suspension arms. Anti-roll bar fitted to all models

Rear suspension

Type . . . . Semi-independent torsion beam axle, with coil springs and telescopic shock absorbers

Steering

Type	Rack-and-pinion with electrically-operated power assistance
Toe setting:	+1.8 mm ± 1 mm
Toe setting (rear – not adjustable)	+ 3.6 mm ± 3 mm
Front camber (not adjustable)	0°34'N ± 30'
Rear camber (not adjustable)	1°10'N ± 30'

Torque wrench settings

	Nm	lbf ft
Front suspension		
Anti-roll bar:		
Mounting bolts	20	15
Link rod nut	50	37
Driveshaft nut:*		
Stage 1	70	52
Stage 2	Angle-tighten a further 55°	
Stage 3	275	203
Front crossmember bolts	40	30
Lower arm balljoint-to-swivel hub	65	48
Lower arm front mounting securing bolt	120	88
Lower arm rear mounting securing bolt	120	88
Subframe bolts:		
Front	120	89
Rear/centre	165	120
Upper	70	52
Subframe extension strut bolts	50	37
Suspension strut piston rod top nut		
Suspension strut-to-swivel hub bolts	75	55
Suspension strut upper mounting (to body)	45	33

Torque wrench settings (continued)

	Nm	lbf ft
Rear suspension		
Hub nut*	310	228
Rear axle mounting brackets to axle	130	96
Rear axle mounting brackets to body	70	52
Shock absorber lower securing bolt	73	54
Shock absorber upper securing bolt	70	52
Stub axle-to-rear axle	73	54
Steering		
Steering column mounting nuts/bolts	15	11
Steering rack mounting bolts	70	52
Steering wheel nut*	50	37
Track rod end-to-swivel hub nut*	40	30
Universal joint clamp bolt*	56	41
Roadwheels		
Roadwheel bolts:		
Steel wheel	85	63
Aluminium wheel	110	81
Do not re-use		

1 General information

Front suspension

The front suspension is independent, comprising transverse lower wishbones, coil spring-over-damper MacPherson strut units and an anti-roll bar. The swivel hubs are bolted to the base of the strut units and are linked to the lower arms by means of balljoints. The entire front suspension assembly is mounted on a subframe, which is in turn bolted to the vehicle body.

Rear suspension

The rear suspension incorporates a torsion beam axle with trailing arms, coil springs and separate double-acting telescopic shock absorbers. The components form a discrete sub-assembly which can be unbolted from

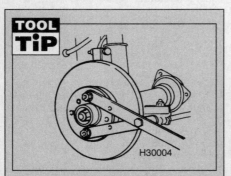

A tool to hold the front hub stationary whilst the driveshaft nut is slackened can be fabricated from two lengths of steel strip (one long, one short) and a nut and bolt; the nut and bolt forming the pivot of a forked tool.

the underside of the vehicle separately or as a complete unit.

Steering

The two-piece steering shaft runs in a tubular column assembly, which is bolted to a bracket mounted on the vehicle bulkhead. The upper shaft is attached to the intermediate shaft by means of a universal joint and the intermediate shaft is similarly connected to the steering gear pinion by a second universal joint.

The rack-and-pinion steering gear is mounted on the front subframe, and is connected by means of track rods to the steering arms projecting rearwards from the swivel hubs. The track rods are fitted with balljoints at their inner and outer ends, to allow for suspension movement, and are threaded to facilitate adjustment.

Electric power steering is fitted to all models. The power assistance is provided by an electric motor and gearbox assembly which is integral with the steering column. The system is controlled by an electronic control unit and is speed sensitive. A lower speeds a greater degree of power assistance is provided for ease of town driving and parking manoeuvres.

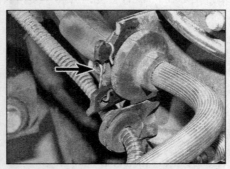

2.4 Release the clip (arrowed) and pull the hose from the strut bracket

2 Front swivel hub assembly – removal and refitting

Note: *A balljoint separator tool will be required for this operation and a new driveshaft retaining nut will be required for refitting.*

Removal

1 Firmly apply the handbrake, then jack up the front of the car and support it securely on axle stands (see *Jacking and vehicle support*). Remove the appropriate front roadwheel.

2 Using a hammer and chisel or similar tool, tap up the staking securing the driveshaft retaining nut in position.

3 The front wheel hub must be held stationary in order to loosen the driveshaft nut. Ideally, the hub should be held by a suitable tool bolted into place using two of the roadwheel bolts **(see Tool Tip)**. Alternatively, have an assistant firmly apply the footbrake to prevent the hub from rotating. Using a socket and extension bar, slacken and remove the driveshaft retaining nut.

⚠️ *Warning: The nut is extremely tight. Discard the nut – a new one must be used on refitting.*

4 Release the brake caliper hydraulic hose from the bracket at the base of the suspension strut **(see illustration)**.

5 Undo the two bolts securing the brake caliper mounting bracket to the swivel hub. Withdraw the caliper and mounting bracket assembly, complete with brake pads, from the disc **(see illustration)**. Suspend the caliper from a convenient place under the wheel arch using string or a cable-tie. Do not allow the caliper to hang unsupported from the brake hydraulic hose.

6 If the swivel hub is being removed for renewal of the bearing, mark the relationship between the brake disc and the hub with

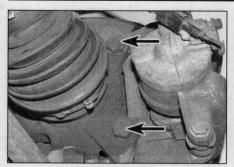

2.5 Undo the bolts (arrowed) and slide the caliper and bracket from the disc

2.7 Disc backplate retaining bolts (arrowed)

2.8 The wheel speed sensor (arrowed) is located on the top of the swivel hub

2.10 Swivel hub-to-suspension strut bolts/nuts (arrowed). Note that the bolts are inserted from the rear

2.12 Undo the nut and remove the balljoint clamp bolt (arrowed)

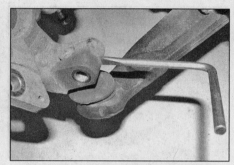

2.13 Use a chisel/screwdriver to spread the clamp slightly, and lift off the hub assembly

chalk or a marker pen, to allow correct refitting. Slacken and remove the disc locating studs, then remove the disc from the wheel hub.

7 Undo the bolts and remove the disc backplate from the swivel hub assembly **(see illustration)**.

8 Release the wheel speed sensor cable from the brackets at the base of the suspension strut. Undo the sensor retaining bolt, withdraw the sensor from the swivel hub and suspend it away from the working area, to avoid the possibility of damage **(see illustration)**.

9 Unscrew the nut securing the track rod end to the swivel hub. Release the track rod end tapered shank using a balljoint separator tool.

10 Unscrew the two nuts and remove the bolts securing the top of the swivel hub to the base of the suspension strut **(see illustration)**.

11 Pull the swivel hub outwards at the top to release the driveshaft outer constant velocity joint from the wheel hub. If necessary, the joint can be tapped free using a soft-faced mallet.

12 Slacken and remove the nut, then withdraw the suspension lower arm balljoint clamp bolt from the swivel hub **(see illustration)**.

13 Tap a small chisel into the split on the swivel hub to spread the hub slightly, then lift the swivel hub assembly up and off the balljoint shank **(see illustration)**.

Refitting

14 Locate the swivel hub over the suspension

lower arm balljoint, pushing it fully into engagement with the balljoint shank. Refit the clamp bolt and secure with the nut tightened to the specified torque.

15 Engage the outer CV joint into the wheel hub, then pivot the top of the swivel hub back towards the car. Screw on the new driveshaft retaining nut, but do not tighten it at this stage.

16 Refit the suspension strut-to-swivel hub bolts, screw on the two nuts and tighten them to the specified torque.

17 Engage the track rod end with the swivel hub, refit the retaining nut and tighten the nut to the specified torque.

18 Ensure that the mating faces of the wheel speed sensor and the swivel hub are clean, and apply a smear of high melting-point brake grease to the sensor location in the swivel hub. Ensure that the end face of the sensor is clean, then locate it in position and secure with the retaining bolt. Refit the sensor cable to the brackets on the suspension strut.

19 Refit the backplate and tighten the retaining bolts securely.

20 Locate the brake disc on the hub so that the roadwheel bolt and locating stud holes are all correctly lined up; use the alignment marks made during removal. Refit the locating studs and tighten them securely.

21 Refit the brake caliper and mounting bracket assembly to the swivel hub. Coat the threads of the mounting bolts with thread-locking compound, then tighten them to the specified torque (see Chapter 9).

22 Refit the brake caliper hydraulic hose to the bracket at the base of the suspension strut.

23 Using the method employed on removal to prevent rotation of the hub, tighten the driveshaft retaining nut to the specified torque. Secure the nut by tapping the staking into the two grooves in the end of the CV joint using a hammer and chisel.

24 Refit the roadwheel, and lower the car to the ground. Depress the brake pedal several times to bring the brake pads into contact with the disc.

25 It is advisable to have the front wheel toe setting checked at the earliest opportunity.

3 Front hub bearings – renewal

Note: *Various special tools, including a hydraulic press, will be required for this operation (see text). If the necessary tools are not available, the swivel hub assembly should be removed as described in Section 2 and taken to a suitably-equipped garage for renewal of the bearing.*

1 Remove the swivel hub assembly as described in Section 2.

2 Press the wheel hub flange from the bearing and extract the hub, together with the bearing inner race **(see illustration)**.

3 The bearing inner race must now be removed from the wheel hub using a suitable puller. To provide sufficient clearance for the

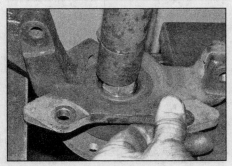

3.2 Press the hub flange from the bearing

3.4 Extract the circlip

3.7a The new bearing is supplied with one side protected by a plastic cap. This indicates which side has the magnetic pulse wheel embedded in the oil seal, which must face inwards against the wheel speed sensor

3.7b Press the new bearing from the inboard side of the hub

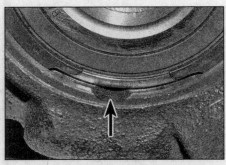

3.8 Locate the new circlip so its ends are either side of the wheel speed sensor location (arrowed)

4 Front suspension strut – removal and refitting

Removal

1 Firmly apply the handbrake, then jack up the front of the car and support it securely on axle stands (see *Jacking and vehicle support*). Remove the appropriate roadwheel(s).
2 Release the brake caliper hydraulic hose and the ABS wheel speed sensor cable from the brackets at the base of the suspension strut.
3 Undo the nut and detach the anti-roll bar link rod from the strut **(see illustration)**. If necessary, counterhold the link rod balljoint shank with an Allen key.
4 Unscrew the two nuts and remove the bolts securing the base of the suspension strut to the top of the swivel hub.
5 Pull the swivel hub outwards at the top to release it from the suspension strut.
6 Remove the windscreen base trim panel as described in Section 22 of Chapter 11.
7 Have an assistant support the strut from underneath the wheel arch. Working in the engine compartment, unscrew the nut securing the upper mounting cup to the strut piston rod while counterholding the piston rod with a suitable Allen key. Lift off the upper mounting cup and withdraw the assembly from under the wheel arch **(see illustration)**.

Refitting

8 Manoeuvre the strut assembly into position under the wheel arch and locate the upper mounting cup over the strut piston. Refit the retaining nut and moderately tighten it at this stage. Final tightening of this nut is carried out with the car resting on its roadwheels.
9 Engage the lower end of the strut with the swivel hub, then fit the securing bolts and nuts. Tighten the nuts to the specified torque.
10 Refit the brake caliper hydraulic hose and the ABS wheel speed sensor cable to the bracket at the base of the suspension strut.
11 Refit the roadwheel, and lower the car to the ground.

puller legs, force the inner race away from the hub flange using a hammer and small chisel inserted between the inner race and the hub flange. When sufficient clearance exists, engage the puller legs behind the inner race and draw the race off the wheel hub.
4 Using a large screwdriver, extract the bearing retaining circlip from the swivel hub **(see illustration)**.
5 Mount the swivel hub on the press bed and press the bearing out of the hub. Note that a flange on the outboard side of the swivel hub means that the bearing can only be removed in one direction.
6 Before installing the new bearing, thoroughly clean the bearing location in the swivel hub.
7 Fit the new bearing from the inboard side the swivel hub and press it fully into position, applying pressure only to the bearing outer

race. Note that one side of the bearing is fitted with a seal which has a magnetic pulse wheel embedded. This side of the bearing must face inwards, against the wheel speed sensor location **(see illustrations)**.
8 Fit the bearing retaining circlip to its groove in the swivel hub so that the circlip's gap is aligned with the aperture for the ABS wheel speed sensor (otherwise the sensor will not function correctly and the ABS failure warning lamp will illuminate) **(see illustration)**.
9 Suitably support the bearing inner race on the press bed and press the wheel hub into the bearing.
10 On completion, check that the wheel hub rotates freely in the bearing without resistance or roughness.
11 Refit the swivel hub assembly as described in Section 2.

4.3 Counterhold the anti-roll bar link with an Allen key

4.7 Undo the strut mounting nut, counterholding with an Allen key/bit

12 With the car resting on its roadwheels, tighten the suspension strut upper mounting cup retaining nut to the specified torque.

5 Front suspension strut – overhaul

Note: *Suitable coil spring compressor tools will be required for this operation.*
Note: *Coil springs should always be replaced as a pair.*

1 Remove the front suspension strut as described in Section 4.
2 Fit suitable spring compressors to the coil spring, and compress the spring sufficiently to enable the upper mounting to be turned by hand **(see illustration)**.

⚠ *Warning: Ensure that the coil spring is compressed sufficiently to remove all the tension from the upper mounting before attempting to remove the piston rod nut.*

3 Unscrew the nut securing the strut piston rod to the upper mounting, while counterholding the piston with a suitable Allen key **(see illustration)**.
4 Withdraw the upper mounting and upper spring seat, then withdraw the spring, complete with the compressors **(see illustration)**.
5 Withdraw the dust cover and bump rubber **(see illustration)**.
6 With the strut assembly now dismantled, examine all the components for wear, damage or deformation. Renew any components as necessary.
7 Examine the strut body for signs of fluid leakage or damage and the piston rod for signs of pitting or scoring. While holding it in an upright position, test the operation of the strut by moving the piston rod through a full stroke, and then through short strokes of 50 to 100 mm. In both cases, the resistance felt should be smooth and continuous. If the resistance is jerky, or uneven, or if there is any visible sign of wear or damage to the strut, renewal is necessary.
8 If any doubt exists about the condition of the coil spring, carefully remove the spring

5.2 Use spring compressors to relieve the tension on the top mounting

5.4 Withdraw the mounting and upper spring seat (arrowed)

5.3 Undo the piston rod nut, counterholding with an Allen key/bit

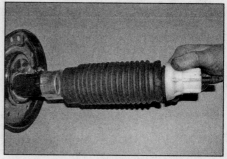

5.5 Withdraw the dust cover and bump rubber

compressors, and check the spring for distortion and signs of cracking. Renew the spring if it is damaged or distorted, or if there is any doubt about its condition.

⚠ *Warning: Coil springs are classified by their height when under load – this is indicated by a coloured paint marking on the side of the coil windings. All coil springs fitted to the vehicle must be of the same classification to ensure the correct ride height.*

9 Begin reassembly by refitting the dust cover and bump rubber.
10 Ensure that the coil spring is compressed sufficiently to enable the upper mounting components to be fitted, then fit the spring over the piston rod, ensuring that the lower end of the spring is correctly located in the recess on the lower spring seat **(see illustration)**.

11 Locate the upper spring seat over the piston rod, ensuring that the raised projection on the spring seat is on the same side as the swivel hub mounting bracket at the base of the strut **(see illustration)**.
12 Refit the upper mounting and position it so that the pointer on the seat flange will be facing the rear of the car when the strut is installed **(see illustration)**.
13 Fit the piston rod top nut, then tighten the nut to the specified torque, counterholding the piston rod in a manner similar to that used during dismantling. Note that a suitable crows-foot adapter or flange-drive socket (Vortex) will be required to tighten the piston rod top nut to the specified torque.
14 Remove the spring compressors and refit the strut to the car as described in Section 4.

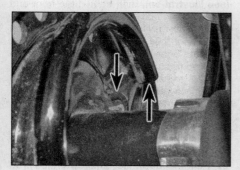

5.10 Ensure the spring end is located against the recess on the lower seat (arrowed)

5.11 The raised projection on the spring seat (arrowed) must align with the swivel hub mounting brackets (arrowed)

5.12 The pointer on the mounting (arrowed) must face the rear of the vehicle

6.3 Remove the support bracket and wheel arch liner panel (arrowed)

6.4 Remove the front, lower crossmember (arrowed)

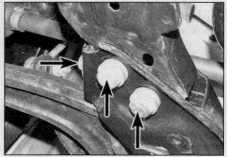

6.5 Undo the bolts (arrowed) and remove the subframe extension strut

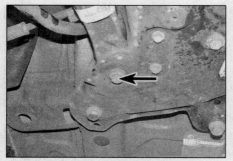

6.8 Lower arm rear mounting bolt (arrowed)

6.9 Lower arm front mounting bolt (arrowed)

6 Front suspension lower arm – removal and refitting

Removal

1 Firmly apply the handbrake, then jack up the front of the car and support it securely on axle stands (see *Jacking and vehicle support*). Remove the relevant roadwheel.

2 Remove the front bumper as described in Chapter 11.

3 Remove the support bracket between the front subframe and the vehicle body, then remove inner wheel arch liner panel (see illustration).

4 Undo the retaining bolts and remove the lower, front crossmember (see illustration).

5 Undo the retaining bolts and remove the extension strut from the front of the subframe on the relevant side (see illustration).

6 Slacken and remove the nut, then withdraw the suspension lower arm balljoint clamp bolt from the swivel hub.

7 Tap a small chisel into the split on the swivel hub to spread the hub slightly, then lever the end of the suspension lower arm down to release it from the base of the swivel hub.

8 Unscrew the bolt securing the suspension lower arm rear mounting to the subframe (see illustration).

9 Slacken and remove the nut from the through-bolt at the lower arm front mounting (see illustration). Withdraw the bolt.

10 Manoeuvre the suspension lower arm from its mounting locations and remove it from under the car.

11 With the lower arm removed, examine the arm itself, and the mounting bushes, for wear, cracks or damage.

12 Check the balljoint for wear, excessive play, or stiffness. Also check the balljoint dust boot for cracks or damage.

13 The mounting bushes and balljoint assembly are integral with the suspension lower arm, and cannot be renewed independently. If either the bushes or the balljoint are worn or damaged, the complete suspension lower arm assembly must be renewed.

Refitting

14 Locate the suspension lower arm in its mountings. Fit the through-bolt to the front mounting bracket and engage it with the lower arm bush. Fit the securing nut, but do not fully-tighten it at this stage.

15 Refit the rear mounting bolt, but do not fully-tighten the bolt at this stage.

16 Using a trolley jack, raise the outer end of the lower arm until it's positioned as shown (see illustration), then tighten the front and rear mounting bolts to the specified torque.

17 Engage the lower arm balljoint with the swivel hub, then refit the balljoint clamp bolt and nut. Tighten the clamp bolt nut to the specified torque.

18 Refit the subframe extension struts, and tighten the retaining bolts to their specified torque.

19 Refit the front crossmember, then tighten the retaining bolts to the specified torque.

20 Refit the wheel arch liner panel, bracket and bumper as described in Chapter 11.

21 Refit the roadwheel, and lower the car to the ground.

22 On completion, have the front wheel toe setting checked at the earliest opportunity.

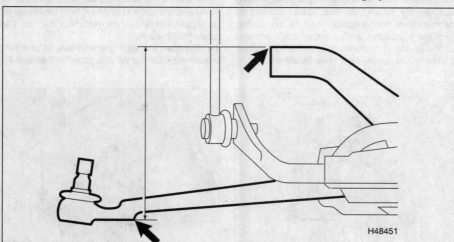

H48451

6.16 Raise the lower arm so the distance between the lower edge and the subframe upper edge is 187 mm

7 Front suspension lower arm balljoint – renewal

The balljoint is integral with the suspension lower arm. If the balljoint is worn or damaged, the complete lower arm must be renewed, as described in Section 6.

8 Front anti-roll bar – removal and refitting

Removal

1 Firmly apply the handbrake, then jack up the front of the car and support it securely on axle stands (see *Jacking and vehicle support*). Remove both front roadwheels.
2 Undo the nut each side, securing the link rods to the ends of the anti-roll bar. Use an Allen key in the balljoint shank to counterhold the nut **(see illustration)**.
3 Undo the bolts and remove the front subframe-to-body bracket each side **(see illustration 6.3)**.
4 Undo the bolts securing the anti-roll bar clamps to the front subframe **(see illustration)**.
5 Undo the bolts securing the steering rack to the subframe **(see illustration 15.10)**.
6 Paint alignment marks between the subframe and vehicle body to aid refitting.
7 Place a workshop/trolley jack under the front subframe, then slacken the retaining bolts and lower the front subframe slightly **(see illustration 9.7)**.
8 Manoeuvre the anti-roll bar assembly through the wheel arch aperture.
9 Inspect the rubber bushes for cracks or deterioration. If renewal is necessary, at the time of writing, it would appear that the complete anti-roll bar must be renewed – the bushes are not available separately. Check with a Ford dealer or parts specialist.
10 Check the anti-roll bar for signs of damage, wear or serious corrosion.

Refitting

11 Refitting is a reversal of removal, bearing in mind the following points:

8.2 Undo the nut (arrowed) securing the anti-roll bar to the link rod

a) Moderately tighten the anti-roll bar mountings initially, then tighten them all to the specified torque after the car has been lowered to the ground and is resting on its roadwheels.
b) Tighten all fasteners to their specified torque where given.
c) Align the previously-made marks prior to tightening the subframe mounting bolts.

9 Front subframe – removal and refitting

Removal

1 Remove both front suspension lower arms as described in Section 6.
2 Undo the bolts and remove the rear, lower engine/transmission link rod.
3 Remove the rear silencer and centre exhaust pipe as described in Chapter 4A.
4 Undo the bolts securing the anti-roll bar clamps to the subframe **(see illustration 8.4)**.
5 Undo the bolts securing the steering rack to the subframe **(see illustration 15.10)**.
6 Paint alignment marks between the subframe and vehicle body to aid refitting.
7 Position a workshop/trolley jack under the subframe, then undo the retaining bolts and lower the subframe from place **(see illustration)**.

Refitting

8 Raise the subframe into position, align the previously-made marks, then tighten the retaining bolts to the specified torque.

8.4 Anti-roll bar clamp bolts (arrowed)

9 The remainder of refitting is a reversal of removal, noting the following points:
a) Tighten all fasteners to their specified torque where given.
b) Moderately tighten the anti-roll bar mountings initially, then tighten them all to the specified torque after the car has been lowered to the ground and is resting on its roadwheels.
c) Have the front wheel alignment checked at the earliest opportunity.

10 Rear hub assembly – removal and refitting

Note: *A new rear hub retaining nut must be used on refitting.*

Removal

1 The rear hub bearings are integral with the hubs themselves, and cannot be renewed separately. If the bearings require renewal, the complete hub assembly must be renewed.
2 Chock the front wheels, then jack up the rear of the vehicle and support securely on axle stands (see *Jacking and vehicle support*). Remove the appropriate rear roadwheel.
3 Remove the brake drum as described in Chapter 9. **Do not** depress the brake pedal whilst the brake drum is removed.
4 Prise the dust cap from the hub, using a mallet and chisel **(see illustration)**.
5 Slacken and remove the hub nut and recover the spacer.
Caution: The nut is tightened to a very high

9.7 Front subframe mounting bolt locations (arrowed)

10.4 Prise off the dust cap

11.3 Rear shock absorber lower mounting bolt...

11.5 ...and upper mounting bolt

torque. *Use a long extension bar to remove the nut and ensure that you have access to torque wrench capable of tightening the new nut to the specified torque before removing the existing nut.*

6 Withdraw the hub and bearing assembly from the stub axle, and recover the inner spacer. Discard the hub nut – a new one must be used on refitting.

7 Thoroughly clean the stub axle, then slide the inner spacer and the hub assembly into position.

8 Fit the outer spacer, then thread a new hub nut onto the end of the stub axle.

9 Tighten the hub nut to the specified torque, then check that the hub spins smoothly and freely. Carefully tap the dust cap into position over the nut.

10 Refit the brake drum as described in Chapter 9.

11 Refit the roadwheel and lower the car to the ground.

11 Rear suspension components – removal and refitting

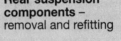

1 Chock the front wheels then jack up the rear of the car and securely support it on axle stands (see *Jacking and vehicle support*). Remove the relevant rear roadwheel(s).

Shock absorber

Removal

2 Using a trolley jack positioned under the rear axle trailing arm, raise the trailing arm to take the strain from the shock absorber.

3 Slacken and withdraw the shock absorber lower retaining bolt **(see illustration)**.

4 Lower the jack and allow the shock absorber to separate from the trailing arm. Take care to avoid displacing the coil spring.

5 Slacken and withdraw the shock absorber upper retaining bolt **(see illustration)**.

6 Withdraw the shock absorber from its upper mounting and remove it from under the car.

7 Examine the shock absorber for signs of fluid leakage or damage.. While holding it in an upright position, test the operation of the shock absorber by moving the piston through a full stroke, and then through short strokes of 50 to 100 mm. In both cases, the resistance

felt should be smooth and continuous. If the resistance is jerky, or uneven, or if there is any visible sign of wear or damage, renewal is necessary. Note that shock absorbers should always be replaced in pairs.

Refitting

8 Refitting is a reversal of removal. Tighten the shock absorber upper and lower retaining bolts to the specified torque, but delay this operation until the full weight of the car is resting on its roadwheels.

Coil spring

Removal

9 Using a trolley jack positioned under the rear axle trailing arm, raise the trailing arm to take the strain from the shock absorbers.

10 Slacken and withdraw the shock absorber lower retaining bolts on both sides.

11 Lower the trailing arm gradually using a trolley jack, until the coil spring is released from its lower seat on the trailing arm and its upper seat on the underbody. Make a note of the orientation of the coil spring, to aid correct refitting later.

Refitting

12 Refitting is a reversal of removal. Tighten the shock absorber retaining bolts to the specified torque, but delay this operation until the full weight of the car is resting on its roadwheels.

Stub axle

Removal

13 Remove the rear hub assembly as described in Section 10.

11.19 Stub axle retaining nuts (arrowed)

14 Remove the rear brake shoes as described in Chapter 9.

15 Using a brake hose clamp, clamp the brake flexible hydraulic hose located adjacent to the rear axle mounting.

16 Clean the brake backplate around the wheel cylinder hydraulic pipe union, then unscrew the union nut and disconnect the hydraulic pipe. Cover the open ends of the pipe and the wheel cylinder to prevent dirt ingress.

17 On models with ABS, slacken and remove the bolt securing the rear wheel speed sensor to the rear of the stub axle and withdraw the sensor from its location. Suspend the sensor away from the working area, to avoid the possibility of damage.

18 Undo the two bolts and remove the brake backplate from the stub axle.

19 Undo the four nuts, withdraw the bolts and remove the stub axle from the rear axle bracket **(see illustration)**.

Refitting

20 Ensure that the stub axle and rear axle bracket mating faces are clean, then locate the stub axle in position. Refit the retaining bolts and nuts and tighten the nuts to the specified torque.

21 Locate the brake backplate on the stub axle, refit the bolts and tighten them securely. Connect the brake pipe to the wheel cylinder and securely tighten the union nut. Remove the brake hose clamp from the flexible hydraulic hose.

22 Refit the rear brake shoes as described in Chapter 9.

23 Refit the rear hub assembly as described in Section 10.

24 Ensure that the mating faces of the wheel speed sensor and the stub axle are clean, and apply a smear of high melting-point brake grease to the sensor location in the stub axle. Clean the end face of the sensor, locate it in place and secure with the retaining bolt.

25 On completion, bleed the brake hydraulic system as described in Chapter 9. Note that if no other part of the system has been disturbed, it should only be necessary to bleed the relevant rear circuit.

Rear axle assembly

Removal

26 Remove the rear brake shoes on both sides as described in Chapter 9.

27 Using brake hose clamps, clamp the brake flexible hydraulic hoses located adjacent to each rear axle mounting.

28 Clean the area around the brake pipe-to-flexible hose union nuts, and unscrew the pipe unions on each side. Extract the retaining clips and detach the flexible hoses from the brackets on the rear axle. Cover the open ends of the pipes and hoses to prevent dirt ingress.

29 Slacken and remove the bolts securing the rear wheel speed sensors to the rear of the stub axles and withdraw the sensors from their location. Suspend the sensors away from the working area, to avoid the possibility of damage.

30 Release the handbrake cables, and where applicable, the rear wheel speed sensor cables, from their clips on the rear axle.

31 Remove both rear coil springs as described previously in this Section.

32 Suitably support the rear axle assembly on a trolley jack and engage the help of an assistant.

33 Undo the bolts securing the rear axle mounting brackets to the underbody on both sides. Slowly lower the jack and guide the axle assembly down and out from under the car.

34 It is possible to renew the axle mounting bushes. Undo the nuts/bolts and remove the mounting bracket from the front end of the axle.

35 Note the fitted position of the bushes, then using a combination of washers, spacers, a length of threaded rod and nuts, draw the bush from place each side.

36 Using soapy water as a lubricant, position the new bushes on the axle, and draw them into place using the same method as removal.

37 Refit the mounting brackets and tighten the nuts/bolts to the specified torque.

Refitting

38 Guide the axle assembly into position, refit the mounting bracket retaining bolts and tighten them to the specified torque.

39 Refit the rear coil springs as described previously in this Section.

40 Ensure that the mating faces of the wheel speed sensors and the stub axles are clean, and apply a smear of high melting-point brake grease to the sensor locations in the stub axles. Clean the end face of the sensors, locate them place and secure with the retaining bolts.

41 Refit the flexible brake hydraulic hoses to their mounting brackets and secure with the retaining clips. Reconnect the brake pipe union to each hose and tighten the union nut securely. Remove the brake hose clamps from the hoses.

42 Secure the handbrake cables, and where applicable, the rear wheel speed sensor cables, in their clips on the rear axle.

43 Refer to Chapter 9 and refit the rear brake shoes then bleed the brake hydraulic system. Note that if no other part of the system has been disturbed, it should only be necessary to bleed the rear circuits.

12 Steering wheel – removal and refitting

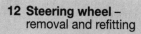

Removal

1 Remove the airbag unit from the steering wheel as described in Chapter 12.

2 Turn the steering wheel to its centre position, so that the roadwheels are pointing straight-ahead.

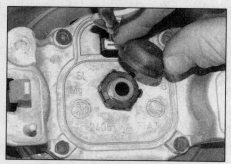

12.3 Lift the protective seal over the retaining nut

3 Lift off the protective seal over the steering wheel retaining nut (see illustration).

4 Open the locking washer tabs and then slacken and remove the steering wheel retaining nut. Discard the nut as a new item must be used on refitting.

5 If no marks are visible, make alignment marks between the steering wheel and the end of the steering column shaft, to aid correct refitting later (see illustration).

6 Lift the steering wheel off the column splines. If it is tight, twist it from side-to-side, whilst pulling upwards to release it from the shaft splines. Once the wheel is free, feed the airbag and horn switch wiring through the aperture in the steering wheel and remove the wheel from the car.

7 With the steering wheel removed, the clock spring assembly should be locked in place. It is advisable to secure the moving and fixed portions of the clock spring together using tape to prevent rotation with the steering wheel removed.

Refitting

8 Check that the airbag clock spring is still centred correctly as described in paragraph 7. Remove the tape used to secure the clock spring moving and fixed portions together.

9 Feed the airbag and horn switch wiring through the steering wheel and locate the wheel on the column splines. Ensure that the marks made on the steering wheel and column shaft are aligned.

10 Screw on a new steering wheel retaining

13.4 Disconnect the wiring plugs

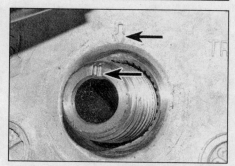

12.5 There should already be alignment marks between the steering wheel and column shaft (arrowed)

nut and tighten the nut to the specified torque. Lock the retaining tabs on the washer in position on the nut using pliers. Refit the protective seal over the retaining nut.

11 Reconnect the horn switch wiring connector.

12 Refit the airbag unit as described in Chapter 12.

13 Steering column – removal and refitting

Removal

1 Remove the steering wheel as described in Section 12.

2 Remove the upper and lower column shrouds as described in Chapter 11.

3 Remove the steering column combination switch assembly as described in Chapter 12.

4 Note their fitted positions and loom routing, then disconnect the various wiring plugs from the column (see illustration).

5 Working in the driver's footwell, unscrew the clamp bolt on the intermediate shaft lower universal joint (see illustration). The joint and rack pinion are equipped with a master spline, so they will only align in one position. Discard the bolt – a new one must be fitted.

6 Undo the steering column retaining nuts/bolts and manoeuvre the assembly away from the bulkhead bracket (see illustrations).

7 Disconnect the universal joint from the

13.5 Intermediate shaft lower clamp bolt (arrowed)

13.6a Steering column upper mounting retaining nuts (arrowed)

13.6b Manoeuvre the steering column assembly away from the bulkhead

steering gear pinion, and with the aid of an assistant, remove the steering column from the car.

Refitting

8 Refitting is a reversal of removal, bearing in mind the following points.
  a) *Ensure that the roadwheels are in the straight-ahead position then engage the universal joint with the steering gear pinion, aligning the marks made on removal.*
  b) *Tighten all retaining nuts and bolts to the specified torque.*
  c) *Refit the steering column stalk switches and airbag clock spring as described in Chapter 12.*
  d) *Refit the steering wheel as described in Section 12.*

14 Power steering electric motor – removal and refitting

Separate parts are not available for the steering column (except for the ignition switch/ steering lock assembly – see Chapter 5A). Consequently, if faulty, the complete steering column assembly must be renewed. Consult a Ford parts specialist.

15 Rack-and-pinion steering gear assembly – removal and refitting

Removal

1 Turn the steering wheel to its centre position, so that the roadwheels are pointing straight-ahead.
2 Firmly apply the handbrake, then jack up the front of the car and support it securely on axle stands (see *Jacking and vehicle support*). Remove both front roadwheels.
3 Remove the front bumper as described in Chapter 11.
4 Remove the support bracket between the front subframe and the vehicle body, then remove inner wheel arch liner panel (see illustrations 6.3).

5 Undo the retaining bolts and remove the lower, front crossmember (see illustration 6.4).
6 Undo the retaining bolts and remove the extension strut from the front of the subframe on the relevant side (see illustration 6.5).
7 Working in the driver's footwell, unscrew the clamp bolt securing the intermediate shaft lower universal joint. Make suitable alignment marks on the steering gear pinion and universal joint to ensure correct orientation when refitting. Discard the bolt – a new one must be fitted.
8 Unscrew the nut securing the track rod end to the swivel hub. Release the track rod end tapered shank using a balljoint separator tool.
9 Undo the bolt securing the rear engine/ transmission mounting to the subframe.
10 Undo the bolts securing the steering rack to the subframe (see illustration).
11 Paint alignment marks between the subframe and vehicle body to aid refitting.
12 Place a workshop/trolley jack under the front subframe, then slacken the retaining bolts and lower the front subframe slightly (see illustration 9.7).
13 Rotate the steering gear downwards to release it from the bulkhead, then withdraw the steering gear through the wheel arch.

Refitting

14 Refitting is a reversal of removal, bearing in mind the following points.
  a) *Centralise the steering gear by turning the pinion so that the rack moves to full left lock. Now move the rack to full right lock, counting the number of turns of the*

15.10 Steering rack mounting bolts (arrowed)

pinion. Turn the pinion back by half the number of turns counted.
  b) *Ensure that the roadwheels are in the straight-ahead position then engage steering gear pinion with the universal joint, aligning the marks made on removal.*
  c) *Align the previously-made marks prior to tightening the subframe mounting bolts.*
  d) *Tighten all retaining nuts and bolts to the specified torque.*
  e) *Have the front wheel toe setting checked at the earliest opportunity.*

16 Steering gear rubber gaiters – renewal

Note: *New gaiter retaining clips should be used on refitting.*
1 Remove the relevant track rod end as described in Section 17.
2 Make an alignment mark between the track rod end locknut and the track rod, to allow the locknut to be accurately positioned when refitting. Unscrew the locknut from the end of the track rod.
3 Mark the correct fitted position of the gaiter on the track rod, then release the gaiter securing clips. Slide the gaiter from the steering gear, and off the end of the track rod.
4 Thoroughly clean the track rod and the steering gear housing, using fine abrasive paper to polish off any corrosion, burrs or sharp edges which might damage the new gaiter sealing lips on installation. Scrape off all the grease from the old gaiter, and apply it to the track rod inner balljoint. (This assumes that grease has not been lost or contaminated as a result of damage to the old gaiter. Use fresh grease if in doubt.)
5 Carefully slide the new gaiter onto the track rod, and locate it on the steering gear housing. Align the outer edge of the gaiter with the mark made on the track rod prior to removal, then secure it in position with new retaining clips.
6 Screw the track rod end locknut onto the end of the track rod and position it accurately in accordance with the mark made on removal.
7 Refit the track rod end as described in Section 17.

17 Track rod end – removal and refitting

Removal

1 Firmly apply the handbrake, then jack up the front of the car and support it securely on axle stands (see *Jacking and vehicle support*). Remove the relevant front roadwheel.
2 Hold the track rod, and unscrew the track rod end locknut by a quarter of a turn. Do not move the locknut from this position, as it will serve as a handy reference mark on refitting.

3 Partially unscrew the nut securing the track rod end to the steering arm **(see illustration)**.
4 Using a balljoint separator tool, separate the track rod end from the steering arm **(see illustration)**. Remove the nut and lift the track rod end from the arm.
5 Counting the **exact** number of turns necessary to do so, unscrew the track rod end from the track rod.

Refitting

6 Carefully clean the track rod end and the track rod threads.
7 Renew the track rod end if the rubber dust cover is cracked, split or perished, or if the movement of the balljoint is either sloppy or too stiff. Also check for other signs of damage such as worn threads.
8 Screw the track rod end onto the track rod by the number of turns noted during removal. This should bring it to within a quarter of a turn from the locknut. Hold the track rod and securely tighten the locknut.
9 Ensure that the balljoint taper is clean, then engage the taper with the steering arm on the swivel hub.
10 Refit the track rod end retaining nut, and tighten the nut to the specified torque.
11 Refit the roadwheel, and lower the car to the ground.
12 Have the front wheel toe setting checked at the earliest opportunity.

18 Wheel alignment and steering angles – general information

Definitions

1 A car's steering and suspension geometry is defined in four basic settings **(see illustration)** – all angles are usually expressed in degrees (toe settings are also expressed as a measurement); the steering axis is defined as an imaginary line drawn through the axis of the suspension strut, extended where necessary to contact the ground.

Camber

2 Camber is the angle between each roadwheel and a vertical line drawn through its centre and tyre contact patch, when viewed from the front or rear of the car. Positive camber is when the roadwheels are tilted outwards from the vertical at the top; negative camber is when they are tilted inwards.
3 The front camber angle is not adjustable, and is given for reference only (see paragraph 5). The rear camber angle is adjustable and can be adjusted using a camber angle gauge.

Castor

4 Castor is the angle between the steering axis and a vertical line drawn through each roadwheel's centre and tyre contact patch, when viewed from the side of the car. Positive castor is when the steering axis is tilted so that it contacts the ground ahead of the vertical;

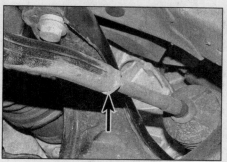
17.3 Use a separator tool to detach the track rod end balljoint from the swivel hub

negative castor is when it contacts the ground behind the vertical.
5 Castor is not adjustable, and is given for reference only; while it can be checked using a castor checking gauge, if the figure obtained is significantly different from that specified, the car must be taken for careful checking by a professional, as the fault can only be caused by wear or damage to the body or suspension components.

Toe

6 Toe is the difference, viewed from above, between lines drawn through the roadwheel centres and the car's centre-line. 'Toe-in' is when the roadwheels point inwards, towards each other at the front, while 'toe-out' is when they splay outwards from each other at the front.
7 The front wheel toe setting is adjusted by screwing the right-hand track rod in or out of its balljoint, to alter the effective length of the track rod assembly.
8 Rear wheel toe setting is also adjustable. The toe setting is adjusted by slackening the trailing arm mounting bracket bolts and repositioning the bracket.

Checking and adjustment

Front wheel toe setting

9 Due to the special measuring equipment necessary to check the wheel alignment, and the skill required to use it properly, the checking and adjustment of these settings is best left to a Ford dealer or similar expert. Note that most tyre-fitting shops now possess sophisticated checking equipment.
10 To check the toe setting, a tracking gauge must first be obtained. Two types of gauge are available, and can be obtained from motor accessory shops. The first type measures the distance between the front and rear inside edges of the roadwheels, as previously described, with the car stationary. The second type, known as a 'scuff plate', measures the actual position of the contact surface of the tyre, in relation to the road surface, with the car in motion. This is achieved by pushing or driving the front tyre over a plate, which then moves slightly according to the scuff of the tyre, and shows this movement on a scale. Both types have their advantages and

17.4 Track rod end locking nut (arrowed)

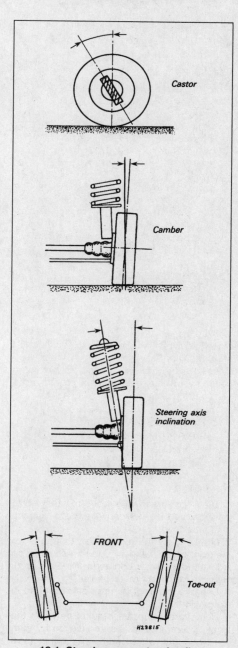
18.1 Steering geometry details

disadvantages, but either can give satisfactory results if used correctly and carefully.

11 Make sure that the steering is in the straight-ahead position when making measurements.

12 If adjustment is necessary, apply the handbrake then jack up the front of the car and support it securely on axle stands.

13 First clean the track rod threads; if they are corroded, apply penetrating fluid before starting adjustment. Release the rubber gaiter outer clips, peel back the gaiters and apply a smear of grease so that both are free and will

not be twisted or strained as their respective track rods are rotated.

14 Retain the track rod with a suitable spanner and slacken the locknut. Alter the length of the track rod, by screwing them into or out of the balljoints by rotating the track rod using an open-ended spanner fitted to the track rod flats provided; shortening the track rods (screwing them onto their balljoints) will reduce toe-in/increase toe-out.

15 When the setting is correct, hold the track rod and tighten the locknut to the specified

torque setting. If after adjustment, the steering wheel spokes are no longer horizontal when the wheels are in the straight-ahead position, remove the steering wheel and reposition it (see Section 17).

16 Check that the toe setting has been correctly adjusted by lowering the car to the ground and rechecking the toe setting; re-adjust if necessary. Ensure that the rubber gaiters are seated correctly and are not twisted or strained, and secure them in position with the retaining clips; where necessary fit a new retaining clip.

Chapter 11
Bodywork and fittings

Contents

Degrees of difficulty

| Easy, suitable for novice with little experience | | Fairly easy, suitable for beginner with some experience | | Fairly difficult, suitable for competent DIY mechanic | | Difficult, suitable for experienced DIY mechanic | | Very difficult, suitable for expert DIY or professional | |

Specifications

Torque wrench settings

	Nm	lbf ft
Front door hinge pin bolt	15	11
Front door hinge (on bodyshell)	27	20
Front seat frame bolts	25	18
Front seat belt inertia reel.	45	33
Front seat belt stalk	45	33
Rear seat belt inertia reel	45	33
Rear seat belt lower anchor on wheel arch	20	15
Rear seat belt stalk.	45	33

1 General information

The bodyshell is composed of pressed-steel sections which are welded together, although some use of structural adhesives is made. In addition, the front wings are bolted on.

The bonnet, door and some other panels vulnerable to corrosion are fabricated from zinc-coated metal. A coating of anti-chip primer, applied prior to paint spraying provides further protection.

Extensive use is made of plastic materials, mainly in the interior, but also in exterior components. The outer sections of the front and rear bumpers are injection-moulded from a synthetic material which is very strong, and yet light. Plastic components such as wheel arch liners are fitted to the underside of the vehicle, to improve the body's resistance to corrosion.

2 Maintenance – bodywork and underframe

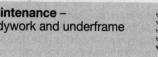

The general condition of a vehicle's bodywork is the one thing that significantly affects its value. Maintenance is easy, but needs to be regular. Neglect, particularly after minor damage, can lead quickly to further deterioration and costly repair bills. It is important also to keep watch on those parts of the vehicle not immediately visible, for instance the underside, inside all the wheel arches, and the lower part of the engine compartment.

The basic maintenance routine for the bodywork is washing – preferably with a lot of water, from a hose. This will remove all the loose solids which may have stuck to the vehicle. It is important to flush these off in such a way as to prevent grit from scratching the finish. The wheel arches and underframe need washing in the same way, to remove any accumulated mud, which will retain moisture and tend to encourage rust. Paradoxically enough, the best time to clean the underframe and wheel arches is in wet weather, when the mud is thoroughly wet and soft. In very wet weather, the underframe is usually cleaned of large accumulations automatically, and this is a good time for inspection.

Periodically, except on vehicles with a wax-based underbody protective coating, it is a good idea to have the whole of the underframe of the vehicle steam-cleaned, engine compartment included, so that a thorough inspection can be carried out to see what minor repairs and renovations are necessary. Steam-cleaning is available at many garages, and is necessary for the removal of the accumulation of oily grime, which sometimes is allowed to become thick in certain areas. If steam-cleaning facilities are not available, there are some excellent grease solvents available which can be brush-applied; the dirt can then be simply hosed off. Note that these methods should not be used on vehicles with wax-based underbody protective coating, or the coating will be removed. Such vehicles should be inspected annually, preferably just prior to Winter, when the underbody should be washed down, and any damage to the wax coating repaired. Ideally, a completely fresh coat should be applied. It would also be worth considering the use of such wax-based protection for injection into door panels, sills, box sections, etc, as an additional safeguard against rust damage, where such protection is not provided by the vehicle manufacturer.

After washing paintwork, wipe off with a chamois leather to give an unspotted clear finish. A coat of clear protective wax polish will give added protection against chemical pollutants in the air. If the paintwork sheen has dulled or oxidised, use a cleaner/polisher combination to restore the brilliance of the shine. This requires a little effort, but such dulling is usually caused because regular washing has been neglected. Care needs to be taken with metallic paintwork, as special non-abrasive cleaner/polisher is required to avoid damage to the finish. Always check that the door and ventilator opening drain holes and pipes are completely clear, so that water can be drained out. Brightwork should be treated in the same way as paintwork. Windscreens and windows can be kept clear of the smeary film which often appears, by the use of proprietary glass cleaner. Never use any form of wax or other body or chromium polish on glass.

3 Maintenance – upholstery and carpets

Mats and carpets should be brushed or vacuum-cleaned regularly, to keep them free of grit. If they are badly stained, remove them from the vehicle for scrubbing or sponging, and make quite sure they are dry before refitting. Seats and interior trim panels can be kept clean by wiping with a damp cloth. If they do become stained (which can be more apparent on light-coloured upholstery), use a little liquid detergent and a soft nail brush to scour the grime out of the grain of the material. Do not forget to keep the headlining clean in the same way as the upholstery. When using liquid cleaners inside the vehicle, do not over-wet the surfaces being cleaned.

Excessive damp could get into the seams and padded interior, causing stains, offensive odours or even rot.

4 Minor body damage – repair

Minor scratches

If the scratch is very superficial, and does not penetrate to the metal of the bodywork, repair is very simple. Lightly rub the area of the scratch with a paintwork renovator, or a very fine cutting paste, to remove loose paint from the scratch, and to clear the surrounding bodywork of wax polish. Rinse the area with clean water.

Apply touch-up paint to the scratch using a fine paint brush; continue to apply fine layers of paint until the surface of the paint in the scratch is level with the surrounding paintwork. Allow the new paint at least two weeks to harden, then blend it into the surrounding paintwork by rubbing the scratch area with a paintwork renovator or a very fine cutting paste. Finally, apply wax polish.

Where the scratch has penetrated right through to the metal of the bodywork, causing the metal to rust, a different repair technique is required. Remove any loose rust from the bottom of the scratch with a penknife, then apply rust-inhibiting paint to prevent the formation of rust in the future. Using a rubber or nylon applicator, fill the scratch with bodystopper paste. If required, this paste can be mixed with cellulose thinners to provide a very thin paste which is ideal for filling narrow scratches. Before the stopper-paste in the scratch hardens, wrap a piece of smooth cotton rag around the top of a finger. Dip the finger in cellulose thinners, and quickly sweep it across the surface of the stopper-paste in the scratch; this will ensure that the surface of the stopper-paste is slightly hollowed. The scratch can now be painted over as described earlier in this Section.

Dents

When deep denting of the vehicle's bodywork has taken place, the first task is to pull the dent out, until the affected bodywork almost attains its original shape. There is little point in trying to restore the original shape completely, as the metal in the damaged area will have stretched on impact, and cannot be reshaped fully to its original contour. It is better to bring the level of the dent up to a point which is about 3 mm below the level of the surrounding bodywork. In cases where the dent is very shallow anyway, it is not worth trying to pull it out at all. If the underside of the dent is accessible, it can be hammered out gently from behind, using a mallet with a wooden or plastic head. Whilst doing this, hold a suitable block of wood firmly against the outside of the panel, to absorb the impact

from the hammer blows and thus prevent a large area of the bodywork from being 'belled-out'.

Should the dent be in a section of the bodywork which has a double skin, or some other factor making it inaccessible from behind, a different technique is called for. Drill several small holes through the metal inside the area – particularly in the deeper section. Then screw long self-tapping screws into the holes, just sufficiently for them to gain a good purchase in the metal. Now the dent can be pulled out by pulling on the protruding heads of the screws with a pair of pliers.

The next stage of the repair is the removal of the paint from the damaged area, and from an inch or so of the surrounding 'sound' bodywork. This is accomplished most easily by using a wire brush or abrasive pad on a power drill, although it can be done just as effectively by hand, using sheets of abrasive paper. To complete the preparation for filling, score the surface of the bare metal with a screwdriver or the tang of a file, or alternatively, drill small holes in the affected area. This will provide a really good 'key' for the filler paste.

To complete the repair, see the Section on filling and respraying.

Rust holes or gashes

Remove all paint from the affected area, and from an inch or so of the surrounding 'sound' bodywork, using an abrasive pad or a wire brush on a power drill. If these are not available, a few sheets of abrasive paper will do the job most effectively. With the paint removed, you will be able to judge the severity of the corrosion, and therefore decide whether to renew the whole panel (if this is possible) or to repair the affected area. New body panels are not as expensive as most people think, and it is often quicker and more satisfactory to fit a new panel than to attempt to repair large areas of corrosion.

Remove all fittings from the affected area, except those which will act as a guide to the original shape of the damaged bodywork (eg headlight shells etc). Then, using tin snips or a hacksaw blade, remove all loose metal and any other metal badly affected by corrosion. Hammer the edges of the hole inwards, in order to create a slight depression for the filler paste.

Wire-brush the affected area to remove the powdery rust from the surface of the remaining metal. Paint the affected area with rust-inhibiting paint, if the back of the rusted area is accessible, treat this also.

Before filling can take place, it will be necessary to block the hole in some way. This can be achieved by the use of aluminium or plastic mesh, or aluminium tape.

Aluminium or plastic mesh, or glass-fibre matting, is probably the best material to use for a large hole. Cut a piece to the approximate size and shape of the hole to be filled, then position it in the hole so that its edges are below the level of the surrounding bodywork.

It can be retained in position by several blobs of filler paste around its periphery.

Aluminium tape should be used for small or very narrow holes. Pull a piece off the roll, trim it to the approximate size and shape required, then pull off the backing paper (if used) and stick the tape over the hole; it can be overlapped if the thickness of one piece is insufficient. Burnish down the edges of the tape with the handle of a screwdriver or similar, to ensure that the tape is securely attached to the metal underneath.

Filling and respraying

Before using this Section, see the Sections on dent, deep scratch, rust holes and gash repairs.

Many types of bodyfiller are available, but generally speaking, those proprietary kits which contain a tin of filler paste and a tube of resin hardener are best for this type of repair. A wide, flexible plastic or nylon applicator will be found invaluable for imparting a smooth and well-contoured finish to the surface of the filler.

Mix up a little filler on a clean piece of card or board – measure the hardener carefully (follow the maker's instructions on the pack), otherwise the filler will set too rapidly or too slowly. Using the applicator, apply the filler paste to the prepared area; draw the applicator across the surface of the filler to achieve the correct contour and to level the surface. As soon as a contour that approximates to the correct one is achieved, stop working the paste – if you carry on too long, the paste will become sticky and begin to 'pick-up' on the applicator. Continue to add thin layers of filler paste at 20-minute intervals, until the level of the filler is just proud of the surrounding bodywork.

Once the filler has hardened, the excess can be removed using a metal plane or file. From then on, progressively-finer grades of abrasive paper should be used, starting with a 40-grade production paper, and finishing with a 400-grade wet-and-dry paper. Always wrap the abrasive paper around a flat rubber, cork, or wooden block – otherwise the surface of the filler will not be completely flat. During the smoothing of the filler surface, the wet-and-dry paper should be periodically rinsed in water. This will ensure that a very smooth finish is imparted to the filler at the final stage.

At this stage, the dent should be surrounded by a ring of bare metal, which in turn should be encircled by the finely 'feathered' edge of the good paintwork. Rinse the repair area with clean water, until all of the dust produced by the rubbing-down operation has gone.

Spray the whole area with a light coat of primer – this will show up any imperfections in the surface of the filler. Repair these imperfections with fresh filler paste or bodystopper, and once more smooth the surface with abrasive paper. Repeat this spray-and-repair procedure until you are satisfied that the surface of the filler, and the

feathered edge of the paintwork, are perfect. Clean the repair area with clean water, and allow to dry fully.

The repair area is now ready for final spraying. Paint spraying must be carried out in a warm, dry, windless and dust-free atmosphere. This condition can be created artificially if you have access to a large indoor working area, but if you are forced to work in the open, you will have to pick your day very carefully. If you are working indoors, dousing the floor in the work area with water will help to settle the dust which would otherwise be in the atmosphere. If the repair area is confined to one body panel, mask off the surrounding panels; this will help to minimise the effects of a slight mis-match in paint colours. Bodywork fittings (eg chrome strips, door handles etc) will also need to be masked off. Use genuine masking tape, and several thicknesses of newspaper, for the masking operations.

Before commencing to spray, agitate the aerosol can thoroughly, then spray a test area (an old tin, or similar) until the technique is mastered. Cover the repair area with a thick coat of primer; the thickness should be built up using several thin layers of paint, rather than one thick one. Using 400-grade wet-and-dry paper, rub down the surface of the primer until it is really smooth. While doing this, the work area should be thoroughly doused with water, and the wet-and-dry paper periodically rinsed in water. Allow to dry before spraying on more paint.

Spray on the top coat, again building up the thickness by using several thin layers of paint. Start spraying at one edge of the repair area, and then, using a side-to-side motion, work until the whole repair area and about 2 inches of the surrounding original paintwork is covered. Remove all masking material 10 to 15 minutes after spraying on the final coat of paint.

Allow the new paint at least two weeks to harden, then, using a paintwork renovator, or a very fine cutting paste, blend the edges of the paint into the existing paintwork. Finally, apply wax polish.

Plastic components

With the use of more and more plastic body components by the vehicle manufacturers (eg bumpers. spoilers, and in some cases major body panels), rectification of more serious damage to such items has become a matter of either entrusting repair work to a specialist in this field, or renewing complete components. Repair of such damage by the DIY owner is not really feasible, owing to the cost of the equipment and materials required for effecting such repairs. The basic technique involves making a groove along the line of the crack in the plastic, using a rotary burr in a power drill. The damaged part is then welded back together, using a hot-air gun to heat up and fuse a plastic filler rod into the groove. Any excess plastic is then removed, and the area rubbed down to a smooth finish. It is

important that a filler rod of the correct plastic is used, as body components can be made of a variety of different types (eg polycarbonate, ABS, polypropylene).

Damage of a less serious nature (abrasions, minor cracks etc) can be repaired by the DIY owner using a two-part epoxy filler repair material. Once mixed in equal proportions, this is used in similar fashion to the bodywork filler used on metal panels. The filler is usually cured in twenty to thirty minutes, ready for sanding and painting.

If the owner is renewing a complete component himself, or if he has repaired it with epoxy filler, he will be left with the problem of finding a suitable paint for finishing which is compatible with the type of plastic used. At one time, the use of a universal paint was not possible, owing to the complex range of plastics encountered in body component applications. Standard paints, generally speaking, will not bond to plastic or rubber satisfactorily. However, it is now possible to obtain a plastic body parts finishing kit which consists of a pre-primer treatment, a primer and coloured top coat. Full instructions are normally supplied with a kit, but basically, the method of use is to first apply the pre-primer to the component concerned, and allow it to dry for up to 30 minutes. Then the primer is applied, and left to dry for about an hour before finally applying the special-coloured top coat. The result is a correctly-coloured component, where the paint will flex with the plastic or rubber, a property that standard paint does not normally possess.

5 Major body damage – repair

Where serious damage has occurred, or large areas need renewal due to neglect, it means that complete new panels will need welding-in, and this is best left to professionals. If the damage is due to impact, it will also be necessary to check completely the alignment of the bodyshell, and this can only be carried out accurately by a Ford dealer using special jigs. If the alignment of the bodyshell is not corrected, the car's handling may be seriously affected. In addition, excessive stress may be imposed on the steering, suspension, tyres or transmission, causing abnormal wear or even complete failure.

6 Bumpers – removal and refitting

Front bumper

1 Apply the handbrake and then jack up the front of the car. Support the car securely on axle stands (see *Jacking and vehicle support*).

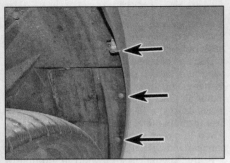

6.3 Remove the fixings (arrowed)

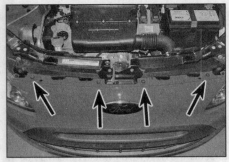

6.5 Slacken the upper screws (arrowed)

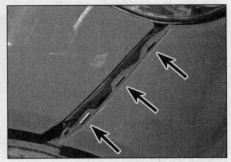

6.6 Note the position of the locating tabs (arrowed)

2 Where front foglights are fitted, open the access doors and disconnect the wiring plugs from each foglight.

3 Undo the fasteners securing the front section of the wheel arch liner on each side and then remove the single upper bolt that secures the front bumper to the front wing **(see illustration)**. Access can be improved by removing the front wheels.

4 Undo the screws at the lower edge of the bumper.

5 Slacken, but do not fully remove the screws at the top edge of the bumper **(see illustration)**.

6 Release the bumper ends from the front wing **(see illustration)**. Note how the locating tabs lock into the support panel.

7 With an assistant supporting the bumper, fully remove the upper mounting screws and then carefully lift the bumper away from the front of the car.

8 Refitting is a reversal of removal.

Rear bumper

9 Chock the front wheels, then jack up the rear of the car and support it securely on axle stands (see *Jacking and vehicle support*). For improved access, remove the rear wheels.

10 Remove the rear lights as described in Chapter 12.

11 Undo the fasteners securing the wheel arch liner to the bumper each side, then pull forwards the liner and then remove the single screw that secures the bumper to the rear wing **(see illustrations)**.

12 Undo the screws on the underside of the bumper.

13 Undo the fasteners on the upper edge of the bumper **(see illustration)**.

14 With the aid of an assistant, carefully lift the bumper away from the car. Disconnect the

wiring plugs from the number plate lamps **(see illustration)** and (where fitted) disconnect the wiring plug from the rear parking sensors, as the bumper is removed.

15 Refitting is a reversal of removal.

7 Radiator grille – removal and refitting

1 Remove the front number plate.

2 Remove the 2 fixing screws from the centre of the grille **(see illustration)**.

3 It is possible to remove the grille with the front bumper on the vehicle, however to avoid damaging the paint work, we removed the bumper, placed it on an old blanket and removed the grille by releasing the locking tabs from the rear **(see illustration)**.

4 Refitting is a reversal of removal.

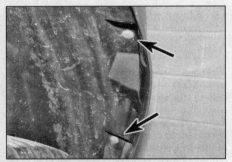

6.11a Undo the wheel arch liner-to-bumper screws (arrowed)...

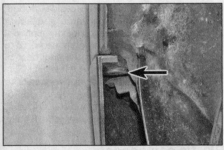

6.11b ...then pull the liner forwards and remove the bumper-to-wing screw each side (arrowed)

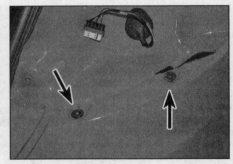

6.13 Remove the screws from the top edge (arrowed) of the bumper each side

6.14 Disconnect the wiring plugs and unclip the loom

7.2 Remove the screws (arrowed)

7.3 Release the locking tabs (arrowed) from the perimeter of the grille

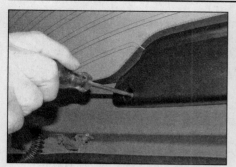

8.4 Remove the high level brake light

8.6 Release the grommet from the tailgate

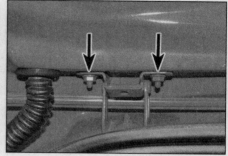

8.10 Remove the nuts (arrowed) from the hinges

8 Tailgate – removal and refitting

Removal

1 Disconnect the battery negative terminal as described in Chapter 5A.
2 Remove the tailgate inner trim panel as described in Section 25.
3 On models fitted with a rear spoiler remove the screws from each end of the spoiler and then work the spoiler free from the adhesive tape. Recover the seal and gasket.
4 Undo the screws and remove the high-level brake light (see illustration). Disconnect the wiring plug.
5 Disconnect the various wiring connectors for the tailgate lock, tailgate handle, heated windscreen and tailgate wiper motor then unbolt any earth leads. Check for any other wiring connectors which must be disconnected to facilitate tailgate removal. **Note:** *Carefully label each wiring harness connector to aid correct refitting.*
6 Tie a length of cord to the wiring harness, then bind the loose ends of the cabling together using PVC tape. Prise the wiring harness grommet from the upper edge of the tailgate (see illustration), then feed the wiring through the aperture in the tailgate. Untie the cord from the harness, but leave it in place in the tailgate, to aid refitting later.
7 Disconnect the fluid hose from the tailgate washer nozzle, then tie a length of cord to

the hose and draw it out of the tailgate, using the same procedure carried out on the wiring harness.
8 Have an assistant support the tailgate in the open position.
9 Detach the upper ends of the support struts from the tailgate as described in Section 9.
10 Slacken and unscrew the nuts securing the hinges to the tailgate (see illustration), then lift the tailgate from the vehicle.

Refitting

11 Refitting is a reversal of removal, bearing in mind the following points.
 a) Tie the cord to the wiring harness and use it to pull the harness through the aperture and into the tailgate. Repeat the procedure on the washer fluid hose.
 b) Do not fully tighten the hinge bolts/nuts until the tailgate adjustment has been checked, as described in the following paragraphs.
 c) On models fitted with a spoiler, clean off the adhesive and the apply new double side adhesive tape before refitting the spoiler.

Adjustment

12 Close the tailgate **carefully**, in case the alignment is incorrect, which may cause scratching on the tailgate or the body as the tailgate is closed, and check for alignment with the adjacent panels. If necessary, slacken the bolts/nuts that secure the hinges to the bodywork and re-align the tailgate to suit. Once the tailgate is correctly aligned, tighten the hinge bolts/nuts securely.

13 Check that the tailgate fastens and releases in a satisfactory manner. If adjustment is necessary, slacken the striker plate retaining bolts, and adjust the position of the striker to suit. Once the lock is operating correctly, securely tighten the striker plate retaining bolts.
14 If necessary, adjust the protrusion of the rubber buffers at the lower edge of the tailgate by screwing them in or out, as appropriate.

9 Tailgate strut – removal and refitting

Removal

1 Open the tailgate and support it using suitable wooden props.
2 At the upper end of each strut, lever out the balljoint spring clip a little. Compress the strut slightly by hand and then prise the strut balljoint from the stud on the tailgate (see illustration).

⚠️ *Warning: The strut may still be under tension and could extend suddenly once detached from its mountings.*

3 Release the lower end of each strut from the studs on the rear wings in the same way.

Refitting

4 Refitting is a reversal of removal.

10 Tailgate lock components – removal and refitting

Lock

1 Remove the tailgate inner trim panel as described in Section 25.
2 Disconnect the wiring plug.
3 Release the retaining clip and then unhook the link rod from the lock.
4 Undo the retaining bolts and manoeuvre the lock from the tailgate (see illustration).
5 Refitting is a reversal of removal.

Exterior handle assembly

6 Remove the tailgate inner trim panel as described in Section 25.

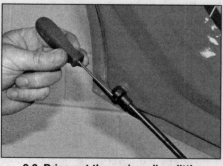

9.2 Prise out the spring clip a little

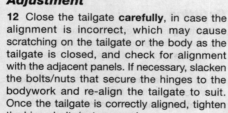
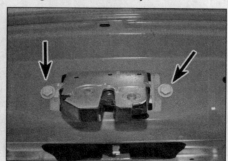

10.4 Lock retaining bolts (arrowed)

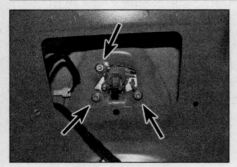

10.8 Remove the nuts (arrowed)

12.2 Remove the mounting bolts (arrowed)

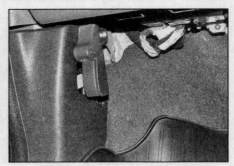

13.4 The bonnet release handle

7 Disconnect the wiring plug and (where fitted) release the link rod from between the lock and the handle.
8 Remove the 3 retaining nuts and remove the lock and handle assembly **(see illustration)**.
9 Refitting is a reversal of removal.

Lock barrel

10 Remove the exterior handle assembly as described previously.
11 Remove the single screw from the barrel.
12 Insert the key into the lock barrel, then prise out the retaining clip and pull the barrel from place. **Do not** remove the key from the barrel.
13 Refitting is the reversal of removal.

Striker plate

14 With the tailgate open, partially release the rear trim panel to expose the striker plate mounting bolts. Mark the position of the striker plate in relation to the bodywork using a pencil or marker pen, to aid accurate refitting.
15 Slacken and unscrew the bolts securing the striker plate to the body.
16 Remove the striker plate from the slam panel.
17 Refitting is a reversal of removal. Use the markings made during removal to give the correct alignment.
18 Check that the tailgate fastens and releases in a satisfactory manner. If adjustment is necessary, slacken the striker plate retaining bolts, and adjust the position of the plate to suit. Once the lock is operating correctly, securely tighten the striker plate retaining bolts.

11 Bonnet –
removal and refitting

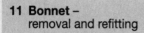

Removal

1 Open the bonnet and prop it up with a stout pole.
2 Mark the relationship between the hinges and the edge of the bonnet using a soft pencil or marker pen. Slacken and unscrew the bolts or nuts (as applicable); have an assistant support the bonnet as the last bolts/nuts are removed.
3 With the help of an assistant, lift off the

bonnet and set it down on its edge, using a dust sheet to protect the paintwork.

Refitting

4 Refit the bonnet and retaining bolts/nuts, using the markings made during removal to achieve the correct alignment. Note that the bolt mounting holes are slotted to allow adjustment if required. On completion, tighten the bolts/nuts securely.
5 If necessary, adjust the bonnet lock assembly, as described in Section 12.

12 Bonnet lock assembly –
removal and refitting

Removal

1 Open the bonnet and mark the relationship between the lock assembly and the front body panel using a soft pencil or marker pen.
2 Slacken and unscrew the two bolts and withdraw the lock assembly from its location **(see illustration)**.
3 Disconnect the lock release cable and remove the lock assembly.

Refitting

4 Refitting is a reversal of removal. Use the alignment markings made during removal to aid accurate refitting. Check that the bonnet fastens and releases in a satisfactory manner, noting that the mounting holes are slotted to allow adjustment of the lock, if required. On completion, tighten the bolts securely.
5 If necessary, adjust the protrusion of the

14.1 Prise free the mirror cover panel

rubber buffers on the front body panel (located above each headlamp unit) by screwing them in or out, as appropriate. When the rubber buffers are correctly adjusted, there should be just enough free movement to allow the bonnet to be closed and locked easily, without using excessive force, but not enough to allow the bonnet to rattle when secured in the locked position.

13 Bonnet release cable –
removal and refitting

Removal

1 Disconnect the release cable from the bonnet lock assembly as described in Section 12.
2 Working around the engine bay, extract the release cable from its securing clips.
3 Remove the glovebox as described in Section 27 of this Chapter.
4 In the passenger's footwell drill out and remove the shear bolts from the Body Control Module (BCM) cover panel. Undo the two bolts securing the release handle mounting bracket to the body **(see illustration)**.
5 Disconnect the cable from the release lever assembly.
6 Tie a length of string to the end of the cable in the engine compartment, then carefully pull the cable through the bulkhead grommet into the passenger's compartment. Untie the string from the cable, but leave it in place in the bulkhead, to aid refitting.

Refitting

7 Refitting is a reversal of removal, using the string to draw the cable through the bulkhead into the engine compartment. Reconnect the cable to the bonnet lock and adjust the lock position as described in Section 12.

14 Door inner trim panel –
removal and refitting

Front door

1 Prise free the cover panel from the door mirror **(see illustration)** and then disconnect the wiring plug (or release the cable).

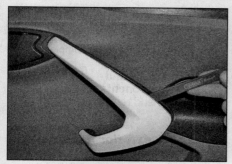

14.2a Prise free and then...

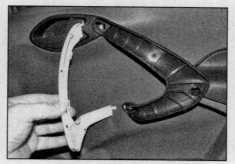

14.2b ...remove the cover

14.3 Remove the cover

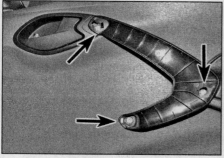

14.4 Remove the screws (arrowed)

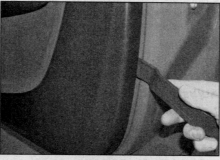

14.5a Release the door panel with a suitable plastic trim tool

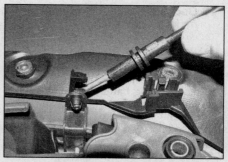

14.5b Support the panel and unhook the lock release cable

2 Using a plastic trim tool prise free the pull handle cover **(see illustrations)** and then on models fitted with manual windows remove the window winder handle retaining clip with a suitable tool. Note the orientation of the retaining clip.

3 Where fitted remove the cover from the release handle retaining screw **(see illustration)** and then remove the screw.

4 Remove the 3 mounting screws from the door pull handle **(see illustration)**.

5 Using a suitable forked tool inserted between the door and the trim panel, release the press-stud

clips located around the edge of the panel, then lift the trim panel upwards. Disconnect the release cable and any wiring plugs as the panel is withdrawn **(see illustrations)**.

6 If work is to be carried out on the door internal components, it will be necessary to remove the plastic membrane from the inside of the door. Start at one corner of the membrane and carefully peel it away, using a sharp blade to split the sealant bead **(see illustration)**. To remove the membrane completely the door speaker will require removal, however for most jobs the membrane

can be folded over the speaker and secured to the A-pillar to keep it out of harms way

7 Refitting is a reversal of removal, bearing in mind the following points:

a) *Ensure that the membrane is correctly refitted, press it on firmly to ensure that it is adequately sealed around its edges. It should be possible to use the original sealant, but if necessary, new sealant can be obtained from a Ford dealer.*

b) *Make sure that the weatherseal engages securely with the top edge of the door as the panel is refitted*

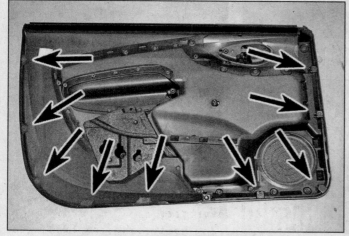

14.5c With the panel removed note the location of the retaining clips (arrowed)

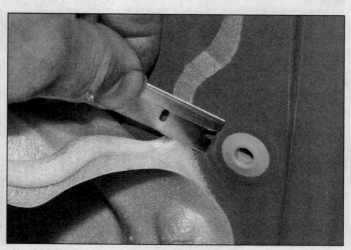

14.6 Use a knife or sharp blade to release the membrane

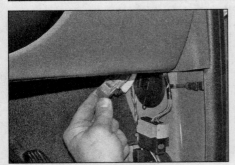

15.3a Disconnect the wiring plug and...

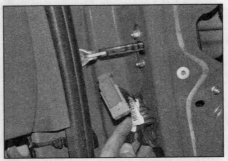

15.3b ...feed the loom through the pillar

15 Door –
removed and refitting

Removal

1 Disconnect the battery negative lead as described in Chapter 5A.

2 Undo the screw/clip and remove the combined door step and footwell kick panel. If removing the passenger's side door, undo the bolts and move the bonnet release lever to one side.

3 Unplug the electrical connector from the inner edge of the A-pillar. Detach the wiring loom rubber gaiter from the outer edge and then feed the wiring loom through the A-pillar **(see illustrations)**.

4 Undo the bolt and release the check strap attachment on the door pillar.

5 Have an assistant support the door and then unscrew the door hinge retaining bolts. Lift the door from the car and store it safely.

Refitting

6 Refitting is a reversal of removal. On completion, tighten the hinge bolts securely.

Adjustment

7 Close the door **carefully**, in case the alignment is incorrect, which may cause scratching on the door or the body as the door is closed, and check the fit of the door with the surrounding panels.

8 If adjustment is required, loosen the hinge-to-body securing bolts (the bolt holes are elongated to allow for adjustment) and move the hinges as required to achieve satisfactory alignment. Tighten the securing bolts securely on completion.

9 Check the operation of the door lock. If necessary, slacken the securing bolts, and adjust the position of the lock striker on the body pillar to achieve satisfactory alignment. Tighten the bolts securely on completion.

16 Door handle and
lock components –
removal and refitting

Front door exterior handle

1 Open the door and remove the small blanking grommet from the door shut **(see illustration)**.

2 Slacken (but do not remove) the now exposed screw. Push on the screw head to release the locking plate from the smaller section of the door handle and then pull the smaller section from the door frame **(see illustration)**. On the drivers door this smaller section of the handle contains the lock barrel.

3 With the smaller section of the handle removed, unhook and remove the main section of the handle **(see illustration)**.

4 Refitting is the reversal of removal.

Front door lock cylinder

5 Remove the exterior handle as described in paragraphs 1 to 3 above and then gently prise free the cylinder cover **(see illustration)**.

6 Insert the ignition key, note the position of the metal retaining clip and then remove it from the cylinder. With care prise free the white plastic cover from the barrel and recover the 2 springs. Finally, extract the lock cylinder from the barrel **(see illustrations)**.

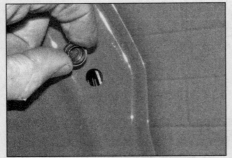

16.1 Remove the blanking plug

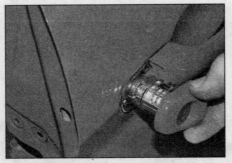

16.2 Release the small section of the exterior handle

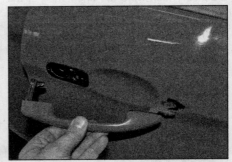

16.3 Unhook the main section of the handle

16.5 Remove the cover

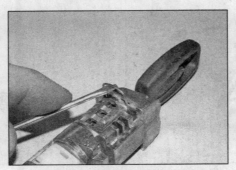

16.6a Release the locking clip

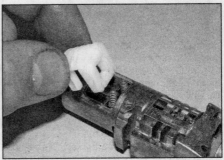

16.6b Prise free the plastic cover (note the position of the springs)...

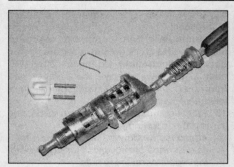

16.6c ...and then pull the cylinder from the barrel

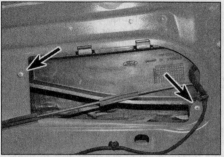

16.11 Drill out the rivets (arrowed)

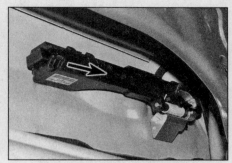

16.12 Release the inner handle support by pushing firmly in the direction shown

7 Locate the lock cylinder in the barrel and secure with the retaining clip. Refit the plastic cover and springs.
8 Refit the door exterior handle as previously described.

Front door exterior handle support

9 Remove the door exterior handle as described above and then remove the small seal from the behind the smaller section of the exterior handle.
10 Remove the door inner trim panel and membrane as described in Section 14.
11 Drill out the rivets and remove the anti-theft cover from the door frame **(see illustration)**. To improve access remove the window guide channel.
12 On the outer side of the door, depress and release the locking tabs from the handle support and then recover the support from the inside of the door frame **(see illustration)**.
13 Partially remove the handle support and unhook the lock release cable.
14 Refitting is a reversal of removal.

Front door interior release handle

15 Remove the door inner trim panel as described in Section 14.
16 Undo the retaining screws and withdraw the handle from the door panel.
17 Refitting is a reversal of removal. Refit the door inner trim panel as described in Section 14.

Front door lock mechanism

18 Disconnect the battery negative lead as described in Chapter 5A.
19 Remove the door inner trim panel as described in Section 14, then drill out the rivets and remove the anti-theft panel.
20 Undo the 2 retaining nuts and remove the window rear guide channel from the door **(see illustration)**.
21 Unhook the lock cylinder link rod from the door lock mechanism.
22 At the trailing edge of the door, remove the three screws that secure the lock mechanism to the door.
23 Manoeuvre the lock mechanism, complete with interior handle release cable out

16.20 Remove the rear window glass guide channel

through the door aperture **(see illustration)**. Disconnect the central locking wiring connectors from the lock motor as the lock is withdrawn. If required, disconnect the release cable.
24 Refitting is a reversal of removal. On completion, refit the door inner trim panel and sealing sheet as described in Section 14.

17 Mirror components – removal and refitting

Door mirror assembly

1 Remove the mirror inner trim panel as described in Section 14.
2 Disconnect the mirror wiring connector (where applicable).

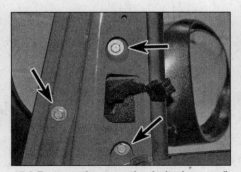

17.3 Remove the mounting bolts (arrowed)

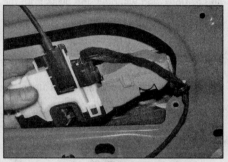

16.23 Manoeuvre the lock from the door frame

3 Hold the mirror securely and then remove the mounting bolts **(see illustration)**.
4 Feed the wiring loom or cable through the door frame and remove the mirror assembly.
5 Refitting is a reversal of removal.

Door mirror glass

6 Push the lower edge of the glass inwards to create an opening between the upper edge of the glass and the mirror body.
7 Insert a blunt, flat-bladed tool between the mirror glass and the mirror body, and carefully release the mirror glass securing clips **(see illustration)**.

 Warning: Protect your hands and eyes from glass splinters.

8 Where applicable, disconnect the heater element wiring from the rear of the glass (see

17.7 Prise between the top of the glass and the mirror body

17.8 Disconnect the wiring plugs (where fitted)

illustration), and withdraw the glass from the mirror assembly.

9 Where applicable, reconnect the wires to the rear of the mirror glass, then push the glass into position to engage the securing clips.

Interior mirror

10 Slide the mirror mounting arm upwards from the bonded base on the windscreen.
11 Refitting is a reversal of removal.

18 Front door window glass and regulator – removal and refitting

Window glass

1 Remove the door inner trim panel and the plastic membrane, as described in Section 14.
2 On models fitted with power windows lower the window until the glass retaining

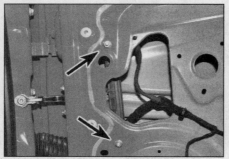

18.3a Remove the bolts (arrowed)...

18.5 Remove the glass

clip is visible through the regulator frame. On models fitted with manual windows, refit the winder handle and lower the window until the retaining clip is visible through the regulator frame.
3 Undo the screws and remove the front window guide channel (see illustrations).
4 Working through the hole in the regulator frame release the locking clip with a suitable screwdriver (see illustration).
5 With care rotate and raise the rear of the window glass. It may be necessary to lower the trailing edge of the glass first to release the plastic clip (fitted to the glass) from the guide channel. Lift up the glass and remove it towards the outside of the vehicle (see illustration).
6 Refitting is a reversal of removal.

Window regulator

7 Separate the window glass from the regulator mechanism, as described above. Note that there is no need to remove the glass guide channel.
8 Fully raise the window glass, and secure the glass in position using suitable tape, or by wedging the glass in position using rags between the glass and the edge of the door – ensure that the glass cannot drop into the door.
9 On models fitted with power windows, disconnect the wiring plug (see illustration).
10 On power window models remove the 2 fixings and on manual window models, unscrew the 5 nuts securing the regulator to the door.

18.3b ...and recover the guide channel

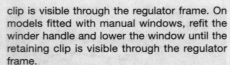

11 Lower the assembly down to the bottom of the door.
12 Manipulate the complete regulator assembly out through the aperture in the door (see illustration). On models fitted with manual windows remove the damper pad from the door frame to extract the regulator mechanism.
13 Refitting is a reversal of removal, bearing in mind the following points:
a) Attach the window glass to the regulator as described previously, before tightening the regulator retaining nuts.
b) Check the operation of the window mechanism before refitting the door inner trim panel.
c) Refit the door inner trim panel and membrane as described in Section 14.

19 Rear window glass – removal and refitting

These areas of glass are secured by the tight fit of the weatherseal in the body aperture, and are bonded in position with a special adhesive. Renewal of such fixed glass is a difficult, messy and time-consuming task, which is considered beyond the scope of the home mechanic. It is difficult, unless one has plenty of practice, to obtain a secure, waterproof fit. Furthermore, the task carries a high risk of breakage. In view of this, owners are strongly advised to have this sort of work carried out by one of the many specialist windscreen fitters.

18.4 Release the glass retaining clip

18.12 Manoeuvre the regulator from the door frame

18.9 Disconnect the wiring plug

20 Windscreen and tailgate glass – general information

These areas of glass are secured by the tight fit of the weatherseal in the body aperture, and are bonded in position with a special adhesive. Renewal of such fixed glass is a difficult, messy and time-consuming task, which is considered beyond the scope of the home mechanic. It is difficult, unless one has plenty of practice, to obtain a secure, waterproof fit. Furthermore, the task carries a high risk of breakage; this applies especially to the laminated glass windscreen. In view of this, owners are strongly advised to have this sort of work carried out by one of the many specialist windscreen fitters.

21 Sunroof – general information

1 Due to the complexity of the sunroof mechanism, considerable expertise is needed to repair, renew or adjust the sunroof components successfully. Removal of the roof first requires the headlining to be removed, which is a complex and tedious operation, and not a task to be undertaken lightly. Therefore, any problems with the sunroof should be referred to a Ford dealer.
2 If the sunroof motor fails to operate, first check the relevant fuse. If the fault cannot be traced and rectified, the sunroof can be opened and closed manually, using the special crank handle supplied in the vehicle tool kit to turn the motor spindle.
3 To gain access to the motor spindle, ensure that the ignition key is in the 'off' position, then carefully prise plastic cap from the headlining. Engage the crank handle with the spindle, and turn the handle to open or close the sunroof.
4 Once the roof is closed, remove the crank handle, and clip the overhead console back into place.

22 Body exterior fittings – removal and refitting

Windscreen scuttle grille panel

1 Open and support the bonnet.
2 Remove the windscreen wiper arms as described in Chapter 12.
3 Pull up the weather seal (see illustration) and then remove the nuts from each end of the panel. Lift up the front of the panel.
4 Move the panel forward to disengage the rear locating clips. Disconnect the washer hose as the panel is withdrawn (see illustration).
5 Before refitting, take the opportunity to

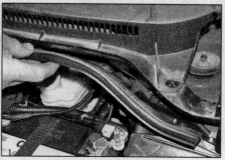

22.3 Remove the seal

clear any leaves/debris from the drain tubes/holes in the base of the scuttle area.
6 Refitting is a reversal of removal.

Wheel arch liners

7 The wheel arch liners are secured by self-tapping screws/fasteners and removal is self-evident and straightforward. Multiple liner panels are used which overlap each other at their edges. In some instances it may be necessary to move aside adjoining panels for access to a specific panel.

Body trim strips and badges

8 The various body trim strips and badges are held in position with a special adhesive tape. Removal requires the trim/badge to be heated, to soften the adhesive, and then cut away from the surface. Due to the high risk of damage to the vehicle paintwork during this operation, it is recommended that this task should be entrusted to a Ford dealer.

23 Seats – removal and refitting

Front seat

⚠️ Warning: Certain models are equipped with side airbags built into the outer sides of the front seats. Refer to Chapter 12 for the precautions which should be observed when dealing with an airbag system. Do

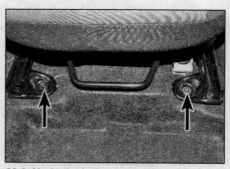

23.3 Undo the bolts at the front of the seat rails (arrowed)

22.4 Disconnect the screen washer hose

not tamper with the airbag unit in any way, and do not attempt to test any airbag system components. Note that the airbag is triggered if the mechanism is supplied with an electrical current (including via an ohmmeter), or if the assembly is subjected to a temperature of greater than 100°C.
1 On models with side airbags in the front seats, de-activate the airbag system, as described in Chapter 12, before attempting to remove the seat.
2 The front seats rails are secured to the floorpan by four bolts.
3 Slide the seat towards the rear of the car to gain access to the two bolts at the front, then slacken and remove them (see illustration).
4 Slide the seat fully forwards and remove the two rearmost bolts (see illustration). Where applicable, disconnect the airbag, and/or seat heater wiring connectors, then remove the seat from the car.
5 Refitting is a reversal of removal.

Rear seat backrest

Fixed rear seat

6 Remove the rear parcel shelf.
7 Release the seat back from its locking catches and tip it forwards.
8 Undo the bolts (2 per side) securing the backrest to the body. Remove the seat back from the car.

Split rear seat backrest

9 Remove the rear parcel shelf.
10 Release the catches and fold the backrests forwards.

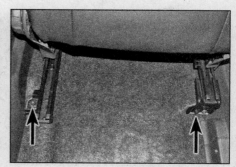

23.4 Remove the rear mounting bolts (arrowed)

23.11 Remove the bracket

23.12 Remove the bolts

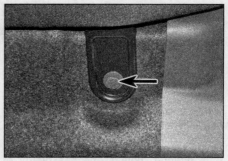

23.15 Undo the bolt (arrowed) each side at the front of the seat cushion

11 Unbolt and remove the central lower mounting bracket **(see illustration)**.
12 Undo the bolts on each side **(see illustration)** and then separate the two sections of the backrest. Recover the spacer from between the backrests.
13 Manoeuvre the backrests from the vehicle.

All models

14 Refitting is a reversal of removal.

Rear seat cushion

15 Undo the 2 bolts at the front lower edge of the cushion **(see illustration)**.
16 Free the seat belt stalks from the cushion and then remove the seat cushion from the vehicle.
17 Refitting is a reversal of removal.

24 Seat belt components – removal and refitting

Note: *Record the positions of the washers and spacers on the seat belt anchors, and ensure they are refitted in their original positions.*

Front seat belt

⚠️ **Warning: On all models, the front seat belt inertia reels are equipped with a pyrotechnic pretensioner mechanism. Refer to the airbag system precautions contained in Chapter 12 which apply equally to the seat belt pretensioners. Do not tamper with the inertia reel pretensioner unit in any way, and do not attempt to test the unit.**

1 Disconnect the battery as described in Chapter 5A and wait a minimum of 10 minutes before working on the seatbelts.
2 Remove the cover from the upper B-pillar mounting and then remove the bolt **(see illustrations)**.
3 Use a small screwdriver and release the lower mounting from the pretensioner **(see illustrations)**.
4 Remove the B-pillar trim panel and the side panel as described in Section 25 of this Chapter.
5 Disconnect the pretensioner wiring plug and undo the mounting bolt **(see illustration)**.
6 Disconnect the wiring plug by depressing the clip and then undo the inertia reel retaining bolt. Withdraw the inertia reel from the centre pillar **(see illustration)** and remove the seatbelt from the vehicle.

24.2a Remove the cover and...

24.2b ...then the bolt

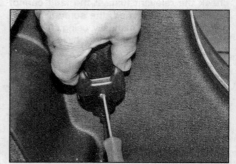

24.3a Release the lower mounting...

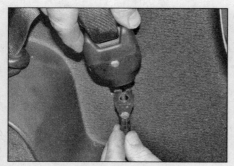

24.3b ...from the pretensioner

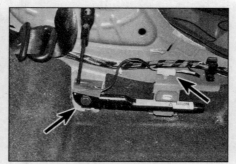

24.5 Remove the wiring plug and then the mounting bolt (arrowed)

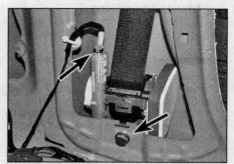

24.6 The inertia reel wiring plug and mounting bolt (arrowed)

7 Refitting is a reversal of removal, ensuring that all mounting bolts are tightened to the specified torque.

Front seat belt stalk

8 Disconnect the battery as described in Chapter 5A and wait a minimum of 10 minutes before working on the seatbelts.
9 Set the seat cushion in its highest position (where possible), then remove the relevant front seat as described in Section 23.
10 Prise the backrest angle adjustment knob from the base of the backrest **(see illustration)**.
11 On the driver's seat, undo the screws, and remove the seat height adjustment lever **(see illustration)**.
12 Carefully pull the front and rear edges of the seat cushion side trim panel from place, then manoeuvre the panel upwards from the retaining clips **(see illustration)**.
13 Release the wiring loom from any retaining clips, then undo the bolt and remove the seat belt stalk **(see illustration)**.
14 Refitting is a reversal of removal, ensuring that all mounting bolts are tightened securely.

Rear seat outer belt

15 Remove the rear seat cushion as described in Section 23.
16 Remove the rear parcel shelf support panel and as described in Section 25.
17 Where fitted, remove the foam cover from the seat belt inertia reel.
18 Undo the inertia reel retaining bolt, the upper bolt and the lower bolt **(see illustrations)**. Remove the seat belt assembly from the car.
19 Refitting is a reversal of removal, but tighten the seat belt anchor bolts to the specified torque.

Rear seat belt stalk

20 Remove the rear seat cushion as described in Section 23.
21 Undo the retaining bolts and remove the seat belt stalks **(see illustration)**.
22 Refitting is a reversal of removal, ensuring that all mounting bolts are tightened to the specified torque.

25 Interior trim panels – removal and refitting

General

1 The interior trim panels are secured by a combination of metal and plastic clips and screws. When releasing certain types of securing clips, a suitable forked tool will prove invaluable to avoid damage to the panel and clips. A degree of force will be necessary to pull some of the panels from their locations, especially where numerous internal retaining clips are used. Be prepared for some of the plastic clips

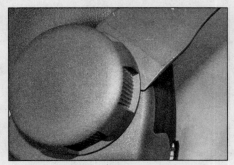

24.10 Prise the backrest angle adjustment knob from place

24.12 Pull out the front and rear edges, then slide the panel upwards from the seat base

to break when their relevant panel is being removed.

Door inner trim panels

2 Refer to Section 14.

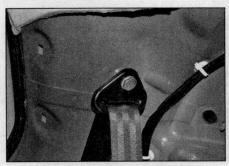

24.18a Remove the upper bolt...

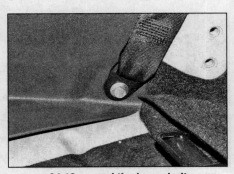

24.18c ...and the lower bolt

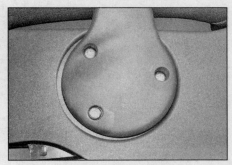

24.11 Undo the screws and remove the height adjustment lever

24.13 Seat belt stalk retaining bolt (arrowed)

Tailgate inner trim panel

3 Unscrew the pull handle and then prise out the push-in clips securing the inner trim panel to the tailgate and remove the panel **(see illustration)**.

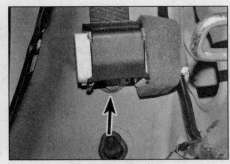

24.18b ...the inertia reel bolt (arrowed)...

24.21 Remove the bolts (arrowed)

25.3 Use a suitable trim tool to remove the clips

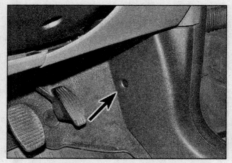

25.5 Remove the screw (arrowed)

25.6 Pull up the trim panel to release it

4 To refit the panel, locate it in position, and push the clips into place.

Door step trim panels

5 Undo the retaining screw at the footwell end of the panel **(see illustration)**.
6 Pull up the door weatherseal and then carefully pull the panel upwards from the sill to release the securing clips **(see illustration)**.
7 To refit the panel, locate it in position, ensuring that the retaining clips engage, and secure with the screw.

A-pillar trim panels

8 On models with side curtain airbags, de-activate the airbag system as described in Chapter 12.
9 Locally remove the front door weatherseal from the edge of the panel.
10 Carefully pull the panel away from the

pillar to release the securing clips. Disconnect the tweeter wiring plug (where fitted)
11 Refitting is a reversal of removal, ensuring the weatherseal is correctly seated.

B-pillar trim panels

12 Locally remove the front door weatherseal from the edge of the B-pillar.
13 Lift up the trim cap over the seat belt upper anchor bolt. Undo the upper anchor bolt and release the seat belt **(see illustrations 24.2a and 24.2b)**. Record the positions of the washers and spacers on the upper anchor bolt to ensure correct refitting.
14 Prise free the upper section of the trim panel **(see illustration)**.
15 The lower section of the B-pillar trim is part of the side trim panel. Removal of the side panel is described below.
16 Refitting is a reversal of removal,

ensuring that all retaining clips are fully engaged. Refit the seat belt upper anchor bolt with the washers and spacers correctly positioned as noted during removal. Tighten the upper anchor bolt to the specified torque.

Side trim panels

17 Remove the sill trim panel as described previously.
18 Locally remove the front door weatherseal from the edge of the centre pillar.
19 Remove the rear seat cushion and seat back as described in Section 23.
20 Remove the B-pillar trim panel as described in this Section.
21 Undo the screw at the lower front edge of the side trim panel and at the upper front edge. Remove a further screw at the rear edge of the panel **(see illustrations)**.
22 Carefully prise the panel away from the body to release the securing clips **(see illustration)**.
23 Refitting is a reversal of removal, ensuring that all retaining clips are fully engaged. Refit the seat belt anchor bolts with the washers and spacers correctly positioned as noted during removal. Tighten the anchor bolts to the specified torque.

C-pillar trim panels

24 Remove the rear parcel shelf, and fold the rear seat backrest forwards.
25 Locally remove the tailgate weatherseal from the edge of the rear pillar.
26 Undo the retaining screws at the lower edge of the combined C-pillar and parcel

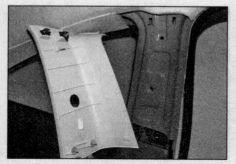

25.14 Remove the upper section of the trim panel

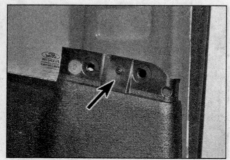

25.21a Remove the upper screw (arrowed)...

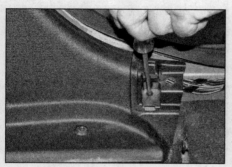

25.21b ...the lower screw...

25.21c ...and the rear screw (arrowed)

25.22 Remove the side panel

shelf support panel **(see illustration)**. Pull the panel inwards to release the retaining clips. If working on the right-hand panel disconnect the wiring plug from the boot light as the panel is removed.

27 If required, undo the rear seat belt lower anchorage bolt and feed the belt through the aperture in the pillar trim panel **(see illustration)**.

28 Refitting is a reversal of removal, ensuring that all retaining clips are fully engaged. Refit the rear seat belt lower anchor bolt with the washers and spacers correctly positioned as noted during removal. Tighten the anchor bolt to the specified torque.

Luggage compartment side trim panel

29 Locally remove the tailgate weatherseal from the edge of the rear pillar.
30 Remove the two screws from the combined parcel shelf and C-pillar trim panel.
31 Remove the side panel.
32 Refitting is a reversal of removal.

Luggage compartment trim panel

33 Lift out the luggage compartment floor covering.
34 Locally remove the tailgate weatherseal from the edge of the trim panel.
35 Remove the screws from the side panel trim as described in this Section.
36 Remove the retaining clips, and manoeuvre the luggage compartment trim panel from place.
37 Refitting is a reversal of removal.

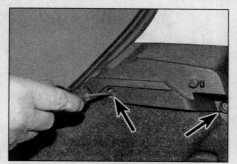

25.26 Remove the screws (arrowed)

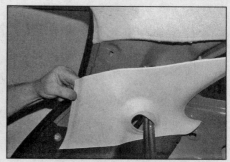

25.27 Feed the seatbelt through the panel

26 Centre console – removal and refitting

Removal

1 Disconnect the battery negative terminal as described in Chapter 5A.
2 At the rear of the handbrake, prise up the cover and remove the single nut **(see illustration)**.
3 With the handbrake applied remove the screw from the front section of the console **(see illustration)**.
4 Pull the console rearward to free it from the front section **(see illustration)** and then manoeuvre the console from the vehicle.

Refitting

5 Refitting is a reversal of removal.

27 Facia panels – removal and refitting

⚠️ *Warning: All models are equipped with an airbag system. The driver's airbag is mounted in the steering wheel centre pad and the passenger's airbag is mounted in the passenger's side of the facia. Make sure that the safety precautions given in Chapter 12 are followed, to prevent personal injury.*

Glovebox

1 Open the glovebox and remove the single centre screw from the rear of the glovebox **(see illustration)**.
2 Close up the glovebox and remove the 3 lower screws. Pull the glovebox from the facia **(see illustrations)**.

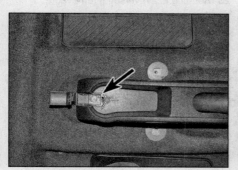

26.2 Remove the single nut at the rear (arrowed)

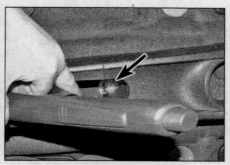

26.3 Remove the front nut (arrowed)

26.4 Separate the rear section of the console

27.1 Remove the single bolt from the rear of the glovebox

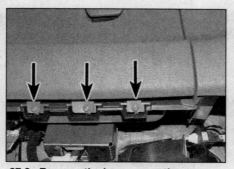

27.2a Remove the lower mounting screws (arrowed)...

27.2b ...and release the glovebox from the facia

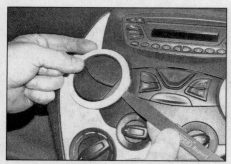
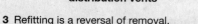

27.7 Use a suitable tool to prise free the air distribution vents

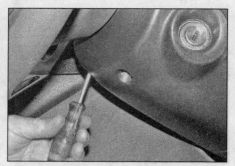

27.10 Remove the lower shroud screws

27.11 Remove the upper shroud retaining screws

3 Refitting is a reversal of removal.

Driver's side lower facia panel

4 Prise free and then pull up the panel to release it.
5 Refitting is a reversal of removal.

Facia vent panels

6 If necessary mask off the surrounding area of the facia to avoid damaging it.
7 Using a suitable plastic trim tool, prise the facia vent panels from place (see illustration).
8 Refitting is a reversal of removal.

Steering column shrouds

9 Fully raise the steering wheel.
10 Undo the 3 lower retaining screws and then remove the lower shroud from the underside of the steering column (see illustration).
11 With the lower shroud removed, locate and remove the 2 screws that retain the upper shroud to the steering column switch assembly (see illustration). Manipulate the shroud out from under the instrument panel and remove the shroud from the column.
12 Refitting is a reversal of removal.

Gearlever trim panel

13 Prise free the gearlever gaiter and then remove the 2 screws from the gaiter support panel (see illustration).
14 Unclip the support panel locking tabs and remove the panel (see illustration), disconnecting the wiring plugs (where fitted) as the panel is removed.
15 Refitting is a reversal of removal.

Gearlever housing panel

16 Remove the gearlever trim panels as described above.
17 On the passenger side prise free the extension panel next to the heater housing (see illustration) and then remove the screws from the main side section of the panel.
18 On the driver's side remove the lower facia panel and then undo the 2 screws and remove the foot rest panel (see illustration). With the foot rest panel removed, remove the screws from the side of the main panel.
19 Remove the centre console as described in Section 26.
20 Remove the 2 lower and 4 upper screws from the panel (see illustrations) and them pull the panel free from the fascia slightly.
21 Where fitted disconnect the wiring plugs from the rear of the panel.
22 Lower the panel slightly and release it from the upper trim panel. Note that it is considerably easier to remove the panel if the facia vents, audio unit, switch panel and the surrounding trim are removed first. Lift the panel out and over the gearlever.
23 Refitting is a reversal of removal.

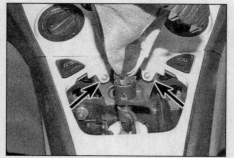

27.13 Remove the screws (arrowed)

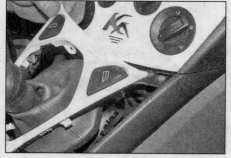

27.14 Release the trim panel

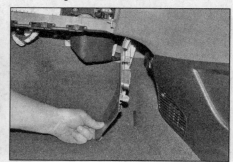

27.17 Remove the extension panel

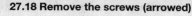

27.18 Remove the screws (arrowed)

27.20a Remove the lower and...

27.20b ...then the upper fixing screws

Complete facia assembly

Note: *This is an involved operation entailing the removal of numerous components and assemblies, and the disconnection of a multitude of wiring connectors. Make notes on the location of all disconnected wiring, or attach labels to the connectors, to avoid confusion when refitting.*

24 Disconnect the battery negative terminal as described in Chapter 5A.

25 If not already done so, remove the audio unit and instrument cluster as described in Chapter 12.

26 Remove the central switch panel as described in Chapter 12.

27 Remove the central air distribution vents as described in paragraphs 6 and 7 of this section.

28 Remove the fixing screws from behind the main switch assembly and then prise free the central trim panel **(see illustration)**.

29 Remove the fixings from the heater/air conditioning control unit **(see illustration)**. Leave the control unit in place.

30 Remove the steering wheel as described in Chapter 10 and then remove the upper and lower column shrouds(as described in paragraphs 9 to 11 of this Chapter).

31 Remove all the facia panels described previously in this Section and then remove the left and right air distribution vents from the ends of the facia panel **(see illustration)**.

32 Remove the instrument panel as described in Chapter 12.

33 Unbolt and move to one side the gearlever mounting bracket.

34 Locate and remove the single bolt from the centre of the facia and then remove the 3 lower bolts from the below the heater control housing.

35 Mark the position of the facia panel in relation to the A-pillars and then remove the mounting bolts from the left and right fascia air vents **(see illustration)**.

36 Remove the lower mounting bolts from the base of the A-pillars.

37 Carefully pull the whole facia moulding away from the bulkhead slightly. Label all remaining wiring connectors to aid correct refitting later, then disconnect them. Check that nothing remains connected between the facia and the crossmember (or bulkhead) and then withdraw the facia and (with the aid of an assistant) remove it from the car.

38 Refitting is a reversal of removal, noting the following points:

a) *Reinstate all electrical connections according to the labels made during removal and ensure that cables are secured in their clips, using the original routing.*

b) *Refer to the Chapters indicated and refit all components disturbed during the removal process.*

c) *On completion, reconnect the battery negative terminal and check the operation*

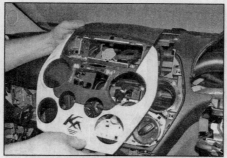

27.28 Remove the trim panel

of all controls, gauges and instruments disturbed during the removal process, including the heating/air conditioning system.

Crossmember

39 Remove the complete fascia panel as previously described.

40 Remove both front doors as described in Section 15.

41 Lift the locking clamp form the Body Control Module (BCM) wiring plugs and then and disconnect the wiring plugs. A drill will be required to remove the shear bolts from the BCM protective cover **(see illustration)**.

42 Remove the earth connection on the front passenger side A-pillar and then disconnect the main wiring plug from the passenger side footwell.

43 Disconnect the wiring plug from the

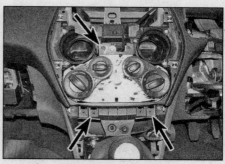

27.29 Remove the heater control unit screws (arrowed)

passenger airbag and then remove the airbag. Store the airbag safely.

44 Depress the locking tab and release the Data Link Connector (DLC) from the crossmember. Some models also have an auxiliary fuse holder adjacent to the DLC; where fitted remove the fuse holder **(see illustration)**.

45 Disconnect the wiring plug from the Airbag control module and then unbolt the adjacent earth connection.

46 Work along the crossmember and release the wiring loom from the multiple retaining clips.

47 Mark the position of the crossmember in relation to the A-pillars and the upper mounting bolts

48 At the transmission tunnel unclip the wiring loom and remove the small support bracket **(see illustration)**.

27.31 Remove the air distribution vents

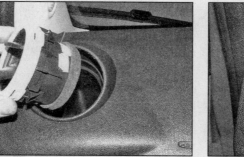

27.35 Remove the screw (arrowed)

27.41 Remove the protective cover from the BCM

27.44 Release the DLC from the crossmember

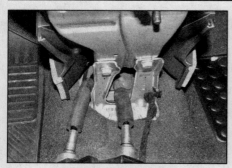

27.48 Remove the bracket

27.50 Remove the bolts (arrowed) from the A-pillars

49 Locate and then remove the bolts that secure the heater housing to the crossmember.

50 Make a final check that all the necessary wiring plugs have been disconnected and

then remove upper mounting bolts. Finally remove the main crossmember bolts from both A-pillars **(see illustration)**.

51 With the aid of an assistant remove the crossmember form the vehicle.

52 Refitting is a reversal of removal, noting the following points:
  a) *Fully wind in the adjustable nuts on each end of the crossmember.*
  b) *Align the crossmember with the previously made alignment marks.*
  c) *Reinstate all electrical connections according to the labels made during removal and ensure that cables are secured in their clips, using the original routing.*
  d) *Refer to the Chapters indicated and refit all components disturbed during the removal process.*
  e) *On completion, reconnect the battery negative terminal and check the operation of all controls, gauges and instruments disturbed during the removal process, including the heating/air conditioning system.*

Chapter 12
Body electrical systems

Contents

Degrees of difficulty

Easy, suitable for novice with little experience	Fairly easy, suitable for beginner with some experience	Fairly difficult, suitable for competent DIY mechanic	Difficult, suitable for experienced DIY mechanic	Very difficult, suitable for expert DIY or professional

Specifications

Bulb ratings

	Watts	Type
Brake light:	21/5	P21/5
Courtesy light	10	C10W
Front direction indicator light	21	PY21W
Front direction indicator side repeater light	5	W5W
Front foglight	55	H1
Front sidelight/running light	5	W5W
Headlights:		
Main beam	55	H4
Dipped beam	55	H4
High-level brake light	5	W5W
Luggage compartment light	5	W5W
Number plate light	5	C5W
Rear direction indicator light	21	PY21W
Rear foglight	21	P21W
Reversing light	21	P21W
Tail light	21/5	P21/5

Torque wrench settings

	Nm	lbf ft
Airbag control unit	10	7
Passenger airbag bolts	10	7

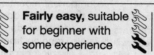

1 General information and precautions

The electrical system is of 12 volt negative earth type. Power for the lights and all electrical accessories is supplied by a lead-acid type battery, which is charged by the alternator.

This Chapter covers repair and service procedures for the various electrical components not associated with the engine. Information on the battery, alternator and starter motor can be found in Chapter 5A.

It should be noted that, prior to working on any component in the electrical system, the battery negative terminal should first be disconnected, to prevent the possibility of electrical short-circuits and/or fires as described in Chapter 5A.

⚠️ *Warning: Before carrying out any work on the electrical system, read through the precautions given in 'Safety first!' at the beginning of this manual, and in Chapter 5A.*

⚠️ *Warning: All models are equipped with an airbag system and pyrotechnic seat belt pretensioners. When working on the electrical system, refer to the precautions given in Section 19, to avoid the possibility of personal injury.*

2 Electrical fault finding – general information

Note: *Refer to the precautions given in 'Safety first!' and in Section 1 of this Chapter before starting work. The following tests relate to testing of the main electrical circuits, and should not be used to test delicate electronic circuits (such as engine management systems and anti-lock braking systems), particularly where an electronic control unit is used.*

General

1 A typical electrical circuit consists of an electrical component, any switches, relays, motors, fuses, fusible links or circuit breakers related to that component, and the wiring and connectors which link the component to both the battery and the chassis. To help to pinpoint a problem in an electrical circuit, wiring diagrams are included at the end of this Chapter.

2 Before attempting to diagnose an electrical fault, first study the appropriate wiring diagram, to obtain a more complete understanding of the components included in the particular circuit concerned. The possible sources of a fault can be narrowed down by noting whether other components related to the circuit are operating properly. If several components or circuits fail at one time, the problem is likely to be related to a shared fuse or earth connection.

3 Electrical problems usually stem from simple causes, such as loose or corroded connections, a faulty earth connection, a blown fuse, a melted fusible link, or a faulty relay (refer to Section 3 for details of testing relays). Visually inspect the condition of all fuses, wires and connections in a problem circuit before testing the components. Use the wiring diagrams to determine which terminal connections will need to be checked, in order to pinpoint the trouble-spot.

4 The basic tools required for electrical fault-finding include a circuit tester or voltmeter (a 12 volt bulb with a set of test leads can also be used for certain tests); a self-powered test light (sometimes known as a continuity tester); an ohmmeter (to measure resistance); a battery and set of test leads; and a jumper wire, preferably with a circuit breaker or fuse incorporated, which can be used to bypass suspect wires or electrical components. Before attempting to locate a problem with test instruments, use the wiring diagram to determine where to make the connections.

5 To find the source of an intermittent wiring fault (usually due to a poor or dirty connection, or damaged wiring insulation), a wiggle test can be performed on the wiring. This involves wiggling the wiring by hand, to see if the fault occurs as the wiring is moved. It should be possible to narrow down the source of the fault to a particular section of wiring. This method of testing can be used in conjunction with any of the tests described in the following sub-Sections.

6 Apart from problems due to poor connections, two basic types of fault can occur in an electrical circuit – open-circuit or short-circuit.

7 Open-circuit faults are caused by a break somewhere in the circuit, which prevents current from flowing. An open-circuit fault will prevent a component from working, but will not cause the relevant circuit fuse to blow.

8 Short-circuit faults are normally caused by a breakdown in wiring insulation, which allows a feed wire to touch either another wire, or an earthed component such as the bodyshell. This allows the current flowing in the circuit to 'escape' along an alternative route, usually to earth. As the circuit does not now follow its original complete path, it is known as a 'short' circuit. A short-circuit fault will normally cause the relevant circuit fuse to blow.

Finding an open-circuit

9 To check for an open-circuit, connect one lead of a circuit tester or voltmeter to either the negative battery terminal or a known good earth.

10 Connect the other lead to a connector in the circuit being tested, preferably nearest to the battery or fuse.

11 Switch on the circuit, bearing in mind that some circuits are live only when the ignition switch is moved to a particular position.

12 If voltage is present (indicated either by the tester bulb lighting or a voltmeter reading,

as applicable), this means that the section of the circuit between the relevant connector and the battery is problem-free.

13 Continue to check the remainder of the circuit in the same fashion.

14 When a point is reached at which no voltage is present, the problem must lie between that point and the previous test point with voltage. Most problems can be traced to a broken, corroded or loose connection.

Finding a short-circuit

15 To check for a short-circuit, first disconnect the load(s) from the circuit (loads are the components which draw current from a circuit, such as bulbs, motors, heating elements, etc).

16 Remove the relevant fuse from the circuit, and connect a circuit tester or voltmeter to the fuse connections.

17 Switch on the circuit, bearing in mind that some circuits are live only when the ignition switch is moved to a particular position.

18 If voltage is present (indicated either by the tester bulb lighting or a voltmeter reading, as applicable), this means that there is a short-circuit.

19 If no voltage is present, but the fuse still blows with the load(s) connected, this indicates an internal fault in the load(s).

Finding an earth fault

20 The battery negative terminal is connected to 'earth' – the metal of the engine/transmission and the car body – and most systems are wired so that they only receive a positive feed, the current returning via the metal of the car body. This means that the component mounting and the body form part of that circuit. Loose or corroded mountings can therefore cause a range of electrical faults, ranging from total failure of a circuit, to a puzzling partial fault. In particular, lights may shine dimly (especially when another circuit sharing the same earth point is in operation), motors (eg, wiper motors or the radiator cooling fan motor) may run slowly, and the operation of one circuit may have an apparently-unrelated effect on another. Note that on many vehicles, earth straps are used between certain components, such as the engine/transmission and the body, usually where there is no metal-to-metal contact between components, due to flexible rubber mountings, etc. Earth connections are made in various places (see illustrations).

21 To check whether a component is properly earthed, disconnect the battery, and connect one lead of an ohmmeter to a known good earth point. Connect the other lead to the wire or earth connection being tested. The resistance reading should be zero; if not, check the connection as follows.

22 If an earth connection is thought to be faulty, dismantle the connection, and clean back to bare metal both the bodyshell and the wire terminal or the component earth connection mating surface. Be careful to

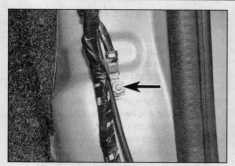

2.20a Some of the earth connections are behind the rear side trim panel (arrowed)...

2.20b ...at the base of the left-hand A-pillar (arrowed)...

2.20c ...camshaft cover (arrowed)...

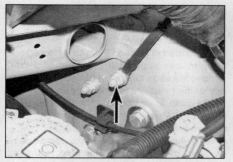

2.20d ...left-hand rear of the engine compartment (arrowed)...

2.20e ...under the heater housing (arrowed)...

2.20f ...and on the left-hand front chassis leg(arrowed)

remove all traces of dirt and corrosion, then use a knife to trim away any paint, so that a clean metal-to-metal joint is made. On reassembly, tighten the joint fasteners securely; if a wire terminal is being refitted, use serrated washers between the terminal and the bodyshell, to ensure a clean and secure connection. When the connection is remade, prevent the onset of corrosion in the future by applying a coat of petroleum jelly or silicone-based grease, or by spraying on (at regular intervals) a proprietary ignition sealer.

3 Fuses and relays –
general information

Fuses

1 Fuses are designed to break a circuit when a predetermined current is reached, in order to protect the components and wiring which could be damaged by excessive current flow. Any excessive current flow will be due to a fault in the circuit, usually a short-circuit (see Section 2).
2 The main fuses are located in the fusebox inside the glove compartment.
3 To gain access to the fuses open the glovebox and open the fusebox cover at the rear of the glovebox. A fuse puller tool is provide in the fusebox cover (see illustrations).
4 Additional fuses and circuit breakers are located in the fuse/relay box in the engine compartment. The fusebox is located next to

the battery on the left-hand side of the engine compartment. Release the clips and lift off the cover to gain access (see illustrations).
5 A blown fuse can be recognised from its melted or broken wire.

6 To remove a fuse, first ensure that the relevant circuit is switched off.
7 Using the plastic tool clipped to the main fusebox, pull the fuse from its location.
8 Spare fuses are provided in the main fusebox.

3.3a Open the fusebox cover and...

3.3b ...use the provided fuse puller to remove the fuse

3.4a Release the clip at the base (arrowed) and slide up the cover...

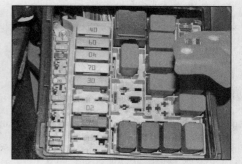

3.4b ...to access the fuses

4.2 Remove the cover

4.3 Remove the headlight bulb

9 Before renewing a blown fuse, trace and rectify the cause, and always use a fuse of the correct rating (fuse ratings are specified on the inside of the fusebox cover panel). Never substitute a fuse of a higher rating, or make temporary repairs using wire or metal foil; more serious damage, or even fire, could result.

10 Note that the fuses are colour-coded as follows. Refer to the wiring diagrams for details of the fuse ratings used and the circuits protected.

Colour	Rating
Orange	5A
Red	10A
Blue	15A
Yellow	20A
Clear or White	25A
Green	30A

Relays

11 A relay is an electrically-operated switch, which is used for the following reasons:
a) *A relay can switch a heavy current remotely from the circuit in which the current is flowing, therefore allowing the use of lighter-gauge wiring and switch contacts.*
b) *A relay can receive more than one control input, unlike a mechanical switch.*
c) *A relay can have a timer function – for example, the intermittent wiper relay.*

12 The main and optional equipment relays are primarily located in the engine compartment fuse/relay box (see *Fuses*). Additional relays may be fitted, depending on model and specification and these are generally mounted adjacent to the component being controlled.

13 If a circuit or system controlled by a relay develops a fault, and the relay is suspect, operate the system. If the relay is functioning, it should be possible to hear it click as it is energised. If this is the case, the fault lies with the components or wiring of the system. If the relay is not being energised, then either the relay is not receiving a main supply or a switching voltage, or the relay itself is faulty. Testing is by the substitution of a known good unit, but be careful – while some relays are identical in appearance and in operation, others look similar but perform different functions.

14 To remove a relay, first ensure that the relevant circuit is switched off. The relay can then simply be pulled out from the socket, and pushed back into position.

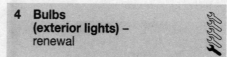

4 Bulbs (exterior lights) – renewal

General

1 Whenever a bulb is renewed, note the following points:
a) *Ensure that the relevant electrical circuit is isolated before removing a bulb. If in doubt, disconnect the battery negative terminal (refer to Disconnecting the battery in the Chapter 5A) before starting work.*
b) *Remember that, if the circuit has just*

been in use, the bulb may be extremely hot.
c) *Always check the bulb contacts and holder, ensuring that there is clean metal-to-metal contact between the bulb and its live contact(s) and earth. Clean off any corrosion or dirt before fitting a new bulb.*
d) *Wherever bayonet-type bulbs are fitted, ensure that the live contact(s) bear firmly against the bulb contact.*
e) *Always ensure that the new bulb is of the correct rating (see Specifications), and that it is completely clean before fitting it; this applies particularly to headlight/ foglight bulbs (see following paragraphs).*

Headlight

Note: *On some models the headlight must be removed completely to change a blown bulb (as described in Section 6 of this Chapter).*
2 Open and support the bonnet and then remove the large centre rubber cover from the rear of the headlight **(see illustration)**.
3 The bulb is removed with the electrical connector. Pull out the connector and then remove the bulb **(see illustration)**.
4 When handling the new bulb, use a tissue or clean cloth to avoid touching the glass with the fingers; moisture and grease from the skin can cause blackening and rapid failure of this type of bulb. If the glass is accidentally touched, wipe it clean using methylated spirit. Avoid knocking or shaking the bulb as this may weaken the filament.
5 Install the new bulb, using a reversal of the removal procedure, ensuring that its locating tabs are correctly located in the light unit cut-outs.

Sidelight/running light

6 Open and support the bonnet.
7 Remove the smaller cover from the rear of the headlight **(see illustration)**.
8 Reach into the aperture and pull the bulb holder to remove it. Using a pair of needle nose pliers to release the bulb holder makes the task easy **(see illustration)**.
9 Remove the push-fit bulb from the bulbholder **(see illustration)**.
10 Fit the new bulb using a reversal of the removal procedure.

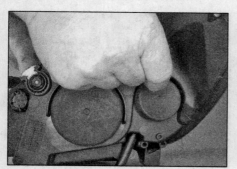

4.7 Remove the cover

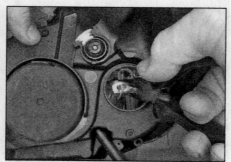

4.8 Use pliers to remove the bulb

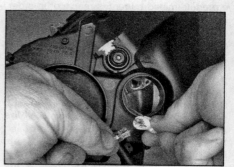

4.9 Pull the bulb from the holder

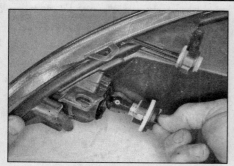

4.12 Twist the indicator bulbholder anti-clockwise and withdraw it

4.17 Push the side repeater forwards to compress the clip (arrowed)

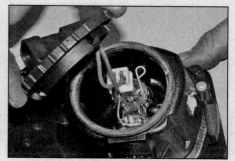

4.23 Twist clockwise to remove the foglight cover

4.25 Release the ends of the retaining clip (arrowed)

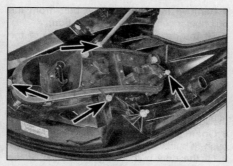

4.28 Undo the screws (arrowed) and remove the bulbholder

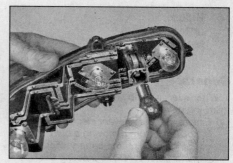

4.29 Remove the relevant bulb from the holder

Front direction indicator

11 Open and support the bonnet.
12 Turn the bulbholder anti-clockwise and remove the bulb holder from the headlight **(see illustration)**.
13 Depress the bulb in the holder and rotate it anti-clockwise to remove the bulb from the bulb holder.
14 Fit the new bulb using a reversal of the removal procedure.

Indicator side repeater

15 If necessary, protect the wing from damage by masking off the paintwork around the lamp.
16 Using a plastic trim tool (or suitable piece of plastic card – a body filler spreader is ideal here) lever the lamp free by first inserting the trim tool at the front edge of the lamp, and then push the lamp towards the rear of the vehicle.
17 Release the rear edge by pushing and levering the lamp towards the front of the vehicle. Remove the lamp **(see illustration)**. Note that the lens is part of the reflector and not a separate assembly
18 Rotate the bulb holder anti-clockwise and remove it from the lamp
19 The bulb is a push-fit in the bulbholder.
20 Fit the new bulb using a reversal of the removal procedure.

Front foglight

21 Jack up and support the front of the vehicle (see *Jacking and vehicle support*).
22 Open the access panel at the rear of

the front bumper and disconnect the wiring plug.
23 Rotate and remove the cover from the rear of the foglight **(see illustration)**.
24 Unplug the wiring connectors from the earth connector and the power supply.
25 Release the retaining clip, hinge it downwards/upwards as applicable, and remove the bulb **(see illustration)**.
26 Fit the new bulb using a reversal of the removal procedure.

Rear light cluster bulbs

27 Remove the rear light cluster as described in Section 6.
28 Undo the 4 retaining screws and remove the bulbholder assembly from the light unit **(see illustration)**.
29 Remove the relevant bulb by pushing it in slightly, and rotating it anti-clockwise **(see illustration)**.

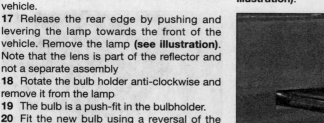

4.31 Prise the number plate light from place

30 Fit the new bulb using a reversal of the removal procedure.

Number plate light

31 Using a small screwdriver, carefully prise the outer edge of the light unit from its location **(see illustration)**
32 Pull the capless bulb from its contacts.
33 Fit the new bulb using a reversal of the removal procedure.

High-level brake light

34 Remove the light unit as described in Section 6.
35 Release the plastic retaining clip at the end of the bulbholder and lift it from the light unit **(see illustration)**.
36 Remove the relevant push-fit bulb from the bulbholder.
37 Fit the new bulb (or bulbs) using a reversal of the removal procedure.

4.35 Release the bulbholder from the lamp

5.2 Prise the courtesy light unit from the headlining

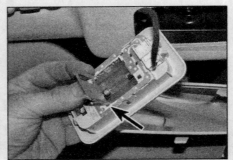

5.4 Lift the cover (arrowed) and pull out the festoon bulb

5.13 Pull the capless bulbs (arrowed) from the heater control assembly

5 Bulbs (interior lights) – renewal

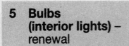

General

1 Whenever a bulb is renewed, note the following points:
- a) *Ensure that the relevant electrical circuit is isolated before removing a bulb. If in doubt, disconnect the battery negative terminal (refer to 'Disconnecting the battery' in Chapter 5A) before starting work.*
- b) *Remember that, if the light has just been in use, the bulb may be extremely hot.*
- c) *Always check the bulb contacts and holder, ensuring that there is clean metal-to-metal contact between the bulb and its live contact(s) and earth. Clean off any corrosion or dirt before fitting a new bulb.*
- d) *Wherever bayonet-type bulbs are fitted, ensure that the live contact(s) bear firmly against the bulb contact.*
- e) *Always ensure that the new bulb is of the correct rating (see Specifications),and that it is completely clean before fitting it.*

Courtesy light

2 Using a small screwdriver, carefully prise the light unit from its location (see illustration).
3 Insert the screwdriver under the tab on the light unit rear cover and open the cover.

4 Remove the festoon type bulb from the bulbholder contacts (see illustration).
5 Fit the new bulb using a reversal of the removal procedure.

Luggage compartment light

6 The light unit (where fitted) is located under the right-hand parcel shelf support panel.
7 Using a small screwdriver, carefully prise the light unit from the support panel.
8 Open the bulbholder and remove the push-fit bulb.
9 Fit the new bulb using a reversal of the removal procedure.

Instrument panel illumination

10 The instrument panel illumination and warning light bulbs are an integral part of the instrument panel cluster and cannot be renewed separately.

Switch illumination

11 The bulbs that illuminate the facia-mounted switches are integral with the switch body and cannot be renewed separately.

Heater/ventilation control illumination

Note: *Not fitted to models with climate control.*

12 Remove the switch assembly from the control panel as described in Chapter 3.
13 Pull the capless bulb from place (see illustration).
14 Fit the new bulb using a reversal of the removal procedure.

6 Exterior light units – removal and refitting

Caution: *Ensure that the relevant electrical circuit is isolated before removing a light unit. If in doubt, disconnect the battery negative terminal as described in Chapter 5A.*

Headlight

1 Open the bonnet and then turn the front wheel outwards (on the appropriate side) to expose the hidden flap. Reach into the wheel arch and open the flap. Remove the headlight retaining screws from the aperture (see illustration).
2 Disconnect the wiring plug from the rear of the lamp (see illustration).
3 Working under the bonnet remove the 2 upper headlight retaining screws (see illustration). Note that the screws are different.
4 Refitting is a reversal of removal. On completion, it is advisable to have the headlight beam alignment checked with reference to Section 8.

Foglights

5 Raise the front of the vehicle and support it securely on axle stands (see *Jacking and vehicle support*).
6 Open the access flap and disconnect the wiring plug
7 Remove the 2 mounting bolts and withdraw the foglight.

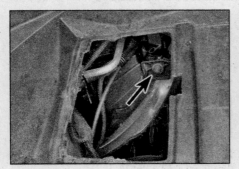

6.1 Remove the lower mounting screw (arrowed)

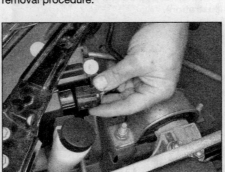

6.2 Depress the clip and disconnect the headlight wiring plug

6.3 Headlight retaining bolts (arrowed)

8 Refitting is a reversal of removal.

Indicator side repeater light

9 The procedure is described as part of the bulb renewal procedure in Section 4.

Rear light cluster

10 Open the tailgate, undo the retaining screws, and pull the light unit directly rearwards to release the clips **(see illustrations)**. Disconnect the wiring plug as the unit is withdrawn.

11 Refitting is a reversal of removal.

High-level brake light

12 Undo the 2 screws and remove the high-level brake light **(see illustrations)**. Pull the trim rearwards to release the clips. Disconnect the wiring plug as the light unit is withdrawn.

13 Refitting is a reversal of removal.

6.10a Remove the screws (arrowed)

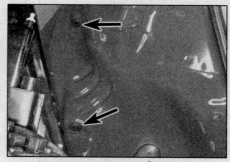

6.10b Note the location of the wing mounted retaining sockets (arrowed)

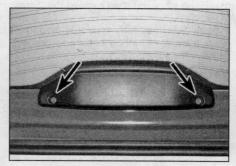

6.12a Remove the screws (arrowed)...

6.12b ...and disconnect the wiring plug

---

7 Instrument panel – removal and refitting

Removal

1 Disconnect the battery negative terminal as described in Chapter 5A.

2 With reference to Chapter 11, remove the fascia lower trim panel and then remove the steering column shroud panels.

3 If not already done so, fully lower the steering wheel. Access can be further improved by slackening (but do not remove) the 2 steering column to cross member bolts.

4 Remove the 2 upper and 2 lower instrument panel mounting bolts **(see illustrations)**.

5 Pull the panel forward, disconnect the wiring plug **(see illustration)** and then carefully manoeuvre the panel from the facia.

Refitting

6 Refitting is a reversal of removal. **Note:** *If a new instrument panel has been fitted, it must be programmed using Ford diagnostic equipment. Entrust this task to a Ford dealer or suitably-equipped garage.*

---

8 Headlight beam alignment – general information

1 Accurate adjustment of the headlight beam is only possible using optical beam-setting equipment, and this work should therefore be carried out by a Ford dealer or suitably-equipped workshop – such as an MOT test centre. Incorrectly adjusted headlamps can dazzle other drivers and cause accidents.

2 For reference, the headlights can be adjusted using the adjuster screws, accessible via the top of each light unit.

---

9 Horn – removal and refitting

Removal

1 Raise the front of the vehicle and support it securely on axle stands (see *Jacking and vehicle support*).

2 Remove the front bumper cover as described in Chapter 11.

3 Undo the nut securing the horn to the mounting bracket **(see illustration)**.

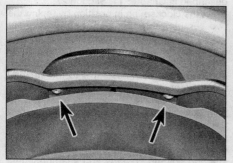

7.4a Remove the upper screws (arrowed)...

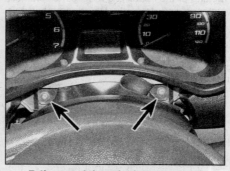

7.4b ...and then the lower screws (arrowed)

7.5 Disconnect the wiring plug

9.3 The horn is located above the radiator on the front panel

10.2 Drill out the rivets

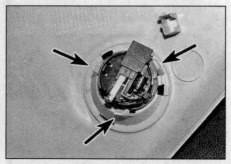

10.4 Release the locking tabs (arrowed)

Disconnect the wiring connector as the horn is withdrawn.

Refitting

4 Refitting is a reversal of removal.

10 Loudspeakers –
removal and refitting

Removal

Front door speaker

1 Remove the door inner trim panel as described in Chapter 11 and then disconnect the wiring plug.
2 Drill out the 3 rivets with an appropriate size drill bit and remove the speaker (see illustration).

Front tweeter

3 Remove the A-pillar trim panel as described in Chapter 11.
4 Release the speaker locking tabs and remove it from the panel (see illustration).

Rear side speaker

5 Remove the rear side trim panel as described in Chapter 11.
6 Disconnect the wiring plug and then drill out the rivets. Remove the speaker.

Subwoofer

7 Where fitted the subwoofer is located beneath the right-hand front seat.
8 Slide the seat fully rearwards and disconnect

the wiring plug and then remove the 2 front mounting bolts.
9 Slide the seat fully forwards and then remove the 2 mounting bolts and bracket. Remove the subwoofer.

Refitting

10 Refitting is a reversal of removal.

11 Radio aerial –
removal and refitting

Removal

1 Unscrew the aerial antenna from the mounting base.
2 Removal of the aerial base requires removal of the headlining. This is considered outside the scope of this manual, as successful refitting of the headlining requires experience, patience and dexterity. We recommend this task is entrusted to a Ford dealer or suitably-experienced repairer.

Refitting

3 Refitting is a reversal of removal.

12 Audio unit –
removal and refitting

Removal

1 Disconnect the battery negative terminal as described in Chapter 5A.

2 Whilst not strictly necessary, removing the facia central air distribution vents (as described in Chapter 11) will avoid damaging them as the audio unit is removed.
3 A special Ford tool (415-008) or suitable equivalent will be required to remove the Audio unit. If the special tool is not available a suitable tool can be fabricated from a suitable length of welding rod.
4 Insert the special extraction tools into the holes on either side of the audio unit. Press them home until the internal clips can be felt to release (see illustration).
5 Pull the unit from the facia, then disconnect the aerial lead and wiring connector from the rear of the unit (see illustrations).

Refitting

6 Refitting is a reversal of removal, ensuring that the wiring is routed freely behind the unit.

13 Switches –
removal and refitting

Note: *Always disconnect the battery before removing any switches - as described in Chapter 5A.*

Steering column combination switches

Note: *The clockspring is an integral part of the switch assembly.*

1 Remove the steering wheel as described in Chapter 10.
2 Remove the steering column shrouds as described in Chapter 11, Section 27.
3 Fix the clockspring in position by taping the two sections together and then disconnect the wiring plug from the clockspring.
4 Release the wiring loom from the side of the steering column and then slacken the screws securing the switch assembly to the steering column (see illustration).
5 Partially remove the switch assembly to gain access to the wiring plugs. Disconnect the wiring plugs and then remove the switch completely from the column.
6 Refitting is a reversal of removal. Refit the steering column shrouds and steering wheel with reference to the Chapters and Sections indicated.

12.4 Note how the release tools (arrowed) engage the spring clip in the audio unit

12.5a Release the audio unit from the facia and...

12.5b ...disconnect the wiring from the rear of the audio unit

Facia switches

7 Protect the surrounding area of the fascia with masking tape, and then using a plastic trim tool prise free the bezels from the central air distribution vents.

8 Using a forked trim tool prise free the switch panel. Disconnect the wiring plug as the switch panel is removed (see illustration).

9 Refitting is a reversal of removal.

Brake light switch

10 Refer to the information contained in Chapter 9.

Electric window switches

11 Remove the gear lever gaiter as described in Chapter 11.

12 Using a small screwdriver depress the locking tabs (see illustration) and then prise the appropriate switch from the panel.

13 Refitting is a reversal of removal.

Door mirror adjustment switch

14 Using a plastic trim tool, prise free the switch panel from the door pillar.

15 Disconnect the wiring plug and then release the switch from the panel.

16 Refitting is a reversal of removal.

Clutch pedal position switch

17 Working under the driver's side of the facia, disconnect the switch wiring plug (see illustration).

18 Prise out the locking element securing the switch arm to the pedal lug.

19 Rotate the locking pin arm forwards, withdraw the lower retaining pin, and disengage the upper locating lug. Manoeuvre the switch from position.

20 Refitting is a reversal of removal.

Steering wheel switches

21 Remove the driver's airbag as described in Section 20 of this Chapter.

22 Disconnect the switch assembly wiring plug, then gently prise the switches from the steering wheel.

23 Refitting is a reversal of removal.

Ignition switch/steering lock

24 Refer to Chapter 5A.

14 Tailgate wiper motor – removal and refitting

Removal

1 Disconnect the battery negative terminal as described in Chapter 5A.

2 Remove the tailgate inner trim panel as described in Chapter 11, Section 25.

3 Remove the wiper arm with reference to Section 17.

4 Working inside the tailgate, disconnect the tailgate wiper motor wiring connector.

5 Unscrew the three bolts securing the motor

13.4 Disconnect the wiring plug and then slacken the mounting screws (arrowed)

13.12 Depress the locking tabs (arrowed)

to the tailgate and remove the motor assembly (see illustration).

Refitting

6 Refitting is a reversal of removal. Refit the wiper arm with reference to Section 17.

15 Windscreen/tailgate washer system components – removal and refitting

Washer fluid reservoir

Removal

1 Firmly apply the handbrake, then jack up the front of the car and support it securely on axle stands (see *Jacking and vehicle support*).

2 Remove the front bumper as described in Chapter 11.

14.5 Remove the bolts (arrowed)

13.8 Disconnect the wiring plug as the switch is removed

13.17 The clutch pedal position switch (arrowed)

3 Release the washer hoses from the pump and disconnect the pump wiring plug.

4 Undo the two reservoir retaining bolts (see illustration) and lower the reservoir from the vehicle.

Refitting

5 Refitting is a reversal of removal.

Washer pump

Removal

6 Firmly apply the handbrake, then jack up the front of the car and support it securely on axle stands (see *Jacking and vehicle support*). Remove the right-hand front roadwheel.

7 Partially remove the wheel arch liner to access the pump, fitted into the reservoir. Disconnect the wiring plug.

8 Place a suitable container beneath the reservoir and then pull the washer pump from

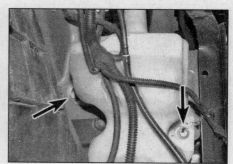

15.4 Remove the bolts (arrowed)

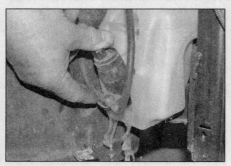

15.8 Remove the screen washer pump

15.11a Disconnect the washer hose...

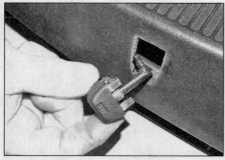

15.11b ...and release the washer nozzle

the reservoir **(see illustration)**. Disconnect the washer hoses. Where applicable, recover the grommet.

Refitting

9 Refitting is a reversal of removal.

16.4 Disconnect the wiper motor wiring plug

16.5b Note the lug (arrowed) on the rear

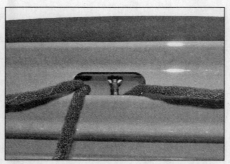

15.13 Access to the nozzle can be gained after removing the high level brake light

Windscreen washer nozzles

Removal

10 Remove the windscreen scuttle grille panel as described in Section 22 of Chapter 11.

16.5a Windscreen wiper motor retaining bolts (arrowed)

17.3 Remove the plastic cover

11 Disconnect the hose from the base of the nozzle, then release the retaining clips and pull the nozzle from place **(see illustrations)**.

Refitting

12 Refitting is a reversal of removal. If necessary, the vertical aim of the nozzles can be adjusted using a screwdriver.

Tailgate washer nozzle

Removal

13 Mask off the paint work around the nozzle and then using a plastic trim tool prise the nozzle free from the tailgate. Alternatively, remove the high level brake light and push the nozzle free from the rear **(see illustration)**.
14 Disconnect the washer fluid hose from the nozzle.

Refitting

15 Refitting is a reversal of removal.

16 Windscreen wiper motor and linkage – removal and refitting

Removal

1 Disconnect the battery negative terminal as described in Chapter 5A.
2 Refer to Section 17 and remove both wiper arms.
3 Remove the windscreen scuttle grille panel as described in Chapter 11, Section 22.
4 Lift the wiper motor protective cover (where fitted) and disconnect the motor wiring connector **(see illustration)**.
5 Undo the two wiper motor and linkage retaining bolts and withdraw the assembly from the scuttle. Note the lug that engages with a grommet in the scuttle **(see illustrations)**.
6 If required the motor can now be unbolted from the linkage.

Refitting

7 Refitting is a reversal of removal.

17 Wiper arm – removal and refitting

Removal

Windscreen wiper

1 Operate the wiper motor, then switch it off so that the wiper arm returns to the at-rest/parked position.
2 Mark the position of the wiper blades on the windscreen with suitable tape
3 Carefully prise the plastic cover from the front windscreen scuttle trim panel to expose the wiper spindle **(see illustration)**.
4 Prise off the wiper arm spindle nut cover, then slacken and remove the spindle nut **(see illustration)**.

17.4 Prise up the spindle cover, and undo the nut beneath

17.5a Pull the wiper arm from the spindle

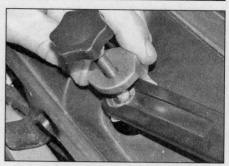

17.5b If necessary, use a puller to release the wiper arm

5 Lift the blade off the glass, and pull the wiper arm off its spindle. If necessary, the arm can be carefully removed using a puller (**see illustrations**). If both windscreen wiper arms are removed, note their locations, as different arms are fitted to the driver's and passenger's sides.

Tailgate wiper

6 Lift up the cover and undo the spindle nut (**see illustration**).
7 Pull the wiper arm from the spindle.

Refitting

Windscreen wiper

8 Ensure that the wiper arm and spindle splines are clean and dry.
9 When refitting a wiper arm, refit the arm to the spindle, aligning the wiper blade with the tape fitted before removal. If both windscreen wiper arms have been removed, ensure that the arms are refitted to their correct positions as noted before removal.
10 Refit the spindle nut, tighten it securely, and refit the nut cover.

Tailgate wiper

11 Fit the wiper arm over the spindle and align the blade with the mark on the screen (**see illustration**).
12 Tighten the spindle nut and fold over the plastic cover.

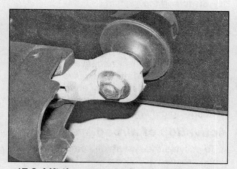

17.6 Lift the cover and undo the spindle nut

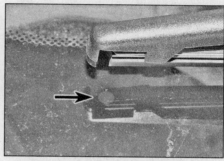

17.11 Align the blade with the mark (arrowed) on the glass

18 Anti-theft system and engine immobiliser – general information

All models in the range are equipped as standard with a central locking system incorporating an electronic engine immobiliser function.

The electronic engine immobiliser is operated by a transponder fitted to the ignition key, in conjunction with an analogue module fitted around the ignition switch.

When the ignition key is inserted in the switch and turned to the ignition 'on' position, the control module sends a pre-programmed recognition code signal to the module on the ignition switch. If the recognition code signal matches that of the transponder on the ignition key, an unlocking request signal is sent to the

engine management ECU allowing the engine to be started. If the ignition key signal is not recognised, the engine management system remains immobilised.

When the ignition is switched off, a locking signal is sent to the ECU and the engine is immobilised until the unlocking request signal is again received.

19 Airbag system – general information, precautions and system de-activation

General information

A driver's airbag and passenger's air bag are fitted as standard on all models, with side airbags, and side curtain airbags available as optional equipment on most models. The driver's airbag is located in the steering wheel centre pad and the passenger's airbag is located above the glovebox in the facia. The side airbags are located in the front seat backs, and the side window airbags are located in the roof headlining on both sides of the car. In addition, pyrotechnic seat belt pretensioners are fitted to the inertia reels of the front seat belts.

The airbag and seat belt pyrotechnic safety systems are armed only when the ignition is switched on, however, a reserve power source maintains a power supply to the systems in the event of a break in the main electrical supply. The airbags are activated by a 'g' sensor (deceleration sensor), and controlled by an electronic control unit located under

the centre of the facia. The side airbags and side window airbags are activated by severe side impact and operate in conjunction with the main system. The pyrotechnic seat belt pretensioners operate independently of the main system.

The airbags are inflated by a gas generator, which forces the bag out from its location in the steering wheel, facia, seat back frame or roof headlining.

Precautions

⚠️ **Warning: The following precautions must be observed when working on vehicles equipped with an airbag system, to prevent the possibility of personal injury. Many of the precautions are equally applicable to the pyrotechnic seat belt pretensioners and should be similarly observed.**

General

The following precautions **must** be observed when carrying out work on a vehicle equipped with an airbag:

a) Do not disconnect the battery with the engine running.
b) Before carrying out any work in the vicinity of the airbag, removal of any of the airbag components, or any welding work on the vehicle, de-activate the system as described in the following sub-Section.
c) Do not attempt to test any of the airbag system circuits using test meters or any other test equipment.
d) If the airbag warning light comes on, or any fault in the system is suspected,

20.1 The Airbag ECU is located below the heater box

consult a Ford dealer without delay. **Do not** attempt to carry out fault diagnosis, or any dismantling of the components.

When handling an airbag

a) Transport the airbag by itself, bag upward.
b) Do not put your arms around the airbag.
c) Carry the airbag close to the body, bag outward.
d) Do not drop the airbag or expose it to impacts.
e) Do not attempt to dismantle the airbag unit.
f) Do not connect any form of electrical equipment to any part of the airbag circuit.

When storing an airbag unit

a) Store the unit in a cupboard with the airbag upward.
b) Do not expose the airbag to temperatures above 80°C.

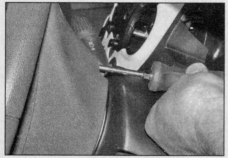

20.4a Insert a screwdriver...

20.4c ...and push the wire clips (arrowed) outwards to release the airbag

c) Do not expose the airbag to flames.
d) Do not attempt to dispose of the airbag – consult a Ford dealer.
e) Never refit an airbag which is known to be faulty or damaged.

De-activation of airbag system

The system must be de-activated before carrying out any work on the airbag components or surrounding area:

a) Switch on the ignition and check the operation of the airbag warning light on the instrument panel. The light should illuminate when the ignition is switched on, then extinguish.
b) Switch off the ignition.
c) Remove the ignition key.
d) Switch off all electrical equipment.
e) Disconnect the battery negative terminal as described in Chapter 5A.
f) Insulate the battery negative terminal and the end of the battery negative lead to prevent any possibility of contact.
g) Wait for at least ten minutes before carrying out any further work.

Activation of airbag system

To activate the system on completion of any work, proceed as follows:

a) Ensure that there are no occupants in the vehicle, and that there are no loose objects around the vicinity of the steering wheel. Close the vehicle doors and windows.
b) Ensure that the ignition is switched off then reconnect the battery negative terminal.

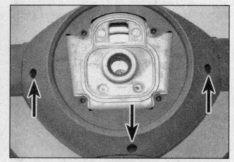

20.4b ...through the 3 holes in the steering wheel boss (arrowed)...

20.5 Disconnect the wiring plug

c) Open the driver's door and switch on the ignition, without reaching in front of the steering wheel. Check that the airbag warning light illuminates briefly then extinguishes.
d) Switch off the ignition.
e) If the airbag warning light does not operate as described in paragraph c), consult a Ford dealer before driving the vehicle.

20 Airbag system components – removal and refitting

Warning: Refer to the precautions given in Section 19 before attempting to carry out work on any of the airbag components. Any suspected faults with the airbag system should be referred to a Ford dealer or suitably equipped specialist – under no circumstances attempt to carry out any work other than removal and refitting of the front airbag unit(s) and/or the airbag clockspring, as described in the following paragraphs.

Electronic control unit

1 The airbag ECU is located under the centre of the facia and is accessible after removal of the footwell kick panels adjacent to the heater air distribution housing **(see illustration)**.

Driver's airbag unit

2 De-activate the airbag system as described in Section 19.
3 With the front wheels in the straight-ahead position, rotate the steering wheel 90° left or right to access the hole in the wheel boss.
4 Ford list a special tool for this operation (501-156), however removal is also possible with a flat bladed screwdriver. Insert a screwdriver and release the airbag retaining clip, by twisting it one way or the other. With the first clip released, turn the steering wheel as necessary to release the other 2 clips, noting which way the wheel is rotated, so that it can be returned to the straight-ahead position **(see illustrations)**.
5 Carefully lift the airbag unit from the steering wheel and disconnect the wiring connector(s) **(see illustration)**.
6 If the airbag unit is to be stored for any length of time, refer to the storage precautions given in Section 19.
7 Refitting is a reversal of removal, bearing in mind the following points:
a) Do not strike the airbag unit, or expose it to impacts during refitting.
b) On completion of refitting, activate the airbag system as described in Section 19.

Airbag clockspring

8 The airbag clockspring is integral with the steering column combination switch assembly. Remove the switch assembly as described in Section 13.

9 Refitting is a reversal of removal, bearing in mind the following points:

a) *Ensure that the centre position indicator window on the outer moving portion of the clockspring is centred over the red indicator tab on the fixed portion* **(see illustration)**.

b) *Ensure that the roadwheels are in the straight-ahead position before refitting the clockspring and steering wheel.*

c) *Refit the steering wheel as described in Chapter 10, and refit the airbag unit as described previously in this Section.*

Passenger's airbag unit

10 De-activate the airbag system as described in Section 19.

11 Remove the complete facia as described in Chapter 11.

12 Disconnect the airbag wiring plug, and remove the single bolt **(see illustrations)**. Manoeuvre the airbag from place.

13 Refitting is a reversal of removal, bearing in mind the following points:

a) *Do not strike the airbag unit, or expose it to impacts during refitting.*

b) *On completion of refitting, activate the airbag system as described in Section 19.*

Side and side window airbags

14 The side, and side window, airbags are located respectively within the front seat backs and roof headlining, and no attempt should be made to remove them. Any suspected problems with the side airbag system should be referred to a Ford dealer.

20.9 We locked the clockspring with a suitably bent split pin (arrowed)

20.12b ...remove the single bolt (arrowed)

Crash sensors

15 Remove the rear side panel as described in Chapter 11.

16 Undo the retaining bolt/nut and remove

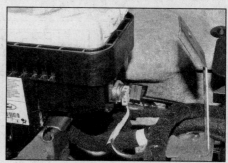

20.12a Disconnect the wiring plug and...

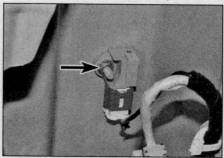

20.16 Side crash sensor retaining nut (arrowed)

the sensor from the pillar **(see illustration)**. Disconnect the wiring plug as the sensor is withdrawn.

17 Refitting is a reversal of removal. Activate the airbag system as described in Section 19.

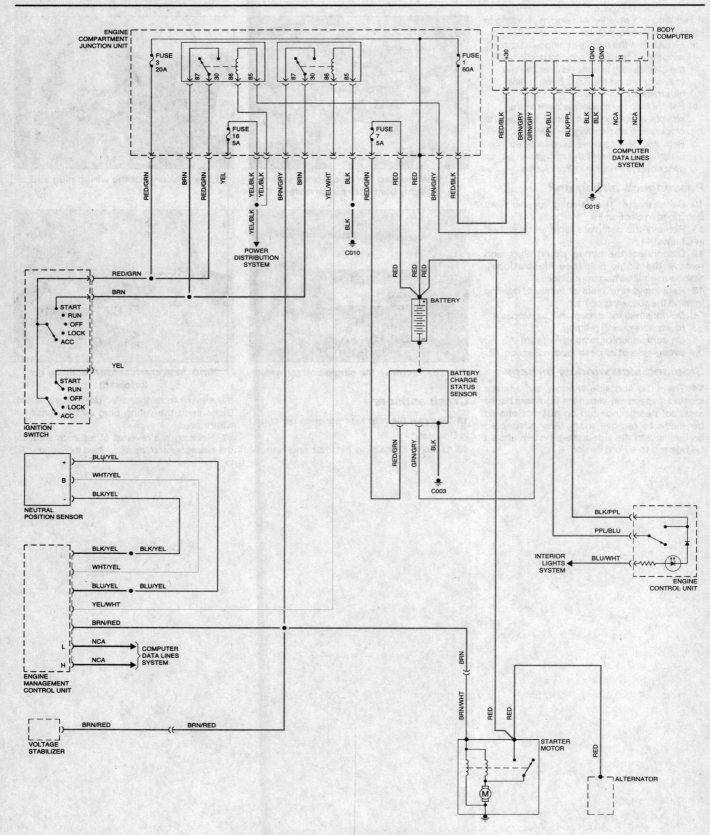

Diagram 1 – Starting circuit (Euro 5 models)

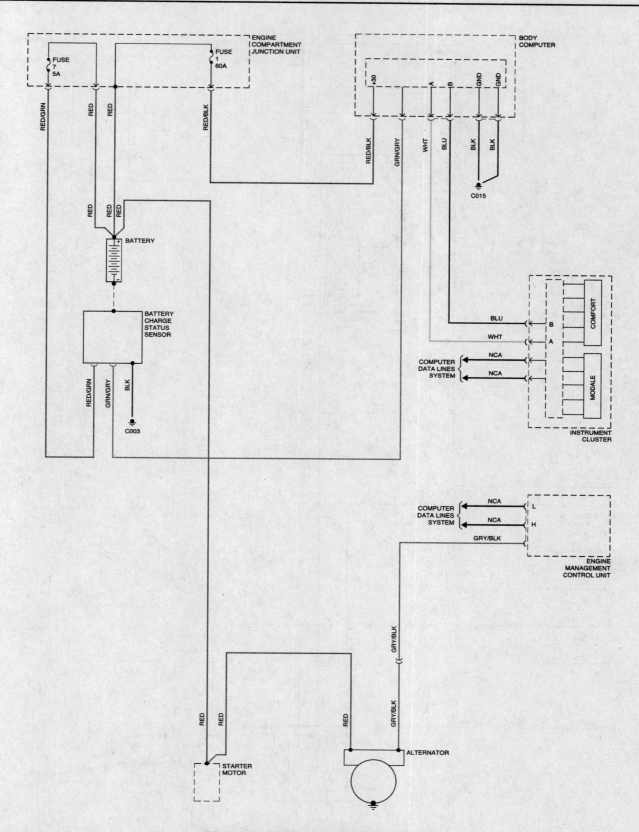

Diagram 2 – Charging circuit (Euro 5 models)

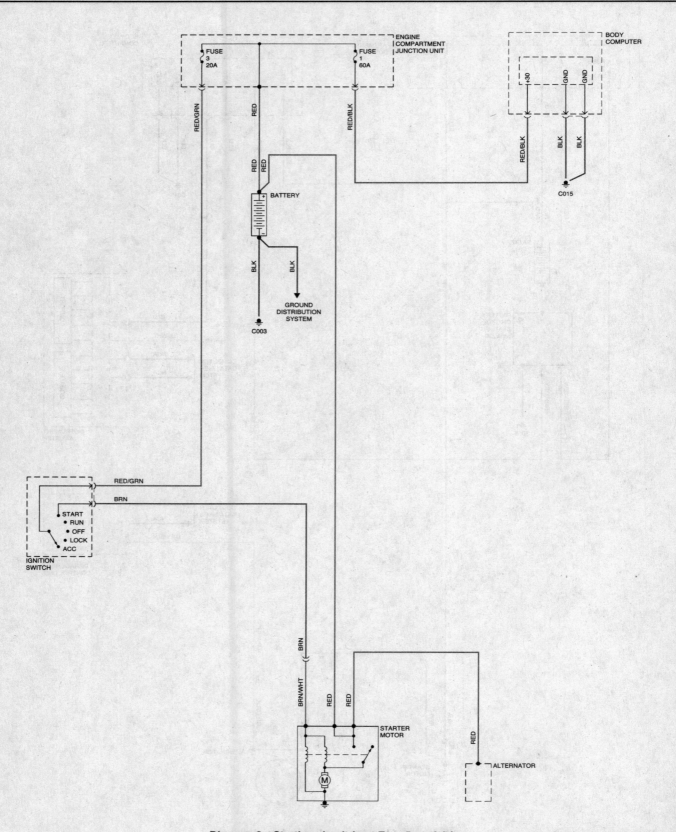

Diagram 3 – Starting circuit (non-Euro 5 models)

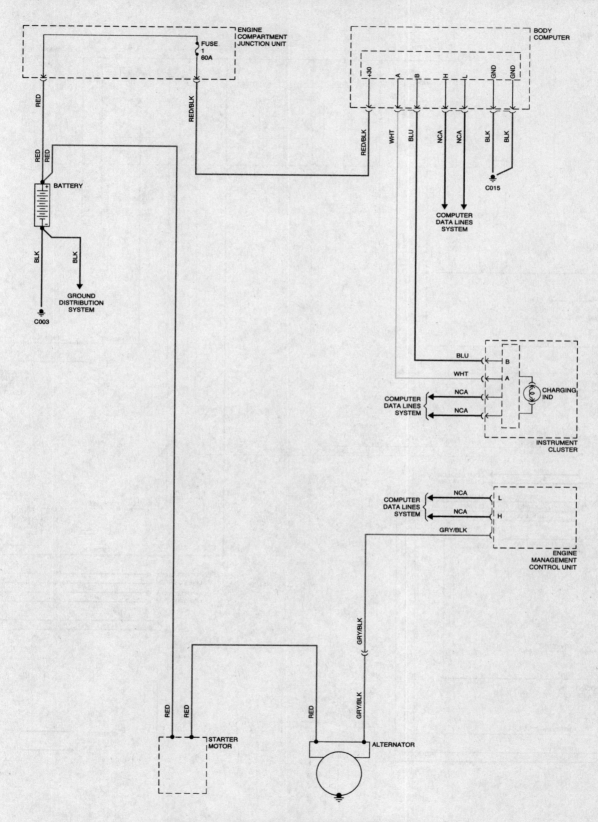

Diagram 4 – Charging circuit (non-Euro 5 models)

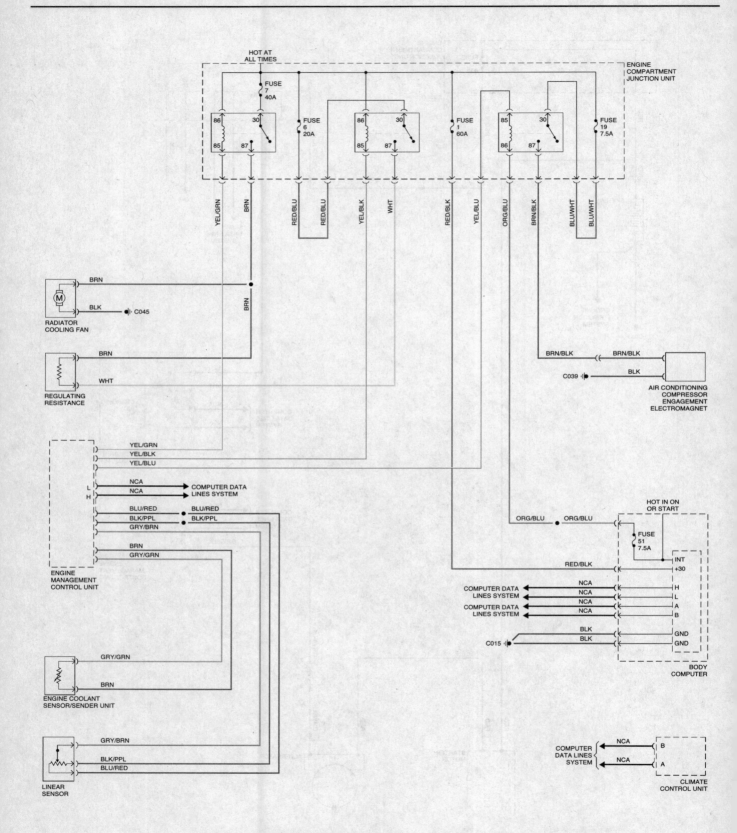

Diagram 5 – Air conditioning and cooling system

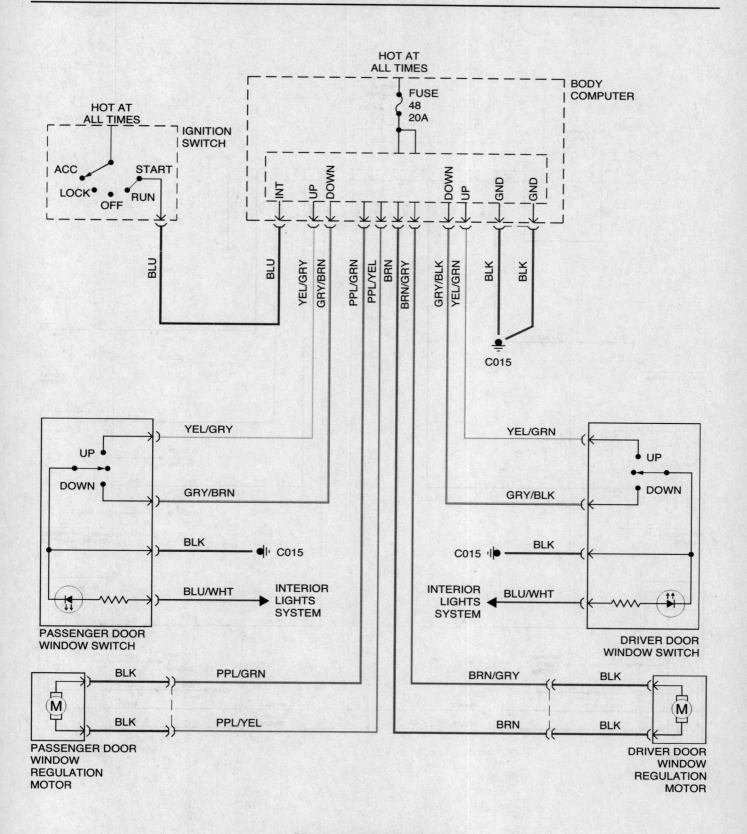

Diagram 6 – Electric windows

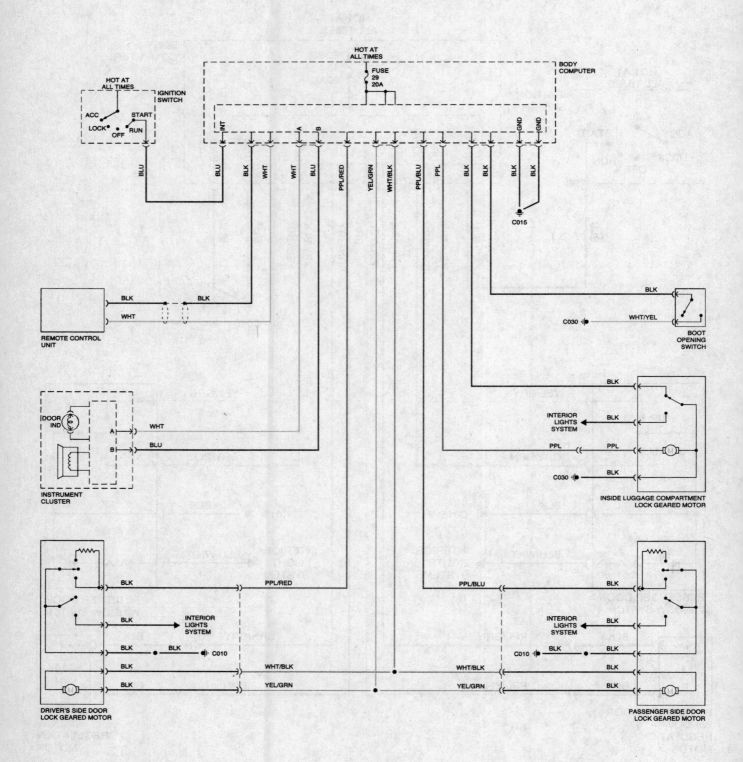

Diagram 7 – Central locking

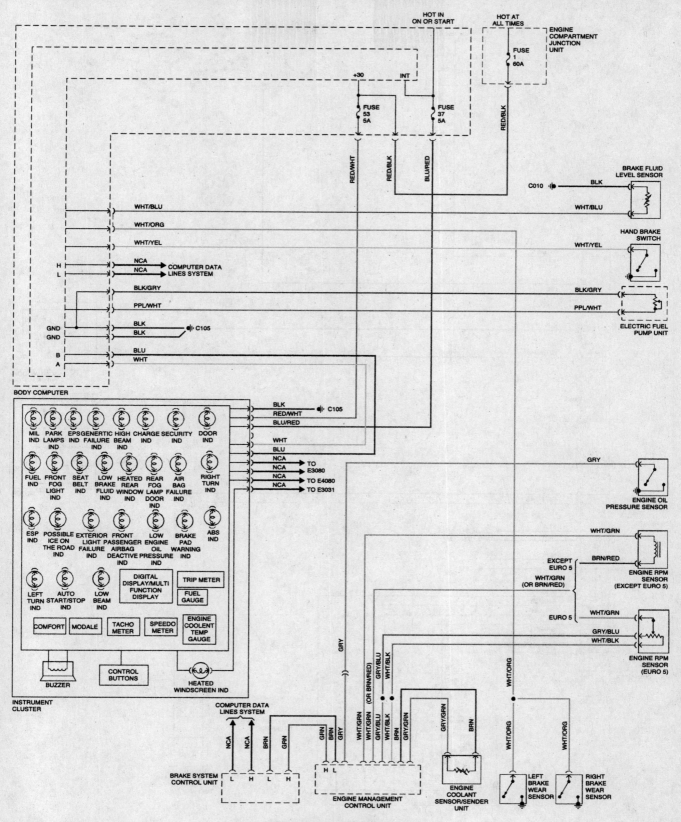

Diagram 8 – Warning lights

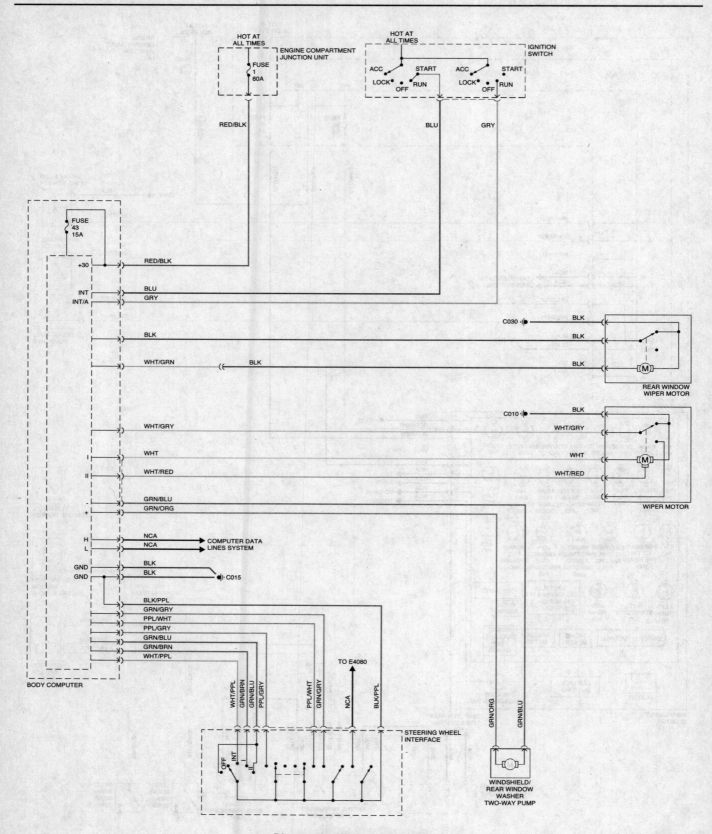

Diagram 9 – Wipers and washers

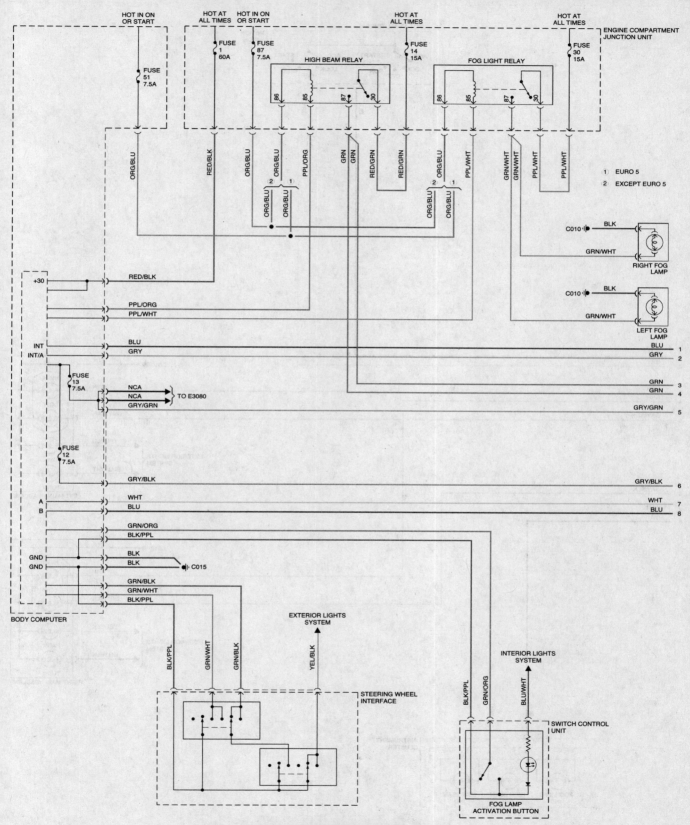

Diagram 10a – Headlights (diagram 1 of 2)

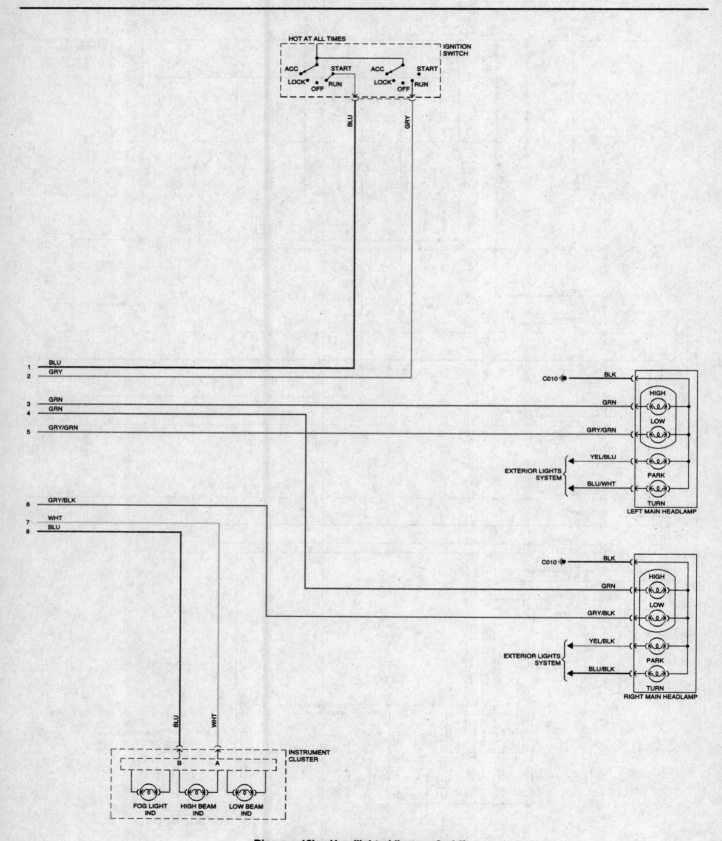

Diagram 10b – Headlights (diagram 2 of 2)

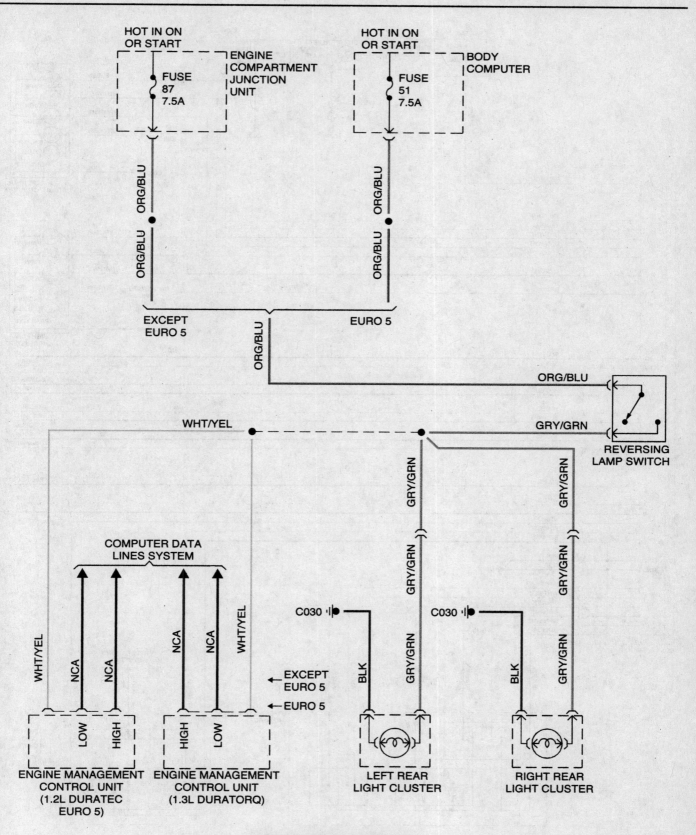

Diagram 11 – Reversing lights

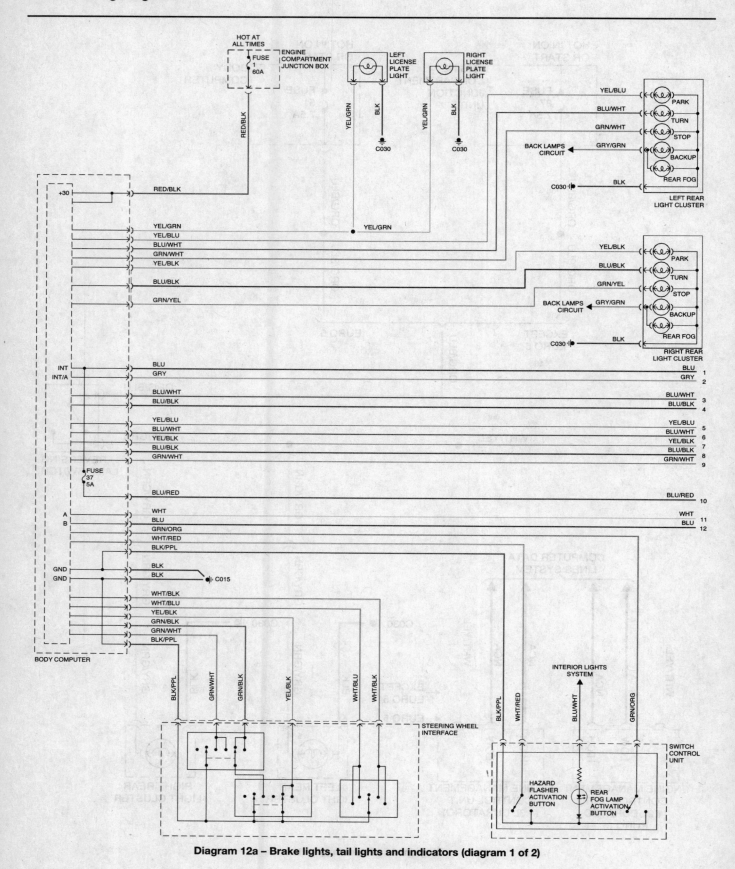

Diagram 12a – Brake lights, tail lights and indicators (diagram 1 of 2)

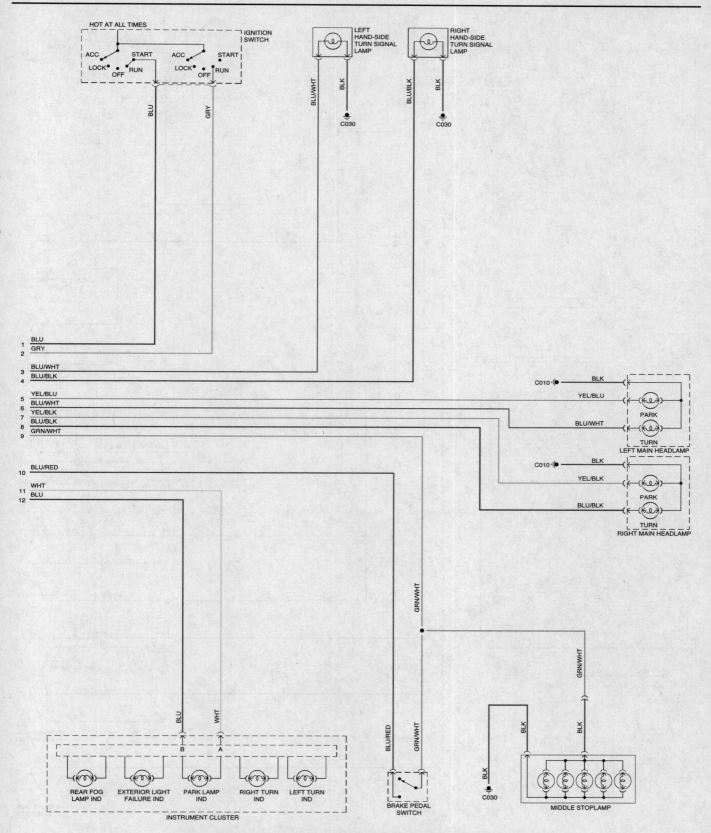

Diagram 12b – Brake lights, tail lights and indicators (diagram 2 of 2)

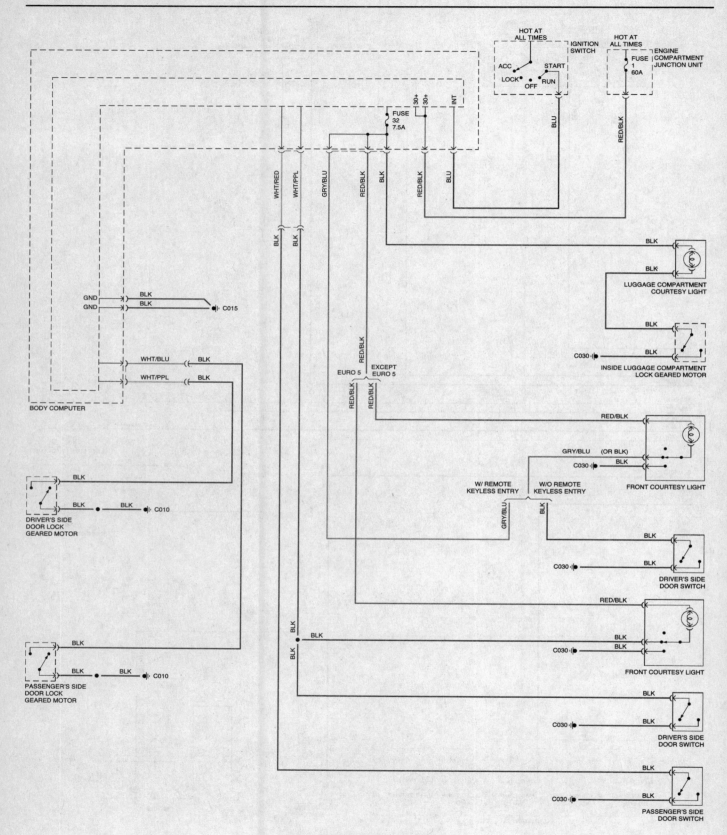

Diagram 13 – Interior lights

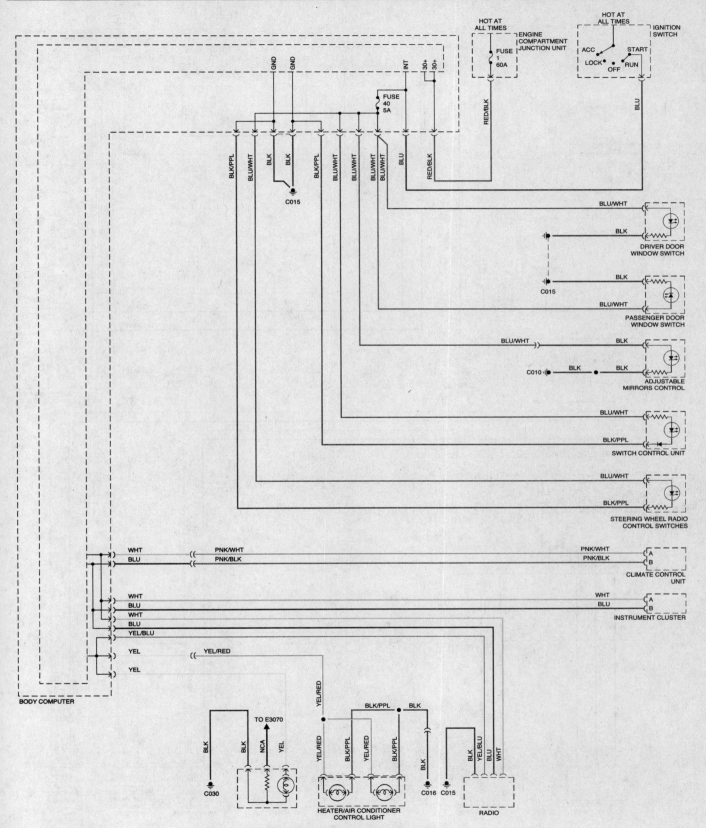

Diagram 14 – Instrument panel illumination

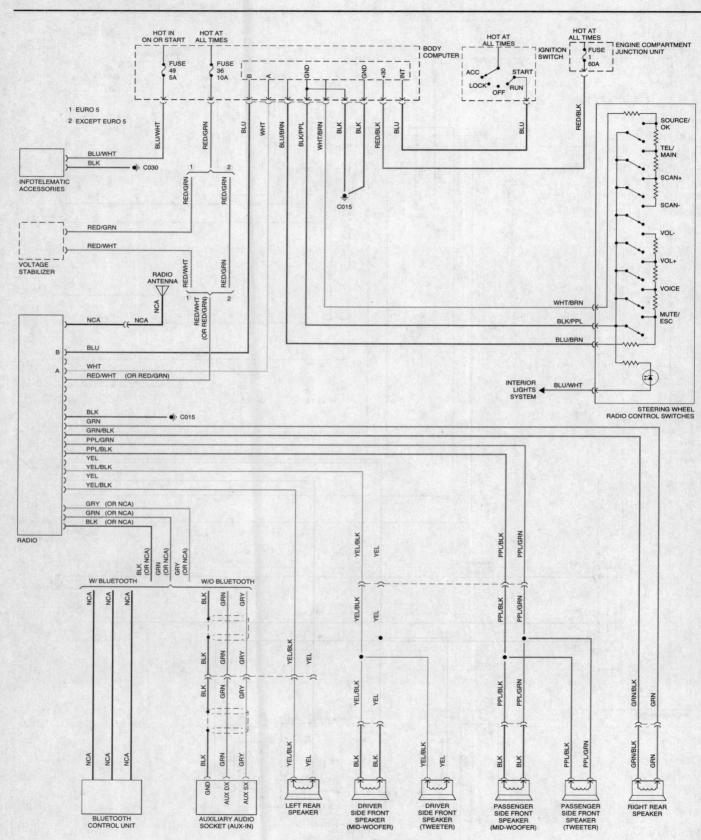

Diagram 15 – Radio

Dimensions and weights

Note: *All figures are approximate, and may vary according to model. Refer to manufacturerís data for exact figures.*

Dimensions

Overall length	3620 mm
Overall width (excluding mirrors)	1658 mm
Overall height	1506 mm
Wheelbase	2300 mm

Weights

Kerb weight	865 kg
Maximum roof rack load	50 kg

Fuel economy

Although depreciation is still the biggest part of the cost of motoring for most car owners, the cost of fuel is more immediately noticeable. These pages give some tips on how to get the best fuel economy.

Working it out

Manufacturer's figures

Car manufacturers are required by law to provide fuel consumption information on all new vehicles sold. These 'official' figures are obtained by simulating various driving conditions on a rolling road or a test track. Real life conditions are different, so the fuel consumption actually achieved may not bear much resemblance to the quoted figures.

How to calculate it

Many cars now have trip computers which will

display fuel consumption, both instantaneous and average. Refer to the owner's handbook for details of how to use these.

To calculate consumption yourself (and maybe to check that the trip computer is accurate), proceed as follows.

1. Fill up with fuel and note the mileage, or zero the trip recorder.
2. Drive as usual until you need to fill up again.
3. Note the amount of fuel required to refill the tank, and the mileage covered since the previous fill-up.
4. Divide the mileage by the amount of fuel used to obtain the consumption figure.

For example:

Mileage at first fill-up (a) = 27,903
Mileage at second fill-up (b) = 28,346
Mileage covered (b - a) = 443
Fuel required at second fill-up = 48.6 litres

The half-completed changeover to metric units in the UK means that we buy our fuel in litres, measure distances in miles and talk about fuel consumption in miles per gallon. There are two ways round this: the first is to convert the litres to gallons before doing the calculation (by dividing by 4.546, or see Table 1). So in the example:

48.6 litres ÷ 4.546 = 10.69 gallons
443 miles ÷ 10.69 gallons = 41.4 mpg

The second way is to calculate the consumption in miles per litre, then multiply that figure by 4.546 (or see Table 2).

So in the example, fuel consumption is:

443 miles ÷ 48.6 litres = 9.1 mpl
9.1 mpl x 4.546 = 41.4 mpg

The rest of Europe expresses fuel consumption in litres of fuel required to travel 100 km (l/100 km). For interest, the conversions are given in Table 3. In practice it doesn't matter what units you use, provided you know what your normal consumption is and can spot if it's getting better or worse.

Table 1: conversion of litres to Imperial gallons

litres	1	2	3	4	5	10	20	30	40	50	60	70
gallons	0.22	0.44	0.66	0.88	1.10	2.24	4.49	6.73	8.98	11.22	13.47	15.71

Table 2: conversion of miles per litre to miles per gallon

miles per litre	5	6	7	8	9	10	11	12	13	14
miles per gallon	23	27	32	36	41	46	50	55	59	64

Table 3: conversion of litres per 100 km to miles per gallon

litres per 100 km	4	4.5	5	5.5	6	6.5	7	8	9	10
miles per gallon	71	63	56	51	47	43	40	35	31	28

Maintenance

A well-maintained car uses less fuel and creates less pollution. In particular:

Filters

Change air and fuel filters at the specified intervals.

Oil

Use a good quality oil of the lowest viscosity specified by the vehicle manufacturer (see *Lubricants and fluids*). Check the level often and be careful not to overfill.

Spark plugs

When applicable, renew at the specified intervals.

Tyres

Check tyre pressures regularly. Under-inflated tyres have an increased rolling resistance. It is generally safe to use the higher pressures specified for full load conditions even when not fully laden, but keep an eye on the centre band of tread for signs of wear due to over-inflation.

When buying new tyres, consider the 'fuel saving' models which most manufacturers include in their ranges.

Driving style

Acceleration

Acceleration uses more fuel than driving at a steady speed. The best technique with modern cars is to accelerate reasonably briskly to the desired speed, changing up through the gears as soon as possible without making the engine labour.

Air conditioning

Air conditioning absorbs quite a bit of energy from the engine – typically 3 kW (4 hp) or so. The effect on fuel consumption is at its worst in slow traffic. Switch it off when not required.

Anticipation

Drive smoothly and try to read the traffic flow so as to avoid unnecessary acceleration and braking.

Automatic transmission

When accelerating in an automatic, avoid depressing the throttle so far as to make the transmission hold onto lower gears at higher speeds. Don't use the 'Sport' setting, if applicable.

When stationary with the engine running, select 'N' or 'P'. When moving, keep your left foot away from the brake.

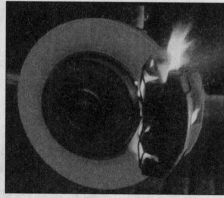

Braking

Braking converts the car's energy of motion into heat – essentially, it is wasted. Obviously some braking is always going to be necessary, but with good anticipation it is surprising how much can be avoided, especially on routes that you know well.

Carshare

Consider sharing lifts to work or to the shops. Even once a week will make a difference.

Electrical loads

Electricity is 'fuel' too; the alternator which charges the battery does so by converting some of the engine's energy of motion into electrical energy. The more electrical accessories are in use, the greater the load on the alternator. Switch off big consumers like the heated rear window when not required.

Freewheeling

Freewheeling (coasting) in neutral with the engine switched off is dangerous. The effort required to operate power-assisted brakes and steering increases when the engine is not running, with a potential lack of control in emergency situations.

In any case, modern fuel injection systems automatically cut off the engine's fuel supply on the overrun (moving and in gear, but with the accelerator pedal released).

Gadgets

Bolt-on devices claiming to save fuel have been around for nearly as long as the motor car itself. Those which worked were rapidly adopted as standard equipment by the vehicle manufacturers. Others worked only in certain situations, or saved fuel only at the expense of unacceptable effects on performance, driveability or the life of engine components.

The most effective fuel saving gadget is the driver's right foot.

Journey planning

Combine (eg) a trip to the supermarket with a visit to the recycling centre and the DIY store, rather than making separate journeys.

When possible choose a travelling time outside rush hours.

Load

The more heavily a car is laden, the greater the energy required to accelerate it to a given speed. Remove heavy items which you don't need to carry.

One load which is often overlooked is the contents of the fuel tank. A tankful of fuel (55 litres / 12 gallons) weighs 45 kg (100 lb) or so. Just half filling it may be worthwhile.

Lost?

At the risk of stating the obvious, if you're going somewhere new, have details of the route to hand. There's not much point in achieving record mpg if you also go miles out of your way.

Parking

If possible, carry out any reversing or turning manoeuvres when you arrive at a parking space so that you can drive straight out when you leave. Manoeuvering when the engine is cold uses a lot more fuel.

Driving around looking for free on-street parking may cost more in fuel than buying a car park ticket.

Premium fuel

Most major oil companies (and some supermarkets) have premium grades of fuel which are several pence a litre dearer than the standard grades. Reports vary, but the consensus seems to be that if these fuels improve economy at all, they do not do so by enough to justify their extra cost.

Roof rack

When loading a roof rack, try to produce a wedge shape with the narrow end at the front. Any cover should be securely fastened – if it flaps it's creating turbulence and absorbing energy.

Remove roof racks and boxes when not in use – they increase air resistance and can create a surprising amount of noise.

Short journeys

The engine is at its least efficient, and wear is highest, during the first few miles after a cold start. Consider walking, cycling or using public transport.

Speed

The engine is at its most efficient when running at a steady speed and load at the rpm where it develops maximum torque. (You can find this figure in the car's handbook.) For most cars this corresponds to between 55 and 65 mph in top gear.

Above the optimum cruising speed, fuel consumption starts to rise quite sharply. A car travelling at 80 mph will typically be using 30% more fuel than at 60 mph.

Supermarket fuel

It may be cheap but is it any good? In the UK all supermarket fuel must meet the relevant British Standard. The major oil companies will say that their branded fuels have better additive packages which may stop carbon and other deposits building up. A reasonable compromise might be to use one tank of branded fuel to three or four from the supermarket.

Switch off when stationary

Switch off the engine if you look like being stationary for more than 30 seconds or so. This is good for the environment as well as for your pocket. Be aware though that frequent restarts are hard on the battery and the starter motor.

Windows

Driving with the windows open increases air turbulence around the vehicle. Closing the windows promotes smooth airflow and reduced resistance. The faster you go, the more significant this is.

And finally . . .

Driving techniques associated with good fuel economy tend to involve moderate acceleration and low top speeds. Be considerate to the needs of other road users who may need to make brisker progress; even if you do not agree with them this is not an excuse to be obstructive.

Safety must always take precedence over economy, whether it is a question of accelerating hard to complete an overtaking manoeuvre, killing your speed when confronted with a potential hazard or switching the lights on when it starts to get dark.

Conversion factors

Length (distance)

Inches (in)	x 25.4	=	Millimetres (mm)	x 0.0394 =	Inches (in)
Feet (ft)	x 0.305	=	Metres (m)	x 3.281 =	Feet (ft)
Miles	x 1.609	=	Kilometres (km)	x 0.621 =	Miles

Volume (capacity)

Cubic inches (cu in; in³)	x 16.387	=	Cubic centimetres (cc; cm³)	x 0.061 =	Cubic inches (cu in; in³)
Imperial pints (Imp pt)	x 0.568	=	Litres (l)	x 1.76 =	Imperial pints (Imp pt)
Imperial quarts (Imp qt)	x 1.137	=	Litres (l)	x 0.88 =	Imperial quarts (Imp qt)
Imperial quarts (Imp qt)	x 1.201	=	US quarts (US qt)	x 0.833 =	Imperial quarts (Imp qt)
US quarts (US qt)	x 0.946	=	Litres (l)	x 1.057 =	US quarts (US qt)
Imperial gallons (Imp gal)	x 4.546	=	Litres (l)	x 0.22 =	Imperial gallons (Imp gal)
Imperial gallons (Imp gal)	x 1.201	=	US gallons (US gal)	x 0.833 =	Imperial gallons (Imp gal)
US gallons (US gal)	x 3.785	=	Litres (l)	x 0.264 =	US gallons (US gal)

Mass (weight)

Ounces (oz)	x 28.35	=	Grams (g)	x 0.035 =	Ounces (oz)
Pounds (lb)	x 0.454	=	Kilograms (kg)	x 2.205 =	Pounds (lb)

Force

Ounces-force (ozf; oz)	x 0.278	=	Newtons (N)	x 3.6 =	Ounces-force (ozf; oz)
Pounds-force (lbf; lb)	x 4.448	=	Newtons (N)	x 0.225 =	Pounds-force (lbf; lb)
Newtons (N)	x 0.1	=	Kilograms-force (kgf; kg)	x 9.81 =	Newtons (N)

Pressure

Pounds-force per square inch (psi; lbf/in²; lb/in²)	x 0.070	=	Kilograms-force per square centimetre (kgf/cm²; kg/cm²)	x 14.223 =	Pounds-force per square inch (psi; lbf/in²; lb/in²)
Pounds-force per square inch (psi; lbf/in²; lb/in²)	x 0.068	=	Atmospheres (atm)	x 14.696 =	Pounds-force per square inch (psi; lbf/in²; lb/in²)
Pounds-force per square inch (psi; lbf/in²; lb/in²)	x 0.069	=	Bars	x 14.5 =	Pounds-force per square inch (psi; lbf/in²; lb/in²)
Pounds-force per square inch (psi; lbf/in²; lb/in²)	x 6.895	=	Kilopascals (kPa)	x 0.145 =	Pounds-force per square inch (psi; lbf/in²; lb/in²)
Kilopascals (kPa)	x 0.01	=	Kilograms-force per square centimetre (kgf/cm²; kg/cm²)	x 98.1 =	Kilopascals (kPa)
Millibar (mbar)	x 100	=	Pascals (Pa)	x 0.01 =	Millibar (mbar)
Millibar (mbar)	x 0.0145	=	Pounds-force per square inch (psi; lbf/in²; lb/in²)	x 68.947 =	Millibar (mbar)
Millibar (mbar)	x 0.75	=	Millimetres of mercury (mmHg)	x 1.333 =	Millibar (mbar)
Millibar (mbar)	x 0.401	=	Inches of water (inH₂O)	x 2.491 =	Millibar (mbar)
Millimetres of mercury (mmHg)	x 0.535	=	Inches of water (inH₂O)	x 1.868 =	Millimetres of mercury (mmHg)
Inches of water (inH₂O)	x 0.036	=	Pounds-force per square inch (psi; lbf/in²; lb/in²)	x 27.68 =	Inches of water (inH₂O)

Torque (moment of force)

Pounds-force inches (lbf in; lb in)	x 1.152	=	Kilograms-force centimetre (kgf cm; kg cm)	x 0.868 =	Pounds-force inches (lbf in; lb in)
Pounds-force inches (lbf in; lb in)	x 0.113	=	Newton metres (Nm)	x 8.85 =	Pounds-force inches (lbf in; lb in)
Pounds-force inches (lbf in; lb in)	x 0.083	=	Pounds-force feet (lbf ft; lb ft)	x 12 =	Pounds-force inches (lbf in; lb in)
Pounds-force feet (lbf ft; lb ft)	x 0.138	=	Kilograms-force metres (kgf m; kg m)	x 7.233 =	Pounds-force feet (lbf ft; lb ft)
Pounds-force feet (lbf ft; lb ft)	x 1.356	=	Newton metres (Nm)	x 0.738 =	Pounds-force feet (lbf ft; lb ft)
Newton metres (Nm)	x 0.102	=	Kilograms-force metres (kgf m; kg m)	x 9.804 =	Newton metres (Nm)

Power

Horsepower (hp)	x 745.7	=	Watts (W)	x 0.0013 =	Horsepower (hp)

Velocity (speed)

Miles per hour (miles/hr; mph)	x 1.609	=	Kilometres per hour (km/hr; kph)	x 0.621 =	Miles per hour (miles/hr; mph)

Fuel consumption*

Miles per gallon, Imperial (mpg)	x 0.354	=	Kilometres per litre (km/l)	x 2.825 =	Miles per gallon, Imperial (mpg)
Miles per gallon, US (mpg)	x 0.425	=	Kilometres per litre (km/l)	x 2.352 =	Miles per gallon, US (mpg)

Temperature

Degrees Fahrenheit = (°C x 1.8) + 32

Degrees Celsius (Degrees Centigrade; °C) = (°F - 32) x 0.56

It is common practice to convert from miles per gallon (mpg) to litres/100 kilometres (l/100km), where mpg x l/100 km = 282

Spare parts are available from many sources, including maker's appointed garages, accessory shops, and motor factors. To be sure of obtaining the correct parts, it will sometimes be necessary to quote the vehicle identification number. If possible, it can also be useful to take the old parts along for positive identification. Items such as starter motors and alternators may be available under a service exchange scheme – any parts returned should be clean.

Our advice regarding spare parts is as follows.

Officially appointed garages

This is the best source of parts which are peculiar to your car, and which are not otherwise generally available (eg, badges, interior trim, certain body panels, etc). It is also the only place at which you should buy parts if the car is still under warranty.

Accessory shops

These are very good places to buy materials and components needed for the maintenance of your car (oil, air and fuel filters, light bulbs, drivebelts, greases, brake pads, touch-up paint, etc). Components of this nature

sold by a reputable shop are usually of the same standard as those used by the car manufacturer.

Besides components, these shops also sell tools and general accessories, usually have convenient opening hours, charge lower prices, and can often be found close to home. Some accessory shops have parts counters where components needed for almost any repair job can be purchased or ordered.

Motor factors

Good factors will stock all the more important components which wear out comparatively quickly, and can sometimes supply individual components needed for the overhaul of a larger assembly (eg, brake seals and hydraulic parts, bearing shells, pistons, valves). They may also handle work such as cylinder block reboring, crankshaft regrinding, etc.

Engine reconditioners

These specialise in engine overhaul and can also supply components. It is recommended that the establishment is a member of the Federation of Engine Re-Manufacturers, or a similar society.

Tyre and exhaust specialists

These outlets may be independent, or members of a local or national chain. They frequently offer competitive prices when compared with a main dealer or local garage, but it will pay to obtain several quotes before making a decision. When researching prices, also ask what extras may be added – for instance fitting a new valve, balancing the wheel and tyre disposal all both commonly charged on top of the price of a new tyre.

Other sources

Beware of parts or materials obtained from market stalls, car boot sales, on-line auctions or similar outlets. Such items are not invariably sub-standard, but there is little chance of compensation if they do prove unsatisfactory. In the case of safety-critical components such as brake pads, there is the risk not only of financial loss, but also of an accident causing injury or death.

Second-hand components or assemblies obtained from a car breaker can be a good buy in some circumstances, but this sort of purchase is best made by the experienced DIY mechanic.

Vehicle identification numbers

Modifications are a continuing and unpublicised process in vehicle manufacture, quite apart from major model changes. Spare parts manuals and lists are compiled upon a numerical basis, the individual vehicle identification numbers being essential to correct identification of the component concerned.

When ordering spare parts, always give

as much information as possible. Quote the vehicle type and year, vehicle identification number (VIN), and engine number, as appropriate.

The vehicle identification number (VIN) is visible through the windscreen and is also located on a plate on right-hand door B-pillar **(see illustrations)**. The model plate also

gives vehicle loading details, engine type, and various trim and colour codes.

The engine number is stamped on the right-hand end of the cylinder block.

The transmission identification numbers are located on a plate attached to the top of the transmission casing, or cast into the casing itself.

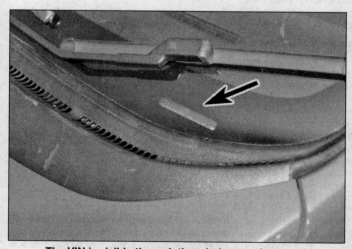

The VIN is visible through the windscreen (arrowed)

...and also repeated on a plate on the B-pillar

General repair procedures

Whenever servicing, repair or overhaul work is carried out on the car or its components, observe the following procedures and instructions. This will assist in carrying out the operation efficiently and to a professional standard of workmanship.

Joint mating faces and gaskets

When separating components at their mating faces, never insert screwdrivers or similar implements into the joint between the faces in order to prise them apart. This can cause severe damage which results in oil leaks, coolant leaks, etc upon reassembly. Separation is usually achieved by tapping along the joint with a soft-faced hammer in order to break the seal. However, note that this method may not be suitable where dowels are used for component location.

Where a gasket is used between the mating faces of two components, a new one must be fitted on reassembly; fit it dry unless otherwise stated in the repair procedure. Make sure that the mating faces are clean and dry, with all traces of old gasket removed. When cleaning a joint face, use a tool which is unlikely to score or damage the face, and remove any burrs or nicks with an oilstone or fine file.

Make sure that tapped holes are cleaned with a pipe cleaner, and keep them free of jointing compound, if this is being used, unless specifically instructed otherwise.

Ensure that all orifices, channels or pipes are clear, and blow through them, preferably using compressed air.

Oil seals

Oil seals can be removed by levering them out with a wide flat-bladed screwdriver or similar implement. Alternatively, a number of self-tapping screws may be screwed into the seal, and these used as a purchase for pliers or some similar device in order to pull the seal free.

Whenever an oil seal is removed from its working location, either individually or as part of an assembly, it should be renewed.

The very fine sealing lip of the seal is easily damaged, and will not seal if the surface it contacts is not completely clean and free from scratches, nicks or grooves. If the original sealing surface of the component cannot be restored, and the manufacturer has not made provision for slight relocation of the seal relative to the sealing surface, the component should be renewed.

Protect the lips of the seal from any surface which may damage them in the course of fitting. Use tape or a conical sleeve where possible. Where indicated, lubricate the seal lips with oil before fitting and, on dual-lipped seals, fill the space between the lips with grease.

Unless otherwise stated, oil seals must be fitted with their sealing lips toward the lubricant to be sealed.

Use a tubular drift or block of wood of the appropriate size to install the seal and, if the seal housing is shouldered, drive the seal down to the shoulder. If the seal housing is unshouldered, the seal should be fitted with its face flush with the housing top face (unless otherwise instructed).

Screw threads and fastenings

Seized nuts, bolts and screws are quite a common occurrence where corrosion has set in, and the use of penetrating oil or releasing fluid will often overcome this problem if the offending item is soaked for a while before attempting to release it. The use of an impact driver may also provide a means of releasing such stubborn fastening devices, when used in conjunction with the appropriate screwdriver bit or socket. If none of these methods works, it may be necessary to resort to the careful application of heat, or the use of a hacksaw or nut splitter device. Before resorting to extreme methods, check that you are not dealing with a left-hand thread!

Studs are usually removed by locking two nuts together on the threaded part, and then using a spanner on the lower nut to unscrew the stud. Studs or bolts which have broken off below the surface of the component in which they are mounted can sometimes be removed using a stud extractor.

Always ensure that a blind tapped hole is completely free from oil, grease, water or other fluid before installing the bolt or stud. Failure to do this could cause the housing to crack due to the hydraulic action of the bolt or stud as it is screwed in.

For some screw fastenings, notably cylinder head bolts or nuts, torque wrench settings are no longer specified for the latter stages of tightening, "angle-tightening" being called up instead. Typically, a fairly low torque wrench setting will be applied to the bolts/nuts in the correct sequence, followed by one or more stages of tightening through specified angles.

When checking or retightening a nut or bolt to a specified torque setting, slacken the nut or bolt by a quarter of a turn, and then retighten to the specified setting. However, this should not be attempted where angular tightening has been used.

Locknuts, locktabs and washers

Any fastening which will rotate against a component or housing during tightening should always have a washer between it and the relevant component or housing.

Spring or split washers should always be renewed when they are used to lock a critical component such as a big-end bearing retaining bolt or nut. Locktabs which are folded over to retain a nut or bolt should always be renewed.

Self-locking nuts can be re-used in non-critical areas, providing resistance can be felt when the locking portion passes over the bolt or stud thread. However, it should be noted that self-locking stiffnuts tend to lose their effectiveness after long periods of use, and should then be renewed as a matter of course.

Split pins must always be replaced with new ones of the correct size for the hole.

When thread-locking compound is found on the threads of a fastener which is to be re-used, it should be cleaned off with a wire brush and solvent, and fresh compound applied on reassembly.

Special tools

Some repair procedures in this manual entail the use of special tools such as a press, two or three-legged pullers, spring compressors, etc. Wherever possible, suitable readily-available alternatives to the manufacturer's special tools are described, and are shown in use. In some instances, where no alternative is possible, it has been necessary to resort to the use of a manufacturer's tool, and this has been done for reasons of safety as well as the efficient completion of the repair operation. Unless you are highly-skilled and have a thorough understanding of the procedures described, never attempt to bypass the use of any special tool when the procedure described specifies its use. Not only is there a very great risk of personal injury, but expensive damage could be caused to the components involved.

Environmental considerations

When disposing of used engine oil, brake fluid, antifreeze, etc, give due consideration to any detrimental environmental effects. Do not, for instance, pour any of the above liquids down drains into the general sewage system, or onto the ground to soak away, as this is likely to pollute your local environment. Many local council refuse tips provide a facility for waste oil disposal, as do some garages. You can find your nearest disposal point by calling the Environment Agency on 03708 506 506 or by visiting www.oilbankline.org.uk.

Note: It is illegal and anti-social to dump oil down the drain. To find the location of your local oil recycling bank, call 03708 506 506 or visit www.oilbankline.org.uk.

The jack available as a Ford accessory should **only** be used for changing the roadwheels in an emergency. When carrying out any other kind of work, raise the vehicle using a heavy-duty hydraulic (or 'trolley') jack, and always supplement the jack with axle stands positioned under the vehicle jacking points. If the roadwheels do not have to be removed, consider using wheel ramps – if wished, these can be placed under the wheels once the vehicle has been raised using a hydraulic jack, and the vehicle lowered onto the ramps so that it is resting on its wheels.

Only ever jack the vehicle up on a solid, level surface. If there is even a slight slope, take great care that the vehicle cannot move as the wheels are lifted off the ground. Jacking up on an uneven or gravelled surface is not recommended, as the weight of the vehicle will not be evenly distributed, and the jack may slip as the vehicle is raised.

As far as possible, do not leave the vehicle unattended once it has been raised, particularly if children are playing nearby.

Before jacking up the front of the car, ensure that the handbrake is firmly applied. When jacking up the rear of the car, place wooden chocks in front of the front wheels, and engage first gear.

When using a hydraulic jack or axle stands, always position the jack head or axle stand head under the relevant jacking points. These are situated directly underneath the vehicle jack location marks in the sill **(see illustrations)**.

The jack supplied with the vehicle locates in the holes provided in the sill. Ensure that the jack head is correctly engaged before attempting to raise the vehicle.

Never work under, around, or near a raised vehicle, unless it is adequately supported in at least two places.

When jacking or supporting the vehicle at these points, always use a block of wood between the jack head or axle stand, and the vehicle body. It is also considered good practice to use a large block of wood when supporting under other areas, to spread the load over a wider area, and reduce the risk of damage to the underside of the car (it also helps to prevent the underbody coating from being damaged by the jack or axle stand). **Do not** jack the vehicle under any other part of the sill, engine sump, floor pan, subframe, or directly under any of the steering or suspension components.

Never work under, around, or near a raised vehicle, unless it is adequately supported on stands. Do not rely on a jack alone, as even a hydraulic jack could fail under load. Makeshift methods should not be used to lift and support the car during servicing work.

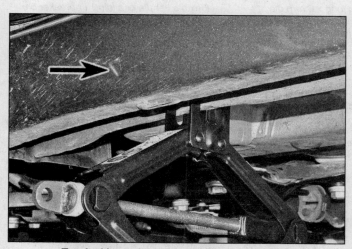

Two jacking points are provided on each side

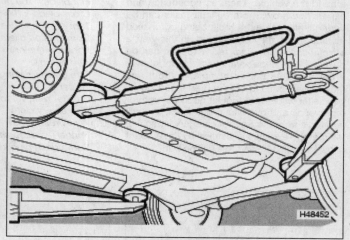

Heavy duty jacking points

Introduction

A selection of good tools is a fundamental requirement for anyone contemplating the maintenance and repair of a motor vehicle. For the owner who does not possess any, their purchase will prove a considerable expense, offsetting some of the savings made by doing-it-yourself. However, provided that the tools purchased meet the relevant national safety standards and are of good quality, they will last for many years and prove an extremely worthwhile investment.

To help the average owner to decide which tools are needed to carry out the various tasks detailed in this manual, we have compiled three lists of tools under the following headings: *Maintenance and minor repair, Repair and overhaul*, and *Special*. Newcomers to practical mechanics should start off with the *Maintenance and minor repair* tool kit, and confine themselves to the simpler jobs around the vehicle. Then, as confidence and experience grow, more difficult tasks can be undertaken, with extra tools being purchased as, and when, they are needed. In this way, a *Maintenance and minor repair* tool kit can be built up into a *Repair and overhaul* tool kit over a considerable period of time, without any major cash outlays. The experienced do-it-yourselfer will have a tool kit good enough for most repair and overhaul procedures, and will add tools from the *Special* category when it is felt that the expense is justified by the amount of use to which these tools will be put.

Maintenance and minor repair tool kit

The tools given in this list should be considered as a minimum requirement if routine maintenance, servicing and minor repair operations are to be undertaken. We recommend the purchase of combination spanners (ring one end, open-ended the other); although more expensive than open-ended ones, they do give the advantages of both types of spanner.

- ☐ *Combination spanners:*
  Metric - 8 to 19 mm inclusive
- ☐ *Adjustable spanner - 35 mm jaw (approx.)*
- ☐ *Spark plug spanner (with rubber insert) - petrol models*
- ☐ *Spark plug gap adjustment tool - petrol models*
- ☐ *Set of feeler gauges*
- ☐ *Brake bleed nipple spanner*
- ☐ *Screwdrivers:*
  Flat blade - 100 mm long x 6 mm dia
  Cross blade - 100 mm long x 6 mm dia
  Torx - various sizes (not all vehicles)
- ☐ *Combination pliers*
- ☐ *Hacksaw (junior)*
- ☐ *Tyre pump*
- ☐ *Tyre pressure gauge*
- ☐ *Oil can*
- ☐ *Oil filter removal tool (if applicable)*
- ☐ *Fine emery cloth*
- ☐ *Wire brush (small)*
- ☐ *Funnel (medium size)*
- ☐ *Sump drain plug key (not all vehicles)*

Repair and overhaul tool kit

These tools are virtually essential for anyone undertaking any major repairs to a motor vehicle, and are additional to those given in the *Maintenance and minor repair* list. Included in this list is a comprehensive set of sockets. Although these are expensive, they will be found invaluable as they are so versatile - particularly if various drives are included in the set. We recommend the half-inch square-drive type, as this can be used with most proprietary torque wrenches.

The tools in this list will sometimes need to be supplemented by tools from the *Special* list:

- ☐ *Sockets to cover range in previous list (including Torx sockets)*
- ☐ *Reversible ratchet drive (for use with sockets)*
- ☐ *Extension piece, 250 mm (for use with sockets)*
- ☐ *Universal joint (for use with sockets)*
- ☐ *Flexible handle or sliding T "breaker bar" (for use with sockets)*
- ☐ *Torque wrench (for use with sockets)*
- ☐ *Self-locking grips*
- ☐ *Ball pein hammer*
- ☐ *Soft-faced mallet (plastic or rubber)*
- ☐ *Screwdrivers:*
  Flat blade - long & sturdy, short (chubby), and narrow (electrician's) types
  Cross blade - long & sturdy, and short (chubby) types
- ☐ *Pliers:*
  Long-nosed
  Side cutters (electrician's)
  Circlip (internal and external)
- ☐ *Cold chisel - 25 mm*
- ☐ *Scriber*
- ☐ *Scraper*
- ☐ *Centre-punch*
- ☐ *Pin punch*
- ☐ *Hacksaw*
- ☐ *Brake hose clamp*
- ☐ *Brake/clutch bleeding kit*
- ☐ *Selection of twist drills*
- ☐ *Steel rule/straight-edge*
- ☐ *Allen keys (inc. splined/Torx type)*
- ☐ *Selection of files*
- ☐ *Wire brush*
- ☐ *Axle stands*
- ☐ *Jack (strong trolley or hydraulic type)*
- ☐ *Light with extension lead*
- ☐ *Universal electrical multi-meter*

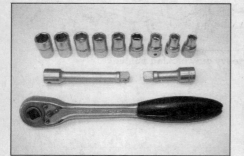

Sockets and reversible ratchet drive

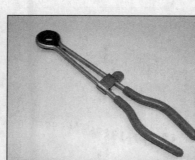

Brake bleeding kit

Torx key, socket and bit

Hose clamp

Angular-tightening gauge

Special tools

The tools in this list are those which are not used regularly, are expensive to buy, or which need to be used in accordance with their manufacturers' instructions. Unless relatively difficult mechanical jobs are undertaken frequently, it will not be economic to buy many of these tools. Where this is the case, you could consider clubbing together with friends (or joining a motorists' club) to make a joint purchase, or borrowing the tools against a deposit from a local garage or tool hire specialist.

The following list contains only those tools and instruments freely available to the public, and not those special tools produced by the vehicle manufacturer specifically for its dealer network. You will find occasional references to these manufacturers' special tools in the text of this manual. Generally, an alternative method of doing the job without the vehicle manufacturers' special tool is given. However, sometimes there is no alternative to using them. Where this is the case and the relevant tool cannot be bought or borrowed, you will have to entrust the work to a dealer.

☐ Angular-tightening gauge
☐ Valve spring compressor
☐ Valve grinding tool
☐ Piston ring compressor
☐ Piston ring removal/installation tool
☐ Cylinder bore hone
☐ Balljoint separator
☐ Coil spring compressors (where applicable)
☐ Two/three-legged hub and bearing puller
☐ Impact screwdriver
☐ Micrometer and/or vernier calipers
☐ Dial gauge
☐ Tachometer
☐ Fault code reader
☐ Cylinder compression gauge
☐ Hand-operated vacuum pump and gauge
☐ Clutch plate alignment set
☐ Brake shoe steady spring cup removal tool
☐ Bush and bearing removal/installation set
☐ Stud extractors
☐ Tap and die set
☐ Lifting tackle

Buying tools

Reputable motor accessory shops and superstores often offer excellent quality tools at discount prices, so it pays to shop around.

Remember, you don't have to buy the most expensive items on the shelf, but it is always advisable to steer clear of the very cheap tools. Beware of 'bargains' offered on market stalls, on-line or at car boot sales. There are plenty of good tools around at reasonable prices, but always aim to purchase items which meet the relevant national safety standards. If in doubt, ask the proprietor or manager of the shop for advice before making a purchase.

Care and maintenance of tools

Having purchased a reasonable tool kit, it is necessary to keep the tools in a clean and serviceable condition. After use, always wipe off any dirt, grease and metal particles using a clean, dry cloth, before putting the tools away. Never leave them lying around after they have been used. A simple tool rack on the garage or workshop wall for items such as screwdrivers and pliers is a good idea. Store all normal spanners and sockets in a metal box. Any measuring instruments, gauges, meters, etc, must be carefully stored where they cannot be damaged or become rusty.

Take a little care when tools are used. Hammer heads inevitably become marked, and screwdrivers lose the keen edge on their blades from time to time. A little timely attention with emery cloth or a file will soon restore items like this to a good finish.

Working facilities

Not to be forgotten when discussing tools is the workshop itself. If anything more than routine maintenance is to be carried out, a suitable working area becomes essential.

It is appreciated that many an owner-mechanic is forced by circumstances to remove an engine or similar item without the benefit of a garage or workshop. Having done this, any repairs should always be done under the cover of a roof.

Wherever possible, any dismantling should be done on a clean, flat workbench or table at a suitable working height.

Any workbench needs a vice; one with a jaw opening of 100 mm is suitable for most jobs. As mentioned previously, some clean dry storage space is also required for tools, as well as for any lubricants, cleaning fluids, touch-up paints etc, which become necessary.

Another item which may be required, and which has a much more general usage, is an electric drill with a chuck capacity of at least 8 mm. This, together with a good range of twist drills, is virtually essential for fitting accessories.

Last, but not least, always keep a supply of old newspapers and clean, lint-free rags available, and try to keep any working area as clean as possible.

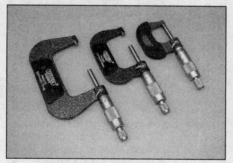

Micrometers

Dial test indicator ("dial gauge")

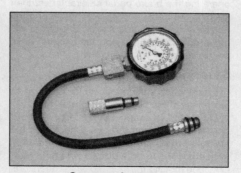

Oil filter removal tool (strap wrench type)

Compression tester

Bearing puller

This is a guide to getting your vehicle through the MOT test. Obviously it will not be possible to examine the vehicle to the same standard as the professional MOT tester. However, working through the following checks will enable you to identify any problem areas before submitting the vehicle for the test.

It has only been possible to summarise the test requirements here, based on the regulations in force at the time of printing. Test standards are becoming increasingly stringent, although there are some exemptions for older vehicles.

An assistant will be needed to help carry out some of these checks.

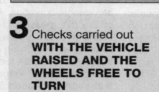

The checks have been sub-divided into four categories, as follows:

1 Checks carried out **FROM THE DRIVER'S SEAT**

2 Checks carried out **WITH THE VEHICLE ON THE GROUND**

3 Checks carried out **WITH THE VEHICLE RAISED AND THE WHEELS FREE TO TURN**

4 Checks carried out on **YOUR VEHICLE'S EXHAUST EMISSION SYSTEM**

---

1 Checks carried out **FROM THE DRIVER'S SEAT**

Handbrake (parking brake)

☐ Test the operation of the handbrake. Excessive travel (too many clicks) indicates incorrect brake or cable adjustment.
☐ Check that the handbrake cannot be released by tapping the lever sideways. Check the security of the lever mountings.

☐ If the parking brake is foot-operated, check that the pedal is secure and without excessive travel, and that the release mechanism operates correctly.
☐ Where applicable, test the operation of the electronic handbrake. The brake should engage and disengage without excessive delay. If the warning light does not extinguish when the brake is disengaged, this could indicate a fault which will need further investigation.

Footbrake

☐ Depress the brake pedal and check that it does not creep down to the floor, indicating a master cylinder fault. Release the pedal,
wait a few seconds, then depress it again. If the pedal travels nearly to the floor before firm resistance is felt, brake adjustment or repair is necessary. If the pedal feels spongy, there is air in the hydraulic system which must be removed by bleeding.

☐ Check that the brake pedal is secure and in good condition. Check also for signs of fluid leaks on the pedal, floor or carpets, which would indicate failed seals in the brake master cylinder.
☐ Check the servo unit (when applicable) by operating the brake pedal several times, then keeping the pedal depressed and starting the engine. As the engine starts, the pedal will move down slightly. If not, the vacuum hose or the servo itself may be faulty.

Steering wheel and column

☐ Examine the steering wheel for fractures or looseness of the hub, spokes or rim.
☐ Move the steering wheel from side to side and then up and down. Check that the steering wheel is not loose on the column, indicating wear or a loose retaining nut. Continue moving the steering wheel as before, but also turn it slightly from left to right.

☐ Check that the steering wheel is not loose on the column, and that there is no abnormal movement of the steering wheel, indicating wear in the column support bearings or couplings.
☐ Check that the ignition lock (where fitted) engages and disengages correctly.
☐ Steering column adjustment mechanisms (where fitted) must be able to lock the column securely in place with no play evident.

Windscreen, mirrors and sunvisor

☐ The windscreen must be free of cracks or other significant damage within the driver's field of view. (Small stone chips are acceptable.) Rear view mirrors must be secure, intact, and capable of being adjusted.

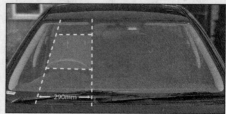

☐ The driver's sunvisor must be capable of being stored in the "up" position.

Seat belts and seats

Note: *The following checks are applicable to all seat belts, front and rear.*

☐ Examine the webbing of all the belts (including rear belts if fitted) for cuts, serious fraying or deterioration. Fasten and unfasten each belt to check the buckles. If applicable, check the retracting mechanism. Check the security of all seat belt mountings accessible from inside the vehicle, ensuring any height adjustable mountings lock securely in place.

☐ Seat belts with pre-tensioners, once activated, have a "flag" or similar showing on the seat belt stalk. This, in itself, is not a reason for test failure.

☐ The front seats themselves must be securely attached and the backrests must lock in the upright position.

Doors

☐ Both front doors must be able to be opened and closed from outside and inside, and must latch securely when closed.

Bonnet and boot/tailgate

☐ The bonnet and boot/tailgate must latch securely when closed.

2 Checks carried out WITH THE VEHICLE ON THE GROUND

Vehicle identification

☐ Number plates must be in good condition, secure and legible, with letters and numbers correctly spaced – spacing at (A) should be 33 mm and at (B) 11 mm. At the front, digits must be black on a white background and at the rear black on a yellow background. Other background designs (such as honeycomb) are not permitted.

☐ The VIN plate and/or homologation plate must be permanently displayed and legible.

Electrical equipment

☐ Switch on the ignition and check the operation of the horn.

☐ Check the windscreen washers and wipers, examining the wiper blades; renew damaged or perished blades. Also check the operation of the stop-lights.

☐ Check the operation of the sidelights and number plate lights. The lenses and reflectors must be secure, clean and undamaged.

☐ Check the operation and alignment of the headlights. The headlight reflectors must not be tarnished and the lenses must be undamaged.

☐ Switch on the ignition and check the operation of the direction indicators (including the instrument panel tell-tale) and the hazard warning lights. Operation of the sidelights and stop-lights must not affect the indicators - if it does, the cause is usually a bad earth at the rear light cluster. Indicators should flash at a rate of between 60 and 120 times per minute – faster or slower than this could indicate a fault with the flasher unit or a bad earth at one of the light units.

☐ Check the operation of the rear foglight(s), including the warning light on the instrument panel or in the switch.

☐ The warning lights must illuminate in accordance with the manufacturer's design. For most vehicles, the ABS and other warning lights should illuminate when the ignition is switched on, and (if the system is operating properly) extinguish after a few seconds. Refer to the owner's handbook.

Footbrake

☐ Examine the master cylinder, brake pipes and servo unit for leaks, loose mountings, corrosion or other damage. If ABS is fitted, this unit should also be examined for signs of leaks or corrosion.

☐ The fluid reservoir must be secure and the fluid level must be between the upper (A) and lower (B) markings.

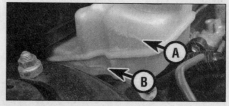

☐ Inspect both front brake flexible hoses for cracks or deterioration of the rubber. Turn the steering from lock to lock, and ensure that the hoses do not contact the wheel, tyre, or any part of the steering or suspension mechanism. With the brake pedal firmly depressed, check the hoses for bulges or leaks under pressure.

Steering and suspension

☐ Have your assistant turn the steering wheel from side to side slightly, up to the point where the steering gear just begins to transmit this movement to the roadwheels. Check for excessive free play between the steering wheel and the steering gear, indicating wear or insecurity of the steering column joints, the column-to-steering gear coupling, or the steering gear itself.

☐ Have your assistant turn the steering wheel more vigorously in each direction, so that the roadwheels just begin to turn. As this is done, examine all the steering joints, linkages, fittings and attachments. Renew any component that shows signs of wear or damage. On vehicles with power steering, check the security and condition of the steering pump, drivebelt and hoses.

☐ Check that the vehicle is standing level, and at approximately the correct ride height.

Shock absorbers

☐ Depress each corner of the vehicle in turn, then release it. The vehicle should rise and then settle in its normal position. If the vehicle continues to rise and fall, the shock absorber is defective. A shock absorber which has seized will also cause the vehicle to fail.

Exhaust system

☐ Start the engine. With your assistant holding a rag over the tailpipe, check the entire system for leaks. Repair or renew leaking sections.

3 Checks carried out
WITH THE VEHICLE RAISED AND THE WHEELS FREE TO TURN

Jack up the front and rear of the vehicle, and securely support it on axle stands. Position the stands clear of the suspension assemblies. Ensure that the wheels are clear of the ground and that the steering can be turned from lock to lock.

Steering mechanism

☐ Have your assistant turn the steering from lock to lock. Check that the steering turns smoothly, and that no part of the steering mechanism, including a wheel or tyre, fouls any brake hose or pipe or any part of the body structure.

☐ Examine the steering rack rubber gaiters for damage or insecurity of the retaining clips. If power steering is fitted, check for signs of damage or leakage of the fluid hoses, pipes or connections. Also check for excessive stiffness or binding of the steering, a missing split pin or locking device, or severe corrosion of the body structure within 30 cm of any steering component attachment point.

Front and rear suspension and wheel bearings

☐ Starting at the front right-hand side, grasp the roadwheel at the 3 o'clock and 9 o'clock positions and rock gently but firmly. Check for free play or insecurity at the wheel bearings, suspension balljoints, or suspension mount-ings, pivots and attachments.

☐ Now grasp the wheel at the 12 o'clock and 6 o'clock positions and repeat the previous inspection. Spin the wheel, and check for roughness or tightness of the front wheel bearing.

☐ If excess free play is suspected at a component pivot point, this can be confirmed by using a large screwdriver or similar tool and levering between the mounting and the component attachment. This will confirm whether the wear is in the pivot bush, its retaining bolt, or in the mounting itself (the bolt holes can often become elongated).

☐ Carry out all the above checks at the other front wheel, and then at both rear wheels.

Springs and shock absorbers

☐ Examine the suspension struts (when applicable) for serious fluid leakage, corrosion, or damage to the casing. Also check the security of the mounting points.

☐ If coil springs are fitted, check that the spring ends locate in their seats, and that the spring is not corroded, cracked or broken.

☐ If leaf springs are fitted, check that all leaves are intact, that the axle is securely attached to each spring, and that there is no deterioration of the spring eye mountings, bushes, and shackles.

☐ The same general checks apply to vehicles fitted with other suspension types, such as torsion bars, hydraulic displacer units, etc. Ensure that all mountings and attachments are secure, that there are no signs of excessive wear, corrosion or damage, and (on hydraulic types) that there are no fluid leaks or damaged pipes.

☐ Inspect the shock absorbers for signs of serious fluid leakage. Check for wear of the mounting bushes or attachments, or damage to the body of the unit.

Driveshafts (fwd vehicles only)

☐ Rotate each front wheel in turn and inspect the constant velocity joint gaiters for splits or damage. Also check that each driveshaft is straight and undamaged.

Braking system

☐ If possible without dismantling, check brake pad wear and disc condition. Ensure that the friction lining material has not worn excessively, (A) and that the discs are not fractured, pitted, scored or badly worn (B).

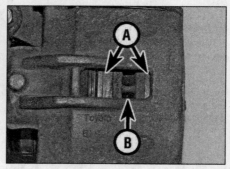

☐ Examine all the rigid brake pipes underneath the vehicle, and the flexible hose(s) at the rear. Look for corrosion, chafing or insecurity of the pipes, and for signs of bulging under pressure, chafing, splits or deterioration of the flexible hoses.

☐ Look for signs of fluid leaks at the brake calipers or on the brake backplates. Repair or renew leaking components.

☐ Slowly spin each wheel, while your assistant depresses and releases the footbrake. Ensure that each brake is operating and does not bind when the pedal is released.

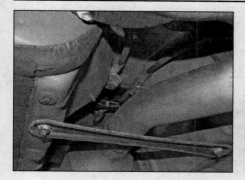

□ Examine the handbrake mechanism, checking for frayed or broken cables, excessive corrosion, or wear or insecurity of the linkage. Check that the mechanism works on each relevant wheel, and releases fully, without binding.

□ It is not possible to test brake efficiency without special equipment, but a road test can be carried out later to check that the vehicle pulls up in a straight line.

Fuel and exhaust systems

□ Inspect the fuel tank (including the filler cap), fuel pipes, hoses and unions. All components must be secure and free from leaks. Locking fuel caps must lock securely and the key must be provided for the MOT test.

□ Examine the exhaust system over its entire length, checking for any damaged, broken or missing mountings, security of the retaining clamps and rust or corrosion.

Wheels and tyres

□ Examine the sidewalls and tread area of each tyre in turn. Check for cuts, tears, lumps, bulges, separation of the tread, and exposure of the ply or cord due to wear or damage. Check that the tyre bead is correctly seated on the wheel rim, that the valve is sound and properly seated, and that the wheel is not distorted or damaged.

□ Check that the tyres are of the correct size for the vehicle, that they are of the same size and type on each axle, and that the pressures are correct.

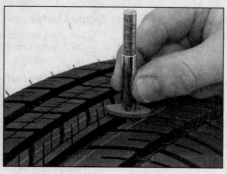

□ Check the tyre tread depth. The legal minimum at the time of writing is 1.6 mm over the central three-quarters of the tread width. Abnormal tread wear may indicate incorrect front wheel alignment or wear in steering or suspension components.

□ If the spare wheel is fitted externally or in a separate carrier beneath the vehicle, check that mountings are secure and free of excessive corrosion.

Body corrosion

□ Check the condition of the entire vehicle structure for signs of corrosion in load-bearing areas. (These include chassis box sections, side sills, cross-members, pillars, and all suspension, steering, braking system and seat belt mountings and anchorages.) Any corrosion which has seriously reduced the thickness of a load-bearing area (or is within 30 cm of safety-related components such as steering or suspension) is likely to cause the vehicle to fail. In this case professional repairs are likely to be needed.

□ Damage or corrosion which causes sharp or otherwise dangerous edges to be exposed will also cause the vehicle to fail.

Towbars

□ Check the condition of mounting points (both beneath the vehicle and within boot/hatchback areas) for signs of corrosion, ensuring that all fixings are secure and not worn or damaged. There must be no excessive play in detachable tow ball arms or quick-release mechanisms.

4 Checks carried out on YOUR VEHICLE'S EXHAUST EMISSION SYSTEM

Petrol models

□ The engine should be warmed up, and running well (ignition system in good order, air filter element clean, etc).

□ Before testing, run the engine at around 2500 rpm for 20 seconds. Let the engine drop to idle, and watch for smoke from the exhaust. If the idle speed is too high, or if dense blue or black smoke emerges for more than 5 seconds, the vehicle will fail. Typically, blue smoke signifies oil burning (engine wear);

black smoke means unburnt fuel (dirty air cleaner element, or other fuel system fault).

□ An exhaust gas analyser for measuring carbon monoxide (CO) and hydrocarbons (HC) is now needed. If one cannot be hired or borrowed, have a local garage perform the check.

CO emissions (mixture)

□ The MOT tester has access to the CO limits for all vehicles. The CO level is measured at idle speed, and at 'fast idle' (2500 to 3000 rpm). The following limits are given as a general guide:

At idle speed – Less than 0.5% CO
At 'fast idle' – Less than 0.3% CO
Lambda reading – 0.97 to 1.03

□ If the CO level is too high, this may point to poor maintenance, a fuel injection system problem, faulty lambda (oxygen) sensor or catalytic converter. Try an injector cleaning treatment, and check the vehicle's ECU for fault codes.

HC emissions

□ The MOT tester has access to HC limits for all vehicles. The HC level is measured at 'fast idle' (2500 to 3000 rpm). The following limits are given as a general guide:

At 'fast idle' – Less then 200 ppm

□ Excessive HC emissions are typically caused by oil being burnt (worn engine), or by a blocked crankcase ventilation system ('breather'). If the engine oil is old and thin, an oil change may help. If the engine is running badly, check the vehicle's ECU for fault codes.

Diesel models

□ The only emission test for diesel engines is measuring exhaust smoke density, using a calibrated smoke meter. The test involves accelerating the engine at least 3 times to its maximum unloaded speed.

Note: *On engines with a timing belt, it is VITAL that the belt is in good condition before the test is carried out.*

□ With the engine warmed up, it is first purged by running at around 2500 rpm for 20 seconds. A governor check is then carried out, by slowly accelerating the engine to its maximum speed. After this, the smoke meter is connected, and the engine is accelerated quickly to maximum speed three times. If the smoke density is less than the limits given below, the vehicle will pass:

Non-turbo vehicles: 2.5m-1
Turbocharged vehicles: 3.0m-1

□ If excess smoke is produced, try fitting a new air cleaner element, or using an injector cleaning treatment. If the engine is running badly, where applicable, check the vehicle's ECU for fault codes. Also check the vehicle's EGR system, where applicable. At high mileages, the injectors may require professional attention.

Engine

☐ Engine fails to rotate when attempting to start
☐ Engine rotates, but will not start
☐ Engine difficult to start when cold
☐ Engine difficult to start when hot
☐ Starter motor noisy or excessively-rough in engagement
☐ Engine starts, but stops immediately
☐ Engine idles erratically
☐ Engine misfires at idle speed
☐ Engine misfires throughout the driving speed range
☐ Engine hesitates on acceleration
☐ Engine stalls
☐ Engine lacks power
☐ Engine backfires
☐ Oil pressure warning light illuminated with engine running
☐ Engine runs-on after switching off
☐ Engine noises

Cooling system

☐ Overheating
☐ Overcooling
☐ External coolant leakage
☐ Internal coolant leakage
☐ Corrosion

Fuel and exhaust systems

☐ Excessive fuel consumption
☐ Fuel leakage and/or fuel odour
☐ Excessive noise or fumes from exhaust system

Clutch

☐ Pedal travels to floor – no pressure or very little resistance
☐ Clutch fails to disengage (unable to select gears)
☐ Clutch slips (engine speed increases, with no increase in vehicle speed)
☐ Judder as clutch is engaged
☐ Noise when depressing or releasing clutch pedal

Manual transmission

☐ Noisy in neutral with engine running
☐ Noisy in one particular gear
☐ Difficulty engaging gears
☐ Jumps out of gear
☐ Vibration
☐ Lubricant leaks

Driveshafts

☐ Vibration when accelerating or decelerating
☐ Clicking or knocking noise on turns (at slow speed on full-lock)

Braking system

☐ Vehicle pulls to one side under braking
☐ Noise (grinding or high-pitched squeal) when brakes applied
☐ Excessive brake pedal travel
☐ Brake pedal feels spongy when depressed
☐ Excessive brake pedal effort required to stop vehicle
☐ Judder felt through brake pedal or steering wheel when braking
☐ Brakes binding
☐ Rear wheels locking under normal braking

Suspension and steering

☐ Vehicle pulls to one side
☐ Wheel wobble and vibration
☐ Excessive pitching and/or rolling around corners, or during braking
☐ Wandering or general instability
☐ Excessively-stiff steering
☐ Excessive play in steering
☐ Lack of power assistance
☐ Tyre wear excessive

Electrical system

☐ Battery will not hold a charge for more than a few days
☐ Ignition/no-charge warning light remains illuminated with engine running
☐ Ignition/no-charge warning light fails to come on
☐ Lights inoperative
☐ Instrument readings inaccurate or erratic
☐ Horn inoperative, or unsatisfactory in operation
☐ Windscreen wipers inoperative, or unsatisfactory in operation
☐ Windscreen washers inoperative, or unsatisfactory in operation
☐ Electric windows inoperative, or unsatisfactory in operation
☐ Central locking system inoperative, or unsatisfactory in operation

Introduction

The vehicle owner who does his or her own maintenance according to the recommended service schedules should not have to use this section of the manual very often. Modern component reliability is such that, provided those items subject to wear or deterioration are inspected or renewed at the specified intervals, sudden failure is comparatively rare. Faults do not usually just happen as a result of sudden failure, but develop over a period of time. Major mechanical failures in particular are usually preceded by characteristic symptoms over hundreds or even thousands of miles. Those components which do occasionally fail without warning are often small and easily carried in the vehicle.

With any fault finding, the first step is to decide where to begin investigations. Sometimes this is obvious, but on other occasions, a little detective work will be necessary. The owner who makes half a dozen haphazard adjustments or replacements may be successful in curing a fault (or its symptoms), but will be none the wiser if the fault recurs, and ultimately may have spent more time and money than was necessary. A calm and logical approach will be found to be more satisfactory in the long run. Always take into account any warning signs or abnormalities that may have been noticed in the period preceding the fault – power loss, high or low gauge readings, unusual smells,

etc – and remember that failure of components such as fuses or spark plugs may only be pointers to some underlying fault.

The pages which follow provide an easy-reference guide to the more common problems which may occur during the operation of the vehicle. These problems and their possible causes are grouped under headings denoting various components or systems, such as Engine, Cooling system, etc. The Chapter and/or Section which deals with the problem is also shown in brackets. Whatever the fault, certain basic principles apply. These are as follows:

Verify the fault. This is simply a matter of being sure that you know what the symptoms are before starting work. This is particularly important if you are investigating a fault for someone else, who may not have described it very accurately.

Don't overlook the obvious. For example, if the vehicle won't start, is there fuel in the tank? (Don't take anyone else's word on this particular point, and don't trust the fuel gauge either). If an electrical fault is indicated, look for loose or broken wires before digging out the test gear.

Cure the disease, not the symptom. Substituting a flat battery with a fully-charged one will get you off the hard shoulder, but if the underlying cause is not attended to, the new battery will go the same way. Similarly, changing oil-fouled spark plugs for a new set will get you moving again, but remember that the reason for the fouling (if it wasn't simply an incorrect grade of plug) will have to be established and corrected.

Don't take anything for granted. Particularly, don't forget that a 'new' component may itself be defective (especially if it's been rattling around in the boot for months), and don't leave components out of a fault diagnosis sequence just because they are new or recently-fitted. When you do finally diagnose a difficult fault, you'll probably realise that all the evidence was there from the start.

Consider what work, if any, has recently been carried out. Many faults arise through careless or hurried work. For instance, if any work has been performed under the bonnet, could some of the wiring have been dislodged or incorrectly routed, or a hose trapped? Have all the fasteners been properly tightened? Were new, genuine parts and new gaskets used? There is often a certain amount of detective work to be done in this case, as an apparently-unrelated task can have far-reaching consequences.

Engine

Engine fails to rotate when attempting to start

- [ ] Battery terminal connections loose or corroded (see *Weekly checks*)
- [ ] Battery discharged or faulty (Chapter 5A)
- [ ] Broken, loose or disconnected wiring in the starting circuit (Chapter 5A)
- [ ] Defective starter solenoid or ignition switch (Chapter 5A or 10)
- [ ] Defective starter motor (Chapter 5A)
- [ ] Starter pinion or flywheel ring gear teeth loose or broken (Chapter 2A or 5A)
- [ ] Engine earth strap broken or disconnected (Chapter 12)
- [ ] Engine suffering 'hydraulic lock' (eg, from water ingested after traversing flooded roads, or from a serious internal coolant leak) – consult a Ford dealer for advice

Engine rotates, but will not start

- [ ] Fuel tank empty
- [ ] Battery discharged (engine rotates slowly) (Chapter 5A)
- [ ] Battery terminal connections loose or corroded (see *Weekly checks*)
- [ ] Ignition components damp or damaged (Chapter 1 or 5B)
- [ ] Immobiliser fault, or 'uncoded' ignition key being used (Chapter 12 or *Roadside repairs*)
- [ ] Crankshaft sensor fault (Chapter 4A)
- [ ] Broken, loose or disconnected wiring in the ignition circuit (Chapter 1 or 5B)
- [ ] Worn, faulty or incorrectly-gapped spark plugs (Chapter 1)
- [ ] Preheating system faulty – diesel models (Chapter 5A)
- [ ] Fuel injection system fault (Chapter 4A)
- [ ] Major mechanical failure (eg, timing belt snapped) (Chapter 2A)

Engine difficult to start when cold

- [ ] Battery discharged (Chapter 5A)
- [ ] Battery terminal connections loose or corroded (see *Weekly checks*)
- [ ] Worn, faulty or incorrectly-gapped spark plugs (Chapter 1)
- [ ] Other ignition system fault (Chapter 1 or 5B)
- [ ] Fuel injection system fault (Chapter 4A)
- [ ] Wrong grade of engine oil used (*Weekly checks*, Chapter 1)
- [ ] Low cylinder compression (Chapter 2A)

Engine difficult to start when hot

- [ ] Air filter element dirty or clogged (Chapter 1)
- [ ] Fuel injection system fault (Chapter 4A)
- [ ] Low cylinder compression (Chapter 2A)

Starter motor noisy or excessively-rough in engagement

- [ ] Starter pinion or flywheel ring gear teeth loose or broken (Chapter 2A or 5A)
- [ ] Starter motor mounting bolts loose or missing (Chapter 5A)
- [ ] Starter motor internal components worn or damaged (Chapter 5A)

Engine starts, but stops immediately

- [ ] Loose or faulty electrical connections in the ignition circuit (Chapter 1 or 5B)
- [ ] Vacuum leak at the throttle body or intake manifold (Chapter 4A)
- [ ] Blocked injectors/fuel injection system fault (Chapter 4A)

Engine idles erratically

- [ ] Air filter element clogged (Chapter 1)
- [ ] Vacuum leak at the throttle body, intake manifold or associated hoses (Chapter 4A)
- [ ] Worn, faulty or incorrectly-gapped spark plugs (Chapter 1)
- [ ] Valve clearances incorrect (Chapter 1)
- [ ] Uneven or low cylinder compression (Chapter 2A)
- [ ] Camshaft lobes worn (Chapter 2A)
- [ ] Timing belt incorrectly fitted (Chapter 2A)
- [ ] Blocked injectors/fuel injection system fault (Chapter 4A)

Engine misfires at idle speed

- [ ] Worn, faulty or incorrectly-gapped spark plugs (Chapter 1)
- [ ] Faulty spark plug HT leads (Chapter 1)
- [ ] Vacuum leak at the throttle body, intake manifold or associated hoses (Chapter 4A)
- [ ] Blocked injectors/fuel injection system fault (Chapter 4A)
- [ ] Uneven or low cylinder compression (Chapter 2A)
- [ ] Disconnected, leaking, or perished crankcase ventilation hoses (Chapter 4B)

Engine misfires throughout the driving speed range

- [ ] Fuel pump faulty, or delivery pressure low (Chapter 4A)
- [ ] Fuel tank vent blocked, or fuel pipes restricted (Chapter 4A)
- [ ] Vacuum leak at the throttle body, intake manifold or associated hoses (Chapter 4A)
- [ ] Worn, faulty or incorrectly-gapped spark plugs – petrol models (Chapter 1)
- [ ] Faulty spark plug HT leads (Chapter 1)
- [ ] Faulty ignition coil (Chapter 5A)
- [ ] Uneven or low cylinder compression (Chapter 2A)
- [ ] Blocked injector/fuel injection system fault (Chapter 4A)
- [ ] Blocked catalytic converter/particulate filter (Chapter 4A)
- [ ] Engine overheating – petrol models (Chapter 3)

Engine (continued)

Engine hesitates on acceleration

- ☐ Worn, faulty or incorrectly-gapped spark plugs – petrol models (Chapter 1)
- ☐ Vacuum leak at the throttle body, intake manifold or associated hoses (Chapter 4A)
- ☐ Blocked injectors/fuel injection system fault (Chapter 4A)

Engine stalls

- ☐ Vacuum leak at the throttle body, intake manifold or associated hoses (Chapter 4A)
- ☐ Fuel pump faulty, or delivery pressure low (Chapter 4A)
- ☐ Fuel tank vent blocked, or fuel pipes restricted (Chapter 4A)
- ☐ Blocked injectors/fuel injection system fault (Chapter 4A)

Engine lacks power

- ☐ Air filter element blocked (Chapter 1)
- ☐ Fuel pipes blocked or restricted (Chapter 4A)
- ☐ Valve clearances incorrect (Chapter 1)
- ☐ Worn, faulty or incorrectly-gapped spark plugs (Chapter 1)
- ☐ Engine overheating – petrol models (Chapter 4A)
- ☐ Accelerator position sensor faulty (Chapter 4A)
- ☐ Vacuum leak at the throttle body, intake manifold or associated hoses (Chapter 4A)
- ☐ Blocked injectors/fuel injection system fault (Chapter 4A)
- ☐ Timing belt incorrectly fitted (Chapter 2A)
- ☐ Fuel pump faulty, or delivery pressure low (Chapter 4A)
- ☐ Uneven or low cylinder compression (Chapter 2A)
- ☐ Blocked catalytic converter/particulate filter (Chapter 4A)
- ☐ Brakes binding (Chapter 1 or 9)
- ☐ Clutch slipping (Chapter 6)

Engine backfires

- ☐ Timing belt incorrectly fitted (Chapter 2A)
- ☐ Vacuum leak at the throttle body, intake manifold or associated hoses (Chapter 4A)
- ☐ Blocked injectors/fuel injection system fault (Chapter 4A)
- ☐ Blocked catalytic converter/particulate filter (Chapter 4A)
- ☐ Spark plug HT leads incorrectly fitted (Chapter 1 or 5B)
- ☐ Ignition coil unit faulty – petrol models (Chapter 5B)

Oil pressure warning light illuminated with engine running

- ☐ Low oil level, or incorrect oil grade (see *Weekly checks*)
- ☐ Faulty oil pressure sensor, or wiring damaged (Chapter 5A)
- ☐ Worn engine bearings and/or oil pump (Chapter 2A)
- ☐ High engine operating temperature (Chapter 3)
- ☐ Oil pump pressure relief valve defective (Chapter 2A)
- ☐ Oil pump pick-up strainer clogged (Chapter 2A)

Engine runs-on after switching off

- ☐ Excessive carbon build-up in engine (Chapter 2A)
- ☐ High engine operating temperature (Chapter 3)
- ☐ Fuel injection system fault (Chapter 4A)

Engine noises

Pre-ignition (pinking) or knocking during acceleration or under load

- ☐ Ignition timing incorrect/ignition system fault (Chapter 1 or 5B)
- ☐ Incorrect grade of spark plug – petrol models (Chapter 1)
- ☐ Incorrect grade of fuel (Chapter 4A)
- ☐ Knock sensor faulty (Chapter 4A)
- ☐ Vacuum leak at the throttle body, intake manifold or associated hoses Chapter 4A)
- ☐ Excessive carbon build-up in engine (Chapter 2A)
- ☐ Blocked injector/fuel injection system fault (Chapter 4A)

Whistling or wheezing noises

- ☐ Leaking intake manifold or throttle body gasket (Chapter 4A)
- ☐ Leaking exhaust manifold gasket or pipe-to-manifold joint (Chapter 4A)
- ☐ Leaking vacuum hose (Chapter 4A or 9)
- ☐ Blowing cylinder head gasket (Chapter 2A)
- ☐ Partially blocked or leaking crankcase ventilation system (Chapter 4B)

Tapping or rattling noises

- ☐ Valve clearances incorrect (Chapter 1)
- ☐ Worn valve gear or camshaft (Chapter 2A)
- ☐ Ancillary component fault (coolant pump, alternator, etc) (Chapter 3, 5A, etc)

Knocking or thumping noises

- ☐ Worn big-end bearings (regular heavy knocking, perhaps less under load) (Chapter 2B)
- ☐ Worn main bearings (rumbling and knocking, perhaps worsening under load) (Chapter 2B)
- ☐ Piston slap – most noticeable when cold, caused by piston/bore wear (Chapter 2B)
- ☐ Ancillary component fault (coolant pump, alternator, etc) (Chapter 3, 5A, etc)
- ☐ Engine mountings worn or defective (Chapter 2A)
- ☐ Front suspension or steering components worn (Chapter 10)

Cooling system

Overheating

☐ Insufficient coolant in system (see *Weekly checks*)
☐ Thermostat faulty (Chapter 3)
☐ Radiator core blocked, or grille restricted (Chapter 3)
☐ Cooling fan faulty, or resistor pack fault (Chapter 3)
☐ Inaccurate coolant temperature sensor (Chapter 3)
☐ Airlock in cooling system (Chapter 3)
☐ Expansion tank pressure cap faulty (Chapter 3)
☐ Engine management system fault (Chapter 4A)

Overcooling

☐ Thermostat faulty (Chapter 3)
☐ Inaccurate coolant temperature sensor (Chapter 3)
☐ Cooling fan faulty (Chapter 3)
☐ Engine management system fault (Chapter 4A)

External coolant leakage

☐ Deteriorated or damaged hoses or hose clips (Chapter 1)
☐ Radiator core or heater matrix leaking (Chapter 3)
☐ Expansion tank pressure cap faulty (Chapter 1)
☐ Coolant pump internal seal leaking (Chapter 3)
☐ Coolant pump gasket leaking (Chapter 3)
☐ Boiling due to overheating (Chapter 3)
☐ Cylinder block core plug leaking (Chapter 2B)

Internal coolant leakage

☐ Leaking cylinder head gasket (Chapter 2A)
☐ Cracked cylinder head or cylinder block (Chapter 2A)

Corrosion

☐ Infrequent draining and flushing (Chapter 1)
☐ Incorrect coolant mixture or inappropriate coolant type (see *Weekly checks*)

Fuel and exhaust systems

Excessive fuel consumption

☐ Air filter element dirty or clogged (Chapter 1)
☐ Fuel injection system fault (Chapter 4A)
☐ Engine management system fault (Chapter 4A)
☐ Crankcase ventilation system blocked (Chapter 4B)
☐ Tyres under-inflated (see *Weekly checks*)
☐ Brakes binding (Chapter 1A or 9)
☐ Fuel leak, causing apparent high consumption (Chapter 1 or 4A)

Fuel leakage and/or fuel odour

☐ Damaged or corroded fuel tank, pipes or connections (Chapter 4A)
☐ Evaporative emissions system fault – petrol models (Chapter 4B)

Excessive noise or fumes from exhaust system

☐ Leaking exhaust system or manifold joints (Chapter 1 or 4A)
☐ Leaking, corroded or damaged silencers or pipe (Chapter 1 or 4A)
☐ Broken mountings causing body or suspension contact (Chapter 1)

Clutch

Pedal travels to floor – no pressure or very little resistance

☐ Air in hydraulic system/faulty master or slave cylinder (Chapter 6)
☐ Faulty hydraulic release system (Chapter 6)
☐ Clutch pedal return spring detached or broken (Chapter 6)
☐ Broken clutch release bearing or fork (Chapter 6)
☐ Broken diaphragm spring in clutch pressure plate (Chapter 6)

Clutch fails to disengage (unable to select gears)

☐ Air in hydraulic system/faulty master or slave cylinder (Chapter 6)
☐ Faulty hydraulic release system (Chapter 6)
☐ Clutch disc sticking on transmission input shaft splines (Chapter 6)
☐ Clutch disc sticking to flywheel or pressure plate (Chapter 6)
☐ Faulty pressure plate assembly (Chapter 6)
☐ Clutch release mechanism worn or incorrectly assembled (Chapter 6)

Clutch slips (engine speed increases, with no increase in vehicle speed)

☐ Faulty hydraulic release system (Chapter 6)
☐ Clutch disc linings excessively worn (Chapter 6)
☐ Clutch disc linings contaminated with oil or grease (Chapter 6)
☐ Faulty pressure plate or weak diaphragm spring (Chapter 6)

Judder as clutch is engaged

☐ Clutch disc linings contaminated with oil or grease (Chapter 6)
☐ Clutch disc linings excessively worn (Chapter 6)
☐ Faulty or distorted pressure plate or diaphragm spring (Chapter 6).
☐ Worn or loose engine or transmission mountings (Chapter 2A)
☐ Clutch disc hub or transmission input shaft splines worn (Chapter 6)

Noise when depressing or releasing clutch pedal

☐ Worn clutch release bearing (Chapter 6)
☐ Worn or dry clutch pedal bushes (Chapter 6)
☐ Worn or dry clutch master cylinder piston (Chapter 6)
☐ Faulty pressure plate assembly (Chapter 6)
☐ Pressure plate diaphragm spring broken (Chapter 6)
☐ Broken clutch disc cushioning springs (Chapter 6)

Manual transmission

Noisy in neutral with engine running

☐ Lack of oil (Chapter 1)
☐ Input shaft bearings worn (noise apparent with clutch pedal released, but not when depressed) (Chapter 7)*
☐ Clutch release bearing worn (noise apparent with clutch pedal depressed, possibly less when released) (Chapter 6)

Noisy in one particular gear

☐ Worn, damaged or chipped gear teeth (Chapter 7)*

Difficulty engaging gears

☐ Clutch fault (Chapter 6)
☐ Worn, damaged, or poorly-adjusted gearchange cables (Chapter 7)
☐ Lack of oil (Chapter 1)
☐ Worn synchroniser units (Chapter 7)*

Jumps out of gear

☐ Worn, damaged, or poorly-adjusted gearchange cables (Chapter 7)
☐ Worn synchroniser units (Chapter 7)*
☐ Worn selector forks (Chapter 7)*

Vibration

☐ Lack of oil (Chapter 1)
☐ Worn bearings (Chapter 7)*

Lubricant leaks

☐ Leaking driveshaft or selector shaft oil seal (Chapter 7)
☐ Leaking housing joint (Chapter 7)*
☐ Leaking input shaft oil seal (Chapter 7)*

* Although the corrective action necessary to remedy the symptoms described is beyond the scope of the home mechanic, the above information should be helpful in isolating the cause of the condition, so that the owner can communicate clearly with a professional mechanic.

Driveshafts

Vibration when accelerating or decelerating

☐ Worn inner constant velocity joint (Chapter 8)
☐ Bent or distorted driveshaft (Chapter 8)
☐ Worn intermediate bearing (Chapter 8)

Clicking or knocking noise on turns (at slow speed on full-lock)

☐ Worn outer constant velocity joint (Chapter 8)
☐ Lack of constant velocity joint lubricant, possibly due to damaged gaiter (Chapter 8)
☐ Worn intermediate bearing (Chapter 8)

Braking system

Note: *Before assuming that a brake problem exists, make sure that the tyres are in good condition and correctly inflated, that the front wheel alignment is correct, and that the vehicle is not loaded with weight in an unequal manner. Apart from checking the condition of all pipe and hose connections, any faults occurring on the anti-lock braking system should be referred to a Ford dealer for diagnosis.*

Vehicle pulls to one side under braking

☐ Worn, defective, damaged or contaminated brake pads/shoes on one side (Chapter 1 or 9)
☐ Seized or partially-seized brake caliper piston/wheel cylinder (Chapter 1 or 9)
☐ A mixture of brake pad/shoe lining materials fitted between sides (Chapter 1 or 9)
☐ Brake caliper/backplate mounting bolts loose (Chapter 9)
☐ Worn or damaged steering or suspension components (Chapter 1 or 10)

Noise (grinding or high-pitched squeal) when brakes applied

☐ Brake pad/shoe friction lining material worn down to metal backing (Chapter 1 or 9)
☐ Excessive corrosion of brake disc/drum (may be apparent after the vehicle has been standing for some time (Chapter 1 or 9)
☐ Foreign object (stone chipping, etc) trapped between brake disc and shield (Chapter 1 or 9)

Excessive brake pedal travel

☐ Faulty master cylinder (Chapter 9)
☐ Air in hydraulic system (Chapter 1, 6 or 9)
☐ Faulty vacuum servo unit (Chapter 9)

Brake pedal feels spongy when depressed

☐ Air in hydraulic system (Chapter 1, 6 or 9)
☐ Deteriorated flexible rubber brake hoses (Chapter 1 or 9)
☐ Master cylinder mounting nuts loose (Chapter 9)
☐ Faulty master cylinder (Chapter 9)

Excessive brake pedal effort required to stop vehicle

☐ Faulty vacuum servo unit (Chapter 9)
☐ Faulty vacuum pump – diesel models (Chapter 9)
☐ Disconnected, damaged or insecure brake servo vacuum hose (Chapter 9)
☐ Primary or secondary hydraulic circuit failure (Chapter 9)
☐ Seized brake caliper/wheel cylinder piston (Chapter 9)
☐ Brake pads/shoes incorrectly fitted (Chapter 9)
☐ Incorrect grade of brake pads/shoes fitted (Chapter 9)
☐ Brake pad/shoe linings contaminated (Chapter 1 or 9)

Judder felt through brake pedal or steering wheel when braking

Note: *Under heavy braking on models equipped with ABS, vibration may be felt through the brake pedal. This is a normal feature of ABS operation, and does not constitute a fault.*

☐ Excessive run-out or distortion of discs/drums (Chapter 1A or 9)
☐ Brake pad/shoe linings worn (Chapter 1A or 9)
☐ Brake caliper/backplate mounting bolts loose (Chapter 9)
☐ Wear in suspension or steering components or mountings (Chapter 1A or 10)
☐ Front wheels out of balance (see *Weekly checks*)

Brakes binding

☐ Seized brake caliper/wheel cylinder piston (Chapter 9)
☐ Incorrectly-adjusted handbrake mechanism (Chapter 9)
☐ Faulty master cylinder (Chapter 9)

Rear wheels locking under normal braking

☐ Rear brake pad/shoe linings contaminated or damaged (Chapter 1 or 9)
☐ Rear brake discs/drums warped (Chapter 1 or 9)

Suspension and steering

Note: *Before diagnosing suspension or steering faults, be sure that the trouble is not due to incorrect tyre pressures, mixtures of tyre types, or binding brakes.*

Vehicle pulls to one side

- [ ] Defective tyre (see *Weekly checks*)
- [ ] Excessive wear in suspension or steering components (Chapter 1 or 10)
- [ ] Incorrect front wheel alignment (Chapter 10)
- [ ] Accident damage to steering or suspension components (Chapter 1)

Wheel wobble and vibration

- [ ] Front wheels out of balance (vibration felt mainly through the steering wheel) (see *Weekly checks*)
- [ ] Rear wheels out of balance (vibration felt throughout the vehicle) (see *Weekly checks*)
- [ ] Roadwheels damaged or distorted (see *Weekly checks*)
- [ ] Faulty or damaged tyre (see *Weekly checks*)
- [ ] Worn steering or suspension joints, bushes or components (Chapter 1 or 10)
- [ ] Wheel bolts loose (Chapter 1)

Excessive pitching and/or rolling around corners, or during braking

- [ ] Defective shock absorbers (Chapter 1 or 10)
- [ ] Broken or weak spring and/or suspension component (Chapter 1 or 10)
- [ ] Worn or damaged anti-roll bar or mountings (Chapter 1 or 10)

Wandering or general instability

- [ ] Incorrect front wheel alignment (Chapter 10)
- [ ] Worn steering or suspension joints, bushes or components (Chapter 1 or 10)
- [ ] Roadwheels out of balance (see *Weekly checks*)
- [ ] Faulty or damaged tyre (see *Weekly checks*)
- [ ] Wheel bolts loose (Chapter 1)
- [ ] Defective shock absorbers (Chapter 1 or 10)

Excessively-stiff steering

- [ ] Seized steering linkage balljoint or suspension balljoint (Chapter 1 or 10)
- [ ] Incorrect front wheel alignment (Chapter 10)
- [ ] Steering rack damaged (Chapter 10)
- [ ] Faulty steering column motor (Chapter 10)

Excessive play in steering

- [ ] Worn steering column/intermediate shaft joints (Chapter 10)
- [ ] Worn track rod balljoints (Chapter 1 or 10)
- [ ] Worn steering rack (Chapter 10)
- [ ] Worn steering or suspension joints, bushes or components (Chapter 1 or 10)

Lack of power assistance

- [ ] Faulty steering column motor (Chapter 10)

Tyre wear excessive

Tyres worn on inside or outside edges

- [ ] Tyres under-inflated (wear on both edges) (see *Weekly checks*)
- [ ] Incorrect camber or castor angles (wear on one edge only) (Chapter 10)
- [ ] Worn steering or suspension joints, bushes or components (Chapter 1 or 10)
- [ ] Excessively-hard cornering or braking
- [ ] Accident damage

Tyre treads exhibit feathered edges

- [ ] Incorrect toe-setting (Chapter 10)

Tyres worn in centre of tread

- [ ] Tyres over-inflated (see *Weekly checks*)

Tyres worn on inside and outside edges

- [ ] Tyres under-inflated (see *Weekly checks*)

Tyres worn unevenly

- [ ] Tyres/wheels out of balance (see *Weekly checks*)
- [ ] Excessive wheel or tyre run-out
- [ ] Worn shock absorbers (Chapter 1 or 10)
- [ ] Faulty tyre (see *Weekly checks*)

Electrical system

Note: *For problems associated with the starting system, refer to the faults listed under ëEngineí earlier in this Section.*

Battery will not hold a charge for more than a few days

☐ Battery defective internally (Chapter 5A)
☐ Battery terminal connections loose or corroded (see *Weekly checks*)
☐ Auxiliary drivebelt worn or incorrectly adjusted (Chapter 1)
☐ Alternator not charging at correct output (Chapter 5A)
☐ Alternator or voltage regulator faulty (Chapter 5A)
☐ Short-circuit causing continual battery drain (Chapter 5A or 12)

Ignition/no-charge warning light remains illuminated with engine running

☐ Auxiliary drivebelt broken, worn, or incorrectly adjusted (Chapter 1)
☐ Internal fault in alternator or voltage regulator (Chapter 5A)
☐ Broken, disconnected, or loose wiring in charging circuit (Chapter 5A or 12)

Ignition/no-charge warning light fails to come on

☐ Warning light bulb blown (Chapter 12)
☐ Broken, disconnected, or loose wiring in warning light circuit (Chapter 5A or 12)
☐ Alternator faulty (Chapter 5A)

Lights inoperative

☐ Bulb blown (Chapter 12)
☐ Corrosion of bulb or bulbholder contacts (Chapter 12)
☐ Blown fuse (Chapter 12)
☐ Faulty relay (Chapter 12)
☐ Broken, loose, or disconnected wiring (Chapter 12)
☐ Faulty switch (Chapter 12)

Instrument readings inaccurate or erratic

Fuel or temperature gauges give no reading

☐ Faulty gauge sender unit (Chapter 3 or 4A)
☐ Wiring open-circuit (Chapter 12)
☐ Faulty gauge (Chapter 12)

Fuel or temperature gauges give continuous maximum reading

☐ Faulty gauge sender unit (Chapter 3 or 4A)
☐ Wiring short-circuit (Chapter 12)
☐ Faulty gauge (Chapter 12)

Horn inoperative, or unsatisfactory in operation

Horn operates all the time

☐ Horn push either earthed or stuck down (Chapter 12)
☐ Horn cable-to-horn push earthed (Chapter 12)

Horn fails to operate

☐ Blown fuse (Chapter 12)
☐ Cable or connections loose, broken or disconnected (Chapter 12)
☐ Faulty horn (Chapter 12)

Horn emits intermittent or unsatisfactory sound

☐ Cable connections loose (Chapter 12)
☐ Horn mountings loose (Chapter 12)
☐ Faulty horn (Chapter 12)

Windscreen wipers inoperative, or unsatisfactory in operation

Wipers fail to operate, or operate very slowly

☐ Wiper blades stuck to screen, or linkage seized or binding (Chapter 12)
☐ Blown fuse (Chapter 12)
☐ Battery discharged (Chapter 5A)
☐ Cable or connections loose, broken or disconnected (Chapter 12)
☐ Faulty relay (Chapter 12)
☐ Faulty wiper motor (Chapter 12)

Wiper blades sweep over too large or too small an area of the glass

☐ Wiper blades incorrectly fitted, or wrong size used (see *Weekly checks*)
☐ Wiper arms incorrectly positioned on spindles (Chapter 12)
☐ Excessive wear of wiper linkage (Chapter 12)
☐ Wiper motor or linkage mountings loose or insecure (Chapter 12)

Wiper blades fail to clean the glass effectively

☐ Wiper blade rubbers dirty, worn or perished (see *Weekly checks*)
☐ Wiper blades incorrectly fitted, or wrong size used (see *Weekly checks*)
☐ Wiper arm tension springs broken, or arm pivots seized (Chapter 12)
☐ Insufficient windscreen washer additive to adequately remove road film (see *Weekly checks*)

Windscreen washers inoperative, or unsatisfactory in operation

One or more washer jets inoperative

☐ Blocked washer jet
☐ Disconnected, kinked or restricted fluid hose (Chapter 12)
☐ Insufficient fluid in washer reservoir (see *Weekly checks*)

Washer pump fails to operate

☐ Broken or disconnected wiring or connections (Chapter 12)
☐ Blown fuse (Chapter 12)
☐ Faulty washer switch (Chapter 12)
☐ Faulty washer pump (Chapter 12)

Washer pump runs for some time before fluid is emitted from jets

☐ Faulty one-way valve in fluid supply hose (Chapter 12)

Electric windows inoperative, or unsatisfactory in operation

Window glass will only move in one direction

☐ Faulty switch (Chapter 12)

Window glass slow to move

☐ Battery discharged (Chapter 5A)
☐ Regulator seized or damaged, or in need of lubrication (Chapter 11)
☐ Door internal components or trim fouling regulator (Chapter 11)
☐ Faulty motor (Chapter 11)

Window glass fails to move

☐ Blown fuse (Chapter 12)
☐ Faulty relay (Chapter 12)
☐ Broken or disconnected wiring or connections (Chapter 12)
☐ Faulty motor (Chapter 11)

Electrical system (continued)

Central locking system inoperative, or unsatisfactory in operation

Complete system failure

☐ Remote handset battery discharged, where applicable
☐ Blown fuse (Chapter 12)
☐ Faulty relay (Chapter 12)
☐ Broken or disconnected wiring or connections (Chapter 12)
☐ Faulty motor (Chapter 11)

Latch locks but will not unlock, or unlocks but will not lock

☐ Remote handset battery discharged, where applicable

☐ Faulty master switch (Chapter 12)
☐ Broken or disconnected latch operating rods or levers (Chapter 11)
☐ Faulty relay (Chapter 12)
☐ Faulty motor (Chapter 11)

One solenoid/motor fails to operate

☐ Broken or disconnected wiring or connections (Chapter 12)
☐ Faulty operating assembly (Chapter 11)
☐ Broken, binding or disconnected latch operating rods or levers (Chapter 11)
☐ Fault in door latch (Chapter 11)

Glossary of technical terms

A

ABS (Anti-lock brake system) A system, usually electronically controlled, that senses incipient wheel lockup during braking and relieves hydraulic pressure at wheels that are about to skid.

Air bag An inflatable bag hidden in the steering wheel (driver's side) or the dash or glovebox (passenger side). In a head-on collision, the bags inflate, preventing the driver and front passenger from being thrown forward into the steering wheel or windscreen.

Air cleaner A metal or plastic housing, containing a filter element, which removes dust and dirt from the air being drawn into the engine.

Air filter element The actual filter in an air cleaner system, usually manufactured from pleated paper and requiring renewal at regular intervals.

Air filter

Allen key A hexagonal wrench which fits into a recessed hexagonal hole.

Alligator clip A long-nosed spring-loaded metal clip with meshing teeth. Used to make temporary electrical connections.

Alternator A component in the electrical system which converts mechanical energy from a drivebelt into electrical energy to charge the battery and to operate the starting system, ignition system and electrical accessories.

Ampere (amp) A unit of measurement for the flow of electric current. One amp is the amount of current produced by one volt acting through a resistance of one ohm.

Anaerobic sealer A substance used to prevent bolts and screws from loosening. Anaerobic means that it does not require oxygen for activation. The Loctite brand is widely used.

Antifreeze A substance (usually ethylene glycol) mixed with water, and added to a vehicle's cooling system, to prevent freezing of the coolant in winter. Antifreeze also contains chemicals to inhibit corrosion and the formation of rust and other deposits that would tend to clog the radiator and coolant passages and reduce cooling efficiency.

Anti-seize compound A coating that reduces the risk of seizing on fasteners that are subjected to high temperatures, such as exhaust manifold bolts and nuts.

Asbestos A natural fibrous mineral with great heat resistance, commonly used in the composition of brake friction materials.

Asbestos is a health hazard and the dust created by brake systems should never be inhaled or ingested.

Axle A shaft on which a wheel revolves, or which revolves with a wheel. Also, a solid beam that connects the two wheels at one end of the vehicle. An axle which also transmits power to the wheels is known as a live axle.

Axleshaft A single rotating shaft, on either side of the differential, which delivers power from the final drive assembly to the drive wheels. Also called a driveshaft or a halfshaft.

B

Ball bearing An anti-friction bearing consisting of a hardened inner and outer race with hardened steel balls between two races.

Bearing The curved surface on a shaft or in a bore, or the part assembled into either, that permits relative motion between them with minimum wear and friction.

Bearing

Big-end bearing The bearing in the end of the connecting rod that's attached to the crankshaft.

Bleed nipple A valve on a brake wheel cylinder, caliper or other hydraulic component that is opened to purge the hydraulic system of air. Also called a bleed screw.

Brake bleeding Procedure for removing air from lines of a hydraulic brake system.

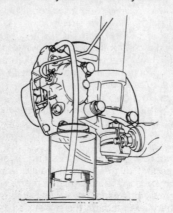

Brake bleeding

Brake disc The component of a disc brake that rotates with the wheels.

Brake drum The component of a drum brake that rotates with the wheels.

Brake linings The friction material which contacts the brake disc or drum to retard the vehicle's speed. The linings are bonded or riveted to the brake pads or shoes.

Brake pads The replaceable friction pads that pinch the brake disc when the brakes are applied. Brake pads consist of a friction material bonded or riveted to a rigid backing plate.

Brake shoe The crescent-shaped carrier to which the brake linings are mounted and which forces the lining against the rotating drum during braking.

Braking systems For more information on braking systems, consult the *Haynes Automotive Brake Manual*.

Breaker bar A long socket wrench handle providing greater leverage.

Bulkhead The insulated partition between the engine and the passenger compartment.

C

Caliper The non-rotating part of a disc-brake assembly that straddles the disc and carries the brake pads. The caliper also contains the hydraulic components that cause the pads to pinch the disc when the brakes are applied. A caliper is also a measuring tool that can be set to measure inside or outside dimensions of an object.

Camshaft A rotating shaft on which a series of cam lobes operate the valve mechanisms. The camshaft may be driven by gears, by sprockets and chain or by sprockets and a belt.

Canister A container in an evaporative emission control system; contains activated charcoal granules to trap vapours from the fuel system.

Canister

Carburettor A device which mixes fuel with air in the proper proportions to provide a desired power output from a spark ignition internal combustion engine.

Castellated Resembling the parapets along the top of a castle wall. For example, a castellated balljoint stud nut.

Castor In wheel alignment, the backward or forward tilt of the steering axis. Castor is positive when the steering axis is inclined rearward at the top.

Catalytic converter A silencer-like device in the exhaust system which converts certain pollutants in the exhaust gases into less harmful substances.

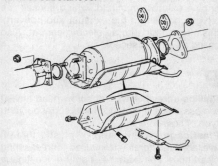

Catalytic converter

Circlip A ring-shaped clip used to prevent endwise movement of cylindrical parts and shafts. An internal circlip is installed in a groove in a housing; an external circlip fits into a groove on the outside of a cylindrical piece such as a shaft.

Clearance The amount of space between two parts. For example, between a piston and a cylinder, between a bearing and a journal, etc.

Coil spring A spiral of elastic steel found in various sizes throughout a vehicle, for example as a springing medium in the suspension and in the valve train.

Compression Reduction in volume, and increase in pressure and temperature, of a gas, caused by squeezing it into a smaller space.

Compression ratio The relationship between cylinder volume when the piston is at top dead centre and cylinder volume when the piston is at bottom dead centre.

Constant velocity (CV) joint A type of universal joint that cancels out vibrations caused by driving power being transmitted through an angle.

Core plug A disc or cup-shaped metal device inserted in a hole in a casting through which core was removed when the casting was formed. Also known as a freeze plug or expansion plug.

Crankcase The lower part of the engine block in which the crankshaft rotates.

Crankshaft The main rotating member, or shaft, running the length of the crankcase, with offset "throws" to which the connecting rods are attached.

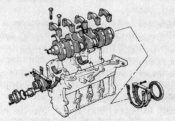

Crankshaft assembly

Crocodile clip See Alligator clip

D

Diagnostic code Code numbers obtained by accessing the diagnostic mode of an engine management computer. This code can be used to determine the area in the system where a malfunction may be located.

Disc brake A brake design incorporating a rotating disc onto which brake pads are squeezed. The resulting friction converts the energy of a moving vehicle into heat.

Double-overhead cam (DOHC) An engine that uses two overhead camshafts, usually one for the intake valves and one for the exhaust valves.

Drivebelt(s) The belt(s) used to drive accessories such as the alternator, water pump, power steering pump, air conditioning compressor, etc. off the crankshaft pulley.

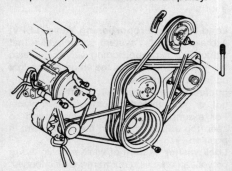

Accessory drivebelts

Driveshaft Any shaft used to transmit motion. Commonly used when referring to the axleshafts on a front wheel drive vehicle.

Drum brake A type of brake using a drum-shaped metal cylinder attached to the inner surface of the wheel. When the brake pedal is pressed, curved brake shoes with friction linings press against the inside of the drum to slow or stop the vehicle.

E

EGR valve A valve used to introduce exhaust gases into the intake air stream.

Electronic control unit (ECU) A computer which controls (for instance) ignition and fuel injection systems, or an anti-lock braking system. For more information refer to the *Haynes Automotive Electrical and Electronic Systems Manual*.

Electronic Fuel Injection (EFI) A computer controlled fuel system that distributes fuel through an injector located in each intake port of the engine.

Emergency brake A braking system, independent of the main hydraulic system, that can be used to slow or stop the vehicle if the primary brakes fail, or to hold the vehicle stationary even though the brake pedal isn't depressed. It usually consists of a hand lever that actuates either front or rear brakes mechanically through a series of cables and linkages. Also known as a handbrake or parking brake.

Endfloat The amount of lengthwise movement between two parts. As applied to a crankshaft, the distance that the crankshaft can move forward and back in the cylinder block.

Engine management system (EMS) A computer controlled system which manages the fuel injection and the ignition systems in an integrated fashion.

Exhaust manifold A part with several passages through which exhaust gases leave the engine combustion chambers and enter the exhaust pipe.

F

Fan clutch A viscous (fluid) drive coupling device which permits variable engine fan speeds in relation to engine speeds.

Feeler blade A thin strip or blade of hardened steel, ground to an exact thickness, used to check or measure clearances between parts.

Feeler blade

Firing order The order in which the engine cylinders fire, or deliver their power strokes, beginning with the number one cylinder.

Flywheel A heavy spinning wheel in which energy is absorbed and stored by means of momentum. On cars, the flywheel is attached to the crankshaft to smooth out firing impulses.

Free play The amount of travel before any action takes place. The "looseness" in a linkage, or an assembly of parts, between the initial application of force and actual movement. For example, the distance the brake pedal moves before the pistons in the master cylinder are actuated.

Fuse An electrical device which protects a circuit against accidental overload. The typical fuse contains a soft piece of metal which is calibrated to melt at a predetermined current flow (expressed as amps) and break the circuit.

Fusible link A circuit protection device consisting of a conductor surrounded by heat-resistant insulation. The conductor is smaller than the wire it protects, so it acts as the weakest link in the circuit. Unlike a blown fuse, a failed fusible link must frequently be cut from the wire for replacement.

G

Gap The distance the spark must travel in jumping from the centre electrode to the side electrode in a spark plug. Also refers to the spacing between the points in a contact breaker assembly in a conventional points-type ignition, or to the distance between the reluctor or rotor and the pickup coil in an electronic ignition.

Adjusting spark plug gap

Gasket Any thin, soft material - usually cork, cardboard, asbestos or soft metal - installed between two metal surfaces to ensure a good seal. For instance, the cylinder head gasket seals the joint between the block and the cylinder head.

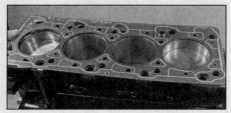
Gasket

Gauge An instrument panel display used to monitor engine conditions. A gauge with a movable pointer on a dial or a fixed scale is an analogue gauge. A gauge with a numerical readout is called a digital gauge.

H

Halfshaft A rotating shaft that transmits power from the final drive unit to a drive wheel, usually when referring to a live rear axle.

Harmonic balancer A device designed to reduce torsion or twisting vibration in the crankshaft. May be incorporated in the crankshaft pulley. Also known as a vibration damper.

Hone An abrasive tool for correcting small irregularities or differences in diameter in an engine cylinder, brake cylinder, etc.

Hydraulic tappet A tappet that utilises hydraulic pressure from the engine's lubrication system to maintain zero clearance (constant contact with both camshaft and valve stem). Automatically adjusts to variation in valve stem length. Hydraulic tappets also reduce valve noise.

I

Ignition timing The moment at which the spark plug fires, usually expressed in the number of crankshaft degrees before the piston reaches the top of its stroke.

Inlet manifold A tube or housing with passages through which flows the air-fuel mixture (carburettor vehicles and vehicles with throttle body injection) or air only (port fuel-injected vehicles) to the port openings in the cylinder head.

J

Jump start Starting the engine of a vehicle with a discharged or weak battery by attaching jump leads from the weak battery to a charged or helper battery.

L

Load Sensing Proportioning Valve (LSPV) A brake hydraulic system control valve that works like a proportioning valve, but also takes into consideration the amount of weight carried by the rear axle.

Locknut A nut used to lock an adjustment nut, or other threaded component, in place. For example, a locknut is employed to keep the adjusting nut on the rocker arm in position.

Lockwasher A form of washer designed to prevent an attaching nut from working loose.

M

MacPherson strut A type of front suspension system devised by Earle MacPherson at Ford of England. In its original form, a simple lateral link with the anti-roll bar creates the lower control arm. A long strut - an integral coil spring and shock absorber - is mounted between the body and the steering knuckle. Many modern so-called MacPherson strut systems use a conventional lower A-arm and don't rely on the anti-roll bar for location.

Multimeter An electrical test instrument with the capability to measure voltage, current and resistance.

N

NOx Oxides of Nitrogen. A common toxic pollutant emitted by petrol and diesel engines at higher temperatures.

O

Ohm The unit of electrical resistance. One volt applied to a resistance of one ohm will produce a current of one amp.

Ohmmeter An instrument for measuring electrical resistance.

O-ring A type of sealing ring made of a special rubber-like material; in use, the O-ring is compressed into a groove to provide the sealing action.

Overhead cam (ohc) engine An engine with the camshaft(s) located on top of the cylinder head(s).

Overhead valve (ohv) engine An engine with the valves located in the cylinder head, but with the camshaft located in the engine block.

Oxygen sensor A device installed in the engine exhaust manifold, which senses the oxygen content in the exhaust and converts this information into an electric current. Also called a Lambda sensor.

P

Phillips screw A type of screw head having a cross instead of a slot for a corresponding type of screwdriver.

Plastigage A thin strip of plastic thread, available in different sizes, used for measuring clearances. For example, a strip of Plastigage is laid across a bearing journal. The parts are assembled and dismantled; the width of the crushed strip indicates the clearance between journal and bearing.

Plastigage

Propeller shaft The long hollow tube with universal joints at both ends that carries power from the transmission to the differential on front-engined rear wheel drive vehicles.

Proportioning valve A hydraulic control valve which limits the amount of pressure to the rear brakes during panic stops to prevent wheel lock-up.

R

Rack-and-pinion steering A steering system with a pinion gear on the end of the steering shaft that mates with a rack (think of a geared wheel opened up and laid flat). When the steering wheel is turned, the pinion turns, moving the rack to the left or right. This movement is transmitted through the track rods to the steering arms at the wheels.

Radiator A liquid-to-air heat transfer device designed to reduce the temperature of the coolant in an internal combustion engine cooling system.

Refrigerant Any substance used as a heat transfer agent in an air-conditioning system. R-12 has been the principle refrigerant for many years; recently, however, manufacturers have begun using R-134a, a non-CFC substance that is considered less harmful to the ozone in the upper atmosphere.

Rocker arm A lever arm that rocks on a shaft or pivots on a stud. In an overhead valve engine, the rocker arm converts the upward movement of the pushrod into a downward movement to open a valve.

Rotor In a distributor, the rotating device inside the cap that connects the centre electrode and the outer terminals as it turns, distributing the high voltage from the coil secondary winding to the proper spark plug. Also, that part of an alternator which rotates inside the stator. Also, the rotating assembly of a turbocharger, including the compressor wheel, shaft and turbine wheel.

Runout The amount of wobble (in-and-out movement) of a gear or wheel as it's rotated. The amount a shaft rotates "out-of-true." The out-of-round condition of a rotating part.

S

Sealant A liquid or paste used to prevent leakage at a joint. Sometimes used in conjunction with a gasket.

Sealed beam lamp An older headlight design which integrates the reflector, lens and filaments into a hermetically-sealed one-piece unit. When a filament burns out or the lens cracks, the entire unit is simply replaced.

Serpentine drivebelt A single, long, wide accessory drivebelt that's used on some newer vehicles to drive all the accessories, instead of a series of smaller, shorter belts. Serpentine drivebelts are usually tensioned by an automatic tensioner.

Serpentine drivebelt

Shim Thin spacer, commonly used to adjust the clearance or relative positions between two parts. For example, shims inserted into or under bucket tappets control valve clearances. Clearance is adjusted by changing the thickness of the shim.

Slide hammer A special puller that screws into or hooks onto a component such as a shaft or bearing; a heavy sliding handle on the shaft bottoms against the end of the shaft to knock the component free.

Sprocket A tooth or projection on the periphery of a wheel, shaped to engage with a chain or drivebelt. Commonly used to refer to the sprocket wheel itself.

Starter inhibitor switch On vehicles with an automatic transmission, a switch that prevents starting if the vehicle is not in Neutral or Park.

Strut See MacPherson strut.

T

Tappet A cylindrical component which transmits motion from the cam to the valve stem, either directly or via a pushrod and rocker arm. Also called a cam follower.

Thermostat A heat-controlled valve that regulates the flow of coolant between the cylinder block and the radiator, so maintaining optimum engine operating temperature. A thermostat is also used in some air cleaners in which the temperature is regulated.

Thrust bearing The bearing in the clutch assembly that is moved in to the release levers by clutch pedal action to disengage the clutch. Also referred to as a release bearing.

Timing belt A toothed belt which drives the camshaft. Serious engine damage may result if it breaks in service.

Timing chain A chain which drives the camshaft.

Toe-in The amount the front wheels are closer together at the front than at the rear. On rear wheel drive vehicles, a slight amount of toe-in is usually specified to keep the front wheels running parallel on the road by offsetting other forces that tend to spread the wheels apart.

Toe-out The amount the front wheels are closer together at the rear than at the front. On front wheel drive vehicles, a slight amount of toe-out is usually specified.

Tools For full information on choosing and using tools, refer to the *Haynes Automotive Tools Manual*.

Tracer A stripe of a second colour applied to a wire insulator to distinguish that wire from another one with the same colour insulator.

Tune-up A process of accurate and careful adjustments and parts replacement to obtain the best possible engine performance.

Turbocharger A centrifugal device, driven by exhaust gases, that pressurises the intake air. Normally used to increase the power output from a given engine displacement, but can also be used primarily to reduce exhaust emissions (as on VW's "Umwelt" Diesel engine).

U

Universal joint or U-joint A double-pivoted connection for transmitting power from a driving to a driven shaft through an angle. A U-joint consists of two Y-shaped yokes and a cross-shaped member called the spider.

V

Valve A device through which the flow of liquid, gas, vacuum, or loose material in bulk may be started, stopped, or regulated by a movable part that opens, shuts, or partially obstructs one or more ports or passageways. A valve is also the movable part of such a device.

Valve clearance The clearance between the valve tip (the end of the valve stem) and the rocker arm or tappet. The valve clearance is measured when the valve is closed.

Vernier caliper A precision measuring instrument that measures inside and outside dimensions. Not quite as accurate as a micrometer, but more convenient.

Viscosity The thickness of a liquid or its resistance to flow.

Volt A unit for expressing electrical "pressure" in a circuit. One volt that will produce a current of one ampere through a resistance of one ohm.

W

Welding Various processes used to join metal items by heating the areas to be joined to a molten state and fusing them together. For more information refer to the *Haynes Automotive Welding Manual*.

Wiring diagram A drawing portraying the components and wires in a vehicle's electrical system, using standardised symbols. For more information refer to the *Haynes Automotive Electrical and Electronic Systems Manual*.

Note: *References throughout this index are in the form* **"Chapter number"** • **"Page number"**. *So, for example, 2C•15 refers to page 15 of Chapter 2C.*

Note: *References throughout this index are in the form "**Chapter number**" • "**Page number**". So, for example, 2C•15 refers to page 15 of Chapter 2C.*

Note: *References throughout this index are in the form* **"Chapter number" • "Page number"**. *So, for example, 2C•15 refers to page 15 of Chapter 2C.*

Haynes Manuals – The Complete UK Car List

Title	Book No.
ALFA ROMEO Alfasud/Sprint (74 - 88) up to F *	0292
Alfa Romeo Alfetta (73 – 87) up to E *	0531
AUDI 80, 90 & Coupe Petrol (79 – Nov 88) up to F	0605
Audi 80, 90 & Coupe Petrol (Oct 86 – 90) D to H	1491
Audi 100 & A6 Petrol & Diesel (May 91 – May 97) H to P	3504
Audi A3 Petrol & Diesel (96 – May 03) P to 03	4253
Audi A3 Petrol & Diesel (June 03 – Mar 08) 03 to 08	4884
Audi A4 Petrol & Diesel (95 – 00) M to X	3575
Audi A4 Petrol & Diesel (01 – 04) X to 54	4609
Audi A4 Petrol & Diesel (Jan 05 – Feb 08) 54 to 57	4885
AUSTIN A35 & A40 (56 – 67) up to F *	0118
Mini (59 – 69) up to H *	0527
Mini (69 – 01) up to X	0646
Austin Healey 100/6 & 3000 (56 – 68) up to G *	0049
BEDFORD/Vauxhall Rascal & Suzuki Supercarry (86 – Oct 94) C to M	3015
BMW 1-Series 4-cyl Petrol & Diesel (04 – Aug 11) 54 to 11	4918
BMW 316, 320 & 320i (4-cyl)(75 – Feb 83) up to Y *	0276
BMW 3- & 5- Series Petrol (81 – 91) up to J	1948
BMW 3-Series Petrol (Apr 91 – 99) H to V	3210
BMW 3-Series Petrol (Sept 98 – 06) S to 56	4067
BMW 3-Series Petrol & Diesel (05 – Sept 08) 54 to 58	4782
BMW 5-Series 6-cyl Petrol (April 96 – Aug 03) N to 03	4151
BMW 5-Series Diesel (Sept 03 – 10) 53 to 10	4901
BMW 1500, 1502, 1600, 1602, 2000 & 2002 (59 – 77) up to S *	0240
CHRYSLER PT Cruiser Petrol (00-09) W to 09	4058
CITROEN 2CV, Ami & Dyane (67 – 90) up to H	0196
Citroen AX Petrol & Diesel (87- 97) D to P	3014
Citroen Berlingo & Peugeot Partner Petrol & Diesel (96 – 10) P to 60	4281
Citroen C1 Petrol (05 – 11) 05 to 11	4922
Citroen C3 Petrol & Diesel (02 – 09) 51 to 59	4890
Citroen C4 Petrol & Diesel (04 – 10) 54 to 60	5576
Citroen C5 Petrol & Diesel (01 – 08) Y to 08	4745
Citroen C15 Van Petrol & Diesel (89 – Oct 98) F to S	3509
Citroen CX Petrol (75 – 88) up to F	0528
Citroen Saxo Petrol & Diesel (96 – 04) N to 54	3506
Citroen Visa Petrol (79 – 88) up to F	0620
Citroen Xantia Petrol & Diesel (93 – 01) K to Y	3082
Citroen XM Petrol & Diesel (89 – 00) G to X	3451
Citroen Xsara Petrol & Diesel (97 – Sept 00) R to W	3751
Citroen Xsara Picasso Petrol & Diesel (00 – 02) W to 52	3944
Citroen Xsara Picasso (Mar 04 – 08) 04 to 58	4784
Citroen ZX Diesel (91 – 98) J to S	1922
Citroen ZX Petrol (91 – 98) H to S	1881
FIAT 126 (73 – 87) up to E *	0305
Fiat 500 (57 – 73) up to M *	0090
Fiat 500 & Panda (04 – 12) 53 to 61	5558
Fiat Bravo & Brava Petrol (95 – 00) N to W	3572
Fiat Cinquecento (93 – 98) K to R	3501
Fiat Panda (81 – 95) up to M	0793
Fiat Punto Petrol & Diesel (94 – Oct 99) L to V	3251
Fiat Punto Petrol (Oct 99 – July 03) V to 03	4066
Fiat Punto Petrol (03 – 07) 03 to 07	4746
Fiat Punto Petrol (Oct 99 – 07) V to 07	5634
Fiat X1/9 (74 – 89) up to G *	0273
FORD Anglia (59 – 68) up to G *	0001
Ford Capri II (& III) 1.6 & 2.0 (74 – 87) up to E *	0283
Ford Capri II (& III) 2.8 & 3.0 V6 (74 – 87) up to E	1309
Ford C-Max Petrol & Diesel (03 – 10) 53 to 60	4900
Ford Escort Mk I 1100 & 1300 (68 – 74) up to N *	0171
Ford Escort Mk I Mexico, RS 1600 & RS 2000 (70 – 74) up to N *	0139
Ford Escort Mk II Mexico, RS 1800 & RS 2000 (75 – 80) up to W *	0735
Ford Escort (75 – Aug 80) up to V *	0280
Ford Escort Petrol (Sept 80 – Sept 90) up to H	0686
Ford Escort & Orion Petrol (Sept 90 – 00) H to X	1737
Ford Escort & Orion Diesel (Sept 90 – 00) H to X	4081
Ford Fiesta Petrol (Feb 89 – Oct 95) F to N	1595
Ford Fiesta Petrol & Diesel (Oct 95 – Mar 02) N to 02	3397
Ford Fiesta Petrol & Diesel (Apr 02 – 08) 02 to 58	4170
Ford Fiesta Petrol & Diesel (08 – 11) 58 to 11	4907
Ford Focus Petrol & Diesel (98 – 01) S to Y	3759
Ford Focus Petrol & Diesel (Oct 01 – 05) 51 to 05	4167
Ford Focus Petrol (05 – 09) 54 to 09	4785
Ford Focus Diesel (05 – 09) 54 to 09	4807
Ford Fusion Petrol & Diesel (02 – 11) 02 to 61	5566
Ford Galaxy Petrol & Diesel (95 – Aug 00) M to W	3984
Ford Galaxy Petrol & Diesel (00 – 06) X to 06	5556
Ford Granada Petrol (Sept 77 – Feb 85) up to B *	0481
Ford Ka (96 – 08) P to 58	5567
Ford Mondeo Petrol (93 – Sept 00) K to X	1923
Ford Mondeo Petrol & Diesel (Oct 00 – Jul 03) X to 03	3990
Ford Mondeo Petrol & Diesel (July 03 – 07) 03 to 56	4619
Ford Mondeo Petrol & Diesel (Apr 07 – 12) 07 to 61	5548
Ford Mondeo Diesel (93 – Sept 00) L to X	3465
Ford Sierra V6 Petrol (82 – 91) up to J	0904
Ford Transit Connect Diesel (02 – 11) 02 to 11	4903
Ford Transit Diesel (Feb 86 – 99) C to T	3019
Ford Transit Diesel (00 – Oct 06) X to 56	4775
Ford 1.6 & 1.8 litre Diesel Engine (84 – 96) A to N	1172
HILLMAN Imp (63 – 76) up to R *	0022
HONDA Civic (Feb 84 – Oct 87) A to E	1226
Honda Civic (Nov 91 – 96) J to N	3199
Honda Civic Petrol (Mar 95 – 00) M to X	4050
Honda Civic Petrol & Diesel (01 – 05) X to 55	4611
Honda CR-V Petrol & Diesel (02 – 06) 51 to 56	4747
Honda Jazz (02 to 08) 51 to 58	4735
JAGUAR E-Type (61 – 72) up to L *	0140
Jaguar Mk I & II, 240 & 340 (55 – 69) up to H *	0098
Jaguar XJ6, XJ & Sovereign, Daimler Sovereign (68 – Oct 86) up to D	0242
Jaguar XJ6 & Sovereign (Oct 86 – Sept 94) D to M	3261
Jaguar XJ12, XJS & Sovereign, Daimler Double Six (72 – 88) up to F	0478
JEEP Cherokee Petrol (93 – 96) K to N	1943
LAND ROVER 90, 110 & Defender Diesel (83 – 07) up to 56	3017
Land Rover Discovery Petrol & Diesel (89 – 98) G to S	3016
Land Rover Discovery Diesel (Nov 98 – Jul 04) S to 04	4606
Land Rover Discovery Diesel (Aug 04 – Apr 09) 04 to 09	5562
Land Rover Freelander Petrol & Diesel (97 – Sept 03) R to 53	3929
Land Rover Freelander (97 – Oct 06) R to 56	5571
Land Rover Series II, IIA & III 4-cyl Petrol (58 – 85) up to C	0314
Land Rover Series II, IIA & III Petrol & Diesel (58 – 85) up to C	5568
MAZDA 323 (Mar 81 – Oct 89) up to G	1608
Mazda 323 (Oct 89 – 98) G to R	3455
Mazda B1600, B1800 & B2000 Pick-up Petrol (72 – 88) up to F	0267
Mazda MX-5 (89 – 05) G to 05	5565
Mazda RX-7 (79 – 85) up to C *	0460
MERCEDES-BENZ 190, 190E & 190D Petrol & Diesel (83 – 93) A to L	3450
Mercedes-Benz 200D, 240D, 240TD, 300D & 300TD 123 Series Diesel (Oct 76 – 85) up to C	1114
Mercedes-Benz 250 & 280 (68 – 72) up to L *	0346
Mercedes-Benz 250 & 280 123 Series Petrol (Oct 76 – 84) up to B *	0677
Mercedes-Benz 124 Series Petrol & Diesel (85 – Aug 93) C to K	3253
Mercedes-Benz A-Class Petrol & Diesel (98 – 04) S to 54	4748
Mercedes-Benz C-Class Petrol & Diesel (93 – Aug 00) L to W	3511
Mercedes-Benz C-Class (00 – 07) X to 07	4780
Mercedes-Benz Sprinter Diesel (95 – Apr 06) M to 06	4902
MGA (55 – 62)	0475
MGB (62 – 80) up to W	0111
MGB 1962 to 1980 (special edition) *	4894
MG Midget & Austin-Healey Sprite (58 – 80) up to W *	0265
MINI Petrol (July 01 – 06) Y to 56	4273
MINI Petrol & Diesel (Nov 06 – 13) 56 to 13	4904
MITSUBISHI Shogun & L200 Pick-ups Petrol (83 – 94) up to M	1944
MORRIS Minor 1000 (56 – 71) up to K	0024
NISSAN Almera Petrol (95 – Feb 00) N to V	4053
Nissan Almera & Tino Petrol (Feb 00 – 07) V to 56	4612
Nissan Micra (83 – Jan 93) up to K	0931
Nissan Micra (93 – 02) K to 52	3254
Nissan Micra Petrol (03 – Oct 10) 52 to 60	4734
Nissan Primera Petrol (90 - Aug 99) H to T	1851
Nissan Qashqai Petrol & Diesel (07 – 12) 56 to 62	5610
OPEL Ascona & Manta (B-Series) (Sept 75 – 88) up to F *	0316
Opel Ascona Petrol (81 – 88)	3215
Opel Ascona Petrol (Oct 91 – Feb 98)	3156
Opel Corsa Petrol (83 – Mar 93)	3160
Opel Corsa Petrol (Mar 93 – 97)	3159
Opel Kadett Petrol (Oct 84 – Oct 91)	3196
Opel Omega & Senator Petrol (Nov 86 – 94)	3157
Opel Vectra Petrol (Oct 88 – Oct 95)	3158
PEUGEOT 106 Petrol & Diesel (91 – 04) J to 53	1882
Peugeot 107 Petrol (05 – 11) 05 to 11	4923
Peugeot 205 Petrol (83 – 97) A to P	0932
Peugeot 206 Petrol & Diesel (98 – 01) S to X	3757

* Classic reprint

Title	Book No.
Peugeot 206 Petrol & Diesel (02 – 06) 51 to 06	4613
Peugeot 207 Petrol & Diesel (06 – July 09) 06 to 09	4787
Peugeot 306 Petrol & Diesel (93 – 02) K to 02	3073
Peugeot 307 Petrol & Diesel (01 – 08) Y to 58	4147
Peugeot 308 Petrol & Diesel (07 – 12) 07 to 12	5561
Peugeot 405 Diesel (88 – 97) E to P	3198
Peugeot 406 Petrol & Diesel (96 – Mar 99) N to T	3394
Peugeot 406 Petrol & Diesel (Mar 99 – 02) T to 52	3982
Peugeot 407 Diesel (04 -11) 53 to 11	5550
PORSCHE 911 (65 – 85) up to C	0264
Porsche 924 & 924 Turbo (76 – 85) up to C	0397
RANGE ROVER V8 Petrol (70 – Oct 92) up to K	0606
RELIANT Robin & Kitten (73 – 83) up to A *	0436
RENAULT 4 (61 – 86) up to D *	0072
Renault 5 Petrol (Feb 85 – 96) B to N	1219
Renault 19 Petrol (89 – 96) F to N	1646
Renault Clio Petrol (91 – May 98) H to R	1853
Renault Clio Petrol & Diesel (May 98 – May 01) R to Y	3906
Renault Clio Petrol & Diesel (June 01 – 05) Y to 55	4168
Renault Clio Petrol & Diesel (Oct 05 – May 09) 55 to 09	4788
Renault Espace Petrol & Diesel (85 – 96) C to N	3197
Renault Laguna Petrol & Diesel (94 – 00) L to W	3252
Renault Laguna Petrol & Diesel (Feb 01 – May 07) X to 07	4283
Renault Megane & Scenic Petrol & Diesel (96 – 99) N to T	3395
Renault Megane & Scenic Petrol & Diesel (Apr 99 – 02) T to 52	3916
Renault Megane Petrol & Diesel (Oct 02 – 08) 52 to 58	4284
Renault Scenic Petrol & Diesel (Sept 03 – 06) 53 to 06	4297
Renault Trafic Diesel (01 – 11) Y to 11	5551
ROVER 216 & 416 Petrol (89 – 96) G to N	1830
Rover 211, 214, 216, 218 & 220 Petrol & Diesel (Dec 95 – 99) N to V	3399
Rover 25 & MG ZR Petrol & Diesel (Oct 99 – 06) V to 06	4145
Rover 414, 416 & 420 Petrol & Diesel (May 95 – 99) M to V	3453
Rover 45 / MG ZS Petrol & Diesel (99 – 05) V to 55	4384
Rover 618, 620 & 623 Petrol (93 – 97) K to P	3257
Rover 75 / MG ZT Petrol & Diesel (99 – 06) S to 06	4292
Rover 820, 825 & 827 Petrol (86 – 95) D to N	1380
Rover 3500 (76 – 87) up to E *	0365
Rover Metro, 111 & 114 Petrol (May 90 – 98) G to S	1711
SAAB 95 & 96 (66 – 76) up to R *	0198
Saab 90, 99 & 900 (79 – Oct 93) up to L	0765
Saab 900 (Oct 93 – 98) L to R	3512
Saab 9000 4-cyl (85 – 98) C to S	1686
Saab 9-3 Petrol & Diesel (98 – Aug 02) R to 02	4614
Saab 9-3 Petrol & Diesel (92 – 07) 52 to 57	4749
Saab 9-3 Petrol & Diesel (07-on) 57 on	5569
Saab 9-5 4-cyl Petrol (97 – 05) R to 55	4156
Saab 9-5 (Sep 05 – Jun 10) 55 to 10	4891
SEAT Ibiza & Cordoba Petrol & Diesel (Oct 93 – Oct 99) L to V	3571
Seat Ibiza & Malaga Petrol (85 – 92) B to K	1609
Seat Ibiza Petrol & Diesel (May 02 – Apr 08) 02 to 08	4889

Title	Book No.
SKODA Fabia Petrol & Diesel (00 – 06) W to 06	4376
Skoda Felicia Petrol & Diesel (95 – 01) M to X	3505
Skoda Octavia Petrol (98 – April 04) R to 04	4285
Skoda Octavia Diesel (May 04 – 12) 04 to 61	5549
SUBARU 1600 & 1800 (Nov 79 – 90) up to H *	0995
SUNBEAM Alpine, Rapier & H120 (68 – 74) up to N *	0051
SUZUKI SJ Series, Samurai & Vitara 4-cyl Petrol (82 – 97) up to P	1942
Suzuki Supercarry & Bedford/Vauxhall Rascal (86 – Oct 94) C to M	3015
TOYOTA Avensis Petrol (98 – Jan 03) R to 52	4264
Toyota Aygo Petrol (05 – 11) 05 to 11	4921
Toyota Carina E Petrol (May 92 – 97) J to P	3256
Toyota Corolla (80 – 85) up to C	0683
Toyota Corolla (Sept 83 – Sept 87) A to E	1024
Toyota Corolla (Sept 87 – Aug 92) E to K	1683
Toyota Corolla Petrol (Aug 92 – 97) K to P	3259
Toyota Corolla Petrol (July 97 0 Feb 02) P to 51	4286
Toyota Corolla Petrol & Diesel (02 – Jan 07) 51 to 56	4791
Toyota Hi-Ace & Hi-Lux Petrol (69 – Oct 83) up to A	0304
Toyota RAV4 Petrol & Diesel (94 – 06) L to 55	4750
Toyota Yaris Petrol (99 – 05) T to 05	4265
TRIUMPH GT6 & Vitesse (62 0 74) up to N *	0112
Triumph Herald (59 – 71) up to K *	0010
Triumph Spitfire (62 – 81) up to X	0113
Triumph Stag (70 – 78) up to T *	0441
Triumph TR2, TR3, TR3A, TR4 & TR4A (52 – 67) up to F *	0028
Triumph TR5 & TR6 (67 – 75) up to P *	0031
Triumph TR7 (75 – 82) up to Y *	0322
VAUXHALL Astra Petrol (Oct 91 – Feb 98) J to R	1832
Vauxhall/Opel Astra & Zafira Petrol (Feb 98 – Apr 04) R to 04	3758
Vauxhall/Opel Astra & Zafira Diesel (Feb 98 – Apr 04) R to 04	3797
Vauxhall/Opel Astra Petrol (04 – 08)	4732
Vauxhall/Opel Astra Diesel (04 – 08)	4733
Vauxhall/Opel Astra Petrol & Diesel (Dec 09 – 13) 59 to 13	5578
Vauxhall/Opel Calibra (90 – 98) G to S	3502
Vauxhall Cavalier Petrol (Oct 88 0 95) F to N	1570
Vauxhall/Opel Corsa Diesel (Mar 93 – Oct 00) K to X	4087
Vauxhall Corsa Petrol (Mar 93 – 97) K to R	1985
Vauxhall/Opel Corsa Petrol (Apr 97 – Oct 00) P to X	3921
Vauxhall/Opel Corsa Petrol & Diesel (Oct 03 – Aug 06) 53 to 06	4617
Vauxhall/Opel Corsa Petrol & Diesel (Sept 06 – 10) 56 to 10	4886
Vauxhall/Opel Corsa Petrol & Diesel (00 – Aug 06) X to 06	5577
Vauxhall/Opel Frontera Petrol & Diesel (91 – Sept 98) J to S	3454
Vauxhall/Opel Insignia Petrol & Diesel (08 – 12) 08 to 61	5563
Vauxhall/Opel Meriva Petrol & Diesel (03 – May 10) 03 to 10	4893
Vauxhall/Opel Omega Petrol (94 – 99) L to T	3510
Vauxhall/Opel Vectra Petrol & Diesel (95 – Feb 99) N to S	3396

Title	Book No.
Vauxhall/Opel Vectra Petrol & Diesel (Mar 99 – May 02) T to 02	3930
Vauxhall/Opel Vectra Petrol & Diesel (June 02 – Sept 05) 02 to 55	4618
Vauxhall/Opel Vectra Petrol & Diesel (Oct 05 – Oct 08) 55 to 58	4887
Vauxhall/Opel Vivaro Diesel (01 – 11) Y to 11	5552
Vauxhall/Opel Zafira Petrol & Diesel (05 -09) 05 to 09	4792
Vauxhall/Opel 1.5, 1.6 & 1.7 litre Diesel Engine (82 – 96) up to N	1222
VW Beetle 1200 (54 – 77) up to S	0036
VW Beetle 1300 & 1500 (65 – 75) up to P	0039
VW 1302 & 1302S (70 – 72) up to L *	0110
VW Beetle 1303, 1303S & GT (72 – 75) up to P	0159
VW Beetle Petrol & Diesel (Apr 99 – 07) T to 57	3798
VW Golf & Jetta Mk 1 Petrol 1.1 & 1.3 (74 – 84) up to A	0716
VW Golf, Jetta & Scirocco Mk 1 Petrol 1.5, 1.6 & 1.8 (74 – 84) up to A	0726
VW Golf & Jetta Mk 1 Diesel (78 – 84) up to A	0451
VW Golf & Jetta Mk 2 Petrol (Mar 84 – Feb 92) A to J	1081
VW Golf & Vento Petrol & Diesel (Feb 92 – Mar 98) J to R	3097
VW Golf & Bora Petrol & Diesel (Apr 98 – 00) R to X	3727
VW Golf & Bora 4-cyl Petrol & Diesel (01 – 03) X to 53	4169
VW Golf & Jetta Petrol & Diesel (04 – 09) 53 to 09	4610
VW LT Petrol Vans & Light Trucks (76 – 87) up to E	0637
VW Passat 4-cyl Petrol & Diesel (May 88 – 96) E to P	3498
VW Passat 4-cyl Petrol & Diesel (Dec 96 – Nov 00) P to X	3917
VW Passat Petrol & Diesel (Dec 00 – May 05) X to 05	4279
VW Passat Diesel (June 05 – 10) 05 to 60	4888
VW Polo Petrol (Nov 90 – Aug 94) H to L	3245
VW Polo Hatchback Petrol & Diesel (94 – 99) M to S	3500
VW Polo Hatchback Petrol (00 – Jan 02) V to 51	4150
VW Polo Petrol & Diesel (02 – May 05) 51 to 05	4608
VW Transporter 1600 (68 – 79) up to V	0082
VW Transporter 1700, 1800 & 2000 (72 – 79) up to V *	0226
VW Transporter (air cooled) Petrol (79 – 82) up to Y *	0638
VW Transporter (water cooled) Petrol (82 – 90) up to H	3452
VW Type 3 (63 – 73) up to M *	0084
VOLVO 120 & 130 Series (& P1800) (61 – 73) up to M *	0203
Volvo 142, 144 & 145 (66 – 74) up to N *	0129
Volvo 240 Series Petrol (74 – 93) up to K	0270
Volvo 440, 460 & 480 Petrol (87 – 97) D to P	1691
Volvo 740 & 760 Petrol (82 – 91) up to J	1258
Volvo 850 Petrol (92 – 96) J to P	3260
Volvo 940 Petrol (90 – 98) H to R	3249
Volvo S40 & V40 Petrol (96 – Mar 04) N to 04	3569
Volvo S40 & V50 Petrol & Diesel (Mar 04 – Jun 07) 04 to 07	4731
Volvo S60 Petrol & Diesel (01 – 08) X to 09	4793
Volvo S70, V70 & C70 Petrol (96 – 99) P to V	3573
Volvo V70 / S80 Petrol & Diesel (98 – 07) S to 07	4263
Volvo V70 Diesel (June 07 – 12) 07 to 61	5557
Volvo XV60 / 90 Diesel (03 – 12) 52 to 62	5630

* Classic reprint

CL 27.08.13

Preserving Our Motoring Heritage

< The Model J Duesenberg Derham Tourster. Only eight of these magnificent cars were ever built – this is the only example to be found outside the United States of America

Almost every car you've ever loved, loathed or desired is gathered under one roof at the Haynes Motor Museum. Over 300 immaculately presented cars and motorbikes represent every aspect of our motoring heritage, from elegant reminders of bygone days, such as the superb Model J Duesenberg to curiosities like the bug-eyed BMW Isetta. There are also many old friends and flames. Perhaps you remember the 1959 Ford Popular that you did your courting in? The magnificent 'Red Collection' is a spectacle of classic sports cars including AC, Alfa Romeo, Austin Healey, Ferrari, Lamborghini, Maserati, MG, Riley, Porsche and Triumph.

A Perfect Day Out

Each and every vehicle at the Haynes Motor Museum has played its part in the history and culture of Motoring. Today, they make a wonderful spectacle and a great day out for all the family. Bring the kids, bring Mum and Dad, but above all bring your camera to capture those golden memories for ever. You will also find an impressive array of motoring memorabilia, a comfortable 70 seat video cinema and one of the most extensive transport book shops in Britain. The Pit Stop Cafe serves everything from a cup of tea to wholesome, home-made meals or, if you prefer, you can enjoy the large picnic area nestled in the beautiful rural surroundings of Somerset.

John Haynes O.B.E., Founder and Chairman of the museum at the wheel of a Haynes Light 12. >

< The 1936 490cc sohc-engined International Norton – well known for its racing success

The Museum is situated on the A359 Yeovil to Frome road at Sparkford, just off the A303 in Somerset. It is about 40 miles south of Bristol, and 25 minutes drive from the M5 intersection at Taunton.
Open 9.30am - 5.30pm (10.00am - 4.00pm Winter) 7 days a week, *except Christmas Day, Boxing Day and New Years Day*
Special rates available for schools, coach parties and outings Charitable Trust No. 292048